Rome: Republic into Empire

By the same author

Women in Ancient Rome (2013)

Roman Women – The Women who Influenced Roman History (2015)

In Bed with the Romans (2015)

Wars & Battles of the Roman Republic (2015)

Roman Military Disasters (2015)

In Bed with the Ancient Greeks (2016)

Ancient Greece in 100 Facts (2017)

Women in Ancient Greece (2017)

When in Rome … A Social History of Rome (2017)

Women at War in Ancient Greece & Rome (2017)

How to be a Roman (2017)

Wars & Battles of Ancient Greece (2018)

Roman Record Keeping & Communications (2018)

Emperors of Rome, from Tiberius to Elagabalus – The Monsters (2018)

Reportage from Ancient Greece and Rome (2019)

Marvels, Mysteries & Magic In The Ancient World (2019)

War in Greek Mythology (2019)

War in Roman Myth and Legend (2019)

The Romans in the North of England (2019)

Rome: Republic into Empire

The Civil Wars of the First Century BCE

Paul Chrystal

Pen & Sword
MILITARY
AN IMPRINT OF PEN & SWORD BOOKS LTD.
YORKSHIRE – PHILADELPHIA

First published in Great Britain in 2019 by
Pen & Sword Military
An imprint of
Pen & Sword Books Ltd
Yorkshire – Philadelphia

ISBN 978 1 52671 009 3

A CIP catalogue record for this book is available from the British Library.

Printed and bound in England by TJ International Ltd, Padstow, Cornwall.

Pen & Sword Books Limited incorporates the imprints of Atlas, Archaeology, Aviation, Discovery, Family History, Fiction, History, Maritime, Military, Military Classics, Politics, Select, Transport, True Crime, Air World, Frontline Publishing, Leo Cooper, Remember When, Seaforth Publishing, The Praetorian Press, Wharncliffe Local History, Wharncliffe Transport, Wharncliffe True Crime and White Owl.

For a complete list of Pen & Sword titles please contact

PEN & SWORD BOOKS LIMITED
47 Church Street, Barnsley, South Yorkshire, S70 2AS, England
E-mail: enquiries@pen-and-sword.co.uk
Website: www.pen-and-sword.co.uk

Or
PEN AND SWORD BOOKS
1950 Lawrence Rd, Havertown, PA 19083, USA
E-mail: Uspen-and-sword@casematepublishers.com
Website: www.penandswordbooks.com

About the author

Paul Chrystal was educated at the Universities of Hull and Southampton where he took degrees in Classics. He has worked in medical publishing sales for over thirty years but now combines this with writing features for national newspapers and history magazines (*Minerva Magazine, BBC History Magazine, Ancient History Magazine, Omnibus and Ad Familiares*) as well as appearing regularly on BBC local radio, BBC Radio 4 and on the BBC World Service. A reviewer for 'Classics for All', he is the author of over 100 books on a wide range of subjects, including many on ancient Greece and Rome. Paul has also contributed to a forthcoming 6-part series for BBC2 'celebrating the history of some of Britain's most iconic craft industries', in this case chocolate in York. He has been history advisor for a number of York tourist attractions. From 2019 he takes over the editorship of *York Historian*, the journal of the Yorkshire Architectural and York Archaeological Society. Also in 2019, he is guest speaker for Vassar College New York's London Programme with Goldsmith University. Paul lives near York.

For more information please visit the author's website: www.paulchrystal.com.

Contents

List of Plates

1. 'Marius Amid the Ruins of Carthage' (1832), John Vanderlyn (1775–1852). The subject is from Plutarch's Lives, of Caius Marius after being expelled from Rome. Marius is seen in reflective mood, sitting in exile amid the ruins of Carthage, which had been destroyed by Romans. The artist aimed to 'reveal in two great instances the instability of human grandeur – a city in ruins and a fallen general'. The Albany Institute's 'Marius' is a small version of a painting of the same subject that won Vanderlyn a gold medal at the prestigious Paris Salon of 1808 and is now in the Fine Arts Museums of San Francisco. (*Albany Institute of History & Art*)

2. The Column of Julius Caesar, where he addressed his army to march on Rome and start the Civil War; Rimini, Italy. (*Photographer Georges Jansoone*)

3. Lecture Diagram, c.1814, 'Caesar's bridge over the Reno' built in 55 BCE during the Gallic Wars. (*London, Sir John Soane's Museum*)

4. This mosaic showing the Battle of Thapsus in 46 BCE is from Praeneste, and now resides in the Staatliche Antikensammlungen, Berlin, between the busts of Caesar and Cleopatra. It is part of another, larger Nilotic mosaic dating to the late first century BCE found at the Temple of Fortuna Primigenia in Palestrina, and which is now in the National Archeological Museum there. Given the Egyptian topography and Alexandrian origin of the work (animals familiar to the Alexandrians have no labels; those that are not, such as giraffes and rhinoceroses, are in Greek), Goudchaux suggests in his comments on the mosaic in the exhibition catalogue to the exhibition 'Cleopatra of Egypt: From History to Myth' that it may have been commissioned by Cleopatra herself to thank the goddess Primigenia for the birth of Caesarion.

5. 'Vercingetorix throws down his arms at the feet of Julius Caesar' by Lionel Royer (1899), Musée Croatzier du Puy-en-Velay. Wonderful as this painting is, the artist has permitted himself much artistic licence. The painting depicts the surrender of Vercingetorix after the Battle of Alesia (52 BCE). One of the warriors (bottom left) has a torque around his neck. In fact, the torque was reserved only for gods and important members of a royal family. The depiction of Gauls with long hair and moustaches is also questionable. The horse is a Percheron, although at that time this breed was not to be found in Gaul. In addition, the Gauls rode bareback, but here the horse is saddled and harnessed. The rectangular shield also does not accord with the time, when they were mostly oval.

6. Woodcut illustration of Porcia Catonis counselling Marcus Junius Brutus, Julius Caesar's death at the hands of Brutus and Gaius Cassius Longinus, and Porcia's suicide, hand-coloured in red, green, yellow and black, from an incunable German translation by Heinrich Steinhöwel of Boccaccio's *De mulieribus claris*, printed by Johannes Zainer at Ulm *c.* 1474. One of seventy-six woodcut illustrations depicting scenes from the life of women. (*Penn Libraries*)

7. 'The Murder of Caesar' (1865) by Karl von Piloty (1826–1886). (*Lower Saxony State Museum, Hanover*)

8. 'The Assassination of Julius Caesar' (1804–1805) by Vincenzo Camuccini (1771–1844). (*Galleria Nazionale d'Arte Moderna, Rome*)

9. 'La Mort de César' (c.1859–1867) by Jean-Léon Gérôme (1824–1904), showing the aftermath of the attack, with Caesar's body abandoned in the foreground as the senators rejoice – but not for long… (*Bequeathed to Walters Art Museum, Baltimore, by Henry Walters, 1931*)

10. 'Julius Caesar. Act IV. Scene III. Brutus's tent, in the camp near Sardis. Brutus and the Ghost of Caesar' (1802). Copperplate engraving by Edward Scriven from a painting by Richard Westall, illustrating Act IV, Scene III, from Shakespeare's *Julius Caesar*.

Maps

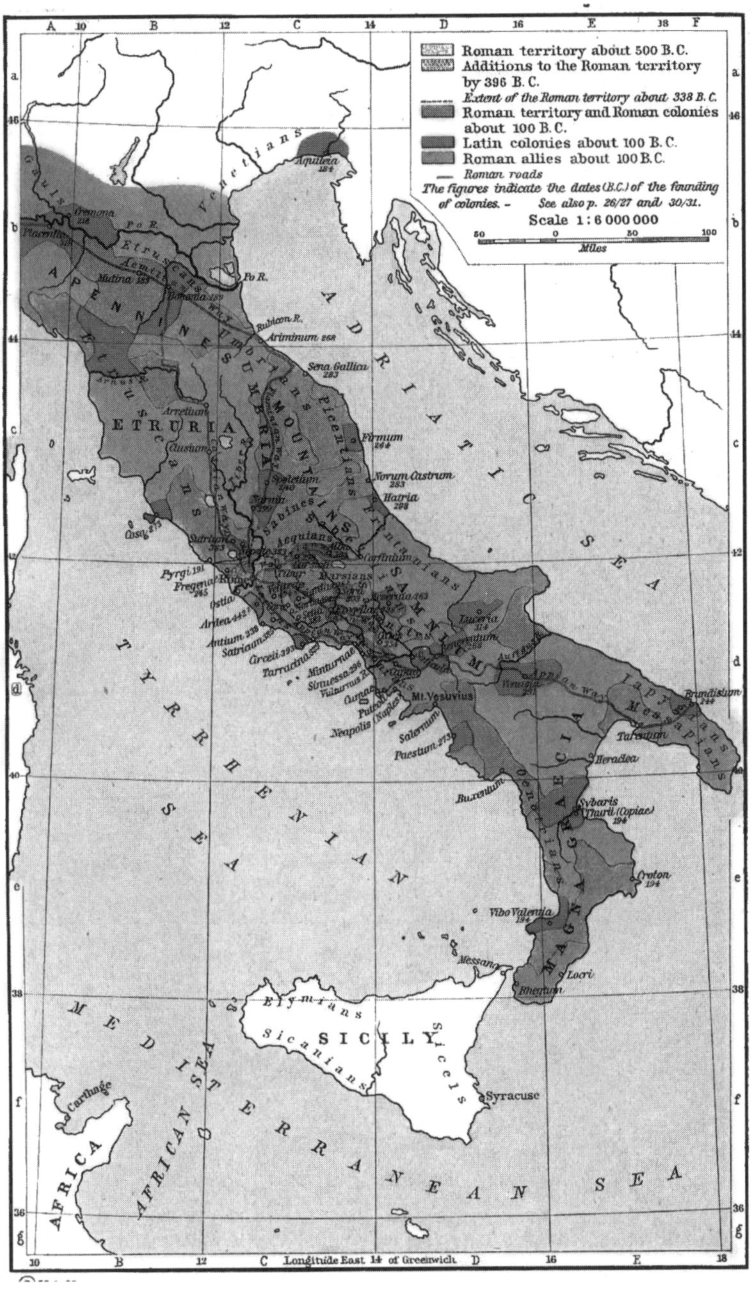
Roman territory about 500 B.C.
Additions to the Roman territory by 396 B.C.
Extent of the Roman territory about 338 B.C.
Roman territory and Roman colonies about 100 B.C.
Latin colonies about 100 B.C.
Roman allies about 100 B.C.
Roman roads
The figures indicate the dates (B.C.) of the founding of colonies. - See also p. 26/27 and 30/31.
Scale 1 : 6 000 000
Miles
ETRURIA
SICILY
AFRICA
ADRIATIC SEA
TYRRHENIAN SEA
MEDITERRANEAN SEA
AFRICAN SEA
APENNINES
UMBRIA
SAMNIUM
MAGNA GRAECIA
Sabines
Aequians
Marsians
Elymians
Sicanians
Sicels
Veneti ans
Aquileia 181
Cremona 218
Placentia 218
Po R.
Mutina 183
Bononia 189
Rubicon R.
Ariminum 268
Sena Gallica 283
Arretium
Clusium
Firmum 264
Spoletium 240
Narnia 299
Novum Castrum 283
Hatria 289
Cosa 273
Sutrium 383
Pyrgi 191
Fregenae 245
Ostia
Ardea 442
Antium 338
Satricum 385
Circeii 393
Tarracina 329
Minturnae
Sinuessa 296
Volturnus
Cumae
Puteoli
Neapolis (Naples)
Mt. Vesuvius
Salernum
Paestum 273
Luceria 314
Beneventum 268
Appian Way
Brundisium 244
Messapians
Tarentum
Heraclea
Buxentum
Sybaris
Thurii (Copiae) 194
Croton 194
Vibo Valentia 194
Messana
Locri
Rhegium
Syracuse
Carthage
Longitude East 14 of Greenwich

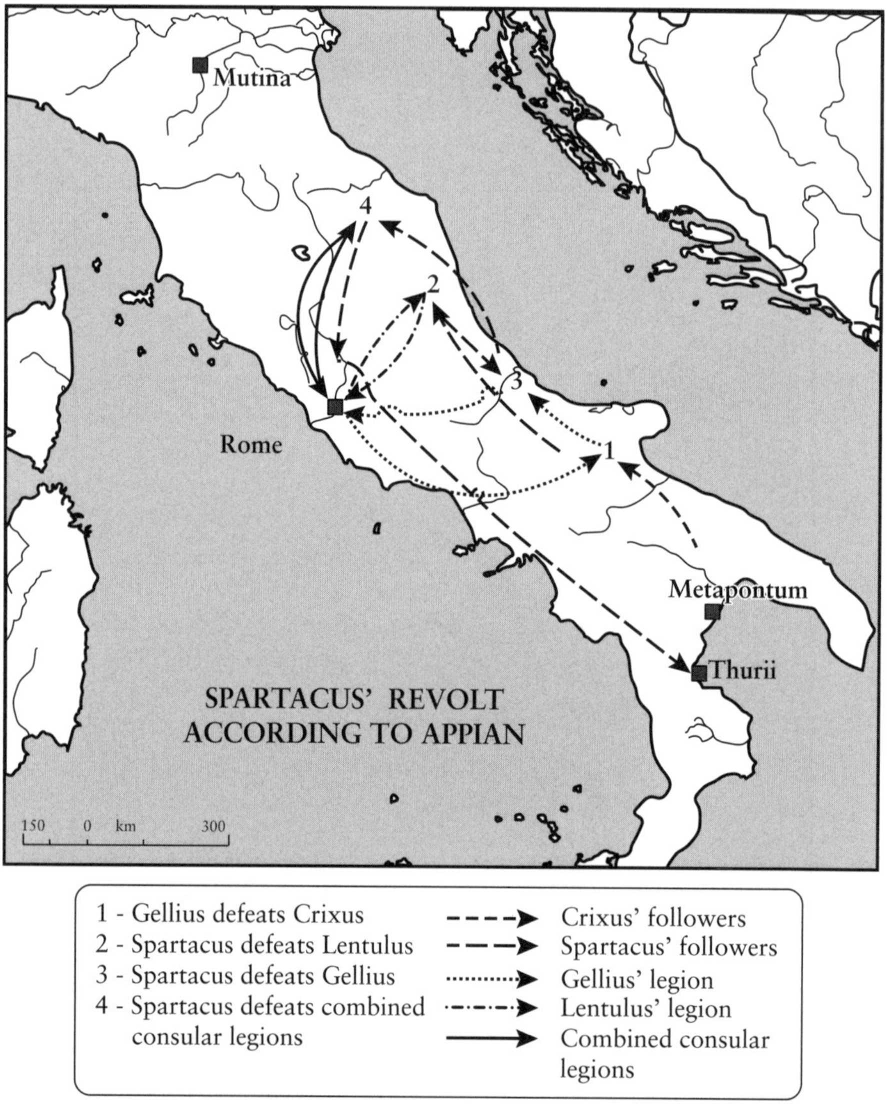
Mutina
Rome
Metapontum
Thurii
SPARTACUS' REVOLT
ACCORDING TO APPIAN
150 0 km 300
1 - Gellius defeats Crixus
2 - Spartacus defeats Lentulus
3 - Spartacus defeats Gellius
4 - Spartacus defeats combined consular legions
Crixus' followers
Spartacus' followers
Gellius' legion
Lentulus' legion
Combined consular legions

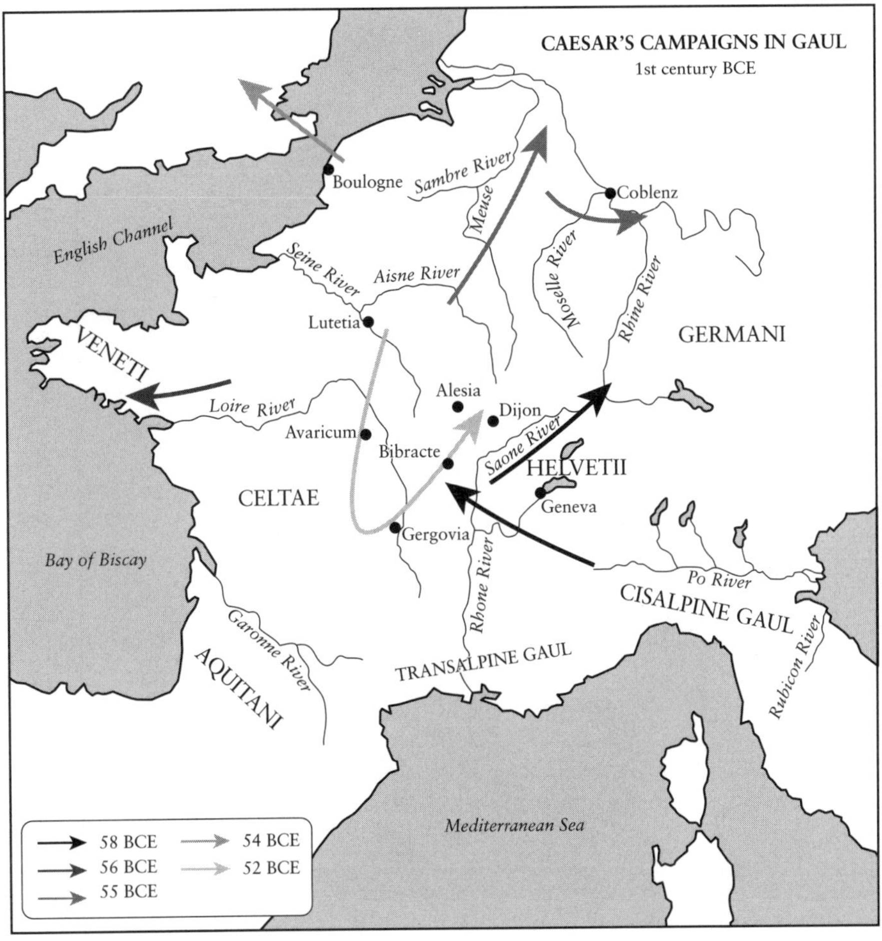
CAESAR'S CAMPAIGNS IN GAUL
1st century BCE
Boulogne
Sambre River
Coblenz
Meuse
English Channel
Seine River
Aisne River
Moselle River
Rhine River
Lutetia
GERMANI
VENETI
Alesia
Loire River
Dijon
Avaricum
Saone River
Bibracte
HELVETII
CELTAE
Geneva
Gergovia
Bay of Biscay
Po River
Rhone River
CISALPINE GAUL
Garonne River
TRANSALPINE GAUL
AQUITANI
Rubicon River
Mediterranean Sea
58 BCE
56 BCE
55 BCE
54 BCE
52 BCE

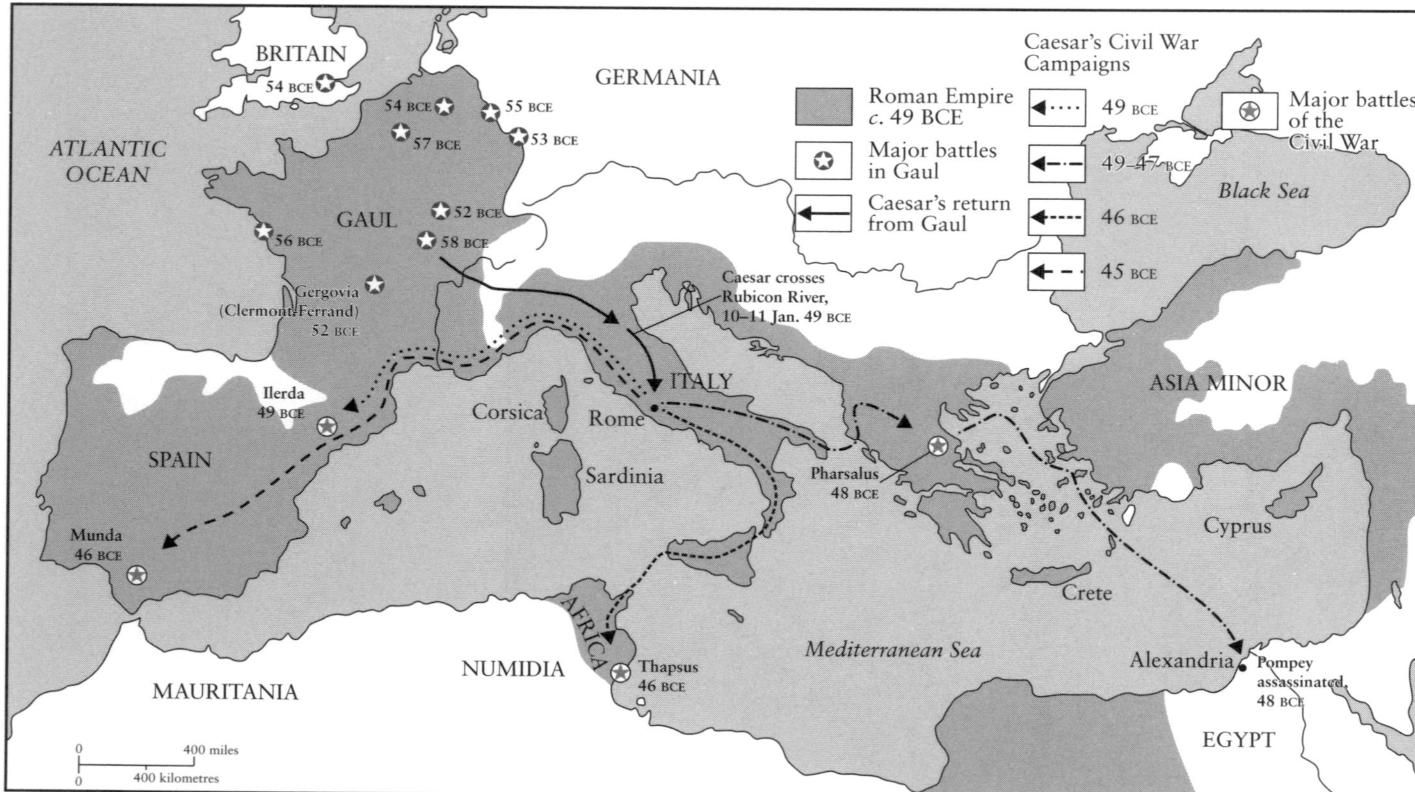

❄ Caesar's wars, first against the Gauls and Germans and then against Pompey, took him as far west as the Atlantic and east through Greece to Egypt.

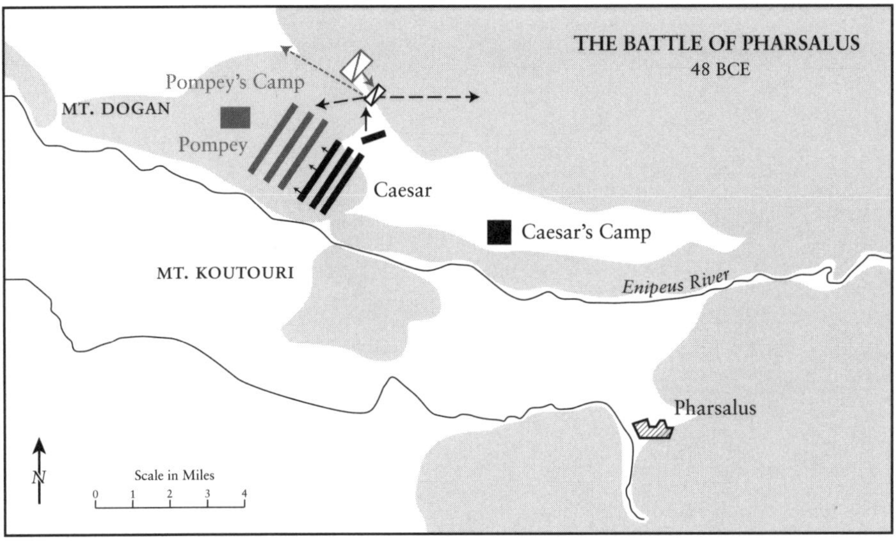
THE BATTLE OF PHARSALUS
48 BCE
Pompey's Camp
MT. DOGAN
Pompey
Caesar
Caesar's Camp
MT. KOUTOURI
Enipeus River
Pharsalus
N
Scale in Miles
0 1 2 3 4

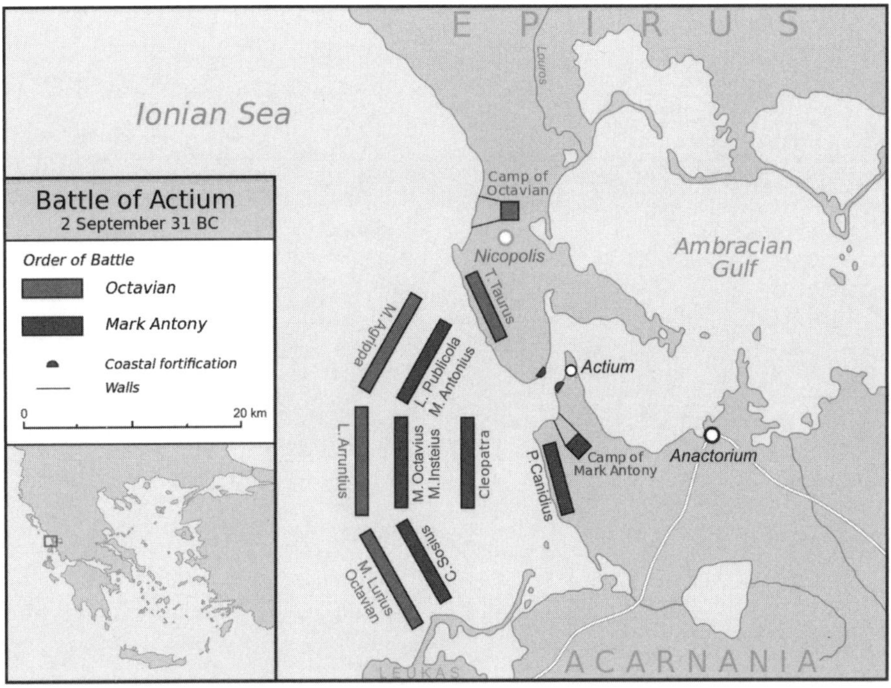
E P I R U S
Louros
Ionian Sea
Battle of Actium
2 September 31 BC
Order of Battle
Octavian
Mark Antony
Coastal fortification
Walls
0
20 km
Camp of Octavian
Nicopolis
Ambracian Gulf
T. Taurus
M. Agrippa
L. Publicola
M. Antonius
Actium
Anactorium
L. Arruntius
M. Octavius
M. Insteius
Cleopatra
P. Canidius
Camp of Mark Antony
C. Sosius
M. Lurius
Octavian
LEUKAS
ACARNANIA

Introduction

R*ome: Republic into Empire* examines the reasons why Rome descended into civil war in the early first century BCE and the political and social ramifications of the civil wars and their associated conflicts. It examines the protagonists, their political aims and the battles they fought and lost; it discusses the consequences of each battle and how the final conflict at Actium triggered a seismic change in the Roman political system with the establishment of an autocratic empire.

Rome: Republic into Empire is not just another arid chronological list of battles, their winners and their losers. Using primary sources provided by contemporary and later historians, other classical writers, official documents, inscriptional evidence and archaeology, the book offers an insight into the wars, battles and politics of this, the most turbulent and consequential of ancient world centuries. In so doing it gives us an eloquent and exciting political, military and social history of ancient Rome during one of its most cataclysmic and crucial periods, and tells us why and how the civil wars led to the establishment of one of the greatest empires the world has known.

The final chapter looks at the social and cultural impact and consequences of the civil wars: their effect on the Roman family – often ignored – and the rise of an anti-war movement of sorts in the face of establishment propaganda and nationalism.

A word about numbers. Numbers, particularly casualty figures, present a particular problem. Bias can easily contort these, inflating, as propaganda, enemy losses and minimizing Roman deaths and injuries. The size of an army was regularly estimated in multiples of 5,000, even though we know – and Dio, Plutarch, Appian and Polybius surely knew too - that the strength of the legions was notoriously inconsistent. If bias or rounding down or up did not bedevil the number, then the copyist may well have done – that inadvertent missing zero could change the complexion and interpretation of many a battle. Caution, therefore, is advised when interpreting troop and casualty figures.

Chapter 1

How did it come to this?

By the time Julius Caesar tore up the statute book and crossed the River Rubicon with his XIII legion on 10 January 49 BCE, the political and constitutional damage to the Roman Republic was already done. Caesar's action here was the culmination of decades of insurrection and internecine conflict stretching back to the later decades of the second century.

Appian wrote that the political crisis at this time was 'the prelude to … the Roman civil wars'. Velleius Paterculus believed that it was Gracchus' unprecedented standing for re-election as tribune in 132 BCE, and the riots and controversy that followed, that triggered the start of a crisis:

> 'This was the beginning of civil bloodshed and of the free reign of swords in the city of Rome. From then on justice was overthrown by force and the strongest was in charge.' (Velleius Paterculus 2.3.3–4)

At the Rubicon, treason was the charge levelled against Caesar and his legion, and civil war the outcome. Refusing to comply with the Senate's demand that he disband his army at this northern frontier of Italy was a conscious and deliberate act of war – a direct threat to the Roman Senate and to its champion, Pompey, who was tasked with dealing with Caesar, now an enemy of the state. According to Suetonius,[1] Caesar, after some deliberation, had grabbed a trumpet on the banks of the Rubicon, sounded the 'Advance!' and crossed the river: 'Let us go where the omens of the Gods and the crimes of our enemies take us! *Iacta alia est*! – the die is cast!' There was no going back: Rome and everything it stood for was in Caesar's sights.

Provincial Roman governors were appointed pro-magistrates with *imperium*, the right to command within their province. At the same time, the governor was the general of the Roman army within his province. According to Roman law, only the elected magistrates - consuls and praetors - could legally hold *imperium* within Italy itself. By crossing over into Italy at the head of an army, a general forfeited his *imperium*, thereby losing his legal right to command his troops. Caesar's illegal action was a capital offence, as was following the orders of a general who did not legally possess *imperium*. Caesar's troops were, therefore, implicated and could suffer the same fate: a sentence of death for treason.

Appian describes that morning's momentous events:

> 'Caesar got into his chariot and drove in the direction of Ariminum with his cavalry following closely behind. When he reached the river Rubicon, which forms the frontier with Italy, he stopped and stared at the stream, contemplating the outrage that would result if he crossed the river bearing arms. Caesar pulled himself together and proclaimed: "My friends, to leave this stream uncrossed will cause me a lot of distress; to cross it, much distress for all mankind." At that he rushed over as if possessed, saying, "The die is cast: bring it on." He then continued his rapid advance and took Ariminum at the break of day, advanced beyond, posting guards at the strategic positions, and subjugated all whom he encountered, either by force or by generosity.'[2]

Back in Rome, the consequences of Caesar's initiative were abundantly clear. Pompey, the consuls C. Claudius Marcellus and L. Cornelius Lentulus Crus, and many members of the Senate fled the city. The days of the Roman Republic were clearly numbered.

How, then, did it come to this? Rome was a victim of her own centuries of success. The pivotal Battle of Sentinum in 295 BCE and the equally decisive defeat of Tarentum and Pyrrhus in 275 marked Rome's dominance in the Italian peninsula, heralding the emergence of Rome as a new power on the world stage. Defeating the powerful army of Pyrrhus was the climax to Rome's systematic and arduous conquering of the Italian peninsula. It was achieved through serial, relentless warfare, extensive colonization, visionary and shrewd alliance-forging diplomacy and ongoing civil engineering projects which saw a network of vital roads and bridges established between the colonies, the allies and Rome. The Romans were now at liberty to flex their imperialistic military muscle overseas.

The first target was a powerful and acquisitive Carthage. Between 264–146 BCE, the two superpowers slogged it out over three wars and, despite catastrophic losses that would have easily floored any force less well organized or replenished, Rome finally emerged victorious and started building up an empire, Sicily and Sardinia being the first gains. To achieve this the Roman war engine required constant refuelling with new recruits, a factor which created something of a vicious circle. By the end of the third century, approximately one-third of Italians south of Rome had already been subdued and were officially Roman citizens; they were, therefore, obliged to do military service.[3] Although these newly enlisted Roman citizens were supported by troops supplied by allies, often as auxiliary forces, the casualties sustained in continuous devastating wars meant that Rome had to keep on conquering if she was to maintain a steady supply of soldiers, and thereby keep her forces up to strength, win battles and act as a deterrent to potential allied insurrection. Italy as a source of manpower was losing steam; Rome had to look further afield.

The wars with Carthage changed everything, forever. Crushing defeats and bitterly fought victories or stalemates resulted in yet more serious manpower shortages, exacerbated by the poverty inflicted on farmers by widespread depredation of Roman land and farms by rampant Carthaginian forces. It is estimated that over 120,000 Roman citizens perished during the three Punic wars - a casualty rate that would have crippled any other nation.

Roman warfare was inextricably linked with politics and economics, with land and the Conflict of the Orders being constant concerns during wars down the years. Economic return on his land gave the soldier-peasant the wherewithal to qualify for service, and to pay for his armour and weapons. The Conflict of the Orders ran from 494–287 BCE and can be described as the 200-year struggle for the plebeians to win political equality. These peasant farmers, of course, with their land and property qualification for army service, had always been the seed corn for recruitment; impoverishing them compromised this vital source. With no land they no longer qualified for army service; with no army service they had no means of support. Consequently, slaves were enlisted, as an emergency measure, to make up the losses.

Nevertheless, Rome was still to some extent able to mitigate the crisis, absorb the wounded and dead, and field armies in various theatres through a policy of enfranchisement of overrun territories and a prudent programme of building alliances. As we have seen, a condition of the former and an obligation of the latter was military service in the Roman army or navy. Between 225–200 BCE, the allies (*socii*) provided between half and three-quarters of Rome's total forces. However, military campaigns generally were increasingly extensive and costly, taking men away from their land and families for longer periods as Rome's expansionism continued apace; new far-away territories required permanent garrisons. With the Italian peninsula under Roman control, booty and land pillaged from earlier conquests was less plentiful, so the pressure to recruit and fight was relentless, as was the need to expand and conquer further afield.

Another factor fuelling the serial war-making was the commonly felt notion, amongst more conservative Romans, that any cessation of war encouraged laxity and moral decay amongst the menfolk of Rome. As a champion of tradition (*mos maiorum*) and a despiser of all things Greek, Cato the Elder (234–149 BCE) had spoken out sternly against what he saw as a period of moral decline and the erosion of the sturdy and rigorous principles on which Rome had lain her foundations. The defeat of Hannibal at Zama in 202 BCE, the victory over the Macedonians at Pydna in 168 BCE and the final extirpation of the Carthaginian threat in 146 BCE all, it was said, allowed Rome to relax and go soft; it encouraged the unprecedented influx of Greek and eastern luxuries, culture and lifestyle into a porous and receptive Rome. In the eyes of many, the waging of war, then, was how to keep Rome strong and the solution to all manner of political and social issues besetting Rome.[4]

Matters were made even worse for farmers and landowners when the elite and the rich began to appropriate the lands neglected, through no fault of their own, by war casualties – dead or disabled - or just left unoccupied by the peasant owners serving far away from home. Slaves were installed to work these 'vacant' lands – slaves who had been taken as prisoners of war, in their droves, by conquest. Much less land was now left for the indigenous farmer and there was little or no work available for the ethnic peasant workforce. These peasants had little choice but to converge on the towns and cities seeking work. Adding to this influx were the demobbed land-owning former soldiers who found their lands devastated or confiscated on their return from the battlefield. Others were faced with rising taxation and mounting debt, which meant that they too upped sticks and headed for the towns.

State land distribution ended in 170 BCE, but demand for land obviously did not. The inevitable and highly significant result of this was that commanders were now able to act and command independently, tempting recruits with their promises of beneficence and distribution of private land.

The wealthy patricians benefitted financially from their land-grabbing investments and, as a result, often became politically more powerful: political office and an easy journey along the *cursus honorum* depended on the ability to pay. The increasingly large estates they built up – the *latifundia* – enabled them also to fund increasingly lavish lifestyles, which in turn had been made possible by overseas conquest and the booty derived therefrom. Employing slave labour protected margins from revenues accrued from the sales of cash crops; grazing land was readily available thanks, as we have noted, to the devastation visited on southern Italy, in particular by Hannibal.[5] That some of this was officially public land - *ager publicus* – went unchallenged by the authorities, who also connived at breaches of the regulations controlling the size of holdings. For the time being, allies and plebeians were largely content so long as they too benefitted from the spoils of war. But something had to give.

The first real manifestation of social tension and conflict came with Tiberius Sempronius Gracchus, a tribune of the plebs, who in 133 BCE courageously introduced a bill limiting holdings in *ager publicus* to 500 iugera, as laid down by ancient law. There was outrage amongst the *optimates*, the rich, conservative senators, and Gracchus was assassinated for his troubles. Ten years later, his brother, Gaius Sempronius Gracchus, unleashed a much wider programme of reform embracing the urban grain supply, provincial administration and taxation, judicial reform and the extension of the franchise to Italian allies. He too was murdered, in 121 BCE, and much of his good work was repealed. The object of the Gracchan reforms was to ensure that the plebeians as well as the patrician class benefitted from the spoils of empire and expansion. Noble as this objective was, amongst the ruling classes it was never going to be on anyone's wish list. The senators, the *optimates*, were aristocrats and among the richest men in Rome; they were the traditional elite and they embodied the *mos maiorum*. Concessions of power, money and influence to the plebeian class - the lower orders, the *proletarii* - were resisted and would have to be fought for. Out of a population of one million or so in Rome, and five times that in greater Italy, the senatorial class probably numbered a mere 600–700; what they lacked in numbers they more than made up for in their tight networking, their exclusiveness and their stolid support of the status quo. But the opposition to the status quo was clearly there: we know that, for example, Caesar at the time could count on an army of 50,000 soldiers, to which we must add their numerous dependants and the businessmen who supplied the legions with provisions, uniforms, arms and other materiel, and the merchants who bought and sold the army's slaves and prisoners of war and converted their booty into cash. The industry created by Caesar has been estimated as benefiting about 20 per cent of Rome's population and contributed handsomely to the city's economy.[6]

The next twenty years or so brought a number of debilitating military challenges for Rome: a war with Jugurtha in Numidian Africa (112–105 BCE); slave revolts in 104 BCE; and incursions into Italy by the Germanic Cimbri, Ambrones and Teutones. All were to some degree mishandled; all highlighted the corruption rooted in those who wielded power. This opened the door for an ambitious *arriviste*, Gaius Marius.

Marius was born into an equestrian family near Arpinum in southern Latium. He is notable for securing the consulship an unprecedented seven times and, significantly for us, in 107 BCE accepting volunteers (*proletarii*) without land or wealth qualification into the army. At the same time, he had the state pay for their equipment and weaponry for the war against Jugurtha.

From the monarchical days of Servius Tullius (578-535 BCE), serving in the military as one of the *assidui* – those qualified to serve – was determined by wealth: the Roman soldier's passport into the army was his wealth and his property, his ability to pay for his arms and armour. Your worth dictated where you stood in the battle line; the richest, the *equites*, made up the cavalry. Wealth was divided into five classes: the top three were heavy infantry, while the fourth and fifth populated inferior ranks, with the men in the fifth valued at a minimum of 11,000 asses.

The traditional economic model on which the Roman army was based was thus turned on its head by Marius. From now on, soldiers could be professional or career soldiers: Roman troops now lived and died for the army; they had little else, with no land to return to. Life in the legion was the totality of their lives, and, accordingly, they sometimes developed an intense loyalty to their commanders and comrades in arms. Hitherto the *proletarii* had only been conscripted as a last resort, in times of crisis (*tumultus*); now they were to be key players, not just in the military but in the associated political machinations of their generals.

The deployment of slaves as navy rowers in 217 BCE presumably indicates that the men who were usually behind the oars – the *proletarii*, the *capite censi* – had been elevated to the ranks of the army. This major policy change was forced on the Romans by the truly devastating casualty figures for the battles of Trebia, Trasimene and Cannae against Hannibal between 218 and 216 BCE, each of which caused a calamitous haemorrhaging of available manpower. In addition, the property requirement was deflated from 11,000 to 4,000 asses. Rome's relentless overseas expansion, the economic depression and crisis in land prices meant that, at the same time, Rome needed more and more troops, but fewer landowners qualified for even the minimum property requirement. To make matters even worse, the population between 163 and 135 BCE declined by 6 per cent, so Rome needed to expand the reservoir of *assidui* at a time when all the available resources were declining. An illustration was in 134 BCE, when Rome was having trouble recruiting for campaigns in Hispania, largely because the province had a reputation for gruelling fighting and was low on the booty scale. Scipio Aemilianus had to rely on 4,000 volunteers, mainly from his client base. After 133 BCE, the bottom fell out of the property requirement when it was reduced further to just 1,500 asses.

Although this added some 75,000 *proletarii* to the ranks of the *assidui*, the problem still did not go away. Rome's supremacy around the Aegean and Mediterranean basin, now that the enemy threats had been extinguished, simply, as noted, allowed the rich to get richer while the poor farmers were depressed even further with the spread of the rich man's *latifundia* and forced by penury off the land into the cities. The Roman army's recruiting grounds were deserted. Free and seemingly limitless slave labour, fed by conquest after conquest, exacerbated the problem and eradicated the supply of recruits, low as the property requirement was.

As we have seen, the valiant attempts to assuage the pauperization of the citizen farmer by the brothers Gracchi and their plans for land redistribution to landless citizens were violently thwarted on the altar of conservative and aristocratic self-interest as civil unrest took hold in the streets of Rome. If the reforms had succeeded, the seedcorn of army recruitment, the *assidui*, may well have increased in numbers sufficient to avert the manpower crisis and obviate the need for Marius' apparent seismic change: the Republic may well have been saved. As it was, political violence took centre stage, the generals became very powerful, the Senate was emasculated and the soldiery assumed a new, albeit indirect, power in the running of the now doomed Roman Republic.

In reality then, the changes Marius made were the culmination and logical conclusion to a process which had been gathering strength and momentum for many decades: legalize army entry for all classes, regardless of property and wealth, pay for their kit and arms, and recruit on a voluntary basis rather than rely on the *dilectus*, the mandatory levy. From now on, 'men of property' did not imply 'soldiers', and vice versa, and your wealth did not dictate where you stood on the battlefield. The military was now being disassociated from the landed classes.

In the ineptitude and confusion which characterizes the Romans' behaviour in the war against Jugurtha, the decisive battle took place at Cirta in 106 BCE. Marius was in command, at the head of an army comprised in part of those volunteer *proletarii* whom he had rigorously trained. Jugurtha's brother-in-law, King Bocchus, ruled in neighbouring Mauretania (roughly modern Morocco), and was persuaded to help by the offer of land. Marius first took the southern fortress of Capsa and levelled it; other cities followed. Marius then took a Jugurthan treasury fort close to the River Moluccha, which compromised Bocchus' ability to pay his mercenaries and laid him exposed to Roman manipulation. Marius wintered some 600 miles to the west; during his march there he was attacked twice by Jugurtha and Bocchus. Marius won a resounding victory in the first, while the second battle took place at Cirta, which was another Roman victory, in which Marius was assisted by the quaestor, Lucius Cornelius Sulla Felix, and his cavalry.

Bocchus, however, read the writing on the wall and slyly defected to the Romans, in delicate negotiations deputed to and adroitly conducted by Sulla; Marius was no diplomat. Sulla persuaded Bocchus that the way into Rome's confidence lay in the betrayal of Jugurtha, and eventually Bocchus put any misgivings or conscience behind him. Jugurtha was kidnapped, sent to Rome, dumped in a pit under the Tullianum prison and left to die. Bocchus received a sizeable part of Numidia in payment for his treachery, and so the Jugurthine War came to an end.[7] The seeds of the enmity between the precocious but talented Sulla and Marius were probably sown here, and exacerbated when Sulla ostentatiously had a signet ring made which showed Jugurtha kneeling in submission to him. He also suggested that the defeat of Jugurtha was down to him, even though the victory officially belonged to Marius.

The appointment of Marius was highly significant in that he was elected by the popular assembly in defiance of the Senate, thus setting a sinister precedent which would eventually lead to a gradual undermining of the Senate's authority.

In 102 BCE, Marius dealt with the menace presented by the Cimbri and Teutones, who had shattered the Romans at Arausio in 105 BCE. He raised another army of *proletarii*, whose rigorous training programme included digging a canal to bypass the silted-up Rhone estuary. The Cimbri, Teutones, Ambrones and Tigurini launched a bold three-pronged attack on the Romans. However, Marius took advantage of the fact that the enemy forces were now split into three manageable armies, and having allowed the huge army to pass (it apparently took six days), he lured the Teutones into an area near Aquae Sextiae from where there could be no retreat. The Teutones were massacred or taken prisoner in droves; their king, Teutobodus, was among the captured. The casualty figures are subject to exaggeration and inflation, but Livy says 200,000 died, with 90,000 made prisoners of war.[8]

In 101 BCE, Marius and Catulus, waiting for the hot and energy-sapping summer to arrive, confronted the Cimbri at Campi Raudii near Vercellae. Here they were also victorious - killing many (60,000) and enslaving even more (120,000). Those who escaped fled back to their camp, only to be killed by their womenfolk, who then killed themselves. Sulla, meanwhile, defeated the Tigurini in the eastern Alpine ranges.[9] With this defeat, the threat posed by the Northmen was extinguished; however, it also served to fan the flames of rivalry between Marius and Sulla. Marius, in true cavalier style, granted Roman citizenship to his Italian allies after the battle, without the permission of the Senate. To Marius, the voice of an ally on the battlefield was indistinguishable from the voice of the law.

The consequences for Rome were profound. The military manpower problem may have been solved by Marius' sweeping change, but a sinister corollary of the Marian reforms was that the plebeians, the proletariat, were for the first time invested with a powerful, unified voice with which to give vent to any grievances. By the same token, the loyalty inculcated by a seemingly more personal and caring type of commander invested in that commander a military power the like of which was unknown in Rome until then.

To achieve the land redistribution promised to veterans, Marius attached himself to the tribune of the people, Lucius Appuleius Saturninus, a man with previous form when it came to exercising political violence. Marius won another consulship in 100 BCE and Saturninus introduced, on Marius' behalf, proposals by which veterans were allocated land on discharge from the army. Roman citizenship was granted to Italian allies who had supported Marius against the Germanic invaders.

The proposals went through, but not without stiff opposition and violence on the streets of Rome. Marius felt obliged to bring his soldiers into Rome to control the unrest, signifying not just an attempt to keep the peace but also a veiled threat as to the consequences should the veterans be denied their land.

Another momentous political and constitutional precedent, this was the first demonstration of the undeniable and uncomfortable fact that now no-one could rule Rome without the support of the army.

The Social War of 91–87 BCE was also to have a major impact. Italian allies (the *socii*) revolted and turned to arms when Rome refused them the vote and denied the right to be Roman citizens. Rome eventually relented, citizenship was granted to inhabitants south of the Po and with the vote came military service. This significantly increased the number of potential recruits available to the Romans and helped unify the peninsula again. But only very briefly.

Chapter 2

The Social War (91–87 BCE)

The name of the Social War derives from the Latin for allies, *socii*. The wars are also known as the Allied War, the Italian War or the Marsic War – a war waged between the Romans and a number of the other Italian cities which had been Roman allies, in some cases for centuries, and had paid tribute and routinely supplied troops to sustain Rome's conquest of the Italian peninsula and beyond. The war had a crucial impact on Roman politics and social history, and on the deconstruction of the Republic.

By the end of the Punic Wars there were more than 150 allied treaties in force up and down the Italian peninsula. The military importance of the allies cannot be understated: by the second century BCE, between half and two-thirds of the troops in Roman armies were sourced from allies. Military obligations were stipulated in the *formula togatorum*, the list of those who wear the toga, establishing precisely the number of troops which could be called upon from each ally. While Rome dictated their foreign policies – to the clear advantage of Rome – the allies were, generally speaking, happy to coexist with Rome as client states in exchange for local autonomy. Loyalty to Rome was amply demonstrated during the wars with Hannibal. Other benefits for the allies included security, a share of booty and tax receipts where appropriate and the (theoretical at least) right to participate in the assignment of land and colonies.

This age-old vexed question of land distribution was at the centre of the Roman relationship with her Italian allies. By the time of Marius, the system had become exploitative and unfair, heavily biased as it was against the allies. Appian gives a bleak assessment of the situation when he tells us that the Romans' policy of land distribution was prejudiced and caused inequality of land-ownership and wealth, leading to the 'Italic people declining little by little into pauperism and paucity of numbers without any hope of remedy'. Smallholders tended to farm wheat and barley, for which the return was far lower than on the cash crops like figs, olives and wine – the preserve of the wealthy owners of the larger estates. The lower prices meant smaller harvests and a fragile food supply. Lucilius, a contemporary poet, pithily sums it up with 'the nourishing grain runs out and there is no bread for the common people'. Add the growing disaffection caused by the ritual exploitation by the rich, and we have the perfect recipe for rebellion.

Over the years, some had tried to avert the inevitable, but meddling with the status quo won no friends; discretion was ever the better part of valour. Scipio Aemilianus – heroic victor over Carthage - was one who tried to resolve the issue, but he pulled out when he saw the hostility he was attracting. Likewise Gaius Laelius, who, in the 140s, withdrew his agrarian bill with the same concerns; as we have seen, the brothers Gracchi died for their troubles. Committees of Action were convened in a number of Italian towns, and one armed force 10,000 strong under Q. Poppaedius Silo, leader of the Marsi, even set off to march on Rome, intent on surrounding the Senate house and demanding citizenship for his people. Discretion won the day again when Silo turned back.

For the allies, Roman citizenship and the right to vote were the clear objectives. The franchise would give the allies political and social parity and entry into the *equites* class, which in turn would provide a say and role in the shaping of Roman foreign and domestic policy. In the words of Appian, they would become partners in empire instead of subjects.[1]

A contemptuous rebuff from the Roman aristocrats provided the litmus paper which, according to Appian, sent the Italic peoples down an inexorable path to poverty with no hope of redress. Unrest increased, fanned unhelpfully by the Lex Licinia Mucia in 95 BCE which gave powers to expel Italic troublemakers from Rome. The law proved ineffective, only serving to increase agitation and act as a recruiting sergeant, harnessing more organized opposition amongst the allies. In 91 BCE, the tribune Marcus Livius Drusus attempted to ease the problem by offering to extend Roman citizenship to the allies, thus giving them a bigger say in national affairs and control of their own lands. In addition, he proposed reforming the corrupt courts by promoting 300 *equites* into the roles of the Senate, also introducing new land and grain laws which were popular with the rural and urban plebs alike. In reality, Drusus' objective in extending the franchise to the Italian allies was to inject a new voting force loyal to traditional senatorial authority. Nevertheless, in return, the allies agreed to join Drusus' clientele, boosting his power considerably. The Senate, however, saw it all very differently, completely missing the point.

Crassus, originally a powerful backer of his in the Senate, deserted him. The Drusus proposals were universally unpopular, particularly and not surprisingly among the landowning elite, and were dismissed out of hand by the Senate. Romans of all classes were urged to pull together against what was seen as the most dangerous threat since Carthage. Drusus was left with nothing except sky and mud (*caelum et caenum*) – mud on his face. He was then assassinated on suspicion of having been in league with Silo. The allies were outraged, declared independence from Rome and started the war in a coalition led by the Marsi and Samnites and spearheaded by the revolt of the Picentes at Asculum. Velleius Paterculus (2, 15) encapsulates the situation:

> 'The [rebels] were totally within their rights. All they wanted was to be citizens in an empire whose lands their weapons defended. Every year and in every war they contributed twice as many infantry and cavalry … the state treated with scorn the people of its own race and kin, rejecting them as strangers and foreigners.'

The rebellion was largely confined to territories in the central and southern Apennines and the central part of the Adriatic coastland. However, these lands could provide some of Italy's best soldiers – veterans from Marius' battle-hardened armies included.

The aim of the allies was to secede from Rome and create their own independent confederation, to be called *Italia*, with its own capital at Corfinium (modern Abruzzo), to be renamed *Italica*. A federal senate was formed from 500 delegates sent from the rebel towns. As for finance, they minted their own coinage to pay for the army; some coins depict eight warriors taking an oath, presumably representing the former allies involved: Marsi, Picentines, Paeligni, Marrucini, Vestini, Frentani, Samnites and Hirpini.[2] The other four rebel allies were the Pompeiani, Venusini, Iapygii and Lucani. Other coins graphically depict the Italian bull goring the Roman wolf. Militarily, the Allies mimicked Roman organization by having two consuls leading two separate armies. Naturally, there were differences in aspirations: the Latin-speaking northern allies wanted an extension of the franchise; the Oscan-speaking Samnites wanted nothing less than total independence.

Rome's strategy was to deal with the immediate military threat and prevent any further defections: one of the two separate theatres of war was assigned to each of the consuls of 90 BCE. In the north, the consul Publius Rutilius Lupus was joined by Gaius Marius and Pompeius Strabo; in the south, the consul Lucius Julius Caesar (Sextus Julius) commanded with Lucius Cornelius Sulla and Titus Didius. Levies of citizens in loyal areas were bolstered by auxiliary units made up of Gauls, Spaniards and Numidians; ex-slaves were recruited to carry out naval patrols. Fifteen legions, or 150,000 men, were signed up in all.

The opening shot turned out well for the allies: the Samnite general Vettius Scaton heavily defeated the army of Lucius Julius Caesar, killing 2,000 of his men. Scaton then laid siege to Aesernia, which fell in 90 BCE. Sulla relieved the town with twenty-four cohorts, inflicting great losses on the allies. The relief was short-lived, however, as the town was back in allied hands later that year.[3] The Romans suffered a further defeat when Marcus Lamponius killed 800 soldiers led by Publius Licinius Crassus and drove the survivors into the town of Grumentum.[4] Meanwhile, in the south, Samnite commander Gaius Papius Mutilus was wreaking havoc in Campania. To bolster his army, he pressed 10,000 infantry and 1,000 cavalry into his service, using them to good effect in his siege of Acerrae (near modern Naples). Pompeii and Nola fell, but Capua, with its arsenal, was successfully defended. A battle then ensued with Lucius Julius Caesar and his 10,000 foot and African cavalry; he slew 6,000 allies and withdrew.[5] The following year, 90 BCE, Vettius Scaton laid a deadly ambush for the Romans, killing 8,000 at the Battle of Tolenus River. The Romans had built two bridges over the river out of sight of each other – one constructed by Rutilius, the other by Marius. When Rutilius crossed the bridge with his army, Vettius Scaton attacked, with deadly consequences. Rutilius died from wounds after the battle.

Marius saw the tell-tale signs of Roman corpses floating down the river; he attacked the Marsi and returned the favour by killing 8,000 of them.[6] Lucius Julius Caesar made the mistake of marching through a gorge at Teanum Sidicinum with 30,000 infantry and 5,000 cavalry. Predictably, he was successfully attacked by a force of Samnites under Marius Egnatius, losing most of his men.[7]

The end to the hostilities, however, was brought about by diplomacy rather than military action. Enough was enough. The intractable Romans finally climbed down and offered concessions to the allies. With the 90 BCE consular elections looming, Lucius Julius Caesar had returned to Rome and introduced the *Lex Iulia de Civitate Latinis et Socii Danda*, granting Roman citizenship to all citizens of Italic towns which had not taken up arms against Rome in the war (notably Etruria and Umbria) to deter them from joining the rebellion. Italians who were currently revolting and agreed to immediately lay down their arms were also offered the franchise.

The next year, 89 BCE, the Romans went a step further and introduced the *Lex Plautia Papiria de Civitate Sociis*, which granted Roman citizenship to the allies who had rebelled in an attempt to extinguish the unrest once and for all. Citizenship might also be granted in recognition of distinguished military service in combat. These concessions were essentially what the allies were fighting for, but many declined to lay down their arms and the war went on.

The allied army fled to Asculum, home town of the Picentes, which was promptly besieged by Pompeius.[8] Allegedly, 60,000 Italians faced 75,000 Romans here. The Marsi lost 18,000 men when they attacked; they were later joined by the Picentes, led by Vidacilius with eight cohorts. He barged his way into the town through the Roman ranks, but had realised that all was lost. He built a huge pyre, had a good meal and committed suicide by taking poison. The pyre was lit and the town fell to the Romans. Archaeology has revealed graffiti-marked sling stones intended for Pompeius: *feri Pompeium* ('hit Pompeius'); some even stipulate where: *ventri* ('in the stomach').

Marius saved the day for Rome when he managed to divert the rebels from marching on Rome down the Via Valeria after the Battle of the Fucine Lake; Rutilius Lupus was killed here. The battle was also notable for the death of Lucius Porcius Cato, who had insulted Marius by comparing and equating their achievements and was surreptitiously murdered during the battle by Marius' son.[9] Later that year, Sulla camped in the Pompeian Hills and was confronted by Lucius Cluentius. An impetuous Sulla attacked the allied army even though he was understrength due to the absence of parties out foraging. Sulla was defeated, but made good in a second attack. Cluentius took reinforcements and challenged Sulla for a third time. Proceedings began with a giant of a Gaul on the allied side offering single combat to a Roman. A diminutive Roman stepped forward and slew the Goliath; the rest of the Gauls turned and fled. Taking advantage of this, Sulla attacked and killed 3,000 allies in their flight to Nola. The allies, however, suffered much greater losses outside the gates of the city when the inhabitants cautiously only opened one of the gates: 20,000 allies died there, including Lucius.[10] At Canusium later that year, the Romans suffered another reverse when Gaius Cosconius laid siege to the town and was routed by the Samnites; he retreated to Cannae. The Social War came to an end after the Battle of the Teanus River, when the allied leaders Poppaedius Silo and Obsidius were killed in a furious clash with the pro-Roman Apulians.[11]

Philip Matyszak sums up the contradictions and paradoxes inherent in the Social War:

> 'Nations so desperate to give up their independence that they fought a war against the state that refused to take it; of the Roman Republic losing that war – itself a rarity – then winning by giving their enemies what they wanted. So the only instance in history of the opposite of a war of independence, was also one of the few cases where surrender brought victory to the losing side.'[12]

Arguably, the Romans had a lucky escape. The allies pursued a policy of wearing down their quarry by sporadic incursions and attacks on the Roman centres of communication. Had they pressed home their notable victories with more direct, aggressive action – particularly with an assault on Rome - then the outcome might have been very different. Rome's eventual, tortuously won victory had the accidental benefit of consolidating Rome with Italy, thus making Rome a stronger power generally, inheriting as she did a fecund supply of able officials and administrators, making her better equipped to deal with the destructive civil wars and the demanding empire which were on the horizon. However, politically and militarily, the Social War was a disaster; losses of manpower and money apart, it widened further the schism between army and state, facilitating the ruinous rise of the triumvirates, expediting the end of the Republic.

It is unlikely that Marius anticipated one of the major consequences of his military reforms. As we have seen, the new non-land-owning class of soldiers had no lands to return to, so they grew dependent on their generals for support.

At the same time, the state had no means of paying adequate discharge payments to its burgeoning armies. Commanders saw an opportunity here: they could recruit and retain armies with the promises of generous pay and pensions which, through long-term mutual loyalty, might well lead to prodigious military and political power for themselves. Marius and Sulla were the first Roman generals to demonstrate the political backing that a military man could expect from the votes lodged by his current soldiers and former army veterans. From now on the soldiery was in the pay of the consuls and generals - and not the state. Individual military leaders could exercise significant political power and influence through their armies, perhaps to effect revolutionary change in Rome. Sulla, in 88 BCE, was the first to try this, but he was by no means the last.

To finance his largesse, the ambitious Roman consul-commander needed money. Booty from foreign conquests was recognized as obvious, easy pickings, fuelling a scramble to overrun and despoil rich new territories, particularly in Greece and the eastern Mediterranean. Money from booty was also needed to support and finance the expanding urban economies that were generated by the influx of agricultural workers from surrounding lands. As increasing numbers of foreign territories fell under Rome's sway, the wealth, extravagance, opulence, tax revenues and ostentatious military triumphs increased. It would all culminate in the bloody civil wars, in which the various triumvirates and their armies relentlessly battled and battered each other, until one general, Octavian, emerged as the victor at the Battle of Actium. By then the Republic was ancient history: the Empire was the future.

Chapter 3

Sulla's First Civil War (88–87 BCE)

Mithridates VI of Pontus must have eyed the turmoil in Italy with delight. Mithridates was keen to expand in the region and carve out *lebensraum* at the expense of his neighbours, Cappadocia and Bithynia – both Roman client states. Here was a chance to build on his plan to expand and eradicate the Roman presence in Asia Minor. He proceeded to foment opposition to the Romans, predicated on the onerous taxes they insisted on levying; this reached its climax in the brutal execution of 80,000 Roman and Italian citizens and other immigrants in Asia Minor. The massacre has become known as the Asiatic Vespers, a name given by analogy with the Sicilian Vespers of 1282 CE in which a bloody rebellion broke out in Sicily against Charles I of France.

The Pontic massacre was planned meticulously and coordinated clinically to occur on the same day in several towns throughout the region. The outraged Roman Senate responded by sending a huge invasion force to cripple Mithridates and annex his territory: this was the First Mithridatic War.

At the beginning of the first century BCE, Mithridates, in expansionist mood, had overrun Cappadocia but, much to his irritiation, was ordered by the Romans to withdraw. He aimed to carve up Paphlagonia and Galatia in league with Nicomedes III of Bithynia. Mithridates, however, soon realized that Nicomedes was nothing more than a Roman puppet intent on an anti-Pontic alliance with the Roman Republic. Mithridates duly clashed with Nicomedes over Cappadocia and defeated him in a series of battles. Nicomedes had no option but to enlist the assistance of Rome. The Romans twice interceded on behalf of Nicomedes (95 and 92 BCE). Mithridates made ready for war with Rome. His sister, Laodice, became Queen of Cappadocia after Mithridates had his brother-in-law, Ariarathes VI, assassinated by Gordius, a Cappadocian nobleman and ally of Mithridates. Laodice ruled as regent for her son Ariarathes VII. Things got very complicated when Laodice married

Nicomedes III, now arch enemy of Pontus. Nicomedes took Cappadocia, but Mithridates removed him. Uncomfortably for Mithridates, he was now virtually surrounded by Roman client states so any empire-building inevitably brought him into conflict with Rome. With Rome preoccupied with the Social War, he flexed his expansionist muscle again, expelling Nicomedes from Bithynia and Ariobarzanes from Cappadocia. The Romans sent Manius Aquilius to restore their puppet leaders. Diplomacy, in the shape of the Aquillian Delegation, came to nothing, so Mithridates attacked Cappadocia again, all the while amassing a huge army of some 250,000 infantry and 40,000 cavalry. Neoptomelus and Archelaus were his generals. Aquilius could only muster 120,000 soldiers, which he divided into three divisions. Nicomedes struck first with 50,000 infantry and 6,000 cavalry at the Amnias River in Paphlagonia against the smaller force of Neoptomelus and Archelaus. The latter, however, were equipped with highly effective scythe-wheeled chariots, literally scything down the Bithynians. The Bithynians were routed by the twin forces of Neoptomelus and Archelaus, but the prisoners that were taken were treated by Mithridates with notable humanity. This defeat by an inferior force gave the Romans pause for thought. Aquilius was captured, with terrible consequences recorded by Appian:

> '[Mithridates] captured Manius Aquilius, one of the ambassadors and the one who was most to blame for this war. Mithridates led him around, bound on an ass, and compelled him to introduce himself to the public as "maniac". Finally, at Pergamon, Mithridates poured molten gold down his throat, thus rebuking the Romans for their bribe-taking.'[1]

The victorious Mithridates was now at liberty to move around the region without impediment. For Rome it was disaster, but worse was to follow: it was at this time that Mithridates ordered the extermination of all Romans and Italians in the Asiatic Vespers.[2] In 88 BCE, Mithridates had received some sinister and mischievous advice from a leading Greek philosopher at his court, Metrodoros of Skepsis, known as *ho misoromaios* – 'the Roman-hater'. Metrodoros convinced the king that if he wanted to bring more communities on side against the Romans, he should simply exterminate all Romans in the province, regardless of age or sex; this was the only way to be rid of the Roman yoke forever. As noted, the massacre was clinically executed and timed to take the victims by surprise, in every community and simultaneously. In a letter to all the civic authorities, Mithridates stipulated that the atrocity was to happen one month after the date of his letter. Appian takes up the gruesome story, its precision and insidious planning:

> '[Mithridates] wrote secretly to all his satraps and magistrates that on the thirtieth day thereafter they should assault all Romans and Italians in their towns, and their wives and children and their slaves of Italian birth, kill them and throw their bodies out unburied, and share their goods with himself. He threatened to punish any who should bury the dead or conceal the living, and offered rewards to informers and to those who should kill persons in hiding, and freedom to slaves for betraying their masters. To debtors for killing money-lenders he offered release from one half of their obligations.'[3]

This is how the atrocity unfurled:

> 'The Ephesians tore fugitives, who had sought sanctuary in the temple of Artemis, from the very statues of the goddess and slew them. The Pergameans shot with arrows those who had fled to the temple of Aesculapius, while they were still clinging to his statues. The Adramytteans followed those who sought to escape by swimming, into the sea, and killed them and drowned their children. The Caunii, who had been made subject to Rhodes after the war against [the Seleucid King Antiochus III] and had been lately liberated by the Romans, pursued the Italians who had taken refuge about the Vesta statue of the senate house, tore them from the shrine, killed children before their mothers' eyes, and then killed the mothers themselves and their husbands after them. The citizens of Tralles, in order to avoid the appearance of blood-guiltiness, hired a savage monster named Theophilus, of Paphlagonia, to do the work. He conducted the victims to the temple of Concord, and there murdered them, chopping off the hands of some who were embracing the sacred images.'[4]

The Romans were now on a war footing. In 88 BCE, Sulla was elected consul and the Senate had to decide on whom to confer the lucrative and prestigious command in the coming war against Mithridates. The Senate chose Sulla, but Marius, with some skulduggery, induced the tribune Publius Sulpicius Rufus to call the *concilium plebis*, which appointed Marius instead. Marius had agreed to annul Rufus' debts. Sulla, quite naturally, was less than pleased.

Sulla left Rome behind for Nola, where his army waited, the very army which the Senate had asked him to assemble and lead against Mithridates. Sulla successfully persuaded his legions to defy the assembly and accept him as their leader. At this critical juncture, Sulla took the momentous decision to order his six legions to march with him on Rome and foment a civil war.

When Marius saw Sulla's intent, he hastily organized a defence of the city by deploying a motley force, including gladiators. This, of course, presented no opposition to Sulla's legions. Sulla crossed the *pomerium* – a religious boundary encircling the city of Rome and defining its legal and physical existence. He occupied the Esquiline Gate while the other consul, Quintus Pompeius, took the Colline Gate. Sulla entered Rome with two of his legions and engaged Marius in the Esquiline forum. Despite offering freedom to any slave who joined his ranks, Marius was subdued and fled Rome for Africa, where he was sentenced to death *in absentia* along with Sulpicius Rufus.[5] Sulla was reconfirmed again as the commander of the campaign against Mithridates. He departed Rome with his legions and marched east.

In 88 BCE Mithridates opened hostilities with the Battle of the River Amnias in Paphlagonia against Nicomedes IV of Bithynia. Mithridates was victorious, thus depriving the Romans of the province of Asia for some years. The Pontic general Archelaus made excellent use of his scythed chariots. According to Appian,

> 'the chariots caused such horrific wounds … cutting some of them in two, and ripping others to shreds. So horrified was the Bithynian army at the sight of men sliced in half while still breathing, or their mangled body parts hanging off the scythes that they were overcome rather by the sheer horror of the spectacle than by the loss of the battle.'

The Romans were alarmed that Archelaus' small force could rout the 50,000 foot and 6,000 horse of Nicomedes.[6]

Mithridates finished the job at the Battle of Protopachium, where Neoptolemus clashed with Manius Aquilius, the Roman legate, and slew 10,000 Romans. Mithridates then expelled Nicomedes from Bithynia and Ariobarzanes from Cappadocia.[7]

Glorying in his success, Mithridates now eyed Europe. His crony, Aristion, stirred up unrest in Athens and was made tyrant there; the city, its port of Piraeus and other parts of southern and central Greece were taken. Sulla came in pursuit and won over most of the Greek states. Athens, nevertheless, remained loyal to Mithridates and was subjected to a brutal, merciless siege through the winter of 87 and 86. Athens fell to Sulla on 1 March 86 BCE when the water ran out and the Athenians were dying of starvation. The city and its citizens were severely punished as a warning to others contemplating such insolent and anti-Roman behaviour:

> 'Knowing that the defenders of Athens were severely pressed by hunger, that they had devoured all their cattle, boiled the hides and skins, and licked what they could get from them, and that some had even eaten human flesh, Sulla directed his soldiers to encircle the city with a ditch so that the inhabitants might not escape secretly, even one by one. This done, he brought up his ladders and at the same time began to break through the wall. The feeble defenders were soon put to flight, and the Romans rushed into the city.
>
> 'A great and pitiless slaughter ensued in Athens, the inhabitants, for want of nourishment, being too weak to escape. Sulla ordered an indiscriminate massacre, not sparing women or children. He was angry that they had so suddenly joined the barbarians without cause, and had displayed such violent animosity toward him. Most of the Athenians, when they heard the order given, rushed upon the swords of the slayers voluntarily. Sulla forbade the burning of the city, but allowed the soldiers to plunder it. In many houses they found human flesh prepared for food. The next day Sulla sold the slaves at auction.'[8]

Sulla recaptured Piraeus, then looted and ransacked the area, most of which had been torched by the departing Archelaus, including Philon's famous arsenal. Sulla now moved into Boeotia and confronted Archelaus' Pontic army at Chaeronea in 86 BCE, soundly defeating it and slaying 10,000 for the reported loss of an unbelievable twelve or thirteen men. Sulla had closed the gap between the armies and rendered the scythe-wheeled chariots useless. Plutarch records a humorous scenario:

> '[Sulla] robbed the scythe-bearing chariots of their efficiency. For these are of most avail over a long distance, which gives them velocity and impetus for breaking through an opposing line; short runs are ineffectual and feeble, as in the case of missiles which do not get full propulsion. And this proved to be true now in the case of the Barbarians. The first of their chariots were driven along feebly and engaged sluggishly, so that the Romans, after repulsing them, clapped their hands and laughed and called for more, as they are wont to do at the races in the circus.'

Sulla then moved north into Thessaly and was met at Orchomenus by 80,000 crack Mithridatic troops who had arrived by sea at Chalcis in Euboea. In a bid to lessen the impact of Archelaus' cavalry by digging trenches down the sides of the plain, his engineers and their guards were cut down. Sulla rallied his army with a solo charge on foot into the ranks of the enemy, where they slew 15,000 troops.[9] Plutarch says that the slaughter was so great that the marshes were clogged with blood; weapons were still being found protruding out of the marshes 200 years later.[10] After the battle Archelaus defected to Rome and Mithridates' designs on Europe evaporated.

Peace was signed at the Treaty of Dardanus, Mithridates accepting terms in which all his gains in Asia, Cappadocia and Bithynia reverted to their original rulers but left him to rule Pontus – a trade-off for a huge indemnity and the loan of seventy ships to Sulla to enable him to return to Rome and face the music.

Ominously, in 87 BCE Gnaeus Octavius, a supporter of Sulla, and Lucius Cornelius Cinna, a supporter of Marius, had been elected consuls. With Sulla away in Greece, street fighting erupted between the conservative faction followers of Sulla, led by Octavius, and the popular supporters of Cinna. That same year, internal strife in Rome led to Cinna's dismissal. Marius, meanwhile, landed in Etruria, raised an army, sacked Ostia and, joining forces with Cinna, laid siege to Rome; along the way he had unscrupulously increased his army by forcibly freeing farm slaves and adding them to the ranks. Plutarch provides some details:

> '[B]y cutting off the grain-ships with his fleet and robbing the merchants, [Marius] took control of Rome's supplies; next, he sailed to the maritime cities and took them, finally seizing Ostia itself, which was treacherously surrendered to him. He plundered all the property there and killed most of its inhabitants; by throwing a bridge across the river he then severed the supply lines from the sea. Then he set off and marched with his army towards the city, and occupied the hill called Janiculum.'[11]

On the promise of a cessation of hostilities from Cinna, the Senate gave in and Marius entered Rome with his army. Despite Cinna's vow, some of the troops went on a five-day rampage, slaughtering prominent supporters of Sulla, including Octavius, displaying their heads in the forum as a warning to others. The Senate exiled Sulla and, under pressure, replaced him as commander in the war against Mithridates with Marius. Both Marius and Cinna were elected consuls for 86; Cinna and the general Quintus Sertorius ordered their less lawless troops to end the slaughter in Rome by killing the rampaging soldiers.

Plutarch records that Marius' resurgence was decidedly savage: his 'anger got worse every day as did his thirst for blood; he went on killing anyone he suspected'. The rising death toll included former consul Q. Lutatius Catulus, Publicus Licinius Crassus and the orator Marcus Antonius, Mark Antony's grandfather. Plutarch goes on to say:

> 'If anyone greeted Marius and was ignored, this in itself was a sign for the man to be slaughtered there and then in the street; even all Marius' friends were filled with trepidation and horror when they approached to greet him.'[12]

Marius nullified and repealed Sulla's reforms and laws, and exiled Sulla. However, Marius died a fortnight later and Cinna was left in sole control of Rome. Sulla, though, was not finished.

Plutarch concludes his biography of Marius with this fitting epilogue:

> 'So, then, Marius died, seventeen days after beginning his seventh consulship. Rome was immediately filled with great rejoicing and a confident hope that she was rid of a grievous tyranny; but in a few days the people saw that they had got a new and vigorous tyrant in exchange for the old one.'

Marius must take some considerable responsibility for the collapse of the Republic and the emergence of the Empire. His cavalier attitude to the law and to Roman tradition, not least in recruiting from the urban proletariat, forced his enemies and subsequent ambitious commanders into positions which, as far as the Republic was concerned, were increasingly untenable, precarious and fragile. Throwing open the doors to the urban poor paved the way for their unprecedented dependence on and loyalty towards military commanders, which, in turn, enabled Julius Caesar to make his decision to cross the Rubicon.

Chapter 4

Sulla's Second Civil War (82–81 BCE)

Sulla defied the Senate when it ordered him to return to Rome to face trial. He was preoccupied with Mithridates until the close of 83 BCE in a successful campaign which he prosecuted with one eye on goings-on back in Rome. The sooner he could bring Mithridates to terms, the sooner he could conclude the unfinished business at home and satisfy his ambitions. Marius may have gone, but neither he nor his cause were forgotten. Cinna, still consul in Rome, took the opportunity to deal with a revolt in Illyria in 84 BCE by interposing his army between Sulla and Rome. Unfortunately, this involved some Hannibal-like high-level, snow-covered mountain trekking, which tested the loyalty of his troops; Cinna became decidedly unpopular as a result and was stoned to death by his own troops as a consequence.

The news of Cinna's death, when it reached him, galvanized Sulla into action. He was anxious to fill the power vacuum which resulted from Cinna's death. In 83 BCE, his three legions – some 40,000 battle-hardened men – landed unopposed at Brundisium and Tarentum, laden with eastern booty.

In Rome, the consuls for the year were L. Cornelius Scipio Asiaticus and C. Norbanus, who set about raising and training armies to confront Sulla and protect the Senate in Rome. Norbanus moved on Sulla at Canusium but was no match for him and, heavily defeated with the loss of 7,000 men to Sulla's seventy, pulled back to Capua, where he was pursued and defeated again by Sulla.[1] Asiaticus was in no mood for battle, his army even less so; they surrendered to Sulla at Teanum Sidicinum without a fight and joined his forces. Asiaticus, however, was not the man Sulla took him for and promptly changed his mind: Sulla made it very clear that such duplicity would not be tolerated.

Amongst the military elite, Sulla was now rapidly becoming the man to side with. Q. Caecilius Metellus Pius, governor of Africa, led a revolt against the Marian forces in Africa with aid from Picenum and Spain. Marcus Licinius Crassus also arrived with an army from Spain, and Pompey, the precocious

23-year-old future triumvirate and son of Pompeius Strabo, the butcher of Asculum, took the initiative by raising an army from his father's veterans and aligned himself with Sulla.

Asiaticus raised another army and moved on Pompey, but once again his army surrendered and went over to the enemy. A desperate Senate re-elected Cinna's old co-consul, Papirius Carbo, to a third term, along with Gaius Marius the Younger, Marius' 26-year-old son, in the hope of motivating and mobilizing Marian supporters, especially the Italian tribes who had been loyal to Marius. The urban praetor L. Junius Brutus Damasippus, meanwhile, instigated the slaughter of pro-Sullan senators.

The year 82 BCE began with Papirius Carbo marching north against Pompey while Marius the Younger took on Sulla in the south. Pompey prevailed with a victory at the River Aesis on the border between Umbria and Picenum, and Metellus successfully defended northern Italy for Sulla.[2] Marius, meanwhile, reinforced with a large contingent of Samnites, camped at Setia in Latium. Sulla took the town and Marius confronted Sulla at Sacriportus, where a bloody and frantic battle ensued. Tragically for Marius, many of his men defected to Sulla, leaving him no choice but to retreat with the remnants of his army to Praeneste, only to be pursued by Sulla, who laid siege to the town. When Sulla arrived, the people of Praeneste closed the gates in the faces of Marius' soldiers. Marius himself was only saved when he was hauled up on ropes over the walls. Sulla had delegated the blockade to a subordinate officer and now advanced north to apply pressure on Carbo, who had retreated to Etruria to take up a position between Rome and Pompey and Metellus.[3] A cavalry battle at the River Clanis resulted in fifty Marian casualties, while 270 more deserted. Carbo then proceeded to kill the remaining cavalrymen to prevent further defections.[4]

A protracted day-long stalemate followed at Clusium, followed by a victory at Spoletium for Pompey and Crassus in which they inflicted 3,000 casualties on Carbo's force. An ambush on reinforcements accounted for a further 2,000 deaths.[5] 'Tangled up in a vineyard' must be one of the most bizarre explanations for a military defeat, but that is exactly what befell Carbo and Norbanus in an aborted night raid on Metellus at Faventia in Gallia Cispadana. The vines, and retaliation from Metellus, accounted for 2,000 casualties.[6] More bad news came when Marcus Lucullus, Sulla's deputy, followed this up with a victory over Norbanus in Gaul. Norbanus then defected to Sulla. Carbo, in a hopeless position, fled to Africa despite his position as consul and still nominally being in command of a sizeable army: 30,000 men were standing by at Clusium, but they were sitting ducks for Pompey, who attacked and despatched 20,000 of them.[7]

But all was not completely lost for the Marians: attempts were made to relieve Marius at Praeneste, but to no avail. The pro-Marian Samnites, commanded by Pontius Telesinus, then advanced north to threaten Rome with 40,000 troops.

Things came to a head on 1 November when the armies clashed at the decisive Battle of the Colline Gate, on the outskirts of Rome. Plutarch tells how Sulla's entry was devastating in the extreme:

> '[Sulla] shouted orders to torch the houses, and seizing a blazing firebrand, led the way himself, ordering his archers to use their fire-bolts and shoot them up at the roofs. This was no calm or collected tactic, but done in passion; having surrendered the control over his actions to his anger … he made his entry by fire, which did not discriminate between the guilty and the innocent.'[8]

Although Sulla suffered an unexpected heavy reverse on his left flank, he won the day in a narrow victory when the Samnites and the Marian army both collapsed: more than 50,000 troops died that day. Sulla systematically murdered what was left of the opposition and emerged as the undisputed master of Rome.[9]

Three thousand Marian troops were taken prisoner, while another 3,000 surrendered; all were imprisoned on the Campus Martius until executed. Their corpses were thrown into the Tiber, which became clogged with bodies – an estimated 10,000 men perished in this way.

After the revolutionary actions of Marius and Sulla, the Republic was in constitutional tatters. At the beginning of 81 BCE, the Senate, thoroughly shaken, reacted by appointing Sulla *dictator legibus faciendis et reipublicae constituendae causa* ('dictator for law-making and for the setting of the constitution'). This radical but, in the circumstances, prudent move under the terms of the Lex Valeria gave him legislative, military and judicial power; it was ratified by the assembly of the people, significantly and unprecedentedly with no time limit set on his tenure. At the same time, they wiped Sulla's slate clean and granted him immunity for his past actions. This effectively gave Sulla complete control of Rome and the Roman Republic: the only exception was Hispania, which Marius' general Quintus Sertorius had established as an independent state.

The appointment of dictators chimed with Rome's policy of not divesting total power in one individual. Until Sulla, a Roman dictator was quite a different animal from later dictators in different ages with connotations of tyranny and absolute, undemocratic power. Roman dictators were appointed for a period of six months as an extraordinary magistrate (*magistratus extraordinarius*) to deal with a specific military or domestic crisis. They were obliged to resign the post once it was dealt with – in short, they were an expedience, and represented a focusing of the powers of the consulship. Sulla's unconventional appointment set the precedent for Julius Caesar's multiple dictatorships.[10]

Sulla had Marius' ashes exhumed and flung into the Tiber. He wasted no time in flexing his new-found political muscle, and he did so with prodigious savagery, inflicting on the Roman people a terrifying programme of proscriptions, the like of which was unprecedented, even by the standards of those set by Marius and Cinna a few years earlier. According to Plutarch,[11] 'Sulla now made the blood flow, filling the city with numberless and limitless deaths without number or limit.' Plutarch added that many of the murdered had nothing to do with Sulla, but he butchered them anyway to 'please his hangers on'. If anyone thought they had escaped the massacre, then there was more to come:

> 'Sulla straightaway proscribed eighty men with no recourse to any magistrate. This evoked a murmur [of disapproval] so he let one day pass, and then proscribed 220 more, with just as many on the third day. Haranguing the people about this he said that he had proscribed everyone he could think of but those who now escaped his memory, he would proscribe them at some time in the future.'[12]

Sulla could indeed now consider himself a very lucky man: his victories over Mithridates and untrammelled success at Rome told him as much. So lucky did he feel that he added the word 'Felix' to his name.

Sulla's proscription policy was ostensibly payback for the atrocities perpetrated by Marius and Cinna and to liquidate anyone whom he considered to have acted against the best interests of the Republic while he was away fighting Mithridates. To that end he ordered the execution, over a number of months, of some 1,500 senators and *equites*, although some put the figure at nearer 9,000.[13] Many others were exiled.

The dictat was nothing if not rigorous and exhaustive: there was literally no hiding place. Aiding or sheltering a proscribed person was a capital offence; on the other hand, murdering a proscribed person attracted a reward of two talents. The aim was simply to have as many people as possible on the proscription lists brought in, dead or alive. Significantly, family members were included in the punishment, and slaves qualified for the rewards. This, of course, made it impossible for normal family life to go on, while making it attractive for slaves to make some easy money. Consequently, as Plutarch tells us, 'husbands were butchered in the arms of their wives, sons in the arms of their mothers'.

It turns out that many of the proscribed had no connection with Sulla or with his faction, and were certainly not his enemies. They were killed for their property, which was confiscated and auctioned off. Sulla made a tidy profit as the proceeds from these sales easily covered the cost of rewarding those who killed the proscribed. Sulla, with an eye on possible future retribution, banned the sons and grandsons of the proscribed from running for political office for the next thirty years.

Amongst the proscribed was one Gaius Julius Caesar, who, on finding himself squarely in Sulla's sights, fled Rome. Caesar's father, also Gaius Julius Caesar, had a sister Julia, Caesar's aunt, who married Gaius Marius. In 85 BCE, Caesar's father died suddenly, leaving the young Caesar head of the family aged just 16. Marius and Cinna ruled Rome when Caesar married Cinna's daughter, Cornelia.[14] This of course implicated Caesar with Marius and left him vulnerable to Sulla's death squads. He was stripped of his inheritance, Cornelia's dowry and his priesthood, but he refused to divorce Cornelia and was forced to flee. Only the intervention of his mother, Aurelia Cotta, and her family, which included supporters of Sulla, along with the influential Vestal Virgins, allowed the threat against him to be lifted. Sulla reluctantly relented, muttering that, 'In this Caesar there are many Mariuses.'

Sulla was a fervent *optimate* and a lifelong enemy of the office of *tribunus plebis*, the main popular assembly. Ironically for a man who spent much of his life undermining and terrorizing the Senate, he worked to strengthen the aristocracy and the Senate, and to diminish the tribunate, in short 'to drain the swamp', or at least what he considered to be the swamp. Perhaps Sulla was still smarting from the action of the tribune Publius Sulpicius Rufus, who, in Marius' pay, relieved him of his command against Mithridates. Among other moves, he retained his earlier reform which required senatorial approval before any bill could be submitted to the popular assembly, thus depriving it of the power to initiate legislation. He also barred ex-tribunes from ever holding any other office, stunting any ambition or desire to seek election to the tribunate, now a political dead end. He revoked the power of the tribunes to veto acts of the Senate. Showing evidence that he had learnt from personal experience, he also passed a new treason law, the *Lex Cornelia Maiestatis*, designed to prevent insurrection by provincial governors and army commanders – more irony.

Sulla increased the number of senators from 300 to 600 and transferred the control of the courts from the *equites* back to the senators. Sulla also codified the *cursus honorum*, which required an individual to be a certain age with a certain level of experience before running for any public office: in particular, any new member of the Senate should at least have already held the position of quaestor, to ensure that the Senate remained a body of political and administrative experience. He confirmed the requirement that an individual wait ten years before being re-elected to any office, and anyone holding office would have to wait at least two years before he could be nominated for the next higher office, the next stage of his *cursus honorum*. He set up a system in which all consuls and praetors spent their year in office in Rome, before going on to command a provincial army as a governor in the year after they left office.

Unfortunately for the survival of the Republic, much of this legislation was ineffective as it only addressed the symptoms and not the root causes of the malaise; so political life went on in the usual way. Later, in 70 BCE, Pompey and Crassus repealed many of the laws, restoring the old powers of the tribunate.

By the end of 81 BCE, Sulla had, perversely for a dictator like Sulla, resigned his dictatorship, paid off his legions and allowed normal consular government to resume. He was elected consul in 80 BCE with Metellus Pius. He dismissed his lictors (traditional bodyguards) and walked around unprotected in public, offering any citizen the opportunity to question him on his actions. The following year, after granting land in Campania and Etruria to veterans of the army – which is, of course, where Marius and he came in – he retired and died one year later, his (largely lost) memoirs unfinished. Sulla had convincingly paved the way for Julius Caesar to follow down the road to dictatorship.

The 70s BCE saw more military crises to stress the Senate. The maverick Marius supporter Quintus Sertorius found much success and popularity in Mauretania and Iberia, where he was welcomed, particularly in Lusitania, ultimately taking up the leadership against the Romans. In 80 BCE, he took on the governor of Further Spain, Lucius Fufidius, on the banks of the River Beatis (modern Guadalquivir) near Corduba, slaying 2,000 men.[15] Other successful battles followed at the Ana River (79 BCE), where Sertorius' second-in-command, Hirtuleius, defeated Marcus Domitius, and at Segovia in 78 BCE, another Hirtuleius victory. By this time, Sertorius held most of Spain. In 76 BCE, he was blockading Lauro when Pompey confronted him with his army, only to be ambushed by a 6,000-strong force of Sertorians.[16] The following year at Italica, Hirtuleius' luck ran out when he was defeated by Metellus Pius with the loss of 20,000 men and fled to Lusitania.[17] Pompey followed this up at Valentia, where he defeated two Roman exiles, Gaius Herennius and Marcus Perperna, killing Herennius and 10,000 others.[18]

Pompey, anxious to get a significant victory under his belt before Metellus arrived, confronted Sertorius at the River Sucro. Sertorius prevailed on day one, but the second day of fighting was inconclusive.[19] A battle at the River Turia saw Pompey and Metellus defeat Sertorius.[20] The three met again at Saguntum: Sertorius was victorious, killing 6,000 of Pompey's men, while Metellus slew 5,000 men under Perperna.[21] The Sertorian War ended in chaos in 74 BCE when Pompey lay siege to Pallantia; Sertorius attacked and relieved the town, at which point Pompey retreated to join Metellus at Calagurris. Sertorius raided their camp, killing 3,000 men. Pompey and Metellus began to enjoy more success and the war was ended when a seemingly jealous Perperna assassinated Sertorius. Pompey then defeated and slew Perperna.[22]

In 77 BCE, the Senate had been destabilized further when Marcus Aemilius Lepidus – consul and an avid supporter of Marius and his legacy – took steps to repeal some of Sulla's legislation. Revolt ensued and he was declared an enemy of the state. Withdrawing to Etruria, he raised an army and marched on

Rome. Opposition came in the form of the other consul, Q. Lutatius Catulus, who, along with Pompey, occupied the Milvian Bridge and the Janiculum. Lepidus was easily repulsed and fled to Sardinia.[23]

The Second Mithridatic War (83–81 BCE) had largely been between Mithridates and the Roman general Lucius Licinius Murena. As part of the settlement of the First Mithridatic War, Sulla was anxious to return to Rome to conduct his political business and agreed to allow Mithridates to retain control of Pontus, but to stay clear of Asia Minor. Independently, Murena invaded Pontus on the pretext that Mithridates was rearming and posed a direct threat to Roman Asia Minor. Mithridates defeated Murena and expelled him from Pontus, after which Sulla ensured that peace was restored.

In 76 BCE, Nicodemus IV of Bithynia died, having bequeathed his kingdom to Rome. This served to rekindle the ire of Mithridates, who invaded Bithynia in 73, thus sparking the Third Mithridatic War with Rome. The war (73–63 BCE) saw victory for the Romans, the demise of Pontus as a power, the death of Mithridates and Armenia absorbed as a client state of Rome.

Mithridates initially had little opposition, the Romans being distracted by Sertorius in Spain. The Senate despatched the consuls Lucius Licinius Lucullus and Marcus Aurelius Cotta: the only other possible general, Pompey, was in Gaul, on his way to Hispania. Lucullus was sent to Cilicia and Cotta to Bithynia.

Things started badly for Rome. The Roman plan was that Cotta should detain Mithridates' fleet while Lucullus attacked by land. To that end, Cotta stationed his fleet at Chalcedon at the mouth of the Bosporus while Lucullus marched through Phrygia on his way to invading Pontus. However, Mithridates surprised and attacked Cotta, forcing him into Chalcedon. Cotta lost sixty-four Roman ships captured or burnt and 3,000 men to Mithridates' mere twenty men. Cotta had no choice but to remain in Chalcedon.[24] He and Lucullus met up in 73 BCE in Nicomedia, while Mithridates sailed down the Bosporus to Heraclea Pontica. Cotta was tasked with securing Lucullus' rear by taking Heraclea, which Mithridates had reinforced with 4,000 troops. Cotta began a blockade of Heraclea, which fell two years later in 71 BCE.

Fortunes changed, however, when Mithridates failed to take Cyzicus by land or sea with his 3,000 men, deterred by Lucullus who had encamped nearby. Lucullus realised that Mithridates, who persisted in the blockade, would have a problem feeding such an army and set about starving them out. Mithridates sent his cavalry, infantry casualties and beasts of burden back to Bithynia, but they were overtaken by Lucullus' men at the River Rhyndacus; many were slain and 6,000 cavalry and 15,000 infantry were taken prisoner.[25] Mithridates was forced through famine to abandon the siege of Cyzicus. He was driven out of Pontus into Armenia by Lucullus. The loyal city was rewarded by grants of land and other benefits. Meanwhile, Mithridates' generals were charged with evacuating the army. Lucullus attacked them at the River Aesepus, slaughtering 20,000 and capturing even more.[26] A sea battle followed at Lemnos, which saw Lucullus victorious again. The following year, Mithridates decamped to Cabira with 40,000 infantry and 4,000 cavalry; Lucullus pursued him but was defeated in a skirmish by the superior Pontic cavalry. Roles were reversed, however, when a Roman foraging party was assailed by the enemy horse, whom they sent packing. Mithridates took the decision to abandon Cabira to Lucullus.[27]

Mithridates took sanctuary with his son-in-law Tigranes II, King of Armenia. Lucullus demanded he be given up, but Tigranes refused. Lucullus attacked at Tigranocerta in 69 BCE; Tigranes had raised an army of biblical proportions, numbering up to 250,000 infantry and 50,000 horse. Lucullus defeated Mithrobarnazes' small cavalry force at Tigranocerta, despite the fact that intelligence was in tatters because Tigranes executed anyone who brought him bad news about Lucullus' advance. Lucullus' army then hurtled down from higher ground, sending Tigranes' baggage train into the ranks of his soldiers, causing utter mayhem. Lucullus' cavalry was able to massacre 100,000 enemy in the confusion, for the loss, allegedly, of just five Romans with 100 more wounded. The royal city of Tigranocerta fell to the Romans.[28] This was in spite of the 25-metre thick walls and the Roman siege engines being repelled by the defenders with naphtha, making Tigranocerta possibly the place where chemical warfare was first deployed in Roman warfare.

Lucullus' army was able to loot and plunder at will. The city was deconstructed stone by stone and the king's treasury, valued at 8,000 talents, was looted and each soldier was gifted 800 drachma. Most of Tigranes' empire to the south of the Taurus now fell to Rome. Appian tells us:

> 'When Lucullus heard of the success of his provision train and observed the enemy's flight, he sent out a large force of cavalry in

> pursuit of the fugitives. Those who were still collecting baggage in the camp he surrounded with his infantry, whom he ordered for the time to abstain from plunder, but to kill indiscriminately. But the soldiers, seeing vessels of gold and of silver in abundance and much costly clothing, disregarded the order. Those who overtook Mithridates himself cut open the pack saddle of a mule that was loaded with gold, which fell out, and while they were busy with it they allowed him to escape to Comona.
>
> 'From thence he fled to Tigranes with 2,000 horsemen. Tigranes did not admit him to his presence, but ordered that royal entertainment be provided for him on his estates. Mithridates, in utter despair of his kingdom, sent the eunuch Bacchus to his palace to put his sisters, wives, and concubines to death. These, with wonderful devotion, destroyed themselves with daggers, poison, and ropes. When the garrison commanders of Mithridates saw these things most went over to Lucullus in droves.' (*The Mithridatic Wars* 17)

In 68 BCE, the bridge at Comana collapsed under the weight of Mithridates' army, thus robbing him of a fight with Valerius Triarius.[29]

By 67 BCE, the Roman army had more or less pulled out of Pontus, leaving two Fimbrian legions amounting to 12,000 men. These were reinforced by Roman slaves, but to no avail. Mithridates attacked, slew 500 men and retreated. Mithridates took an arrow wound to the face but soon recovered.

The Romans tried to reassert their dominance at the Battle of Zela in 67 BCE, which was preceded by a tornado. Both sides interpreted this omen as a definite call to battle, which the Romans initiated by a night attack on the camp of Mithridates. This was repulsed: the Romans were driven back into their trenches, which were soon 'clogged up with dead Romans'. Mithridates was badly wounded again, but was quickly restored to action by a shaman called Agari who applied snake venom to the wound. The Romans were forced to flee, leaving 7,000 dead, including twenty-four tribunes and 150 centurions.

As if the new war with Mithridates was not unsettling enough for the Senate, piratical activity throughout the Mediterranean, not without a little encouragement from Mithridates, had reached such a level that their raids were beginning to cause serious food shortages in Italy. Pompey was tasked with the job of eradicating them in 67 BCE and given control of the navy.

The Senate, of course, were cautious of Pompey and the power he derived from his popularity amongst the plebeians, largely because of his earlier successes against Sertorius and the allies of Marius. Voting him extensive powers might ease the way for him to seize power as dictator, as Sulla had done. But the plebeians cared little for such political niceties. They were exercised more by the bread shortages the pirates were causing, and the fact that in the previous year the pirates had torched Rome's port and grain warehouses at Ostia, destroyed the war fleet and kidnapped two prominent senators, along with their staff. Pompey, seeing an opportunity here, had Aulus Gabinius introduce the Lex Gabinia. This extraordinary measure gave him proconsular powers in any province within 50 miles of the Mediterranean without holding a properly elected magistracy. It gave him a substantial fleet and army, which Appian estimates at 270 warships, 120,000 infantry and 4,000 cavalry.[30] He was also voted 144 million sesterces, and twenty-five legates of praetorian rank and a generous three years to eradicate Rome's pirate problem.

Sulla's laws as dictator, of course, were intended to strengthen the power of the Senate, to prevent one man assuming great power and weaken the tribunes of the people. The Lex Gabinia demonstrated that this was not happening; the law was passed despite almost universal opposition in the Senate and to a backdrop of violence. It was, therefore, a significant factor in the demise of the Roman Republic. Hitherto, military commands were awarded for single provinces; the Lex Gabinia was unprecedented in that it gave command over a significant part of the empire to one man.

When he moved on the eastern Mediterranean, Pompey astutely offered beneficial terms to those pirates who surrendered to him personally, rather than to his other commanders. Some pirates surrendered their ships, even their families as well as themselves, to Pompey. From these he gleaned invaluable intelligence about the secret locations of other pirates.

According to Plutarch, Pompey was particularly successful at Coracesium (modern Alanya). Here he won a decisive victory over the pirates and blockaded the town. Around 20,000 Cilician pirates surrendered all their harbours and fortified islands, allowing the Romans to take the booty that the pirates had amassed and release many of the prisoners awaiting ransom. Strabo records that Pompey destroyed 1,300 pirate vessels. Appian has it that they gave up without a fight and were dispersed to inland locations.[31]

Within three short months, Pompey had completed his task with consummate efficiency, drastically reducing the pirates' spheres of operation.

In 66 BCE, after his successful campaign against the pirates, Pompey was, under the Lex Manilia, appointed sole commander to deal once and for all with Mithridates. Defeats at Nicopolis, Cyris River and Abas River in 66 and 65 BCE spelled the end for Mithridates. Mithridates was deserted and betrayed by his two sons. Machares, king of Cimmerian Bosporus, refused to help his father; Mithridates had him killed and took his land. Pharnaces II, under pressure from a war-weary population, rebelled against his father. Mithridates was deeply wounded by all of this and attempted suicide by poison in Panticapaeum. However, his prudence earlier in life got the better of him. Mithridates was in the habit of taking sub-lethal doses of all known poisons to build up immunity against assassination, So the poison he took now was ineffective.

Appian describes the scene:

> 'Mithridates then took out some poison that he always carried next to his sword, and mixed it. There two of his daughters, who were still girls growing up together, one of whom was also named Mithridates and the other Nyssa – who had been betrothed to the kings of Egypt and Cyprus – asked him to let them have some of the poison first, and insisted strenuously and prevented him from drinking it until they had taken some and swallowed it. The drug took effect on them at once; but upon Mithridates, although he walked around rapidly to hasten its action, it had no effect, because he had accustomed himself to other drugs by continually trying them as a means of protection against poisoners. These are still called the Mithridatic drugs.'[32]

Dio has a different version of events:

> 'Mithridates had tried to make away with himself, and after first removing his wives and remaining children by poison, he had swallowed all that was left; yet neither by that means nor by the sword

> was he able to perish by his own hands. For the poison, although deadly, did not prevail over him, since he had inured his constitution to it, taking precautionary antidotes in large doses every day; and the force of the sword blow was lessened on account of the weakness of his hand, caused by his age and present misfortunes, and as a result of taking the poison, whatever it was. When, therefore, he failed to take his life through his own efforts and seemed to linger beyond the proper time, those whom he had sent against his son fell upon him and hastened his end with their swords and spears. Thus Mithridates, who had experienced the most varied and remarkable fortune, had not even an ordinary end to his life. For he desired to die, albeit unwillingly, and though eager to kill himself was unable to do so; but partly by poison and partly by the sword he was at once self-slain and murdered by his foes.'[33]

Appian tells us that Mithridates ordered his Gallic bodyguard and friend, Bituitus, to stab him with his sword. Whatever the actual course of events, Mithridates' body was buried in Sinope, his capital city, on the orders of Pompey. Pompey admired the king's achievements and paid for a royal funeral in the cave tombs of his ancestors in Amasya, the old capital of Pontus. Appian's epitaph, however, is uncompromising:

> 'He was bloodthirsty and cruel to all - the slayer of his mother, his brother, three sons, and three daughters … When the Romans heard of his death they held a festival because they were delivered from a troublesome enemy.'[34]

Chapter 5

The Spartacus Revolt (73–71 BCE)

Italy was thronged with slaves – mainly former prisoners of war but many also from the bustling slave markets, some of which were enthusiastically supplied by pirates. Estimates suggest two million slaves in the early first century BCE against an Italian-Roman population of six million. One of the lucrative sidelines and benefits of owning slaves was their potential as combative gladiators – or as wild animal fodder in gladiatorial contests. Much money could be made here, particularly with the rise in celebrity amongst the more successful stars of the arena. One such celebrity was a slave called Spartacus.

Gladiatorial contests were serious business. The gladiators had to be at the top of their game if the baying crowds which flocked to the shows all around the Roman world were to be satisfied. Gladiators underwent training in gladiatorial schools. In 73 BCE, seventy-eight of these escaped from the fighting school of Gnaeus Lentulus Batiatus at Capua in southern Italy. Initially, the breakout was inspired more by the hope of freedom than anything else. According to Plutarch, the gladiators were only armed with stolen kitchen utensils: meat cleavers and spits. As luck had it, the escapees came upon a wagon filled with gladiatorial weaponry; now heavily armed, they occupied a slope on Mount Vesuvius. Their nominated leaders were Spartacus, Oenomaus and Crixus: a Thracian, a Greek and a German.

Plutarch gives us some detail:

> 'Spartacus was a Thracian from the nomadic tribes and not only had a great spirit and great physical strength, but was, much more than one would expect from his condition, most intelligent and cultured, being more like a Greek than a Thracian.'[1]

His physical and military prowess were no doubt honed by his former experience fighting for Rome as an auxiliary. His small band was soon bolstered by other runaway slaves and disaffected farm workers, and they quickly cut their combat teeth on a militia despatched from Capua to deal with them. Rome could not afford to ignore Spartacus, even though she was preoccupied with two other wars: Pompey was fighting against Sertorius in Hispania and Lucullus was at war with Mithridates VI of Pontus in the east. At home, there was mounting unrest at the grain shortages caused by these far-away conflicts. Florus picks up the story, showing revenge as an additional element as the revolt rapidly snowballed:

> 'When, by summoning the slaves to their standard, they had quickly collected more than 10,000 adherents, these men, who had been originally content merely to have escaped, soon began to wish to take their revenge also.'[2]

The propraetor Gaius Claudius Glaber hastily raised an army of 3,000 untrained men to quell the revolt. Things started well for Claudius, who quickly isolated the gladiators on a hill high up on Vesuvius and looked to be in control. However, with tactical ingenuity the slaves made ladders from the branches of vines, enabling them to get down from the mountain by night and penetrate the rear of Claudius' lines. The armies of Lucius Cossinus, Lucius Furius and Caius Toranius were all also soundly defeated. The praetor Publius Varenius managed to surround the slave army, but they escaped, leaving dead sentries lashed to stakes guarding an empty camp.[3] The Romans panicked and fled, deserting their camp and allowing it to be looted by the gladiators, who armed themselves with the weapons they found there. The Romans regrouped and attacked a second time, now under the command of Varenius. Oddly, Varenius split his forces, enabling the rebels to defeat them comfortably. Varenius' humiliation and shame were complete when he lost not only the horse he was sitting on but both his lictors, who were taken prisoner, and their *fasces*, which Spartacus triumphantly paraded through his camp. Florus tells us:

> 'The first position which attracted them (a suitable one for such ravening monsters) was Mt. Vesuvius. Being besieged here by Clodius Glabrus [*sic*], they slid by means of ropes made of vine-twigs through a passage in the hollow of the mountain down into its very depths,

> and issuing forth by a hidden exit, seized the camp of the general by a sudden attack which he never expected. They then attacked other camps, that of Varenius and afterwards that of Thoranus; and they ranged over the whole of Campania. Not content with the plundering of country houses and villages, they laid waste Nola, Nuceria, Thurii and Metapontum with terrible destruction.'

The rebels became more like a regular army every day, reinforced as they were by more and more malcontents.[4] Nothing if not industrious, Spartacus and his slave army spent the winter of 73-72 BCE productively, making crude shields of wicker-work and animal skins, and swords and other weapons by melting down the iron in the slave jails they liberated. A cavalry unit was formed with the horses they rounded up. The plan was to cross the Apennines and head north so that his soldiers could exit Italy and head back to their homes in Germania or the Balkans. The logistic difficulties of moving 70,000 men over mountainous terrain were not lost on Spartacus, and he was forced to split his forces.

The Romans saw their chance. In the spring of 72 BCE, consul Lucius Gellius Publicola launched a surprise attack on a unit which Plutarch called 'the German contingent' and Appian 'the force of Crixus'. Appian records that Crixus was killed and lost two-thirds of his 30,000 Germans and Gauls in the battle, which took place at Mount Garganus near modern Foggia. Crixus and Spartacus had fallen out over whether to leave Italy or engage the Romans, as Crixus wanted.[5] Simultaneously, the consul Gnaeus Cornelius Lentulus Clodianus intercepted Spartacus' main force in the Apennines. The strategy was to wait for Gellius before engaging so as to attack Spartacus from both sides. Spartacus scuppered this by defeating both armies in detail, looting their equipment and pressing on to the Adriatic Sea. Here is Plutarch's account of these moves:

> 'The consul Gellius, falling suddenly upon a party of Germans, who through contempt, and confidence had straggled from Spartacus, cut them all to pieces. But when Lentulus with a large army besieged Spartacus, he sallied out upon him, and, joining battle, defeated his chief officers, and captured all his baggage. As he made toward the Alps,

Cassius, who was praetor of that part of Gaul that lies about the Po, met him with ten thousand men, but being overcome in the battle, he had much ado to escape himself, with the loss of a great many of his men.'

Our sources differ here. Appian records:

'In the aftermath the consuls retreated in confusion, while Spartacus, first sacrificing 300 Roman prisoners to Crixus, made for Rome with 120,000 foot soldiers after burning the useless equipment and putting all the prisoners to death and slaughtering the draught animals to free himself of all encumbrances.'[6]

Florus and Orosius differ again, the former writing:

'He [Spartacus] also celebrated the obsequies of his officers who had fallen in battle with funerals like those of Roman generals, and ordered his captives to fight at their pyres, just as though he wished to wipe out all his past dishonour by having become, instead of a gladiator, a giver of gladiatorial shows.'[7]

Spartacus rubbed salt in the Romans' wounds when he mocked the Romans and turned the tables by making them perform in gladiatorial contests and by imitating their funeral rites in honour of Crixus.

Cato the Younger volunteered for service in this battle and, unlike the bungling Gellius, acquitted himself well. The Romans retreated back to Rome, pursued for a while by Spartacus, who turned and headed for the Alps along the Adriatic coastline. This time the Romans followed Spartacus and reached Ancona first, where the slave army was victorious again.

The way to the Alps was almost clear; they only had to defeat the army of governor Gaius Cassius Longinus at Modena in Gallia Cisalpina. Spartacus won yet again. He had convincingly achieved his objective. But it did not go quite to plan:

'Spartacus' view was that they should cross the mountains and then disperse to their own homes … His men, however, would not listen to

> him. They were strong in numbers and full of confidence, and they went about Italy ravaging everything in their way.'[8]

Plutarch tells us that some at least of the slaves chose not to leave and proceeded to lay waste to the northern cities of Roman Italy. No doubt they were seduced by the promise of booty and rapine, only too happy to prolong the camaraderie which had built up between the slaves.

For Rome this was all an embarrassing and humiliating disaster. The eyes of the Roman world would be on Spartacus and his victories. Rumour spread that slaves could defeat the Roman military; slaves everywhere would be taking note. Highly trained and battle-hardened Roman armies were being beaten by nothing more than a rabble of headstrong amateurs. The demonstration of slave power had gone on too long. Roman military prestige had to be restored at all costs. An unsettled and concerned Senate had to act: if this continued to spread, the Republic was in peril.

Marcus Licinius Crassus, praetor in 72 BCE, was sent to deal with Spartacus and duly defeated him at Camalatrum with ten legions, six of which were newly recruited. Crassus ordered the commander of the remnants of the army, Mummius, to head south but to avoid contact with the enemy at all costs. Mummius thought he knew better and attacked Spartacus with his legion, but he was defeated. Crassus proceeded to decimate the legion as an example to anyone else thinking about insubordination. He picked out the 500 men who were the first to run away and divided them into fifty groups of ten: one man from each was doomed to die by lot, 'with a variety of appalling and terrible circumstances, presented before the eyes of the whole army, assembled as spectators', according to Plutarch.[9]

After the dilemma in the north, Spartacus had headed south at the end of 72 BCE and took Thurii – the only town to be captured by the slaves in the whole campaign. He made camp at Rhegium. The intention was to escape to Sicily, which had an enduring reputation for slave rebellion.

Not surprisingly, there were no ships available to the rebels. In desperation they tried to make rafts from beams and barrels bound together. Spartacus has no choice but to collaborate with the notorious Cilician pirates; the prospect of what would have been a coalition from hell must have enraged and terrified the Romans even more. A base on Sicily founded with Spartacus' help would benefit the pirates enormously, allowing them to pillage the Italian coast with virtual impunity. Money changed hands, a meeting was arranged – but the pirates, being what pirates are, did not show. Instead, Crassus turned up and ordered that a 60km trench with a high wall be dug right across Bruttium in the 'toe' of Italy, from the Tyrrhenian to the Ionian Sea. Crassus' legions made short work of the project. Plutarch writes of this great feat of civil engineering and the strategy behind it.[10]

Not only did the wall give the Roman soldiers something constructive to do, it prevented Spartacus from foraging for food. Spartacus was perilously boxed in, but he was up to the challenge. During a stormy, snowy night, he filled in part of the ditch with earth, branches and the corpses of soldiers, horses and cattle to create a bridge, over which he crossed with a third of his army. Spartacus attacked, but is said to have lost 6,000 men to the Romans' (incredible) three. Spartacus resorted to guerrilla tactics. Desperate to maintain discipline, he crucified a Roman prisoner in no-man's land to show his troops what awaited them if they were defeated.[11]

Crassus now had Spartacus just where he wanted him over the winter; the slaves' provisions would be exhausted come the spring, leaving just a starving and undernourished army to attack. However, a bungling Senate was having none of it, and invited the recently victorious Pompey from Hispania to get involved. Nothing could be sure to galvanize Crassus more than the prospect of his arch enemy raining on his parade. According to Plutarch,

> 'News was already brought that Pompey was at hand; and people began to talk openly that the honour of this war was reserved to him, who would come and at once oblige the enemy to fight and put an end to the war. Crassus, therefore, eager to fight a decisive battle, encamped very near the enemy, and began to make lines of circumvallation; but the slaves made a sally and attacked the pioneers.'

As it happened, Spartacus attacked first and, at the Battle of Cantenna on the Lucanian Lake, punctured Crassus' lines, but with only a third of his army; serious divisions and mutiny had split his forces. The remaining two-thirds were then picked off by the legions under Quintus Marcius Rufus and Lucius Pomptinus. Even worse for Spartacus, the slave force which had punched through the Roman lines was split, and one of these groups suffered serious casualties. Spartacus appeared just in time to prevent the annihilation of his whole army, but he reputedly lost 35,000 men that day, including his generals Castus and Cannicus.[12]

The Romans now had a significant numerical superiority. Crassus boldly attacked Spartacus and won the day. Around 12,300 slaves were killed. Apparently, only two of these were wounded in the back, the rest all dying holding their ground according to Livy in his *Periochae*. The casualties were a massive, but exaggerated, 60,000. Spartacus made a futile attempt to negotiate a peace with Crassus, but he was snubbed. He then retreated further south, to Petelia, where he defiantly defeated both Quintus Marcius Rufus and Gnaeus Tremellius Scrofa. These victories, however, were to be the death of the slaves, according to Plutarch:

> '[S]ince it filled [Spartacus'] slaves with over-confidence. They refused any longer to avoid battle and would not even obey their officers. Instead they surrounded them with arms in their hands as soon as they began to march and forced them to lead them back through Lucania against the Romans.'[13]

In March 71 BCE, Spartacus attempted to seize Brundisium, perhaps with a view to sailing to Sicily or Epirus. However, the governor of Macedonia, Marcus Teretius Varro Lucullus, had been recalled by the Senate and was lying in wait for him there. Spartacus knew that all was up. His horse was brought to him, and Spartacus drew out his sword and killed it in front of the army, saying: 'If we win the day I shall have a great many better horses from the enemy, and if we lose, I shall have no need of one.' It was win or die. The rebels paid for their incaution and over-enthusiasm at the conclusive Battle of the River Silarus, where the 35,000 rebels remaining were heavily defeated. Crassus recovered five legionary eagle-standards, twenty-six other standards and five *fasces*. Spartacus died in the battle; his body was never recovered.[14] Appian writes:

> 'Spartacus was wounded in the thigh with a spear and sank upon his knee, holding his shield in front of him and contending in this way

> against his assailants until he and the great mass of those with him were surrounded and slain.'

The scattered remnants of Spartacus' army took refuge in the mountains of Bruttium, where, led by one Publior, they organized themselves into four groups on the banks of the River Silarus and conducted a guerrilla war against the Romans until they were finally wiped out by Pompey and Crassus.

The Romans captured 6,000 unfortunate slaves alive. As a stark reminder of the fate which awaited the rebellious slave, they were all crucified on crosses placed every 40 metres or so along the 150 miles of the Via Appia between Rome and Capua. The corpses were gradually eaten away by wild dogs and carrion, reduced to grimacing and grinning skeletons. Pompey butchered a further 5,000 survivors. By contrast, 3,000 Roman prisoners of war were found alive and well at Spartacus' camp at Rhegium.

A duplicitous Pompey claimed credit for ending the war. He was awarded a triumph for defeating Sertorius in Spain, but a disappointed and angry Crassus had to make do with an *ovation* - a low-rent triumph.[15] Crassus never forgave Pompey. This lesser decoration reflected the official embarrassment and shame felt in Rome at the humiliating runaround a bunch of slaves had given them for two years. The Romans had needed an excessive seventy-one legions to quell the rebellion. It was inconceivable that a victory, essential as it was, over a rabble of a slave army could merit a glorious triumph. Members of the establishment like Cicero naturally thought Spartacus was comparable to the worst of Romans, fit only to be despised, deserving of everything he got; to Horace he was a devastator and fierce (*acer*).[16] Down the years he was dragged out as a bogeyman by Roman mothers to frighten naughty children into obedience. Spartacus had threatened everything Rome and the Romans stood for and cherished. The disaster that was the revolt of Spartacus was quietly consigned to history.

It was suggested above that the rebellion was born more of a desperate bid for freedom than anything else. It was never going to succeed in erasing slavery from Roman society, if it was ever intended to achieve that end. If a number of the slaves were repatriated after the quandary in northern Italy, then that was a limited success, but the fact remains that the tens of thousands of slaves toiling away in Roman towns and cities did not flock to Spartacus' cause as he and his army strutted and pillaged up and down the peninsula. The Roman army, as we have observed, had a seemingly endless source of recruits: when one army was depleted it was immediately replaced by another. Spartacus was not the first and he was not the last to suffer from this relentless regeneration of Roman armies. Indeed, Varinia, Spartacus' perceptive wife, in Stanley Kubrick's 1960 film shows a resigned appreciation of this: 'No matter how many times we beat them, they always seem to have another army to send against us. And another.'

The Romans seemed to have learnt their lesson. Mile after mile of putrifying roadside crucifixions would have kept memories fresh for many years – a salutary reminder to slaves of the folly of running away and of rebellion. During the Catiline conspiracy crisis in 63 BCE, gangs of gladiators were removed to Campania from Rome for security reasons. In 49 BCE, Julius Caesar relocated 5,000 gladiators to Capua: Lucius Cornelius Lentulus wanted to recruit them into his army, but Pompey, according to Cicero, 'very sensibly distributed [them] … among the population, two per household'.[17]

Chapter 6

The Catiline Conspiracy (63–62 BCE)

If the prospect of a wholesale revolt by the servile classes was not destabilising and disturbing enough for the Senate and for the Republic itself, the conspiracy led by Lucius Sergius Catilina (Catiline) to seize the consulship and destroy the Republic shook the establishment to the core. The coup d'état took place against a background of economic gloom and uncertainty. Trade was sluggish, and with it a concomitant loss of tax revenue; debt among many affluent Romans debt was on the increase. Unemployment in Rome was high.

Catiline (108–62 BCE) had something of a reputation for trouble. His career started well, though, when he served with distinction in the Social War alongside Pompey and Cicero under Gnaeus Pompeius Strabo in 89 BCE.[1] He later took the side of Sulla in the civil war of 84–81 BCE. During Sulla's proscriptions, Catiline maimed and then killed and beheaded his brother-in-law, Marcus Marius Gratidianus; he then carried the head through the streets of Rome and placed it at Sulla's feet at the temple of Apollo. The aim was to have Sulla add the name of Gratidianus to the proscription lists, thereby making the murder and subsequent seizing of his assets legal. Cicero also alleged the murder by Catiline of Quintus Caecilius, Marcus Volumnius and Lucius Tanusius. In addition, Catiline faced accusations of murdering his first wife and son so that he could marry the wealthy and vivacious Aurelia Orestilla, daughter of Gnaeus Aufidius Orestes (consul in 71 BCE). After serving in Cicilia in the early 70s BCE, he faced trial in 73 for adultery with the Vestal Virgin, Fabia, a half-sister of Cicero's wife, Terentia. Quintus Lutatius Catulus, leader of the *optimates*, testified on his behalf, and eventually Catiline and Fabia were acquitted.[2] Conviction would have meant live entombment for Fabia and execution for Catiline.

The year 68 BCE saw Catiline as praetor, followed by two years as propraetorian governor for Africa. On his return he stood for consul, but a delegation from Africa indicted him for abuses and he was disqualified. He was brought to trial in 65 BCE, only to be acquitted after bribing the judges.[3] Catiline lost out in the consular elections for 63 BCE due to his economic policy: the *optimates* were appalled that he exposed the shocking plight of the plebs and by his policy of *tabulae novae*, the cancellation of debts, wiping the slate clean.[4]

Catiline's macabre treatment of Gratidianus during the proscriptions soon caught up with him when he was accused by Cato the Younger of murder. He was, nevertheless, acquitted again and was ready to stand for consul in 62 BCE. Catiline lost out again, and having exhausted legal methods, his only option now was to win the consulship by illegal means and thereby overturn the Republic and the consulships of Cicero and Gaius Antonius Hybrida.[5] He was able to attract a number of disaffected aristocrats, and many plebeians who were afflicted by debt, particularly those who had lost their farms in the economic crisis. Plebs apart, the second Catiline oration identifies six specific groups:

> Wealthy men who are heavily in debt and who could repay their debt by selling land but are reluctant to do so.
>
> Men who are in debt and see revolution as the path to power.
>
> Veterans of Sulla's army who had been settled in colonies, but have lived beyond their means, are bankrupt and now seek new proscriptions from which to recover their fortunes.
>
> Men deep in financial straits who seek to resolve their problems by joining Catiline.
>
> Criminals.
>
> Rome's dissolute youth.

Publius Cornelius Lentulus Sura, the most powerful conspirator after Catiline, had been consul in 71 BCE but in the following year was consigned to the political wilderness by the Senate in a political purge on trumped-up charges of debauchery. Publius Autronius Paetus came over when he was banned from holding further office. Cassius Longinus, who was praetor in 66 BCE with Cicero, joined up after he failed to obtain the consulship in 64 BCE with Catiline. Gaius Cethegus joined too. Many of the conspirators were looking to rekindle their political power and restore their status as senators.

The conspirators' plan was to send Gaius Manlius, a former Sullan centurion, to raise an army in Etruria, while others were despatched throughout Italy stirring up civil unrest. In Rome, Catiline planned arson attacks and the murder of many senators before joining up with Manlius' army. Then they would return to Rome and mount a coup against the government. Gaius Cornelius and Lucius Vargunteius were deputed to assassinate Cicero on 7 November 63 BCE. However, Quintus Curius, a senator who became one of Cicero's chief informants, warned Cicero of the threat through his mistress, Fulvia; by posting guards at his house, Cicero deterred the would-be assassins. Fulvia was not one of those vulnerable women whom Catiline recruited as informants and *agents provacateurs* – former prostitutes who had fallen on hard times towards the end of their careers, and were thus open to exploitation by the conspirators. Fulvia, on the other hand, was of good birth.[6] After sitting through a thoroughly hostile speech in the Senate, Catiline left, pretending he was going into voluntary exile in Massilia so as to spare his country the horrors of civil war. However, he arrived at Manlius' camp in Etruria to stoke the fires of his revolution.

The conspirators then implicated a delegation of Allobroges who happened to be in Rome complaining about the oppression of their governor. Publius Gabinius Capito met with them and revealed the conspiracy, and their envoys quickly informed Cicero. Cicero, however, needed physical proof of the conspiracy, which came in the form of letters written by five of the leading conspirators to the Allobroges describing the benefits that would accrue from joining the conspiracy. The letters were intercepted at the Milvian Bridge. Cicero now had his evidence and read out the incriminating letters to the Senate the following day. The five conspirators were condemned to death without trial, despite opposition from Julius Caesar: Cicero had them strangled in the Tullianum.[7] If he thought that that was the end of the matter, then he would be forced to think again; these summary executions came back to haunt Cicero in the form of the First Triumvirate.

Catiline's conspiracy had failed. What had been a force of some 10,000 men shrank through desertion to a mere 3,000 when it was learnt that Publius Cornelius Lentulus Sura and others had been slain. Catiline, on the way to the border with Gaul, was reluctantly brought to battle against Gaius Antonius' army near Pistoia, avoiding the stronger force of Quintus Caecilius Metellus

Celer with his three legions. Despite a brave fight, with Catiline courageously leading from the front, the rebellion was quashed.[8]

Cicero tries to explain the enigma that was Catiline:

> 'He had many things about him which served to entice men to satisfy their passions; he had also many attributes which acted as incentives to hard work and industry. The vices of lust raged in him; but at the same time he was conspicuous for great energy and military skill. Nor do I believe that there ever existed so strange a prodigy upon the earth, made up in such a manner of the most various, and different and inconsistent studies and desires.'[9]

Chapter 7

The Carrhae Disaster (53 BCE)

Destabilizing conflicts continued to break out and beset the Republic. An uprising by the Allobroges had to be subdued at a place called Solonium in 61 BCE by Gaius Pomptinus, the governor of Gallia Narbonensis.[1] In 57 BCE, the Romans were forced to quell an uprising by the Jews when the sons of Alexander of Judaea – Aristobolus II and Hyrcanus II - squabbled over the succession. Pompey arrived on the scene, made Hyrcanus high priest, imprisoned his brother and took Jerusalem. Alexander, the son of Aristobolus, made a bid for the throne with 10,000 infantry and 1,500 cavalry against Aulus Gabinius, commander in Syria. Gabinius deployed Mark Antony with the cavalry first, and followed with his legion. At the pitched battle which followed outside Jerusalem, Alexander lost 3,000 men and had another 3,000 captured. But Alexander was not to be subdued: in 55 BCE, with 30,000 men, he attacked Gabinius at Mount Tabor, only to lose a further 10,000 casualties.[2]

The last thing that the Roman Republic needed at this point was a significant military disaster. Yet Carrhae was the worst Roman disaster, and Rome's darkest day (*dies ater*) since the catastrophic battle of Cannae in 216 BCE some 163 years earlier. Not only was Carrhae an unwelcome, destabilizing military reverse, but the battle had huge symbolic importance for the Republic: Roman standards were lost in the conflict, a matter of great consequence for morale, status and prestige in the Roman world.

The battle was fought against the Parthians, a monarchy founded about 250 BCE when a band of migrants settled on the northern extremity of the Persian plateau. After the Battle of Magnesia in 190 BCE, the Parthians took the whole of Persia from the dying Seleucid monarchy and extended their western border to the banks of the Euphrates. Negotiations with the expansive Chinese empire took place around 100 BCE, and a few years later Tigranes of Armenia took western Mesopotamia from them. Thirty years after this, King Phraates III regained the lost provinces. Mutual distrust of Mithridates and

Tigranes united Rome and the Parthians, which led to an alliance with Sulla, then governor of Cilicia. A further agreement with Pompey should have led to the recovery of all the lost territory in Mesopotamia, but Pompey reneged and partitioned the land between Armenia and Parthia. This soured the relationship and marked the start of years of animosity and conflict between Rome and Parthia. Pompey's second in command, Gabinius, made the situation worse when he unsuccessfully supported a usurper for the Parthian crown against King Orodes II (r. 57–37 BCE) in 56 BCE.

The arrogance of Marcus Licinius Crassus was largely to blame for the calamity in which the battle and the precious Roman standards were lost. He was still bitter and smarting from the slight he received from Pompey when Pompey took credit for extirpating the Spartacus slave revolt. He was anxious to score a military victory of his own to compare with the military victories of Caesar and Pompey. Crassus had no mandate from the Roman Senate when he invaded Mesopotamia; moreover, to many he epitomized obscene wealth and ruthless materialism, the worst of all Roman characteristics. Crassus' fortune started to build when he greedily bought up and made a killing on the properties of Sulla's proscription victims: these had been confiscated with their contents and sold at knock-down prices to Crassus, who sold them on at eye-watering profits. He used his money to raise and keep a troop of 500 slaves, all skilled builders and other tradesmen, whom he would put to work rebuilding houses (and any damaged buildings adjacent) that had burnt down in Rome's frequent fires. Some believe that Crassus was also a serial arsonist. Again, these rebuilt houses would be sold at high profit or leased out at extortionate rents. Add to this his lucrative silver mines in Spain, the cash cows that were the *latifundia* and his luxury, prestigious property in the city of Rome and we have a very rich man. Crassus maintained his own private army and used his money to magnetize political allies amongst obsequious senators and powerful men such as Julius Caesar and Pompey, his co-triumvirs. In the war against Spartacus, he revived the much-feared punishment of decimation and made crucifixion the slow death of choice when he lined the road to Rome with 150 miles of prisoners rotting away on their crosses.

But Crassus was not just the inordinately wealthy, odious monster of a man who bungled his way around Parthia, as is often portrayed. Over the years before Carrhae, which he fought when he was about 60 years old, he exhibited considerable political and military skill. We have seen how he supported Sulla with a private army in the First Civil War, winning the decisive Battle of the Colline Gate in 82 BCE, and was ruthlessly effective in his terrible programme of proscriptions. He defeated Spartacus and brought an end to the slave rebellion, even though Pompey stole the glory and took the credit. He also helped overthrow Sulla, and was censor and consul twice. He was, of course, one third of the First Triumvirate.

There was much opposition to the conflict at the highest level. Cicero said there was *nulla causa* ('no justification') for the war with the Parthians because the two nations were bound by treaty. Cicero's was not the only voice of discontent: the tribune Gaius Ateius Capito was so violently opposed that he conducted a public ritual of execration in November 55 BCE as Crassus prepared to leave Rome. Crassus was on the Capitoline performing the required ritual vows before his army's departure. Ateius claimed to have seen *dirae* – the most calamitous of portents. Crassus ignored him, so Ateius tried to arrest Crassus before he could set sail:

> 'Ateius then ran on ahead to the city gate where he set up a brazier containing lighted fuel. When Crassus came to the gate, [Ateius] threw incense and libations on the brazier and called down on [Crassus] curses which were dreadful and frightening enough in themselves and made still more dreadful by the names of certain strange and terrible deities … The Romans believe that these mysterious and ancient curses are so powerful that no one who has had them laid upon him can escape from their effect … So on this occasion people blamed Ateius for what he had done; he had been angry with Crassus for the sake of Rome, yet he had involved Rome in these curses and in the terror which must be felt of supernatural intervention.'[3]

Ateius Capito's execration won a reputation as an instance of a successful curse with unintended consequences.

The prospect of confrontation between Rome and Parthia had been simmering away for decades. Parthia had moved to restore the Persian empire in a cavalier fashion, ignoring the interests of neighbouring nations as it annexed at will. Rome, on the other hand, was moving inexorably eastwards, absorbing

Parthian lands through force and deception. Mithridates and Pontus, for example, saw Lucullus marching on the Armenian capital Tigranocerta (near Mardin); when he reached Parthia, he encouraged the Parthian king, whom Mithridates and Tigranes had asked for help, to remain neutral. The king suggested to Lucullus that the Euphrates should be recognized as the frontier between Parthia and Rome. Lucullus dissimulated and pretended to be taking note, but instead planned an attack on Parthia, which was only thwarted by the rebellion of his troops.[4] Pompey showed an interest in subjugating the East when he enquired about the distance to India later invaded by Parthian Gorduene.[5] Gabinius, who commanded Syria, Arabia, Persia and Babylonia, aided Mithridates of Parthia in his rebellion against his newly crowned brother, Orodes.[6] This interference led to clashes between the Romans and Parthians, who had hitherto remained allies. To the Romans, Parthia was nothing more than just another Asiatic state: such dismissive, arrogant judgement betrayed a serious lack of geopolitical understanding and no appreciation of Parthia's strong national identity, its prodigious natural resources and the determination of the Parthians to defend their independence. Indeed, Parthia was more like Rome than the Romans could ever believe. The Romans assumed that the successful subjugation of the East was an inevitablility. This is the mindset that Crassus inherited.

The Parthians, however, were militarily shrewd and had good intelligence of Roman expansionist strategies; they planned their defensive strategy accordingly. Crucially, Crassus was desperate to match the military prowess of his co-triumvirs, Julius Caesar and Pompey. He insulted the Parthians' military achievements when he pompously wrote them off as 'kid's stuff', declaring his ambition to conquer the East as far as Bactria and India.[7] Despite defeating Spartacus and a creditable victory at the Battle of the Colline Gate, Crassus still had precious little to show on his military *curriculum vitae*.

The Battle of Carrhae was fought on an open, hot and dusty plain east of Harran in northern Mesopotamia. Here the Roman army was exposed and vulnerable – the last in a series of blunders which began when Crassus invaded and garrisoned the towns of western Mesopotamia with one-fifth of his army: all surrendered to the Romans, except for Zenodotia. Crassus had reached Syria in late 55 BCE, using his prodigious wealth to raise an army. He passed his first year there fortifying towns, and no doubt training his troops, but he also cultivated local opposition and enmity when he rashly looted native sanctuaries. Crassus then returned to winter quarters in Syria instead of the more sensible option of advancing on Seleucia or booty-rich Ctesiphon, the capital of the Parthian Empire. He was joined in Syria by his son, Publius, a promising soldier who had served with distinction under Caesar in Gaul. Publius brought with him 1,000 Gallic cavalry. During the winter of 54–53 BCE, Crassus' rapacity knew no bounds, weighing out the treasures from the temples he had captured and accepting cash from the citizens in lieu of military service in the forthcoming campaign. The temple at Jerusalem was just one of the sanctuaries remorselessly looted. Plutarch takes up the developments:

> 'When he drew his army out of winter quarters, ambassadors came to him from Arsaces, with this short speech: If the army was sent by the people of Rome, he denounced mortal war, but if, as he understood was the case, against the consent of his country, Crassus for his own private profit had invaded his territory, then their king would be more merciful, and taking pity upon Crassus's dotage, would send those soldiers back who had been left not so truly to keep guard on him as to be his prisoners. Crassus boastfully told them he would return his answer at Seleucia, upon which Vagises, the eldest of them, laughed and showed the palm of his hand, saying, "Hair will grow here before you will see Seleucia"; so they returned to their king, Hyrodes, telling him it was war.'

Crassus faced the Parthian general Surena, fighting for his king, Orodes I. Crassus knew that Surena was in the desert east of the Euphrates, but he unwisely left the cover of the river, ignoring the advice of his Armenian allies under Artavasdes, King of Armenia. Unlike Crassus, Artavasdes was blessed with indisputable local knowledge; he recommended Crassus invade from the mountains to the north and so maximize the cover they would give against the Parthian cavalry. Instead, the bull-headed Crassus crossed the Euphrates at Zeugma to link up with his new garrisons. The objective was Seleucia, the commercial capital of Babylonia, brimming with booty potential. His large force comprised 34,000 men in seven legions of heavy-armed infantry, 4,000 cavalry and some 4,000 lightly armed foot soldiers. His quaestor Gaius Cassius Longinus saw the folly in this and warned that Crassus should advance along the river to Seleucia, where his flank would be protected and his water supply guaranteed by the river. The omens could not have been worse, according to Plutarch in Dryden's translation:

> '[H]e encountered preternaturally violent thunder, and the lightning flashed in the faces of the troops, and during the storm a hurricane broke upon the bridge, and carried part of it away; two thunderbolts fell upon the very place where the army was going to encamp; and one of the general's horses, magnificently caparisoned, dragged away the groom into the river and was drowned. It is said, too, that when they went to take up the first standard, the eagle of itself turned its head backward … And when at the last general sacrifice the priest gave him the entrails, they slipped out of his hand.'[8]

Crassus blundered on and ingratiated himself with a local Arab chieftain called Ariamnes (or Abgar of Osrhoene), 'a cunning and wily fellow' who promised to escort the Romans across the Balicha (Balīḵ) river and Ḵabūr toward Ctesiphon, and to provide him with cavalry.[9] Ariamnes duped Crassus into believing that he faced only a token force of Parthians, led not by King Orodes but by Surena; Crassus seriously underestimated the military skill of the precocious Surena. Surena was an adept cavalryman, and cavalry was Parthia's strong suit; he clearly saw the advantages of deploying cavalry in the open plain - 'a brilliant idea', according to Mommsen. The Parthian nobility sponsored heavily armoured cuirassiers, whose horses were specially bred to support their riders in terms of weight and strength; they were the forerunners of the heavily mailed medieval cavalries. Unfortunately, Crassus' army consisted mainly of infantry; apart from the cavalry brought from Gaul by Publius, Crassus was dependent on the horse promised by his ally Artavasdes.

Futhermore, according to Tarn,[10] Surena saw that,

> 'archers were useless without arrows; this does not seem to have occurred to anyone before … For the first time in history, so far as is known, there had appeared a trained professional force dependent solely on long-range weapons and with enough ammunition for a protracted fight.'

Surena's vision ensured that the Parthian quivers were always replenished. Camels were crucial to the Parthian victory: Surena had shrewdly brought along 1,000 Arabian camels, one for every ten men, laden with arrows, enabling the Parthians to replenish their quivers in a kind of relay.

Plutarch had the measure of Crassus' quaestor, Gaius Cassius Longinus, having Caesar say of him: 'I am not much in fear of these fat, long-haired fellows, but rather of those pale, thin ones.' This was famously paraphrased by Shakespeare in *Julius Caesar,* just before the assassination.[11]

Crassus blindly pursued the Parthian army into the desert under the dubious guidance of Ariamnes, who turned out to be a double agent, leading the Romans into the deep sand before he promptly melted away into the baking hot desert. The promised Armenian support failed to materialise, as Artavasdes was himself under attack by Orodes and needed help from the Romans. Artavasdes advised a withdrawal into Armenia, from where the Romans could launch a new attack. Crassus was furious and threatened revenge on what he considered to be perfidious Armenians. He refused to allow his tired, hungry and increasingly nervous army to rest, opting instead to continue his pursuit of what he thought was the retreating Parthian army, but was actually just a squadron of scouts. Crassus' army, inexperienced in desert warfare and not acclimatized to the searing heat, was routed. The priceless legionary standards were lost. Cassius, together with 500 cavalry, escaped that night and reached Syria. A destroyed and distraught Crassus ceded command to his legates, Vargunteius, Octavius and Cassius.

It took until 20 BCE before Emperor Augustus negotiated the return of the precious and prestigious standards from the Parthians. Just how crucial a feat of diplomacy this was can be seen by it being regarded as a national triumph celebrated in 19 BCE by the dedication of the Arch of Augustus.

Plutarch and Cassius Dio are our sources for Carrhae, although there are snippets of information from Cicero, Julius Caesar, Velleius Paterculus, Josephus and Appian. Tarn claims that the battle was witnessed at first-hand by an unknown historian whose account is now lost, but who provided the material for Plutarch's *Life of Crassus.*[12] According to Tarn, it 'gives us a better account of the battle of Carrhae and its preliminaries than we possess of most battles of antiquity; also we know what both sides were doing'.[13] Plutarch tells us that Crassus marched into Parthia with seven legions, almost 4,000 cavalry and 4,000 light-armed troops; in total about 44,000 troops. He came out with 30,000 fewer men, 10,000 of whom were taken prisoner. The Romans had been confronted by a much smaller force of 10,000 Parthian cavalry – heavily armed and armoured cataphracts, and mounted archers who were skilled in shooting even in retreat. Those arrow-carrying camels were also key to the Parthian victory. Crassus realised his predicament and, lacking provisions, tried to negotiate, but in vain. Dust also proved an important factor in the ensuing battle – raised in clouds by the Parthians to blind the Romans and exacerbate the intense June heat – and to cap it all the psychologically disturbing and relentless rhythmic beating of drums drove the Romans out of their minds. Here is Plutarch's terrifying account of the one-sided encounter:

> 'All the field rung with a hideous noise and terrible clamour. For the Parthians do not encourage themselves to war with cornets and trumpets, but with a kind of kettle-drum, which they strike all at once in various quarters. With these they make a dead, hollow noise, like the bellowing of beasts, mixed with sounds resembling thunder, having, it would seem, very correctly observed that of all our senses hearing most confounds and disorders us, and that the feelings excited through it most quickly disturb and most entirely overpower the understanding. When they had sufficiently terrified the Romans with their noise, they threw off the covering of their armour, and shone like lightning in their breastplates and helmets of polished Margianian steel, and with their horses covered with brass and steel trappings … Now as long as they had hopes that the enemy would exhaust their missiles and desist from battle or fight at close quarters, the Romans held out; but when they perceived that many camels laden with arrows were at hand, from which the Parthians who first encircled them took a fresh supply, then Crassus, seeing no end to this, began to lose heart … Then the Romans halted, supposing that the enemy would come to close quarters with them, since they were so few in number. But the Parthians stationed their mail-clad horsemen in front of the Romans, and then with the rest of their cavalry in loose array rode round them, tearing up the surface of the ground, and raising from the depths great heaps of sand which fell in limitless showers of dust,

> so that the Romans could neither see clearly nor speak plainly, but, being crowded into a narrow compass and feeling upon one another, were shot, and died no easy nor even speedy death. For, in the agonies of convulsive pain, and writhing about the arrows, they would break them off in their wounds, and then in trying to pull out by force the barbed heads which had pierced their veins and sinews, they tore and disfigured themselves the more. Thus many died, and the survivors also were incapacitated for fighting. And when Publius urged them to charge the enemy's mail-clad horsemen, they showed him that their hands were riveted to their shields and their feet nailed through and through to the ground, so that they were helpless either for flight or for self-defence.'[14]

Dio's version is no less horrific:

> 'For if they decided to lock shields for the purpose of avoiding the arrows by the closeness of their array, the pikemen were upon them with a rush, striking down some, and at least scattering the others; and if they extended their ranks to avoid this, they would be struck with the arrows. Hereupon many died from fright at the very charge of the pikemen, and many perished hemmed in by the horsemen. Others were knocked over by the pikes or were carried off transfixed. The missiles falling thick upon them from all sides at once struck down many by a mortal blow, rendered many useless for battle, and caused distress to all. They flew into their eyes and pierced their hands and all the other parts of their body and, penetrating their armour, deprived them of their protection and compelled them to expose themselves to each new missile. Thus, while a man was guarding against arrows or pulling out one that had stuck fast he received more wounds, one after another. Consequently it was impracticable for them to move, and impracticable to remain at rest. Neither course afforded them safety but each was fraught with destruction, the one because it was out of their power, and the other because they were then more easily wounded … Finally, as the enemy continually assaulted them from all sides at once, and they were compelled to protect their exposed parts

> by the shields of those who stood beside them, they were shut up in so narrow a place that they could no longer move. Indeed, they could not even get a sure footing by reason of the number of corpses, but kept falling over them. The heat and thirst (it was midsummer and this action took place at noon) and the dust, of which the barbarians raised as much as possible by all riding around them, told fearfully upon the survivors, and many succumbed from these causes, even though unwounded.'[15]

Eran Spahbodh Rustaham Suren-Pahlav, or Surena, was no ordinary general, or *spahbed*. His name means 'heroic one'; he is still popular in Armenia and Iran today. Plutarch wrote:

> 'Surena was an extremely distinguished man. In wealth, birth, and in the honour paid to him, he ranked next after the king; in courage and ability he was the foremost Parthian of his time; and in stature and personal beauty he had no equal. When he travelled about the country on his own affairs, he was always accompanied by a baggage train of 1,000 dromedaries; 200 wagons carried his harem; 1,000 armoured cavalry and still more light armed cavalry acted as his escort. The total number of his cavalry, his vassals, and his slaves came to at least 100,000 men. He had, as an ancient privilege of his family, the right to be the first to set the crown on the head of the king of Parthia at the coronation … he, also, took the great city of Seleucia, was the first man that scaled the walls, and with his own hand beat off the defenders. And though at this time he was not above thirty years old, he had a great name for wisdom and sagacity, and, indeed, by these qualities chiefly, he overthrew Crassus, who first through his overweening confidence, and afterwards because he was cowed by his calamities, fell a ready victim to his subtlety.'

But Plutarch also said that looks could be deceiving:

> 'Surena was the tallest and finest looking man himself, but the delicacy of his looks and effeminacy of his dress did not promise so much

> manhood as he really was master of; or his face was painted, and his hair parted after the fashion of the Medes.'[16]

Publius Crassus fought valiantly on behalf of his father. He managed to rally his Gauls: some seized the Parthian cataphracts' lances and dragged them to the ground, where their heavy armour immobilized them. Some dismounted and crawled under the Parthian horses, which they promptly disembowelled. Publius, perhaps inevitably, was badly wounded and dragged off the field for a last stand. Two local Greeks, Hieronymus and Nicomachus, urged him to flee to nearby Ichnae, a town friendly to the Romans, but he refused, preferring to stay and die with his troops. Publius ordered his armour-bearer to run him through with his sword, his promising career tragically cut short.

The entrancing, persistent drum beating resumed as the Parthians rode towards Crassus with Publius' head on the end of a spear, asking where on earth could his parents be – so brave and courageous a soldier could not possibly be the son of so wretched a coward as Crassus.

Octavius and his 5,000 men escaped, but sly Cassius and his 500 cavalry deserted, managing to get away that night and make their way to Syria. The Parthians let them go, but next morning they butchered 4,000 surviving wounded and stragglers lost on the night march to Carrhae. Refusing to negotiate with Surena and to be bound by the shackles the Parthians demanded as a prerequisite, Crassus enlisted the help of another guide, Andromachus (who was later rewarded with the governorship of Carrhae for his duplicity), to help him and his 1,500 survivors to escape through the tricky terrain. Andromachus too was a double agent and misled the Romans straight into marshes. The Parthians attacked, but Crassus was saved when Octavius' unit, also lost, joined up with him and saved the day. Surena then offered Crassus a truce: peace, safe conduct and the restoration of relations with Rome; urged on by his troops, Crassus accepted. He parleyed with Surena, who gave him a horse as he could not negotiate with an enemy leader on foot, and asked for the treaty to be signed on the banks of the Euphrates, now the boundary between Rome and Parthia. Octavius, however, totally misread the situation, drew his sword and killed the groom who was helping with Crassus' horse. The Romans were killed in the ensuing skirmish.

Crassus suffered the fate of all treaty-breakers: his head and hands were cut off by a Parthian, Pomaxathres, and sent to Orodes. According to Dio, the Parthians poured molten gold down his throat as a symbol of his avarice. Legend has it that his head arrived at an opportune moment, during the wedding ceremony of Artavazd's sister to Orodes II's son and heir, Pacorus, while they were enjoying a performance of Euripides' *The Bacchae*. A quick-witted actor, Jason of Tralles, took the head and quoted these appropriate lines from *The Bacchae* – 'We bring from the mountain a tendril fresh-cut to the palace a wonderful prey' – to bring the performance to a happy conclusion.

Of the 42,000 Romans who started the war with Crassus, 10,000 eventually made it back to Syria and were reorganized into a fighting force by Cassius. Another 10,000 were taken prisoner and held at Marv; the rest died. Some did escape with Cassius, who lived to conspire against Caesar and assassinate him in 44 BCE.[17] So ended one of the worst disasters ever suffered by the Roman Army.

Surena enjoyed his victory to the full and revelled in his success. He led his army back to Seleucia to celebrate a mock Roman triumph, in which a Roman prisoner of war, Gaius Paccianus Paccianus - who bore a passing resemblance to Crassus - was placed at the head of the humiliated army, forced to wear women's clothes and to answer to the name of Crassus. Surena's soldiers marched behind, each carrying a decapitated Roman head, followed by Parthian women singing abusive songs about the cowardice and effeminacy of Crassus. But Surena got no thanks for this spectacle and was later executed by an increasingly jealous Orodes. Orodes suffered the same fate in 38 BCE, at the hands of his own son, Phraactes, who strangled him when the poison he administered failed.

The disaster of Carrhae has been called 'without doubt the most celebrated episode of Parthian history'.[18] On the other hand, it brought far-reaching and long-lasting humiliation and disgrace for Rome, and another serious loss of prestige. The only consolation for the Romans, who greeted the news with 'unwonted apathy', was that the disgrace was mitigated somewhat because Crassus' action was independent of the Senate and not officially sanctioned by them. Nevertheless, the allies in the region and the tricky client kingdoms cannot have been impressed by Rome's performance. The evidence of Roman ignominy must have been there for all to see for a long time. Visiting traders, officials and diplomats would have been made only too aware of the bodies littering the battlefield and on the route of the disorderly retreat. The temples would have been filled with Roman booty and the captured standards will have taken pride of place in Parthia. The war between Parthia and Rome then slowly 'died of inanition'.[19] The campaign left the province of Syria undefended and leaderless: Crassus had deployed its legions in Parthia, and all that now remained were 10,000 stunned survivors from Carrhae. In 52 BCE, Orodes successfully attacked Syria.

Most crucially for our narrative, Carrhae was also responsible for destabilizing the delicate balance of power held by the First Triumvirate. Pompey had married Caesar's daughter, Julia, and when she died in childbirth in 54 BCE, Caesar married the widow of Publius Crassus: a strong bond between the surviving triumvirs (now the duumvirs) had been irreparably broken. Where there were three, there was now two. A stand-off was inevitable.

Surena had put a decisive stop to Roman expansion in the East, restored Mesopotamia to the Parthians and established the Euphrates as the boundary between the two empires. Carrhae put Parthia on an equal footing with Rome, making them political and military rivals for the next 700 years. The Romans did not go away completely empty-handed: they learnt the benefits and value of the fleet and mobile Parthian cavalry, and adapted it to their own needs.

Whatever was thought of Crassus at the time, his reputation seems to have been restored quite soon after the disaster. Some Roman poets of the early Empire were unanimous in their praise. Ovid says 'the pride of the nation had been fostered by the deaths of Crassus and his son' and 'Parthia, thou shalt pay the penalty; rejoice you buried Crassi, and your standards that shamefully endured barbarian violence'. Propertius chimes in with a reference to the cavalry skills of the Parthians: 'No longer does the Euphrates allow Parthian horsemen to glance behind their backs, and regrets keeping possession of the Crassi.' He adds: 'Rejoice Crassus, if any consciousness be yours amid the grave's black sands: now we may cross the Euphrates to your tomb.'[20]

Chapter 8

The First Triumvirate: Julius Caesar, Pompey the Great and Marcus Licinius Crassus (59–53 BCE)

The term 'triumvirate' is modern and is used nowadays to describe the fractious coalition between Caesar, Pompey and Crassus, formed in 59 BCE Essentially, these three giants of mid-first-century Roman politics and warfare were united, not by any common purpose or agenda of benefit to the common good, but by a desire to pursue their individual political objectives for their own personal benefit and advancement. The three believed that, by this means, they could undermine and replace the Senate, Rome's traditional vehicle of government, and dictate policy, lead the army and monopolize the consulship. The only glue holding the alliance together was the belief that they, as a threesome, could and would bring strength and stability where there was only weakness and vulnerability.

Enmities between each other were laid aside in pursuit of the greater prize, enhanced *gloria*, *auctoritas* and *dignitas* – glory, authority and prestige or dignity. Such lofty ideals were unlikely to be achieved independently, so collaboration, however tenuous or unpopular, was the only way. If there was one single thing that they agreed on, it was swearing to oppose collectively any legislation of which any one of them might disapprove.[1]

Looked at another way, the coalition represented a provocative challenge by the *populares* to the deeply conservative *optimates* (the *boni*). The former relied on the plebeians for support and championed policies which addressed the problems of the urban poor and enshrined reforms that would improve their lot – debt relief and redistribution of land for the landless poor to farm, for example. Central to their ideology was a challenge to the power of the aristocratic *nobiles* and the power they exerted over Roman politics in the Senate. Julius Caesar was a leading figure in the *populares* camp. Pompey tended to look both ways, committing himself entirely to neither camp. The *optimates* favoured the nobles; they did not favour reform. Where the *optimates* were active was in trying to limit the power of the plebeian tribunes and the assembly of the plebeians, thus maintaining or bolstering the power of the Senate and preserving the status quo.

It was about this time that Cicero's summary executions of the Catiline conspirators came back to haunt him and his fellow *optimates*. Although Cicero's actions may have been seen at the time as a genuine expedient to discourage further revolution and violence, the *populares* had a different perpective; their view was that it constituted a violation of the right to a trial and was an example of repressive government, an expression of the Senate's aristocratic dominance in politics. The power and status of the *optimates* were now being called into question. In 63 BCE, Cicero came very close to being dragged through the courts when the plebeian tribunes Quintus Caecilius Metellus Nepos Iunior and Calpurnius Bestia, supported by Caesar, attacked Cicero's actions.[2]

After eradicating the Pontic threat and having reorganized the Asian provinces into client states, Pompey, contrary to the fears of the Senate about another march on Rome, disbanded his army and returned to Rome in 62 BCE very much a hero, celebrating a two-day triumph. His priority now was to ask the Senate to approve two things: that his troops be given land and that the Senate ratify his settlement of the East. There was nothing unreasonable about either, but Pompey's enemy, the tribune Lucius Licinius Lucullus, led the Senate's rejection of both of these requests with the support of Cato the Younger.[3]

Meanwhile, Crassus, as noted, clamoured for a military command. Julius Caesar returned triumphant from Spain looking for a consulship and the military command in Gaul. For the triumvirs, consolidating the pact, the *amicitia* – not least by cooling the rivalry between Pompey and Crassus – was the priority. Caesar then married off his daughter Julia to Pompey and was named consul for 59 BCE, with the *optimate* Marcus Calpurnius Bibulus, who, unfortunately for the pact, was a good friend of Cato. To enable him to stand for the consulship, Caesar had to forego a triumph for his achievements in Spain – another annoying obstacle laid in his way by the troublesome Senate.

Caesar's first action as consul was to improve radically the transparency of senatorial business, passing a law that required the public release of all debates and procedures of the Senate, a kind of Roman *Hansard*. This move would see him apparently working on the part of the people against the exclusive, opaque Senate and aristocracy; at the same time, it had the benefit of reducing the power of the Senate.

The first test for the Triumvirate and the Senate came when Caesar put Pompey's land settlement proposal through the Senate in a land bill that was meticulous in its detail. To minimize and deflect opposition, Caesar diplomatically made it clear that the terms were open to debate and that he was happy to amend or delete any clauses that the Senate disliked. Unused land in other parts of Italy outside Campania would be redeveloped for the purpose, which would have the dual benefit of relocating the mobs of unemployed and underemployed in Rome while, at the same time, satisfying Pompey and his veterans.

However, traditionally, any form of land redistribution was anathema to the conservative nobility. Predictably then, Marcus Calpurnius Bibulus proved a thorn in the Triumvirate's collective side and exercised his right to veto. Caesar sidestepped him by taking the proposal to the popular assembly. Bibulus tried to interfere using omens and public holidays as delaying tactics, but, for his troubles, his *fasces* were broken in front of him and he was unceremoniously thrown down the steps of the Temple of Castor and Pollux, followed by a bucketful of faeces.[4] Bibulus spent the rest of his term at home looking out for omens with which he might invalidate all legislation passed that year. First Triumvirate supporters pilloried Bibulus by asserting that the two consuls were really 'Julius and Caesar'; Bibulus retorted bitchily by referring to Caesar as the 'Queen of Bithynia', an allusion to Caesar's alleged dalliance with the King of Bithynia when he apparently lived the life of a girl in the court of King Nicomedes, and was later referred to behind his back as 'Queen of Bithynia', 'every woman's man and every man's woman'.

Bibulus also alleged that Caesar had been involved in the first conspiracy of Catiline. For the time being, that was the end of Bibulus' political career, ominously leaving Caesar to rule as consul alone.

Cato the Younger surrendered and accepted the bill, and the veterans got their land. So far so good for the Triumvirate.

But Rome was descending inexorably into political violence. A murder attempt on Caesar and Pompey in the forum by Vettius was averted; Vettius was a plebeian put up to the scheme by Bibulus, Cicero and Cato – and perhaps

Lucullus as well. Whatever the facts, Vettius died soon after in prison.[5] The eccentric and unpredictable Publius Clodius Pulcher (93–52 BCE) became embroiled in events when Caesar enlisted him to act against Cicero because of his suspicions about the Vettius affair. Caesar had decided that Clodius was in his debt because Caesar had not testified against him when Clodius was tried for sacrilege in 62 BCE. But Caesar need not have worried about Clodius' loyalty: Clodius harboured a pathological grudge against Cicero because he had testified against him at the same trial. Dio relates how, after the trial, Clodius came to despise the *optimates*; Suetonius described Clodius as the enemy of Cicero; and Appian recorded that Clodius had already supported Caesar when he helped him to secure the governorship of Gaul. Clodius was also an ally of Pompey.[6]

As tribune, Clodius aimed his legislation directly at Cicero: he introduced a law, punishable with exile, criminalizing anyone who executed a Roman citizen without a trial. Cicero, of course, had done just that when he had members of the Catiline conspiracy strangled while in prison. In vain, Cicero argued that he was indemnified by the *senatus consultum ultimum* from punishment and cast around for support from senators and consuls, including Pompey. None was forthcoming, and Cicero was duly exiled to Thessalonica on 29 May 58 BCE. That same day, Clodius passed a law which forbade Cicero to approach within 400 miles of Italy, and permitted confiscation of his property. Cicero's house on the Palatine was trashed and torched by Clodius' supporters, his villas in Tusculum and Formiae likewise.[7] Clodius then had a temple of Libertas built on the site of Cicero's house so that even when, or if, Cicero returned, he could not reclaim the site.

Clodius warmed to the violence and thuggery that was now pervading the streets of Rome, and which had replaced the rule of law and democracy to become the most efficacious means of exerting political power. To that end, he abolished the restrictions on establishing new *collegia* – social and political clubs or guilds of workmen – and established new ones. These were thinly disguised gangs of thugs which Clodius deployed to control and dominate the streets by intimidating and chasing off opponents by various forms of harassment, accosting and beating in the streets, booing, showering with excreta at the games, throwing rocks at their houses and attempting to burn down their houses.

Clodius, however, soon became an embarrassment to the triumvirs. Things turned sour when Pompey criticized Clodius' actions and policies, and even suggested recalling Cicero from exile. Clodius was apoplectic and turned on Pompey; he organized an assassination attempt in August 58 BCE, in which his henchmen, laying siege to the Pompey household, forced Pompey into virtual house arrest. Clodius then turned on Caesar by declaring illegal his consular legislation during 59 BCE. However, all that this achieved was the recall of Cicero, which in turn produced the expected violence, making it all too clear that gang violence had to be met with gang violence. Pompey gave his approval for the tribunes Milo and Publius Sestius to raise mobs, including gladiator trainers and ex-gladiators, to oppose Clodius' thugs. The street fighting continued apace and Clodius was beaten. However, he recovered and attacked the workmen who were rebuilding Cicero's house, assaulted Cicero himself in the street and set fire to the house of Cicero's younger brother, Quintus Tullius Cicero.

Clodius was voted the aedileship for 57 BCE and instigated proceedings against Milo for inciting violence, the very same charge Milo had brought against him. Clodius had his rent-a-mob heckle Pompey in the assemblies and continued his attacks on Cicero. Clashes between the two factions went on.

His consulship over, Caesar, with the help of the tribune Publius Vatinius, passed the '*Lex Vatinia*' which gave Caesar the Proconsulship of Cisalpine Gaul and Illyricum – a five-year posting unprecedented for a region that was relatively secure. Coincidentally, the current governor of neighbouring Gallia Narbonensis, Quintus Caecilius Metellus Celer, died and his province was assigned to Caesar. Caesar left Rome for Gaul, where he spent the next ten years honing his military expertise and seeking glory.

Pompey was awarded command over Rome's grain supply – becoming *praefectus annonae* (prefect of the provisions) – in 57 BCE, in a bid by the Senate to quell a series of food riots. Pompey executed this with his usual professionalism, sending agents to various locations and sailing to Sardinia, Sicily and Africa – Rome's breadbaskets – to collect grain. So much did he collect that the markets were glutted. Both Plutarch and Dio say that the law bestowing the prefectorship made Pompey 'the master of all the land and sea under Roman possession'. Appian records that this success accorded Pompey reputation and power.

Pompey and Crassus were elected joint consuls in 55 BCE, and Pompey was made governor of Spain, which he ruled at arm's length from Rome. Things went from bad to worse when Julia, Pompey's wife and Caesar's daughter, died while giving birth to a girl in 54 BCE; another of the fragile bonds holding the Triumvirate together had evaporated.[8] Crassus, as we have seen, took on the Parthians, led his army to a disastrous rout at Carrhae and, most calamitously, lost Rome her prestigious standards. His death effectively marked the end of the coalition, despite it having been renewed at Luca in 56 BCE when Caesar's time in Gaul was extended.

Chapter 9

Caesar's Gallic Wars (58–50 BCE)

In 52 BCE, Caesar was still preoccupied with his wars in Gaul and had concluded two speculative reconnoitres of Britannia in 55 and 54. His co-duumvir, Pompey, was left to deal with a Rome that was engulfed in bribery scandals, gang warfare, cancelled elections and street fighting. Caesar, our source for the Gallic campaign, would have us believe that his war was a pre-emptive, defensive war. In reality, it was used by Caesar as another step on his *cursus honorum* and a means of paying off his substantial debts through booty. Caesar's *Gallic War* comprises seven 'books', each devoted to one year of campaigning. The first book covers 58 BCE and opens with the battles against the Helvetians.

Before Caesar's wars, Roman and Italian merchants and Roman commanders communicated what was known about Gaul. But there still remained much mystery, in common with other lands which were largely *terra incognita*. The writing of the Greek sailor Pytheas, in Caesar's time some three centuries old, were the best that might be expected, with the exception of the fantastic description given by Xenophon of Lampsacus. He told the world, as quoted by Pliny the Elder in his *Natural History* (4, 95), that in the Gallic north there were people with horses' hooves and huge ears; on the Birds Islands, Xenophon said, people lived on oats and eggs.

Gaul was of considerable strategic importance to Rome and Caesar was doing the state a rare favour when he quelled the troublesome natives and secured the Rhine as a natural frontier of the empire. Caesar's war against the Gauls lasted from 58-50 BCE, the decisive battle of which was at Alesia in 52 BCE, in which total Roman victory resulted in the expansion of the Republic over the whole of Gaul, largely present-day France and Belgium.

Caesar launched his campaign with four veteran legions –:*Legio* VII, *Legio* VIII, *Legio* IX *Hispana* and *Legio* X – with which he was familiar from his governorship of Hispania Ulterior in 61 BCE and his successful campaigns with them against the Lusitanians. Caesar was also at liberty to levy additional legions and auxiliary units as required.

The tribes of Gaul were civilized and wealthy after years of commercial contact with Roman merchants; some even were constitutionally advanced, like the Aedui and Helvetii, which were republics and had enjoyed stable political alliances with Rome. Past conflict with the Gallic tribes had instilled in the Romans a healthy respect for and fear of some of the Gauls. Memories of 109 BCE were still fresh, when Italy was invaded from the north and saved at great expense in lives by Gaius Marius.

In 62 BCE, a Roman client state, the Arverni, conspired with the Sequani and Suebi nations east of the Rhine to attack the Aedui, another Roman client state of some standing. Rome turned a blind eye. The Sequani and Arverni defeated the Aedui in 63 BCE at the Battle of Magetobriga.

Discontent had been brewing amongst the Gallic tribes for all the usual reasons: heavy-handed Roman rule and depradation, oppressive taxation and unrealistic quotas for auxiliaries.

The Helvetii and their land were at the forefront of early trouble in 58 BCE. The Helvetii was a confederation of five or so related Gallic tribes that lived on the Swiss plateau, between the Alps and the rivers Rhine and Rhone. Other German tribes to the north and east were exerting pressure on the Helvetii in their quest for *lebensraum*. Helvetiian plans for a mass migration and its provisioning were well advanced under Orgetorix. The plan was to traverse Gaul to the west coast through the lands of the Aedui, a staunch Roman friend, in the Roman province of Transalpine Gaul.

No one can accuse the Helvetii of neglecting the due diligence for this huge project. They sent envoys to all affected neighbouring tribes to ensure peaceful transit. Orgetorix entered into an alliance with the Sequani chieftain, Casticus; he also arranged to marry his daughter to an Aedui chieftain, Dumnorix. But there was an ulterior motive for their new-found clannishness. According to Caesar, the three covertly planned to establish themselves as kings of their respective tribes, and, worse for Rome, as masters of all of Gaul.[1] Orgetorix was found out and put on trial, destined to burn at the stake if convicted; but Orgetorix happened to have numerous debtors, and these helped him to escape. However, he never made it: according to Caesar, the demise of Orgetorix was 'not without suspicion that he had decided upon death for himself', or, in other words, he committed suicide.[2] The migration proceeded, with the Helvetii burning their towns and villages behind them.[3]

Caesar was in Italy at the time and vulnerable, for there was only one legion in Transalpine Gaul, so he repaired to Geneva, levied a number of auxiliary units and destroyed the Rhone bridge. When the Helvetii sent diplomats to negotiate a peaceful and safe passage, Caesar stalled the negotiations for fifteen days, using the time to build up fortifications with a 19-mile rampart and parallel trench.[4]

When the embassy came back, Caesar refused their request, warning them that he would oppose any forceful attempt to cross the river. Several attempts were made but quickly beaten off. The Helvetii retreated and started negotiations with the Sequani, and with Dumnorix of the Aeduans, in their search for an alternate route.[5]

Caesar left his solitary legion under the command of his second-in-command, Titus Labienus, and hastened to Cisalpine Gaul, where he took command of the three legions stationed in Aquileia and enrolled two new legions, the *Legio* XI and *Legio* XII. He returned through the Alps, through the lands of several hostile tribes, fighting skirmishes on the way.[6]

The Helvetii, meanwhile, had already advanced through the territories of the Sequani, and were busy plundering the lands of the Aedui, Ambarri and Allobroges. These tribes were unable to do anything to prevent this, other than request Caesar's help. Caesar agreed, and attacked the Helvetii as they crossed the River Arar (modern Saône). Most of the Helvetii had already crossed, but about a quarter, the Tigurine, remained on the east bank. Three legions under Caesar attacked and defeated the Tigurine in the Battle of the Arar. The remaining Tigurini fled.[7]

After the battle, the Romans built a bridge over the Saône to enable them to pursue the remaining Helvetii. The Helvetii responded with an embassy led by Divico, but were refused. The Romans continued to harry them for a number of weeks with 4,000 Roman and allied Aedui cavalry, until supplies ran short. Dumnorix did everything he could to hinder the supplies; the Romans headed for the Aedui town of Bibracte where the tables were turned, and the Helvetii pursued the Romans, harassing their rearguard. Caesar then offered battle.

In the Battle of Bibracte, the Romans carved out a hard-fought victory. The Helvetii offered to surrender, which Caesar accepted, but 6,000 men of the

Helvetian Verbigeni tribe fled. Other Gallic tribes rounded up and returned the fugitives. Caesar had them executed, but those who had complied and surrendered were sent back to their homeland to rebuild it in order to create a buffer between the Romans and the Celtic tribes from the north.

Caesar refers to the Suebi as a single, identifiable Germanic tribe existing within an alliance with other tribes. Tacitus, Pliny the Elder and Strabo, however, made the important distinction that the Suebi 'do not, like the Chatti or Tencteri, constitute a single nation. They actually occupy more than half of Germania, and are divided into a number of distinct tribes under distinct names, though all generally are called Suebi.'[8] Indeed, from an ethnographical aspect in the first centuries CE, Suebi was applied to so many Germanic tribes that it could easily have replaced the name 'Germans'.

In 61 BCE, Ariovistus, then chief of the Suebi tribe, resumed the tribe's migration from the east of Germania to the Marne and Rhine region, a movement which encroached on Sequani territory. Despite this, the Sequani formed an alliance with Ariovistus against the Aedui and repaid Ariovistus with land following his victory in the Battle of Magetobriga. Ariovistus moved 120,000 of his people onto the new land, soon joined by 24,000 Harudes:

> 'But worse was to come for the victorious Sequani than the vanquished Aedui, for Ariovistus, a king of the Germani, had settled in their territories, and had seized upon a third of their land, which was the best in the whole of Gaul, and was now ordering them to depart from another third part, because a few months previously 24,000 men of the Harudes had come to him, for whom room and settlements must be provided.'[9]

Ariovistus demanded more land from the Sequani to accommodate the Harudes, a demand which made the Romans anxious lest Ariovistus then swallowed up all of the Sequani land from which to attack the rest of Gaul. There were rumblings of discontent, too, amongst other German tribes, not least Diviciacus, leader of the Aeduas and spokesman for the Gallic delegation. Diviciacus pressed Caesar to defeat Ariovistus, in order to remove his threat of invasion, or they too would be forced to migrate. Caesar was obliged to protect the Aedui and their alliance, but there was another aspect to the problem: it was an opportunity to expand Rome's borders, reinforce loyalty within Caesar's army and establish him as *the* commander of Rome's overseas armies.

The situation was further complicated because in 59 BCE the Senate had declared Ariovistus a 'king and friend of the Roman people', so tying Caesar's hands because he could not attack the the Suevis. Consequently, Caesar declared that he could not ignore the plight the Aedui were in and delivered an ultimatum to Ariovistus demanding that no German cross the Rhine, the return of Aedui hostages and the protection of the Aedui and other friends of Rome. Ariovistus pointed out that Rome had no jurisdiction over him: the Harudes attacked the Aedui. Caesar now had good reason to declare war on Ariovistus in 58 BCE.

Ariovistus had designs on Vesontio, the Sequani's largest town, which Caesar marched toward. Ariovistus tried diplomacy, requesting a truce and a meeting with Caesar, but Ariovistus violated the truce. Two days later, Ariovistus requested another meeting: Caesar sent Valerius Procillus, his friend, and Caius Mettius, a merchant with a commercial track record of trading with Ariovistus. Ariovistus was insulted by the status of the delegates and clapped them in chains. He then encamped 2 miles behind Caesar, cutting off Caesar's communication and supply lines. Caesar had a second camp built near Ariovistus' position. Ariovistus attacked but was repulsed.

The next day, Caesar advanced towards Ariovistus and came out victor in the battle, with no small contribution from Publius Crassus and his cavalry, who broke the German line. The majority of Ariovistus' 120,000 men were slain; the remnants escaped crossed the Rhine, never to trouble Rome again.

The Belgae were a large Gallic confederation settled from the third century BCE in northern Gaul, between what we now call the English Channel, the west bank of the Rhine and northern bank of the Seine. Caesar famously describes Gaul at the time of his campaigns as being divided into three parts: the Aquitani in the south-west, the Gauls in the centre – who were called Celtae – and the Belgae in the north. Each of these had different characteristics relating to customs, laws and language. To Caesar, the Belgae were:

> 'the bravest of the three peoples, being farthest removed from the highly developed civilization of the Roman Province, least often

> visited by merchants with enervating luxuries for sale, and nearest to the Germans across the Rhine, with whom they are continually at war.'[10]

Trouble started here for Caesar when, in 58 BCE, his intelligence reported rumours that the Belgic tribes were forming an alliance against Rome because they feared Roman interference in their affairs. This union included the Bellovaci, Suessiones, Nervii, Atrebates, Ambiani, Morini, Menapii, Caleti, Veliocasses, Viromandui, Aduatuci, Condrusi, Eburones, Caeroesi and Paemani tribes, and was under the leadership of Galba, a king of the Suessiones. The reports gave Caesar a pretext for conquering more of Gaul, to which end he raised two legions in Cisalpine Gaul (the XIII and XIV) and persuaded the Remi tribe to side with him.[11]

This caused various Belgic and Celtic tribes to attack Bibrax, the *oppidum* (fortified town) of the Remi, near the Aisne River. Caesar sprang to its defence and won a battle at the Aisne, causing the tribal union to collapse and disperse back to their own lands, with the agreement to come to the support of any tribe attacked by the Romans. Caesar continued his advance. Tribes surrendered one by one, but four tribes – the Nervii, Atrebates, Aduatuci and Viromandui – held out.[12] Of the four, the Nervii showed most hostility to Roman rule. They had a reputation for tenacity and bravery, and did not allow luxury items as they believed these to be corrupting and feminizing. They had no intention of parleying with the Romans, so Caesar planned to move on them.

Intelligence provided by the Remi told Caesar he was up against 50,000 Nervii, 15,000 Atrebates, 10,000 Veromandui and 19,000 Aduatuci.[13] He himself commanded eight legions, comprising the VII, VIII, IX Triumphalis, X Equestris, XI, XII Victrix, XIII and XIV – plus auxiliaries, archers and cavalry. Gallic intelligence reported back that the legionary baggage trains were mixed up between the legions, making it easy to cut off the leading legion from the rest and destroy it before help could arrive.

In 57 BCE, the Nervii launched a swift surprise attack on Caesar's army. The Battle of the Sabis was fought near modern Saulzoir in northern France while Caesar was making camp near the River Sambre. The disorganized Romans found themselves on the verge of a humiliating defeat: Caesar lost all of his standards and most of his centurions were killed or wounded. Only a courageous stand by the *Legio* X and the timely arrival of reinforcements allowed Caesar to regroup and eventually repel the Nervii, Atrebates and Viromandui. Peltasts, slingers and archers were deployed to good effect for the specific purpose of overcoming the Gauls' shield wall tactics, mass attack and close combat.

Caesar made effective use of fixed projectile weaponry like the 'scorpion' and light ballista, as well as the archers and peltasts, against the Nervii, a tribe whose military skills and determination he admired. Indeed, the Nervii habitually caught Roman javelins in flight and hurled them back at the legionaries. Victory handed Caesar control of what is now modern Belgium.

The following year, 56 BCE, saw Caesar focus on the tribes of the Atlantic seaboard, especially the Veneti in Armorica (modern Brittany), who had put together and led a confederacy of anti-Roman tribes. The Veneti were seafarers and made good use of their fleet. This obliged the Romans to build their own galleys for a protracted land and sea campaign, in which Caesar was eventually able to subdue these tribes.

Britain was next in line for Caesar in 55 BCE, an enticing island over the intimidating English Channel. He was attracted by the kudos its conquest held and by the Gallic connection with the island: the Belgae of north-eastern Gaul had raided Britain, establishing settlements, and Diviciacus, King of the Suessiones, had wielded power in Britain as well as in Gaul.[14] Gallo-Belgic coins found in Britain predate 100 BCE, and perhaps are as early as 150 BCE; they were minted in Gaul and found mainly in Kent. More significantly, Caesar had reason to believe that the Britons had compromised his campaigns in Gaul. They had lent support to the efforts of the mainland Gauls against him and provided safe harbour for fugitives from the Gallic Belgae fleeing to Belgic settlements in Britain. Moreover, he believed that the Veneti of Armorica, who controlled seaborne trade to the island, depended on military aid from their British allies in their conflict against Caesar in 56 BCE.[15] Strabo adds that the Venetic rebellion was fomented to prevent Caesar from travelling to Britain and disrupting their trade.[16]

Caesar sent a tribune, Gaius Volusenus, as a scout in a single warship to reconnoitre the Kent coast between modern Hythe and Sandwich, but he was unable to land, since he 'did not dare leave his ship and entrust himself to the barbarians',[17] and after five days returned to give Caesar what intelligence he had.

Envoys from some British tribes, tipped off by merchants, came to offer alliances, but Caesar sent them back, along with his ally Commius, King of the Gallic Atrebates, to win over as many other states as possible.

At Portius Itius (Boulogne), Caesar assembled a fleet of eighty transport ships, big enough to carry *Legio* VII and *Legio* X, along with warships. Another eighteen transports of cavalry were due to sail from Ambleteuse. That the legions travelled without baggage or heavy siege machinery suggests that the invasion was for surveillance only. Dubris (Dover), with its natural harbour, was rejected at the last minute as a landing point because the Britons on the cliffs above could rain down their javelins on the Romans.[18] Walmer would appear to be the actual disembarkation point.

The exploratory, fact-finding mission was beset by bad luck, with atrocious weather wrecking most of the fleet. The massed chariots of the Britons on the Kent clifftops put the fear of the gods into the two legions as they approached in their boats. The Roman ships were sitting too low in the water due to their loads, which prevented them from getting close inshore and the troops had to disembark in deep water, while under attack from the enemy. They had to be urged on by the *aquilifer* (standard bearer) of the *Legio* X, who jumped into the shallows shouting: 'Jump down comrades, unless you wish to betray your eagle to the enemy. I, for my part, will perform my duty to the republic and to my general.'[19]

The Romans finally repulsed the British with *catapultae* and slings, but the Britons came back at the Romans, intent on detaining Caesar in Britain over the winter and starving him into defeat. The Britons ambushed one of his legions as it foraged near the Roman camp. The foraging party was relieved and the Britons were again driven off, only to regroup after several days of storms with a larger force to attack the Roman camp. This ended in a rout for the Britons.

The British sent ambassadors, but Caesar, to avoid a winter crossing, set off back to Gaul.

Before Caesar – and this may have been another motive for the expedition – Britain to the Romans meant tin. Early reconnaissance visits included those by the Greek geographer Pytheas in the fourth century BCE, and in the fifth century by the Carthaginian navigator Himilco. To most Romans, however, Britannia was shrouded in mystery, a misty island located beyond the Ocean at the edge of the known world ('ultima Thule'). Such was the trepidation it caused the highly suspicious Romans that its very existence was denied and Pythias was dismissed as a hoaxer.[20]

Caesar returned in 54 BCE, this time better prepared, having learned from his mistakes and with a much larger force: five legions instead of the previous year's two, plus 2,000 cavalry, conveyed in ships specially designed with the latest Venetic shipbuilding technology. They were better suited to amphibious beach landings, being broader and lower. Portus Itius in the Pas de Calais was the port of departure.

Caesar left Labienus at Portus Itius to ensure the lines of supply. The naval ships were joined by a trade delegation in the shape of a flotilla of trading ships looking to secure business with the Britons. The fleet totalled 800 ships.

The Britons offered no opposition to the landing. Caesar delegated protection of the beachhead to Quintus Atrius and made an immediate night march some 12 miles inland, where he clashed with British forces somewhere on the River Stour. The Britons were driven back and regrouped at the hill fort at Bigbury Wood in Kent, only to be defeated again.

Caesar heard from Atrius that his anchored ships had been smashed against each other in a storm, with the loss of forty vessels.[21] He returned to the coast to repair his fleet, working day and night for ten days, and building a fortified camp around them. Labienus was ordered to send more ships.

When Caesar returned to the Stour river crossing he found the British forces waiting for him there. Cassivellaunus, leader of the British combined forces, had a chequered past, having previously been at war with most of the British tribes; he had recently deposed King Mandubracius of the mighty Trinovantes and exiled his son. A Roman tribune, Quintus Laberius Durus, died in the fighting, but the Britons were repelled and routed by the Roman cavalry when they attacked a three-legion foraging party under Gaius Trebonius.

Cassivellaunus knew his limitations. Realising he was unlikely to defeat Caesar in open battle, he resorted to guerrilla warfare, relying on the mobility and speed of his 4,000 chariots and his superior knowledge of the local terrain. Caesar reached the Thames at the one fordable place available to him, only to find that it had been fortified with sharpened stakes, both on the shore and under the water, and the far bank was defended. The second-century CE writer Polyaenus tells us that Caesar deployed a huge combat elephant, heavily armoured and carrying archers and slingers in its tower, to terrify the defenders and put them to flight. The Roman army crossed over the river and invaded Cassivellaunus' territory.[22]

British opposition then collapsed. The Trinovantes sent envoys promising Caesar aid and materiel, grain and hostages. Mandubracius was restored as their king. Five more tribes – the Cenimagni, Segontiaci, Ancalites, Bibroci and Cassi – surrendered to Caesar, and revealed to him the location of Cassivellaunus' stronghold, the hill fort at Wheathampstead, which he besieged.

Cassivellaunus responded by sending word to his allies in Kent, Cingetorix, Carvilius, Taximagulus and Segovax – the 'four kings of Cantium'[23] – to stage a diversionary attack on the Roman beachhead to entice Caesar away. This ruse failed, and Cassivellaunus sent ambassadors to negotiate a surrender. Caesar was anxious to get back to Gaul, so an agreement was mediated by Commius, the terms of which were that Cassivellaunus give hostages, agree an annual tribute and undertake not to make war against Mandubracius or the Trinovantes. Commius later switched sides, fighting in Vercingetorix's Gallic rebellion.

What the two British expeditions lacked in military success or benefit, they more than made up for in propaganda, although many back in Rome criticized them as expensive and over-ambitious exercises in expansionism. The Senate decreed a *supplicatio* (thanksgiving) of twenty days when it received Caesar's report of the first expedition. Furthermore, Caesar learnt a lot from his invasions: he found that as well as infantry and cavalry, the Britons deployed chariots, something new to the Romans. Caesar describes the Britons as follows:

> 'The way they fight with their chariots is this: firstly, they drive about in all directions and throw their weapons and generally break the ranks of the enemy with the very dread of their horses and the noise of their wheels; and when they have worked themselves in between the troops of horse, leap from their chariots and engage on foot. The charioteers in the meantime withdraw some little distance from the battle, and so place themselves with the chariots that, if their masters are overpowered by the number of the enemy, they may have a ready retreat to their own troops. Thus they display in battle the speed of horse, [together with] the firmness of infantry; and by daily practice and exercise attain to such expertness that they are accustomed, even

> on a declining and steep place, to check their horses at full speed, and manage and turn them in an instant and run along the pole, and stand on the yoke, and then take themselves with the greatest speed to their chariots again.'[24]

During the civil wars, Caesar made use of a kind of boat he had seen used in Britain, similar to the Irish currach or Welsh coracle. He describes them as follows:

> '[T]he keels and ribs were made of light timber, then, the rest of the hull of the ships was wrought with wicker work, and covered over with hides.'[25]

Caesar then returned to Gaul and started to build bridges; two were constructed, in 55 and 53 BCE. From a strategic point of view they were highly successful and are considered masterpieces of military engineering. The first bridge – between Andernach and Neuwied, downstream of modern Koblenz on the Rhine – was built to secure the eastern border against marauding Germanic tribes and to demonstrate support for the Ubians, an ally of Rome.

Book 4 of Caesar's *Gallic Wars* gives the engineering detail. However, the important thing was that with 40,000 soldiers at his disposal, Caesar was able to build the bridge in only ten days. Once it was up, he crossed over to the eastern side and torched some villages, but found that the Sugambri and Suebi had moved east in readiness for a clash with the Romans. Caesar vacated the region after taking down the bridge behind him.

In 53 BCE, Caesar built a second bridge 'in a few days', as described in Book 6 of the *Gallic Wars*, close to the site of the first bridge at today's Urmitz. Brief forays against the Suebi proved inconclusive, so Caesar retreated and again took the bridge down.

Over time, more permanent bridges were built, for example at Castra Vetera (Xanten), Colonia Claudia Ara Agrippinensium (Köln), Confluentes (Koblenz) and Moguntiacum (Mainz).

In 53 BCE, Ambiorix, leader of the Eburones in the Ardennes, ambushed and massacred a legion and five cohorts at Atuatuca Tungrorum (modern Tongeren in Belgium) after he had enticed them out from their winter quarters in Liege. This had the effect of exciting other tribes to revolt. Another legion led by Quintus Tullius Cicero, the famous orator's brother, was holed up by the Nervii and only saved from destruction by a forced march by Caesar to rescue them. Eventually, all the rebellious tribes were subdued, but not for long. The savagery with which Caesar conducted these reprisals served only to inflame the Gauls yet further.

Caesar's forces won a victory at Solonium at the start of the Gallic uprising in 61 BCE, followed by success at Admagetobriga, the Arar River, Bibracte and Plain of Alsace in 58, the rivers Axona and Sabis and Octodurus in 57, Morbihan Gulf and Sotium in 56 and at Noviodunum Biturigum in 52, where Caesar encountered Vercingetorix for the first time.

Caesar was to meet Vercingetorix again later that year at Gergovia, capital of the Averni tribe. This Gallic leader presented Caesar with a dilemma when, having been expelled from Gergovia the previous year, he attacked the *oppidum* that winter.[26] Should Caesar wait until the spring and appear indecisive to his allies, the Aedui, or should he respond but risk running out of supplies? He chose the latter. After defeating Vercingetorix at Noviodunum, Caesar then took Avericum, where he resupplied and prepared to face his quarry at Gergovia, an easily defendable plateau 400 metres high with just one way in and one way out.[27] It was crucial to get to Gergovia before Vercingetorix and assume the advantage of such a strong fortress position. Vercingetorix shadowed Caesar, destroying the bridges over the River Allier as he went. At Varennes, Caesar split his forces and ordered a third of his army to move north under Labienus to attack the Senones and Parisii; he himself took the remaining six legions south. Vercingetorix followed, believing that he was pursuing the whole force. Caesar then rebuilt the bridge at Varennes and recalled the larger contingent: the whole army was now able to cross the river and proceed to Gergovia. Caesar then laid siege and, in a night attack, took a small hill at the foot of the mountain which provided running water and grain. He then built a double trench, 12ft wide, between the newly captured hill and his main camp. The plan was to encircle Gergovia and starve the Gauls inside. Vercingetorix, meanwhile, through a chief called Litavicus, had persuaded the Aedui, Rome's most loyal ally in the region, to desert Caesar and join him, aided by the untrue story that Caesar had butchered Aedui hostages surrendered with immunity in a peace treaty. Caesar reports the treachery:

> 'Caesar soon got the Aedui back on side in a meeting some twenty-five miles from Gergovia. Eporedirix, a high ranking cavalry commander was one of the men Litavicus claimed had been killed; his physical presence disabused Caesar of this; Caesar led four of his six legions to confront the 10,000 Aeduan infantry. Caesar sent Eporedirix into the Aeduan camp, at which point Litavicus's plan turned to dust. He fled to Vercingetorix; the Aedui returned to Caesar. Meanwhile, Gaius Fabius who was left in Gergovia, got word to Caesar that he was under attack; Caesar sped back to relieve his colleague. In the ensuing battle Caesar was successful, but at a heavy price in terms of casualties.'

Using one of his legions as a decoy, Caesar moved to tempt the Gauls from the plateau by feigning a retreat. Unfortunately for Caesar, most of his men failed to hear the signal and continued their attempt to dislodge the Gauls from the mountain top. The resulting frontal assault was a disaster for the Romans: forty-six centurions and 700 legionaries died in the rout that followed, and over 6,000 were wounded, compared with a few hundred Gauls killed and wounded. A furious Caesar harangued his surviving men for (apparently) disregarding his order to retreat, ordering them back into battle the next day.

Caesar describes the mayhem as the adrenalin rushed through the Roman soldiers:

> 'Elated, however, by the hope of a speedy victory, by the flight of the enemy, and their successful engagements on previous occasions, they thought that nothing was so difficult as to be unattainable by their valour, and they did not make an end of pursuing until they neared the wall and the gates of the town. Then, indeed, shouting arose from all parts of the city, and those who were farther away were terror-struck at the sudden uproar, and, believing that the enemy was within the gates, flung out of the town. Matrons threw clothing and silver from the wall, and with bare breasts and outstretched hands begged the Romans to spare them, and then not to do as they had done at Avaricum, where they slaughtered even women and children. Some of the women were lowered by hand from the wall, and gave themselves up to the troops. Lucius Fabius, a centurion of the Eighth Legion,

> who was known to have said that day among his company that he was spurred on by the rewards at Avaricum, and would allow no one to mount the wall before him, got three men of his company, was lifted up by them, and mounted the wall. Then he in turn took hold of them one by one and pulled them up on to the wall.'

The Romans had little chance:

> 'When a great host of the [Gauls] had assembled, the matrons who a moment before were stretching out their hands to the Romans from the wall began to turn on their own men and, in Gallic fashion, to show dishevelled hair and to bring their children forward into view. The Romans had no fair contest in ground or numbers; they were tired out by the speedy march and the duration of the battle, and could not easily resist men that were fresh and unhurt.'[28]

Vercingetorix was triumphant. Caesar had to accept that, humiliating as it was, this was a defeat. He built a bridge across the Allier, and then, somewhat resignedly, advanced into Aedui territory:

> '[Caesar] decided that enough had been done to reduce the bravado of the Gauls and to establish the spirit of the troops, and he moved camp accordingly into the territory of the Aedui. Even then the enemy did not pursue; and on the third day he reached the river Allier, rebuilt the bridge, and brought the army across to the other side.'[29]

This was, nevertheless, Caesar's only serious reverse in Gaul. He won back his pride and the army's reputation at Lutetia Parisiorum, at the decisive Battle of Alesia and finally at Uxellodunum. Vercingetorix opted to occupy Alesia, at which point Caesar successfully besieged him, also fending off a huge Gallic relief force.

The *oppidum* of the Parisii's Lutetia Parisiorum was originally believed to be on the Île de la Cité in modern-day Paris. In 52 BCE, the Parisii burned the bridges leading onto the Île de la Cité. Vercingetorix's lieutenant, Camulogenus, whose army camped on the Mons Lutetius, was defeated by Roman forces led by Titus Labienus. The Romans then subdued the Gauls at nearby Melun and took control of Lutetia.

The Battle (or siege) of Alesia took place in September 52 BCE, the Gallic *oppidum* of Alesia being a key town for the Mandubii tribe. Alesia is considered one of Caesar's greatest military achievements, a classic example of siege warfare and investment.

Alesia boasted excellent natural fortification, so Caesar opted for a siege to effect surrender by starvation of the 80,000 men garrisoned there, along with the civilian population. Vercingetorix's cavalry, in the meantime, was exhorting Gallic tribes to reinforce him at Alesia. In anticipation of this, Caesar ordered a double circumvallation around Alesia that was 11 Roman miles long (16km), with twenty-four redoubts (towers). All the while, the Gallic cavalry sallied out to harry the Roman engineers,[30] as the besiegers were getting ready to be besieged themselves.

Vercingetorix commanded that all the grain be brought to him and rationed. It was decided that the old and the sick should be evicted, along with wives and children, to save food for the fighters; the hope was that Caesar would treat them as prisoners and feed them. Caesar, however, refused, and they were left to slowly starve between the opposing forces.

The Gallic reinforcements arrived and camped on a hill a mile from the Roman fortification, moving nearer to the town the next day and attacking the outer fortification, while the besieged attacked the inner one. The combined attack failed. The next day, the Gauls attacked by night, but Mark Antony and Caius Trebonius brought in troops to support their hard-pressed comrades. The besieged Gauls, led by Vercingetorix, retreated.

There was, however, a weak spot in the Roman fortification which the Gauls identified and targetted. The Gauls picked 60,000 men and appointed Vercassivellaunus to lead an attack there. Caesar sent Labienus to support the defence of the weak area with six cohorts of cavalry, and then despatched Brutus with six cohorts of cavalry and Caius Fabius with a further seven to defend the inner fortification. The Gallic attack was repelled. The Roman cavalry was suddenly at the rear of the Gauls; the Roman troops attacked rapidly and the Gauls fled, only to be intercepted by the cavalry and slaughtered.[31]

The following day, Vercingetorix offered to be killed or surrendered alive to the Romans. Caesar ordered the Gauls to surrender their weapons and deliver their chieftains over to him. The chieftains were brought before him and Vercingetorix was surrendered. The Aedui and Arverni handed over captives as part of the spoils of war.

The 51 BCE siege of Uxellodunum was the last major conflict of the Gallic Wars. After the fall of the town and the decisive Roman victory, Gaul was under Roman rule.

Luciterius, the chief of the Carduci, and Drapes, chief of the Senones, had retired to the secure, virtually impregnable hill fort of Uxellodunum to see out the governorship of Caesar. Here they plotted a new rebellion against the Romans. The legatus in charge of Uxellodunum, Gaius Caninius Rebilus, divided his legions into three strategicaly sited camps designed to prevent any Gauls from escaping the city. In so doing he sealed off the city.

However, Luciterius and Drapes had other plans: they would leave the fort at night to forage for food and provisions, leaving a garrison of around 2,000 men inside Uxellodunum. When the Gauls then tried to slip back past the Roman sentries set by Rebilus, they were spotted. Rebilus attacked the Gauls: Luciterius fled, but omitted to tell Drapes. The Gauls were massacred to a man; 12,000 Gauls perished that night.

Rebilus pursued and caught Drapes, and had him executed. Rebilus then strengthened his siege works around Uxellodunum. Gaius Fabius, recently victorious at the Battle of the Loire, arrived with two-and-a-half legions. Roman forces now amounted to four-and-a-half legions, enough to run an effective siege. Caesar hurried to Uxellodunum from the territory of the Belgae; learning that the city could not be carried by force and that it was well provisioned, he focussed on the water supply, positioning archers and *ballista* near the river to fire on any Gauls attempting to collect water.

To plug a spring which provided another source, Caesar ordered a ramp of earth and rock be built to support a ten-storey siege tower, which he used to bombard the spring. Simultaneously, he built a series of tunnels that finished at the source of the spring. The Gauls fell for the tower decoy and attacked it, setting it on fire under a barrage of missiles to prevent the Romans from extinguishing the flames. Caesar then sent a diversionary attack up the ramp.

Soon after, Caesar's engineers tunnelled through to the water source and cut off the Gauls from their water sources, forcing them to surrender. Caesar decided to set an example and dispensed with the usual punishment of execution or selling the survivors into slavery. Instead, he had the hands of all surviving men of military age cut off, dispersing them throughout the province so that they could demonstrate only too vividly what happened to those who rebelled against Rome and how they were unable to take up arms again.

Caesar then took two legions and marched into Aquitania. Confident that there would be no further Gallic insurrection, he marched with the *Legio* XIII for Italy, the Rubicon in his sights.

This was effectively the end of Caesar's Gallic Wars. The last year of his procosulship was spent in reconciliation, winning back the trust and loyalty of the Gallic tribes – another lesson learnt. Additionally, Caesar imposed little more than a nominal tribute, which also helped to bring the province to a state of peace and calm, allowing him to withdraw most of his forces by 49 BCE and later to enlist Gauls in the armies he needed to fight the civil wars.

To put Caesar's achievement into perspective, the Transalpine Gaul he subdued and brought into Rome's orbit was double the size of the whole Italian peninsula and more populous than the province of Hispania. Caesar got the military glory he wanted at a critical juncture in his career, and the prodigious booty he acquired paid off some of his enormous debts, allowing him to buy political favours and alliances on a scale that would not have disappointed Crassus. Rome also got stability in Gaul, which lasted until the second century CE. Caesar returned to Italy, cast his die, crossed the Rubicon and eventually died amidst a salvo of stabbing daggers in the Forum on the Ides of March 44 BCE.

Chapter 10

Caesar's Civil War (49–45 BCE)

As we have seen, the deaths of Julia and Crassus in 54 and 53 BCE exacerbated the deteriorating relationship between Pompey and Caesar.[1] Florus sums up the mutual envy and enmity:

> 'Caesar's power now inspired the envy of Pompey, while Pompey's eminence was offensive to Caesar; Pompey could not brook an equal or Caesar a superior.[2]

More civil strife and discord accompanied the consular elections for 53 and 52 BCE. Lucillius proposed Pompey as dictator, but Cato vehemently opposed the proposal. The *optimates*, nevertheless, favoured Pompey to restore order: Marcus Calpurnius Bibulus no less, the one-time enemy of the Triumvirate, proposed in the Senate that Pompey should be elected as sole consul. Cato did a u-turn and gave his support, on the basis that any government was better than no government. Pompey invited him to be his adviser and colleague; Cato agreed to do so in a private capacity. Pompey had clearly moved to the right into the *optimates* camp, putting ground between himself and the *populares*.[3]

Pompey then married Cornelia, widow of Publius Crassus and one of the daughters of Quintus Caecilius Metellus Pius Scipio. This was but one example of the prevalent use of marriage as a political expedient amongst the male political classes.

Pompey successfully restored order and chose his father-in-law, Metellus Scipio, as his colleague for the last five months of 52 BCE. Pompey was granted an extension of his command in Syria and was voted an annual budget for the maintenance of his troops. Cato, meanwhile, was warning Pompey about Caesar's manoeuvres and machinations to increase his power, using the money he made from the Gallic war booty – widely extending his patronage in Rome. Cato encouraged Pompey to act. Pompey hesitated, but Cato stood for the consulship so as to deprive Caesar of his military command and have him brought to book and put on trial. In the event, Cato was not elected.

In keeping with such a volatile and mercurial character in life, the death, and its aftermath, of Publius Clodius Pulcher was particularly melodramatic, reflecting as it did the disorder reigning in and around Rome. Clodius was murdered in January 52 BCE and the *populares* vented their outrage on the Curia, the Senate House, the emblem of senatorial rule. The burning of the Curia demonstated very clearly the impotence of the Senate and the mob's potential for civil unrest. When the senators called in Pompey to quell the riots, he did so by deploying veterans from his eastern campaigns. The mob that despatched Clodius had as it leader Milo, ally of Cicero and anathema to the *populares*.

The Senate ruled that Caesar and Pompey must each contribute one legion apiece to Syria's defence. Pompey, however, shrewdly decided that his contribution would be the one legion he had lent Caesar some years earlier during the Gallic Wars. Faced with this chicanery, Caesar had no choice but to send two of his veteran legions, VI and XV, to Italy, while Pompey's army was left intact.

In 50 BCE, a victorious Julius Caesar returned to find a Rome in which Pompey was in the ascendant. Caesar, though, was a war hero and ever popular with the people, factors which made the Senate nervous. In a bid to prevent him from being voted consul *in absentia* on the conclusion of his governorship, the Senate demanded he resign command of his army.[4] In December 50 BCE, Caesar wrote to the Senate agreeing to do this if Pompey did likewise. An outraged Senate repeated its demand to Caesar, saying he must agree or be declared an enemy of the people. This was an illegal move, since Caesar was entitled to retain his command until the expiry of his governorship.

But Caesar too was nervous and anxious. The much-coveted second consulship would bring with it the welcome safety of *imperium* and immunity against the inevitable prosecutions which awaited him for alleged irregularities during his consulship and in his Gallic campaigns. These prosecutions, if brought and proven, would render Caesar politically impotent and marginalize him. When Caesar's supporters – the tribunes Mark Antony and Quintus Cassius Longinus – vetoed the bill against Caesar, they were expelled from the Senate. They joined Caesar, who had by now assembled his army ready for action.

Pompey levelled charges of insubordination and treason against Caesar. The agonising decision for Caesar as to whether or not to ford the Rubicon with his troops beckoned.

The rift between the two widened further when Pompey fell ill in Naples in 50 BCE. His recovery was met with public rejoicing and sacrifices of thanksgiving throughout Italy. Nothing could have been more galling for Caesar; indeed, Plutarch records that this was said 'to have done more than anything else to ignite the subsequent civil war'. However, the adulation and dancing in the streets that Pompey enjoyed on his journey back to Rome made him arrogant, careless and contemptuous of Caesar.[5] The following year would see the two men fighting each other in a civil war.

On 7 January 49 BCE, the Senate demanded that Caesar, then in Ravenna, surrender his ten legions to a new Cisalpine Gaul governor. Caesar chose not to, quoting Menander: 'the die is cast' (*alea iacta est*). During the night of 10/11 January, the *Legio* XIII advanced to Rimini.

If the Senate believed that the northern Italians would oppose Caesar, then they were mistaken. If anything, the Italians were quite blasé, unexcited because the coming conflict was not going to destroy their fields and towns. Moreover, the establishment Senate was up against a legion, the XIII, that was highly incentivized and motivated. They were fighting for significant bonuses and for their pensions: no win, no pension payments. All the Senate could depend on was the *Legio* XV – which was far from dependable as it had fought with Caesar in Gaul. The *Legio* V, VIII, XII and XVI soon joined Caesar. Aware of Pompey's seven veteran legions in Spain, Caesar posted three legions to the Pyrenees to block any Republican moves from the west.

Caesar also had the problem that his general, Labienus, still felt aggrieved by the secondary role he had been assigned in the Gallic Wars and was ready to defect to the patricians. Moreover, the people would not rise in support of him where there was still uncertainty; neither could Caesar's grain supply from Gaul be guaranteed during a long Italian campaign.

Pompey held three legions in Italy, as well as his main army in Spain, with access to thousands of recruits from African and Asian provinces, whose rulers owed their sovereignty to him. Pompey was also at the helm of Rome's fleet of

500 warships and light galleys, maximizing his mobility and enabling him to quickly transfer forces from one theatre according to events.

When Caesar cast his metaphorical die on 10 January 49 BCE and made his decision to cross the Rubicon at the head of *Legio* XIII Gemina, he was only too aware of the associated aftermath and of its irrevocable consequences. The river was the boundary between Cisalpine Gaul and Italy; crossing it with an army was a legally proscribed action, forbidden to every commander. The prohibition and the proscription were designed as a last-resort protection for the Roman Republic from a *coup d'état*; Caesar was on the verge of deliberately compromising that.

Caesar then crossed the Rubicon and precipitated years of civil war.

The response was immediate and decisive. The *populares* were jubilant. The Senate, who could not have known at this point that Caesar was leading only a single legion, panicked, over-reacted and threw in their lot with Pompey. Pompey, pronouncing that Rome could not be defended, fled to Capua with his supporters, the aristocratic *optimates* and the consuls.

Ariminum was the first town to fall to Caesar, without a fight. Caesar progressed south, capturing three more towns, while Mark Antony, leading five cohorts, captured Arretium on the *Via Cassia*, opening a second route south to Rome. Other northern Italian towns fell to the *populares*, who soon numbered some 20,000 battle-hardened veterans.

On 17 January, Pompey ordered all senators to evacuate Rome or be officially regarded as Caesar's allies: 'If you're not with us you're against us.' He then relocated the government of Rome to Brundisium on the Adriatic coast. With no opposition in Rome, Caesar helped himself to the treasury and raised additional troops, sending them to Sicily and Sardinia to secure Italy's grain supply. Carelessly, the republicans in their haste had failed to secure the 15,000 bars of gold, 30,000 bars of silver and 30 million sesterces which fell into Caesar's hands.

There was unrest in Hispania to be dealt with, fomented by Pompey's forces there. Caesar saw this as an opportunity to inflict some damage on Hispania's leaderless Pompeian army, and elected to confront Pompey's main army in Spain.

At this time, Pompey's Spanish army – under Marcus Petreius, Lucius Afranius and Marcus Varro – was divided, with five legions and another 5,000 cavalry in the north, and two legions in southern Spain. Pompey's northern generals made no efforts to block the Pyrenees when Caesar approached. Instead, they took up positions at Ilerda, only to be besieged by Caesar's army, supported by 7,000 cavalry.

Caesar had made an astonishing twenty-seven-day forced march to Spain, all the more astounding because it was interrupted and delayed by a revolt and subsequent siege in Massilia led by Ahenobarbus. Caesar delegated the siege to Gaius Trebonius and Decimus Junius Brutus Albinus, and proceeded on his march to Hispania Citerior with the *Legio* VI, VII, VIIII, X, XI, XIV, XXVIII, XXIX and XXX to join the three legions he had sent there as an advance guard under his legate Fabius. In late July, the Pompeians attempted a retreat south of the Ebro. At one point the opposing armies were encamped so close to each other that they began to fraternize. Petreius would have none of it, and had the Caesarian soldiers who had wandered into his camp rounded up and murdered. By 30 July, however, Caesar had completely surrounded Afranius and Petreius's army at Ilerda (modern Lérida),[6] and on 2 August, cut off from water sources and besieged in open terrain, the Pompeian legions under Afranius and Petreius surrendered to Caesar. Caesar then sent two legions under Gaius Cassius Longinus to subdue Pompey's forces under Marcus Terentius Varro in Cordoba. One of Varro's legions mutinied at Cadiz and went over to Caesar. Varro then surrendered, so in less than forty days Caesar had captured and eliminated the Spanish threat with barely a fight.

Characteristically, Caesar spared the opposing commanders and pardoned his enemies, and established a new Senate, a puppet government sympathetic to his policies, in April 49 BCE. For example, legislation passed included a law granting Roman citizenship to the inhabitants of Cisalpine Gaul. Caesar then deputed his legate Quintus Cassius Longinus – the brother of Gaius Cassius Longinus – to take charge of Spain with four of the legions, and returned with the rest of his army to the siege of Massilia.

Caesar describes in detail the siege works he deployed there:

> 'But there had been in the town from early days such huge military stores of every kind, and such a multitude of engines, that no penthouses woven with osiers could withstand their assault. For beams twelve feet long with spiked ends, discharged by enormous

> catapults, often fixed themselves in the earth after passing through four layers of hurdles. So the roofs of the penthouses were protected by timbers a foot square clamped together and beneath this shelter material for the earthwork was carried forward from hand to hand. In front went a tortoise sixty feet in height, for the levelling of the ground, also made of very stout timbers, and wrapped over with everything that could serve to keep off showers of firebrands and stones. But the greatness of the works, the height of the wall and the towers, the multitude of engines, hindered the whole of our operations. Moreover, frequent sorties from the town were made by the Albici, and firebrands were flung upon the earthwork and the towers – all of which assaults our troops repelled with ease, and kept driving back into the town those who had made a sortie, even inflicting great losses on them.'[7]

By the end of the mutiny, the Caesarian forces – six legions, 3,000 cavalry who were Gallic campaign veterans and Caesar's 900-horse personal bodyguard – suffered seventy men killed in action, while the Pompeian forces lost 200 men killed and 600 wounded.

Caesar now set his sights on Pompey in Greece.

Caesar should have been worried. While he was in Spain, Pompey had enlisted troops from Asia Minor, Pontus, Judea, Syria, Arabia, Palestine and Egypt – places where the name of Pompey the Great still carried kudos and respect.

Pompey formed them into nine legions, with the promise of two additional legions from Syria, led by Metellus Scipio. Pompey's total strength was roughly 36,000 infantry, with 7,000 cavalry and 4,200 archers and slingers. With his grain supplies from Egypt and Thessaly secure, Pompey assembled a fleet of 300 ships under the command of Caesar's former co-consul and lifetime enemy, Marcus Calpurnius Bibulus.

Pompey reached Brundisium, en route to Epirus in Greece. He was joined at the port by *optimate* forces, having left a rearguard at Capua. Caesar followed Pompey to Brundisium, hoping to renew their pact, but Pompey refused on the grounds that Caesar was his junior and was thus obliged to disband his armies before any negotiations. Pompey sailed to Epirus.

On returning to Rome in December 49 BCE after a six-month absence, Caesar was appointed dictator with Mark Antony as his Master of the Horse. The tenure, however, was intentionally short-lived: the eleven days were enough to allow him to procure a second term as consul, with Publius Servilius Vatia Isauricus as his colleague. Caesar then resumed his pursuit of Pompey, now in pro-Pompey Greece, in early 48 BCE.

Caesar's main problem was a lack of transportation facilities – he had insufficient ships, having previously lost some forty vessels to Bibulus' fleet, and had only enough transports to take half his army to Greece. Caesar embarked seven depleted legions (about 15,000 men) with some 500 cavalry and supplies, and sailed for Greece on 4 January 48 BCE. He safely landed his troops near Apollonia, but the return trip was less fortunate. Upon landing at Palaeste, he sent his ships back to Brundisium to pick up Mark Antony and the remaining five legions. Bibulus, to whom Pompey had given the command of his 600-ship fleet, saw all of this and intercepted Caesar's fleet, marooning Caesar from the other half of his army. Antony, with Caesar's remaining forces along with most of the supplies, was stuck near Brundisium. Caesar and his depleted army, now isolated in Greece, were in serious trouble. Caesar sent Vibullius Rufus to negotiate peace with Pompey, but there was to be no deal and the two armies went into winter quarters, evading the winter storms battering the Adriatic. But what was bad for Caesar was equally bad for Bibulus, as the storms confined most of the latter's ships to port.

The two forces clashed at Dyrrhachium. Caesar could count on 34,000 infantry and some 1,300 cavalry in the vicinity of Dyrrhachium; Pompey outnumbered him by about 8,000 men. Caesar managed to outmanoeuvre Pompey and set himself between Pompey and his base at Dyrrhachium, but Caesar had no supply ships and Pompey's superior cavalry prevented foraging, so Caesar's troops resorted to digging up roots and baking them into hard bread.

If Dyrrhachium was to be taken, Caesar first had to deal with Pompey's defence, so he surrounded Pompey's army and erected siege works to prevent Pompey's cavalry from limiting his foraging. He isolated Pompey from his food supplies, but although Pompey's provisions began to run low, evacuation was not an option: Greece was the only theatre of war where he outnumbered Caesar.

On 9 July, Caesar tried to take Dyrrhachium. Pompey then despatched sixty cohorts plus light infantry and archers in a two-pronged attack on the southern end of Caesar's fortifications. Caesar's *Legio* IX was being driven back until Antony arrived with twelve cohorts and stabilized the front. Caesar counter-attacked and retook most of his original siege works. Caesar then tried to surround Pompey, but his thirty-three cohorts were outflanked by five patrician legions and several cavalry units from the north. Caesar was unable to control his men, who panicked and fled. By the end he had lost nearly 1,000 troops and thirty-two standards, and was forced to retreat. Pompey took this as a feint and missed the chance to follow up his victory and inflict yet further significant damage on Caesar. When he realized that Pompey would, astonishingly, not press home his advantage, Caesar remarked to his officers: 'The enemy would have won the war today, if they had a commander who knew how to use a victory.'

Caesar withdrew to Apollonia. Pompey followed. Caesar made a move by night into Thessaly, where food was more plentiful and he could rendezvous with his XI and XII legions under Domitius Calvinus. En route, the town of Gomphi made the error of closing its gates to Caesar's army; inevitably, it was stormed and looted, providing a good example of the fate that awaited other Thessalian towns who failed to welcome Caesar.

A suitable place on the north bank of the Enipeus River in Thessaly, near the town of Pharsalus (modern Fersala), was chosen for the clash of the armies. Caesar commanded 30,000 infantry and some 1,000 Gallic and German cavalry, plus 2,000 light infantry and auxiliaries. Pompey marched into the Enipeus valley and camped his legions on the slopes of Mount Dogantzes, about 3½ miles from Caesar's camp. He commanded 40,000 infantry and more than 3,000 cavalry and supporting troops, all made up of a kaleidoscope of Mediterranean nations: Italians, Bithynians, Phoenicians, Jews, Arabs, Cypriots, Cretans, Syrians, Egyptians, Thracians, Ionians and others.

Nothing much happened for a number of days. Caesar moved south and camped near Pharsalus. According to Caesar, Pompey's soldiers were bullish in the extreme, confident that total victory was at hand. Labienus, Caesar's former ally now fighting for Pompey, motivated them further:

> 'Don't think that this is the army that conquered Gaul and Germany. I was there for all those battles, and I know what I'm talking about. A

very small part of that army survives. Most of it is dead – the autumn epidemics killed many in Italy, and others have deserted or been left behind.'

Oaths were sworn that the combatants would only leave the battlefield as victors, tents were draped with laurel wreaths and slaves were detailed to prepare victory banquets for their glorious return.

Pompey attacked but, despite his superior numbers, was soundly defeated by Caesar's troops. Caesar was never going to repeat Pompey's failure to follow up his victory at Dyrrhachium, and urged his troops to win the war, not the battle. The next day, Pompey's remaining four legions surrendered, beaten by thirst in the midday sun. Caesar again showed mercy to his enemies, pardoning many prominent patricians, including Marcus Junius Brutus, who would loom back into Caesar's life as one of his assassins.

According to Caesar, Pompey lost 15,000 killed and 24,000 captured. Ten senators, including Domitius Ahenobarbus, were among the patrician dead. Caesar estimated his own losses at an improbably low 200 troops. Pharsalus was the decisive battle of the Civil War; when Caesar surveyed the battlefield at sunset and saw the bodies of the dead senators, he laconically remarked: 'Well, that's what they wanted.'

For Pompey, the prelude to Pharsalus had been loaded with ill omen and superstition. On the morning of 9 August, Pompey was unnerved by a meteor shooting across the sky near his camp the previous night. Pompey retired to his tent, only to dream of being applauded by Rome's citizens as he dedicated a temple to the goddess Venus: this too made him nervous, as Venus was the goddess from whom Caesar's *gens*, the Julians, were descended. Unknown to Pompey, Caesar had vowed at the same time that if Venus gave him victory at Pharsalus, he would dedicate a great temple to her in Rome.

Pompey's surviving soldiers were enlisted in four of Caesar's new legions, the XXXIV, XXXV, XXXVI and XXXVII, which were sent east to defend Syria. Caesar's own legions were sent back to Italy, except for *Legio* VI.

Seeking refuge and support, Pompey sailed to Egypt, where Cleopatra VII was queen. Pompey and Egypt went back a long way – to the Mithridatic Wars in fact, when Cleopatra's father, Ptolemy XII Auletes, assisted Pompey against Mithridates VI. A coup led by Cleopatra V and another daughter, Berenike IV, in

58 BCE forced the exile of Auletes and daughter Cleopatra to Rome via Rhodes and Athens. In 55 BCE, after much bribery and intrigue between Auletes and the Romans, alternately playing and paying Berenike off, Alexandria was recaptured and Ptolemy XII restored to the throne – but only at a price: it was with the support of the Roman general Aulus Gabinius and Mark Antony, sent to Egypt by Pompey. Auletes slew Berenike and her supporters, and Cleopatra, aged 14, was made joint ruler with her father. After her father's death in 51 BCE, Cleopatra assumed control with her precocious 14-year-old brother Ptolemy XIII, destined not to be the happiest of joint monarchies. Later that year, relations between brother and sister broke down irreparably, with Ptolemy virtually ostracized and Cleopatra defying the Ptolemaic tradition that made female rulers subservient to male.

After the Rubicon in 49 BCE, Pompey had requested military support from Egypt. Cleopatra responded by sending a detachment of the Gabiniani and warships. The Gabiniani were originally 2,000 Roman legionaries and 500 auxiliary cavalry, with Gallic and German horsemen, left behind in Egypt by Aulus Gabinius, proconsul of Syria, after his restoration of Ptolemy XII to the Egyptian throne in 55 BCE. The function of these soldiers was to guard and protect the king, but it was not long before they were immersed in the culture and manners of their new country and became completely estranged from Rome. According to Caesar, they soon adopted the dissipated way of life of the Alexandrians, shunning Roman discipline. Nevertheless, they remained a potent fighting force in the Alexandrinian war. Upon Ptolemy XII's death in 51 BCE, they helped his son Ptolemy XIII in his power struggle against his sister Cleopatra VII, embroiling Caesar in conflict. After the Parthians humiliated the Romans at the Battle of Carrhae in 53 BCE, and the governor of Syria, Marcus Calpurnius Bibulus, sent two of his sons to Egypt in 50 BCE to enlist the Gabiniani for the war against the Parthians, the Gabiniani, loathe to give up their comfortable life, simply killed the sons of Bibulus.

In 48 BCE, Cleopatra incurred the wrath of the Gabiniani when she handed the murderers over to Bibulus. This led to Cleopatra's temporary fall from power: she fled Egypt while Ptolemy XIII assumed sole rule. Pompey ingratiated himself with Ptolemy.

As stated, after Pharsalus, Pompey demanded help and support from the Ptolemaic regime and sought sanctuary in Alexandria with the remnants of his army. The real power was held by the eunuch Pothinus, Ptolemy XIII's political minister and official regent, rhetorician Theodotus of Chios, Ptolemy's tutor, and Achillas, the Egyptian-born Greek commandant of the Ptolemaic army. Ptolemy XIII's men were reluctant to get involved in the Roman civil war, concerned that Egypt would become the next battleground in a conflict that had already destroyed central Greece.

They resolved to murder Pompey in an attempt to please the victorious Caesar. Pothinus also feared that Pompey would try to incite the former Roman soldiers in the Ptolemaic army to gain control over Egypt. An inappropriately small boat was sent out to bring Pompey ashore. On board was Achillas, Lucius Septimius – a former Roman tribune and a veteran of Pompey's eastern campaigns, now on the Ptolemaic books – and a centurion under his command named Salvius. The boy Ptolemy XIII haughtily watched Pompey's arrival from a specially erected throne in the harbour. On disembarkation, Pompey was stabbed in the back and beheaded in front of his wife and children; his body was burnt, his head embalmed. The deed was committed by Achillas and Lucius Septimius at the bidding of the eunuch Pothinus and Theodotus of Chios.[8]

Plutarch provides the detail in his biography of Pompey:

> 'So, when they saw a reception that was neither royal, nor splendid, nor in accordance with the hopes of Theophanes, but just a few men sailing up in a single fishing-boat, they viewed this lack of respect with suspicion, and advised Pompey to have his ship rowed back into the open sea, while they were beyond reach of missiles. But meanwhile the boat drew near, and first Septimius rose up and addressed Pompey in Latin as Imperator. Then Achillas saluted him in Greek, and invited him to come aboard the boat, telling him that the shallows were extensive, and that the sea, which had a sandy bottom, was not deep enough to float a trireme. At the same time some of the royal ships were seen to be taking their crews aboard, and men-at-arms were occupying the shore, so that there seemed to be no escape even if they changed their minds; and besides, this very lack of confidence might give the murderers an excuse for their crime. Accordingly, after embracing Cornelia [Pompey's wife], who was bewailing his

approaching death, he ordered two centurions to go into the boat before him, besides Philip, one of his freedmen, and a servant named Scythes, and while Achillas was already stretching out his hand to him from the boat, turned towards his wife and son and repeated the verses of Sophocles: "Whatever man upon a tyrant takes his way, His slave he is, even though a freeman when he goes."

'After these last words to his friends, he went into the boat. And since it was a long way from the trireme to the land, and none of his companions in the boat had any friendly word for him, turning his eyes upon Septimius he said: "Surely I am not mistaken, you are an old comrade of mine!" Septimius nodded merely, without saying anything to him or showing any friendliness. So then, as there was profound silence again, Pompey took a little scroll containing a speech written by him in Greek, which he had prepared for his use in addressing Ptolemy, and began to read it. Then, as they drew near the shore, Cornelia, together with his friends, stood anxiously on the trireme watching for the outcome, and began to take heart when she saw many of the king's people assembling at the landing as if to give him an honourable welcome. But at this point, while Pompey was clasping the hand of Philip that he might rise to his feet more easily, Septimius, from behind, ran him through the body with his sword, then Salvius next, and then Achillas, drew their daggers and stabbed him. And Pompey, drawing his toga down over his face with both hands, without an act or a word that was unworthy of himself, but with a groan merely, submitted to their blows, being sixty years of age less one, and ending his life only one day after his birthday.'

This half-baked attempt by Ptolemy to curry favour with Caesar backfired. Ptolemy assumed that Caesar would be pleased by the removal of his arch-enemy. Caesar had sailed to Egypt to collect an outstanding debt owed to him by Auletes, but instead he was presented with Pompey's head. He was incensed, visibly upset by the atrocity – after all, Pompey, although an enemy, was still a Roman consul and the widower of Caesar's daughter, Julia, who had died in childbirth giving birth to Pompey's daughter.

The atmosphere between Caesar and the Ptolemaic faction went from cool to frigid. Caesar demanded a repayment of debts owed to the Roman state dating from the reign of Ptolemy XII of about 10 million drachmas – a lot of money but not unfeasible. Indeed, the real debt was over 17 million drachmas, but Caesar discounted the debt as the current pharaoh did not incur it.

Pothinus and his team were highly indignant over Caesar's demands. Tactlessly, they served mouldy old grain to the Roman troops and set out plain simple pottery at official diplomatic dinners between Caesar and the courtiers instead of the usual gold and silver.

Caesar's reaction was to take Alexandria and set himself up as mediator between Ptolemy and Cleopatra in what was known as the Alexandrine Civil War, a consequence of which was his liaison with Cleopatra.

Cleopatra saw the tension between Caesar and her brother as an opportunity. Her envoys had achieved little or nothing with Caesar, so she resolved to meet Caesar to plead her case. Caesar agreed to a meeting, despite Ptolemy's attempts to thwart it.[9] Arriving regally at the palace in the royal boat (Ptolemy had blocked all the roads), Lucan says that she bribed the guards to unchain the harbour; Plutarch, improbably, insists that she, less than regally, inveigled her way in, rolled up in a carpet carried by Apollodorus the Sicilian, her faithful acolyte, to make the meeting with Caesar. According to Plutarch, it was Cleopatra's ingenuity here, her 'provocative impudence', that enthralled Caesar.[10] Caesar cannot have failed to be impressed by the appearance of Cleopatra: Lucan describes her as 'wearing the spoils of the Red Sea, treasures in her hair and around her neck, great pains taken on her refinement'.[11] Nine months later, in June 47 BCE, Cleopatra gave birth to their son, Ptolemy XV Caesar, nicknamed Caesarion ('little Caesar'). Caesar's paternity is doubted and was strenuously denied by him, possibly pending changes to the Roman laws of marriage which Caesar promised in order to have his 'marriage' to Cleopatra officially recognized.

Meanwhile, Pothinus and Achillas plotted to assassinate Caesar at the state dinner at the Royal Palace in Alexandria formally reuniting Cleopatra and Ptolemy as joint rulers. However, Caesar's barber overheard gossip about the plot; he informed Caesar, who took the initiative. Caesar had one of his guards leave the banquet hall in search of Pothinus; when he found him, he killed him. Theodotus of Chios fled Egypt in 42 or 43 BCE, was captured in Anatolia by

Brutus and Cassius and executed for his role in the death of Pompey. Achillas left the city and raised the Ptolemaic army.

At this crucial and sensitive time, Caesar named Octavian, his grandnephew, as his heir and main beneficiary, despite Cleopatra's insistence on Caesarion. As with the crossing of the Rubicon, Caesar had changed the course of history.

Caesar was now clearly backing Cleopatra's claim to the Egyptian throne, but was blockaded in Alexandria by Achillas and Pothinus, allies of Ptolemy XIII. Mithridates of Pergamum raised the siege and Caesar defeated Ptolemy's army at the Battle of the Nile, where Ptolemy drowned in the river. Caesar restored Cleopatra to her throne, with her younger brother Ptolemy XIV as co-ruler. Caesar and Cleopatra married according to Egyptian rites – a bigamous union, as Caesar was still married to Calpurnia Pisonis, his third wife. Furthermore, it was illegal for a Roman citizen to marry any foreigner.

After the Alexandrine War, Caesar replaced the Gabiniani with three regular legions, the XXVII, XXVIII and XXIX – in effect, the Roman occupation army of Egypt responsible for protecting Cleopatra and ensuring her continued loyalty to Rome.

A luxury cruise down the Nile afforded Caesar the opportunity to display Rome's naval might. Cleopatra reciprocated by showing Caesar the extent of her prodigious wealth and the treasures of Egypt. Suetonius describes the almost party atmosphere, a virtual holiday midst a crisis:

> 'He [Caesar] had love affairs with queens too … but above all with Cleopatra, with whom he often feasted until daybreak, and he would have gone through Egypt with her in her state-barge almost to Aethiopia, had not his soldiers refused to follow him.'[12]

Two centuries later, Appian adds:

> 'He made a voyage on the Nile to look at the country with a flotilla of 400 ships in the company of Cleopatra, and enjoyed himself with her in other ways as well.' (Appian, *The Civil Wars*, 2, 90)[13]

When Caesar left Egypt some weeks later to prosecute the Civil War, he left behind him three legions (the *Legio* XXVII, XXXVII and XXXIX) under the command of Rufio, as much to keep Cleopatra under watch as to ensure the security of Egypt.[14]

At the age of 21, Cleopatra had started to exert real influence on Rome. In 46 BCE, Cleopatra, Ptolemy XIV and Caesarion visited Rome, staying for two years in one of Caesar's houses on the fashionable Janiculum Hill[15] - an ill-judged move on Caesar's part, as people were beginning to wake up to the fact that he was, scandalously, still married to Calpurnia. More indiscretion and arrogance followed when he erected a golden statue of the queen in the guise of Isis in the temple of Venus Genetrix, the ancestor of his *gens*, situated in the prestigious new Forum Julium which he built after the Battle of Pharsalus.[16] The shock of a statue in honour of a living person, a woman at that, a foreigner and a monarch - and the religious association with Roman Venus - all in the centre of Rome, was incalculable.

Cleopatra and her retinue were still in Rome when Caesar was assassinated on 15 March 44 BCE.[17] She returned to Egypt via Cyprus to re-establish Egyptian control on the island; Cyprus had been restored to her by Caesar in 48 BCE. Cicero, and many other Republicans besides, despised the foreign queen, Horace's *fatale monstrum* (doom monster), and was glad to see the back of her.

There were two significant battles in north Africa in 49 BCE. The first, the Battle of Utica, was a clash between Julius Caesar's general, Gaius Scribonius Curio, and Pompeian forces commanded by Publius Attius Varus, supported by cavalry and infantry sent by King Juba I of Numidia, a client state, whose father owed his position to Pompey. Juba himself harboured a grudge against Curio: as plebeian tribune, Curio had once proposed that Numidia become a Roman province. Curio defeated the Pompeians and Numidians, driving Varus back into Utica.

Varus had been propraetor some years before, and now took possession of the province on behalf of Pompey. Varus raised two legions. In early August, Curio embarked from Lilybaeum; his fleet of 100 transports and twelve galleys transported two legions and 500 cavalry, and, chasing off the patrolling ships of Lucius Caesar, disembarked at Thonara Bay on Cape Bon. Curio scouted out a camp near Utica, the Castra Cornelia, situated on a hill to the west of the town. From there he had a good view of Varus' camp, from where he noticed a column of fugitives fleeing to the safety of Utica, which he decided to attack to create panic. Varus sent 1,000 Numidian troops to their rescue. Curio and Varus clashed and the Numidians were defeated, losing 120 men, as the remainder of the troops retreated into the town.

Curio then spotted that 200 of Varus' supply ships were berthed unprotected in Utica's harbour. Curio simply ordered the captains of the vessels to unload their cargoes onto the quay and took possession of the stores.

The next day, Curio commanded his forces to march on Utica, but instead of heading towards the Castra Cornelia which he had spied out for his camp, he went on the offensive and took up position on a ridge to the south-west of the town. Patrols reported Numidian reinforcements on their way. Curio's cavalry engaged the Numidians, who were dispersed with heavy losses.

The following day, Curio led his men out for battle. Curio sent in his cavalry, supported by two cohorts, and they launched themselves at Varus' advancing troops. The Numidian cavalry turned and fled. The auxiliaries were surrounded and slaughtered where they stood. Following up, Curio led the charge in pursuit of the survivors, only to discover that Varus' men had broken and run. Many of Varus' troops were trampled to death by their own men in their flight, while others were killed by Curio's forces. Varus lost some 600 men, while another 1,000 were wounded; Curio's tally of injured was 100.

Curio was encouraged to take the town before Varus could regroup, but he delayed as he did not have the resources to launch an attack. The next day, however, he formed a contravallation of Utica, intending to starve the town into submission. Varus then received welcome information that King Juba was on his way with a large force, less than 23 miles from Utica. Curio heard likewise and abandoned the siege, making his way to the Castra Cornelia and the Battle of the Bagradas River.

At the Castra Cornelia, Curio, intending to defend his position until the reinforcements arrived, urgently requested that his officers send the two legions and the cavalry he had left behind in Sicily. He quickly changed his mind, though, when deserters from Utica reported that King Juba was actually 120 miles away near Leptis, putting down an uprising there, and his force was a mere squadron of troops under Juba's military commander, Saburra. Curio sent his cavalry out under darkness with orders to locate Saburra's camp and then to wait for Curio and the rest of the army. Leaving some of his forces

'Marius Amid the Ruins of Carthage' (1832), John Vanderlyn (1775–1852). The subject is from Plutarch's Lives, of Caius Marius after being expelled from Rome. Marius is seen in reflective mood, sitting in exile amid the ruins of Carthage, which had been destroyed by Romans. The artist aimed to 'reveal in two great instances the instability of human grandeur – a city in ruins and a fallen general'. The Albany Institute's 'Marius' is a small version of a painting of the same subject that won Vanderlyn a gold medal at the prestigious Paris Salon of 1808 and is now in the Fine Arts Museums of San Francisco. (*Albany Institute of History & Art*)

The Column of Julius Caesar, where he addressed his army to march on Rome and start the Civil War; Rimini, Italy. (*Photographer Georges Jansoone*)

Above: Lecture Diagram, *c.*1814, 'Caesar's bridge over the Reno' built in 55 BCE during the Gallic Wars. (*London, Sir John Soane's Museum*)

Below: This mosaic showing the Battle of Thapsus in 46 BCE is from Praeneste, and now resides in the Staatliche Antikensammlungen, Berlin, between the busts of Caesar and Cleopatra. It is part of another, larger Nilotic mosaic dating to the late first century BCE found at the Temple of Fortuna Primigenia in Palestrina, and which is now in the National Archeological Museum there. Given the Egyptian topography and Alexandrian origin of the work (animals familiar to the Alexandrians have no labels; those that are not, such as giraffes and rhinoceroses, are in Greek), Goudchaux suggests in his comments on the mosaic in the exhibition catalogue to the exhibition 'Cleopatra of Egypt: From History to Myth' that it may have been commissioned by Cleopatra herself to thank the goddess Primigenia for the birth of Caesarion.

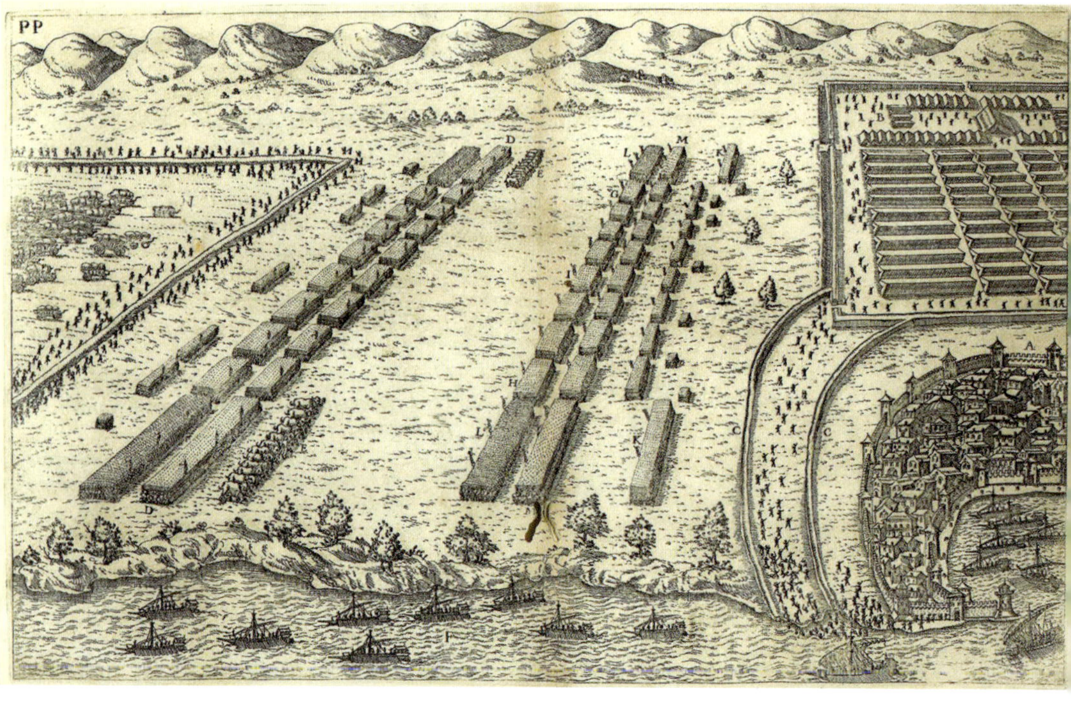

Above: 'Vercingetorix throws down his arms at the feet of Julius Caesar' by Lionel Royer (1899), Musée Croatzier du Puy-en-Velay. Wonderful as this painting is, the artist has permitted himself much artistic licence. The painting depicts the surrender of Vercingetorix after the Battle of Alesia (52 BCE). One of the warriors (bottom left) has a torque around his neck. In fact, the torque was reserved only for gods and important members of a royal family. The depiction of Gauls with long hair and moustaches is also questionable. The horse is a Percheron, although at that time this breed was not to be found in Gaul. In addition, the Gauls rode bareback, but here the horse is saddled and harnessed. The rectangular shield also does not accord with the time, when they were mostly oval.

Below: Woodcut illustration of Porcia Catonis counselling Marcus Junius Brutus, Julius Caesar's death at the hands of Brutus and Gaius Cassius Longinus, and Porcia's suicide, hand-coloured in red, green, yellow and black, from an incunable German translation by Heinrich Steinhöwel of Boccaccio's De mulieribus claris, printed by Johannes Zainer at Ulm c. 1474. One of seventy-six woodcut illustrations depicting scenes from the life of women. (*Penn Libraries*)

Above: 'The Murder of Caesar' (1865) by Karl von Piloty (1826–1886). (*Lower Saxony State Museum, Hanover*)

Below: 'The Assassination of Julius Caesar' (1804–1805) by Vincenzo Camuccini (1771–1844). (*Galleria Nazionale d'Arte Moderna, Rome*)

Above: 'La Mort de César' (*c*.1859–1867) by Jean-Léon Gérôme (1824–1904), showing the aftermath of the attack, with Caesar's body abandoned in the foreground as the senators rejoice – but not for long …. (*Bequeathed to Walters Art Museum, Baltimore, by Henry Walters, 1931*)

Right: 'Julius Caesar. Act IV. Scene III. Brutus's tent, in the camp near Sardis. Brutus and the Ghost of Caesar' (1802). Copperplate engraving by Edward Scriven from a painting by Richard Westall, illustrating Act IV, Scene III, from Shakespeare's *Julius Caesar*.

Left: 'An Audience at Agrippa's' (1876) by Lawrence Alma-Tadema (1836–1912). (*Dick Institute, Kilmarnock*)

Below: 'Fulvia With the Head of Cicero' by Pavel Svedomsky, Павел Александрович Сведомский, (1849–1904). (*Pereslavl-Zalessky History and Art Museum, Russian Federation – Pereslavl-Zalessky*)

Above: 'The Death of Cleopatra' by Reginald Arthur (1871–1934). Note the asp as bracelet on her right wrist. (*Roy Miles Gallery, London*)

Below: 'The Battle of Actium, 2 September 31 BC' (1672) by Lorenzo A. Castro (fl. 1664–1700). (*National Maritime Museum, London*)

Right: The odious and repellent 'Erichtho' by John Hamilton Mortimer, one of Lucan's less attractive characters in his epic *Bellum Civile*. Detail from 'Sextus Pompeius consulting Erichtho before the Battle of Pharsalia' by John Hamilton Mortimer.

Below: The Ara Pacis Augustae, 'Altar of Augustan Peace', is dedicated to *Pax*, commissioned by the Roman Senate on 4 July 13 BCE to celebrate the return of Augustus to Rome after three years in Hispania and Gaul. It was reassembled in its current location, now the Museum of the Ara Pacis in Rome, in 1938. (*Photograph by Manfred Heyde*)

guarding his camp under the command of Marcius Rufus, Curio marched to the Bagradas River about two hours before sunrise.

Saburra's advance party had already reached the river. Curio's cavalry came upon them and attacked as they slept in their tents. Most of the Numidians were either killed or captured. Curio, meanwhile, ordered a forced march towards the river, leaving behind most of his cavalry, whose horses were exhausted.

Juba, meanwhile, whose camp was 6 miles to the rear of Saburra, immediately dispatched his Spanish and Gallic mercenary bodyguard, comprising some 2,000 cavalry, together with a specially picked infantry force, to reinforce Saburra. Juba then forded the river with the remainder of his troops and proceeded northward. Saburra, who was convinced that Curio would attack swiftly, gave orders to pretend to retreat as soon as the Romans appeared, warning his men to be ready for a signal to turn around and attack.

Curio fell for the ploy and attacked the Numidians. Baking and thirsty under a hot sun, Saburra gave the signal, and his forces did an about turn and engaged the exhausted Romans. Despite valiant resistance, fatigue began to tell against Curio's troops, who were too tired to pursue the Numidians who were steadily falling back. The Numidian cavalry returned and overran the Roman line; Juba continually reinforced Saburra with fresh reserves, while the Romans continued to weaken as the battle progressed. With Roman resolve gone, Curio ordered his army to retreat northward, but Saburra sent his cavalry to cut off Curio's forces. The Romans scattered, scythed down as they ran, while others simply fell to the ground exhausted, waiting for inevitable death.

Curio fought on until he was killed; only a handful of soldiers managed to escape the ensuing massacre. Marcius Rufus, left in charge at Castra Cornelia, ordered the captains of the transports and the other ships to have their boats ready to embark the troops back onto the ships. But Juba's army was approaching and discipline rapidly broke down. The resulting evacuation was utter mayhem: with Juba's army rapidly approaching, and Varus' legions poised to attack, chaos ensued when most of the galleys and transports set sail without the stranded soldiers. Those that did pick up soldiers were soon swamped by panicking troops, and many sank in the process, with soldiers fighting each other to get on the boats. Some sailors agreed to take a few of those who were married - soldiers with families back home - while other troops swam out to the ships and were pulled aboard. Those who had been deserted sent their centurions as delegates to Varus, who promised they would not be harmed. But when Juba turned up, he executed many of Curio's remaining soldiers as an example. Caesar and the Roman Senate declared him an enemy of the state; Juba returned to Numidia, taking with him senators he had captured, and executed them there.

In 47 BCE, Caesar effectively dealt with a troublesome Pharnaces II, a client king of Pompey and son of Mithridates VI of Pontus. An expansionist Pharnaces took advantage of the distractions caused by the Civil War to expand his Kingdom of the Bosporus into his father's old Pontic empire. In 48 BCE, he invaded Cappadocia, Bithynia and Armenia Parva. Deotarus, ruler of Galatia, felt threatened by this and appealed for help to Gnaeus Domitius Calvinus, Caesar's man in Asia. The Romans moved to do battle with Pharnaces: the two armies clashed at Nicopolis in Anatolia, where Pharnaces II defeated the Roman army and overran Pontus.

Calvinus mustered his forces at Comana, comprising the *Legio* XXXVI and two recently levied local legions recruited in Armenia Parva, armed, trained and organized the Roman way by King Deiotarus. Local auxiliary skirmishers and cavalry from Cilicia completed the force. Despite being outnumbered by Pharnaces, Calvinus advanced toward Pontus. Pharnaces tried to delay Calvinus by feigning diplomacy, but, failing in this, retired to Nicopolis in Armenia Parva, where he waited for the Romans to advance.

Calvinus advanced, but the battle did not start well for him when his Pontic troops fled. Calvinus had little choice but to retreat. Although the *Legio* XXXVI escaped with light losses, Calvinus had lost nearly two-thirds of his army by the end of the battle. Pharnaces followed up his victory with a series of atrocities visited on the Roman prisoners and any Roman civilians found in the region.

The Romans responded quickly, and a further battle ensued at Zela. Here Caesar had two cohorts of the veteran *Legio* VI, the full *Legio* XXII, an allied force of Galatians and vexillations from the *Legio* XXXVI. He also had a small contingent of cavalry. Pharnaces had an army approximately 20,000 strong, mostly tribal and levied infantry, but also containing a core of professional phalangites, legionaries and cavalry. Pharnaces also deployed scythed chariots.

The battle took place in Zile, in what is now the Tokat province of northern Turkey. The Pontic army positioned itself near the hilltop town of Zela, but as Caesar's men were digging in on high ground the Pontic army suddenly, and unaccountably, launched an attack. Pharnaces had counter-intuitively surrendered his strong position to attack uphill. Confusion reigned, but Caesar soon drove the Pontic army back down the hill, where it was soundly routed.

Pharnaces II fled back to his Bosporan Kingdom, where he managed to assemble a small force of Scythian and Sarmatian troops, with which he was able to gain control of a few cities. His former governor and son-in-law, Asander, then attacked his forces and killed him.

It was after this convincing and comprehensive defeat of Pharnaces at Zela that Caesar, encapsulating the speed of the victory, famously and pithily concluded '*veni, vidi, vici*'.

Meanwhile, a number of prominent *optimates* were still keen to continue the fight and assembled in Africa to launch resistance, led by Cato the Younger and Caecilius Metellus Scipio. Others included Titus Labienus, Publius Attius Varus, Lucius Afranius, Marcus Petreius and Pompey's sons, Sextus and Gnaeus Pompeius. King Juba I of Numidia was on hand to provide invaluable local support. Caesar pursued them to Africa, landing in Hadrumetum (modern Sousse in Tunisia) on 28 December 47 BCE. The *optimates*, led by Petreius and Labienus, confronted Caesar, but the outcome was indecisive and both sides retreated.

The *optimates* rallied: their forces included 40,000 infantry, a powerful cavalry force led by Caesar's former right-hand man, Titus Labienus, forces of allied local kings and sixty war elephants. A number of strength-gauging skirmishes followed, in which two legions defected to Caesar. In February, Caesar reached Thapsus (modern Ras Dimas) and blockaded the city with three lines of fortifications. The *optimates*, under Metellus Scipio, were forced into battle.

Caesar's archers let fly at the elephants, causing them to panic and crush their own men. After the early loss of the elephants, Metellus Scipio lost ground. Caesar's cavalry destroyed the fortified camp and forced its enemy to retreat. King Juba's allied troops abandoned the site and the battle was over.

Around 10,000 soldiers lost their lives; unfortunate survivors were slaughtered. Scipio escaped to commit suicide in a later naval battle near Hippo Regius.

Caesar then successfully renewed the siege of Thapsus and pursued Cato to Utica, where he committed suicide. The Battle of Thapsus marked the last large-scale use of combat elephants in the West.

The following year saw Caesar pursue Gnaeus and Sextus Pompeius, who had been joined by Titus Labienus, Caesar's former second-in-command in the Gallic War. They had fled to Hispania, where Caesar defeated this final opposition in the Battle of Munda in March 45 BCE. Caesar's legions took the upper hand when the Pompeian legions broke their lines and fled in disarray, and a rout ensued: 30,000 Pompeians died to Caesar's 1,000. All thirteen standards of the Pompeian legions were captured.[18]

Gnaeus Pompey was executed and Labienus died in the battle, but Sextus Pompey escaped to take command of the remnants of the Pompeian fleet.

In the meantime, Caesar had been elected to his third and fourth terms as consul, in 46 BCE with Marcus Aemilius Lepidus and in 45 BCE *sine collega* (without a colleague). For the *optimates*, this was unpalatable enough, but Caesar's record as a dictator was even more disturbing. We have noted how he was dictator for eleven days in 49 BCE, and again for the year 48/47 BCE. In 46 BCE, he was elected dictator for the next ten years. Between January and February 44 BCE, he was appointed *dictator perpetuo*. To many he could not have been further removed from that fifth-century BCE paragon of Roman *virtus*, Lucius Quinctius Cincinnatus.

To other Romans, it seems that the conferment of this monarchy, this permanent dictatorship or tyranny even, was the better of two evils, preferable to yet more internecine civil war.[19]

Chapter 11

Power Politics and Assassination (44–43 BCE)

Even while he was still fighting in Spain, honours for Caesar bestowed by the Senate came in thick and fast. Caesar had frequently shown clemency and did not proscribe his enemies – on the contrary, he pardoned most of them. Generally, there was currently little or no apparent serious public opposition to him. For the victory at Munda, spectacular and lavish games were held in the April, although, according to Plutarch, many Romans blanched at the extravagant triumph that Caesar received since it was a Roman victory over Romans: those vanquished in the Civil War were not foreigners, but fellow Romans.[1] The authorities then added some 'spin', focussing on victories won over Gaul, Egypt, Pharnaces and Juba, rather than against Caesar's Roman opponents.

But Roman audiences were not to be fooled, especially when Arsinoë IV, Egypt's capable former queen and co-ruler of Egypt with Ptolemy XIII from 48–47 BCE, was rolled out, ostentatiously paraded in chains behind a burning effigy of the Lighthouse of Alexandria, the scene of her victory over him. Caesar would normally have had her strangled, as was the fate for such prisoners at triumphs, but he was pressured into mercy, granting her sanctuary at the temple of Artemis in Ephesus. The crowds had applauded her dignified mien and demonstrated their sympathy towards her.[2]

Arsinoë IV (who reigned in 68 and 59-41 BCE) was the half-sister of Cleopatra VII and younger sister of Ptolemy XIII. When Ptolemy XII died in 51 BCE, he left Egypt to his eldest son and daughter, Ptolemy and Cleopatra, as joint rulers. Ptolemy soon turned on Cleopatra and forced her to flee from Alexandria. When, as we have seen, Caesar arrived in Alexandria in 48 BCE, he was shocked and appalled to be presented with Pompey's head: this contributed to his decision to side with Cleopatra and, in line with Ptolemy XII's will, ordain that Cleopatra and Ptolemy would, after all, rule Egypt jointly. Cyprus, annexed by Rome in 58 BCE, was restored to Egypt at the same time, as a gift to

Arsinoë and her youngest brother, Ptolemy XIV. In the meantime, Caesar had Ptolemy's regent, the eunuch Pothinus, executed, while the general Achillas escaped.

Caesar called on his allies; he sent to Rhodes, Syria and Cilicia, and summoned archers from Crete and cavalry from Malchus, King of the Nabateans. He fortified the southern end of the small peninsula in Alexandria where the Royal Palace stood, and made it his fortress.

The Alexandrians dammed up the city's canals to cut off potential routes of escape, and erected walls in the city streets. Impressive and innovative siege equipment was built on the spot. Egyptian slaves were armed by wealthy citizens to join in the fight, and arms and armour were forged by local artisans.

Achillas marched on Alexandria with 20,000 infantry and 2,000 cavalry.[3] Caesar could not match these forces and so resorted to diplomacy, only to see Achillas murder the envoys and close all avenues to conciliation. Achillas marched into Alexandria and took the best part of the city; and so began the siege of Alexandria in 47 BCE.

Meanwhile, Arsinoë escaped from Caesar and joined Achillas. But the concord did not last very long: Arsinoë fled Alexandria with the eunuch Ganymedes and took command of the Egyptian army, proclaiming herself Queen Arsinoë IV. Achillas, meanwhile, had assumed the title of pharaoh, but Arsinoë had him executed and promoted Ganymedes to second-in-command of her army.

Arsinoë enjoyed some notable success against Caesar. She cornered him and built walls to trap him, while Ganymedes flooded the area by drawing water from the sea and pouring it into the canals that supplied Caesar, causing panic among Caesar's troops. Caesar reacted by digging wells into the porous limestone beneath the city containing fresh water, and despatched ships out along the coast to search for more fresh water. Caesar knew he had to break out from the city, so he attacked the island of Pharos with its famous lighthouse. Arsinoë's forces repelled him in a humiliating defeat, which at one point saw Caesar, in desperation, tear off his armour and purple cloak, and, holding a sheaf of important documents above the water, swim for refuge and his life to a nearby Roman ship moored in the bay. Negotiations then brought about the exchange of Arsinoë for Ptolemy XIII.[4] Ptolemy continued to prosecute the war until Roman reinforcements arrived in the shape of Mithridates of

Pergamum and Antipater from Judea. Mithridates reached the Nile delta in early 47 BCE and defeated one Egyptian force sent to stop him. Caesar joined Mithridates, and their combined force of 20,000 men engaged the Egyptians in February of that year at the Battle of the Nile. Caesar and Mithridates were victorious; Ptolemy drowned while attempting to cross the river.

The temple of Artemis in Ephesus was home to Arsinoë for a number of years until, in 41 BCE, at the ever-suspicious Cleopatra's prompting, Mark Antony ordered Arsinoë's execution on the steps of the temple – a huge act of sacrilege which ignited scandal and shock back in Rome.

In addition to the spectacle provided by Arsinoë at Caesar's triumph, beast-hunts were held featuring 400 lions, along with gladiator contests. A *naumachia* (simulated sea battle) was organized on a flooded basin at the Field of Mars. At the Circus Maximus, two armies of prisoners of war, each comprising 2,000 combatants, with 200 horses and twenty elephants, fought to the death. This extravagance was not universally appreciated and a riot broke out, which was only quelled when Caesar had two of the rioters sacrificed by the priests on the Field of Mars.

A priority for Caesar on his return to Italy in September 45 BCE was to finalize and file his will with the Vestal Virgins. In this, he named his adoptive grandnephew, Gaius Octavius (Octavian, later known as Augustus Caesar), as his principal heir, bequeathing his immense estate and property, including his potent name. If Octavian predeceased Caesar, then Decimus Junius Brutus Albinus – a future assassin - would be next in line. The citizens of Rome also did well out of the will: 'his gardens were given to the people as a place of recreation, and to every Roman still living in the city he gave seventy-five Attic drachmas.'[5]

The chaos, lameness and dysfunctionality inherent in the present Roman administration were plain for all to see. The machinery of state was no longer fit for purpose, the Senate was enfeebled and the provinces were allowed to act independently of central government in Rome; the army, under their commanders, effectively dictated things. Corruption was rife, as was fear, but the status quo was still welcomed by conservative factions in the Senate.

Caesar resolved to put things right. He came up with a three-point plan to extirpate all armed resistance in the provinces, restoring order and strength to the Republic; simultaneously create a strong central government in Rome;

and harness all provinces into a single cohesive political unit. This would prevent any recurrence of the problems which sparked the Social Wars, when individuals outside Rome and Italy were not considered 'Roman' and were denied full citizenship rights.

When Caesar defeated Pompey and his supporters, he had dealt with the first matter. Absolute and unquestioned sway over the government was required to achieve the second and third points, so he set about augmenting his personal power and, simultaneously, eroding the authority of Rome's other political institutions. He also put in place reforms intended to address several issues that had long been neglected, the most important of which was his reform of the Roman calendar.

More legislative and constitutional housekeeping followed: Caesar conducted a census, which led to a reduction in the state-subsidised grain dole, imposing a fixed number of recipients, all of whom were entered into a register. Laws decreed that jury service be restricted to the Senate or the equestrian ranks. A sumptuary law restricted the purchase of certain luxuries. A fertility law rewarded families for producing certain numbers of children, to expedite the repopulation of Italy. He banned professional guilds, except those which could claim an ancient foundation; guilds were often hotbeds of anti-government sedition. The length of time governors could hold office in the provinces was restricted, to close down the risk that another general might attempt to challenge him. Debts were restructured, wiping out about a quarter of all outstanding debt.

Caesar turned his attention to public works. Among other projects, he built the Forum of Caesar, with its Temple of Venus Genetrix. Between 47-44 BCE, he organized the distribution of land to around 15,000 of his veterans. He set up a police force, appointed officials to officiate on his land reforms and ordered that Carthage and Corinth be rebuilt. The prevailing tax system was abolished, reverting to an earlier version that allowed cities the freedom to collect tribute independently, without involving Roman bureaucrats. Other plans included the construction of a temple to Mars, a large theatre and a library to match the Library of Alexandria – all of which were abandoned after Caesar's assassination.

Plans were also in place to upgrade Ostia to a major port, and cut a canal through the Isthmus of Corinth. Military campaigns against the Dacians and

Parthians, to avenge the catastrophic loss at Carrhae, were on the drawing board, resulting in a huge recruitment push. Encouraged by Caesar, the Senate honoured him with the post of censor for life, Father of the Fatherland and *imperator*.

Some of these actions and honours clearly had about them more than a whiff of monarchy, divinity and despotism, and were later used to justify his assassination. Most blatantly and obviously, the Senate named Caesar *dictator perpetuo* ('dictator in perpetuity'). Caesar now wielded real power. As *dictator perpetuo*, Caesar elected the other magistrates, selected the provincial governors and, in doing so, the army commanders. He enjoyed the support of the many to whom he had shown clemency in the recent past. To add to this, in 47 BCE, Caesar misused his powers as censor to replenish the membership of the Senate, which had been badly depleted through proscription and exile. New senators were appointed to bring membership up to 900 – all the novices were, of course, Caesar's men. While this strengthened Caesar's arm immeasurably, it also further diluted the democratic nature of the Senate and compromised its status and prestige.

All of this was decidedly counter *mos maiorum* ('ancestral custom'), it rode roughshod over tradition, it was devoid of 'Romanitas' (the concept by which Romans defined themselves) and, of course, it had more than just a hint of monarchism about it. Mark Antony, who had been elected co-consul with Caesar, seemed to confirm this when he delivered a speech from the Rostra at the 44 BCE Lupercalia and tried to place a diadem on Caesar's head – a botched attempt to confer royalty on Caesar; Caesar laid it aside to use as a sacrifice to Jupiter Optimus Maximus.

Denarius coins were minted bearing his image, the text '*dictator perpetuo*' and with an image of the goddess Ceres and Caesar's title of Augur Pontifex Maximus on the reverse. Dio records how when a senatorial delegation went to inform Caesar of his new honours in 44 BCE, Caesar hubristically, tactlessly and arrogantly remained sitting in the Temple of Venus Genetrix, rather than standing to meet them.[6] A statue of him was placed in the company of those of the old, dreaded kings of Rome. Obsequiously, he was granted a golden chair in the Senate, a gesture smacking of regal orientalism, and was allowed to wear triumphal dress whenever he pleased: Caesar was now the constant *triumphator*. He was offered a popular cult, with Mark Antony as his high priest. More toadying came when he was privileged with the right to speak first during senatorial debates.

In 46 BCE, Caesar rewarded himself with the title of 'Prefect of the Morals' (*praefectura morum*), a censor by any other name, which allowed him censorial powers but exemption from the checks and balances to which the regular censors were subject.

Back in 48 BCE, permanent tribunician powers had been conferred on Caesar, which rendered him sacrosanct and allowed him power of veto over the Senate. Suetonius tells how when a crowd gathered to greet Caesar on his return to Rome, one of them placed a laurel wreath on the statue of Caesar on the Rostra. Tribunes Gaius Epidius Marullus and Lucius Caesetius Flavus ordered the wreath be removed as it was a symbol of Jupiter and of royalty. Caesar reacted by having the tribunes stripped of their powers and removed from office.[7] Suetonius believes that, from this point on, Caesar was not able to disassociate himself from 'royalness'.[8] After this, Caesar was never bothered again by annoying members of the Tribunician College.

Suetonius also relates how a crowd on the Alban Hill shouted, calling him '*rex*' ('king'), to which Caesar replied, 'I am Caesar, not *Rex*'. The tribunes arrested a member of this crowd, but the plebeians protested his right to freedom of speech; Caesar had the tribunes removed from office and erased their names from the public records.

In early 44 BCE, Caesar made plans for a war against the Parthians. This, of course, would involve his lengthy absence from Rome and the seat of power, and would compromise his ability to install his own consuls. Accordingly, he put in place legislation which gave him the right to appoint all magistrates for 43 BCE and all consuls and tribunes in 42 BCE. The Roman constitution was thus turned on its head: the magistracies were no longer representatives of the people, but were now representatives of a dictator.

The Ides of March came. Caesar's diary had him down to appear at a session of the Senate. Led by Gaius Cassius Longinus, Decimus Junius Brutus, and Marcus Junius Brutus, several senators, 'liberators', had other plans for Caesar's day: they had had enough of his despotic behaviour and conspired to assassinate him. Mark Antony had picked up vague rumblings and rumours of a plot the previous night from a petrified liberator and future assassin, the 'envious' Servilius Casca, tribune of the people. Antony went to warn Caesar, but the conspirators had taken such a move into account and arranged for Gaius Trebonius to intercept him as he approached the portico of the Theatre of Pompey, the temporary home of the Senate where the session was to be held, and detain him outside. As it happened, Antony fled when he heard the din coming from the Senate chamber. Trebonius had been a loyal friend of Caesar, but later defected to the assassins.

More importantly, the omens were, predictably, decidedly bad. Calpurnia, his wife, dreamt of him bleeding to death; Spurinna – a soothsayer – gave him the clearest of advice, telling him, 'beware the Ides of March'. Regal hubris led him to ignore her.

Plutarch reports that when Caesar arrived at the Senate, Tillius Cimber presented him with a diversionary and spurious petition to recall his exiled brother. Cimber, like Trebonius, had been a loyal supporter of Caesar, but he too had defected. The other conspirators milled around to feign support. When Caesar motioned Cimber away, Cimber grabbed his shoulders and pulled Caesar's tunic down. Caesar then indignantly cried to Cimber, '*Ista quidem vis est*!' ('Why, this is some violence!'). Casca drew his dagger and thrust at Caesar's neck, only to have Caesar spin around and catch him by the arm, protesting, 'Casca, you scoundrel, what are you doing?' A frightened Casca could only call for his brother, 'Help, brother!' ('ἀδελφέ, βοήθει'). At this the conspirators, as a man, lashed out at the dictator. Caesar attempted to get away, but to no avail: blinded by blood amidst a blizzard of daggers, he fell. The assassins plunged in their daggers time and again as he lay bleeding, helpless and defenceless, on the steps of the portico. Eutropius records that the killers numbered about sixty men, inflicting between them twenty-three stab wounds.

If Suetonius is to be believed, a doctor later established there had been only one fatal wound to Caesar's chest, the second strike, which pierced his aorta. Caesar's last words, if indeed he uttered any, have been a matter of dispute ever since. Suetonius maintains that he said nothing, but that others believe his dying words to have been 'καὶ σύ, τέκνον' ('You too, child?') when he saw Brutus amongst the mob of assassins.[9]

Plutarch agrees, adding that Caesar pulled his toga over his head when he caught sight of Brutus among the conspirators.[10] The most famous, unhistorical, version comes down from Shakespeare's *Julius Caesar*: '*Et tu, Brute*?'– ('And you as well, Brutus?').

The assassins could not have predicted the consequences of their actions. To them, the murder of Caesar was a short-term expedient, ridding Rome of a tyrant. Now that he was gone, they presumably thought that things would revert more or less to as before the civil wars: the *mos maiorum* would be resumed and life with the status quo would take over again. Good Romans would be free once more to continue their journeys unhindered along their personal *cursus honorum*.

With nearly a century's worth of hindsight to help him, the epic poet Lucan (39–65 CE) would see the civil wars and the Triumvirate very differently – in keeping with his penchant for melodrama and hyperbole, they were to him nothing less than apocalyptic and cataclysmic. His poem tells what drove to arms 'A maddened nation and from all the world struck peace away'.

> 'So when that hour,
> The last in all the centuries, shall sound
> The world's disruption, all things shall revert
> To that primaeval chaos, stars on stars
> Shall crash; and fiery meteors from the sky
> Plunge in the ocean. Earth shall then no more
> Front with her bulwark the encroaching sea:
> The moon, indignant at her path oblique,
> Shall drive her chariot 'gainst her brother Sun
> And claim the day for hers; and discord huge
> Shall rend the spheres asunder. On themselves
> The great are dashed: such end the gods have set
> To height of power: nor ever Fortune shares
> With other lands the weapons of her spite
> Against a nation lord of land and sea.
> Thou, Rome, degraded, sold, the common prey
> Of triple despots, of a tyrant rule
> Partnered as ne'er before – thyself art cause
> Of all the ills.'[11]

In the immediate aftermath, Plutarch reports that the assassins fled the Theatre of Pompey.[12] Brutus and his co-conspirators marched on the Capitol, exclaiming: 'People of Rome, we are free again!' The ensuing silence must have been deafening, for the people of Rome, stunned and frightened, had barricaded themselves inside their homes as rumours and panic spread. Caesar's blood-soaked corpse lay where it fell for nearly three hours before three slaves loaded him on a litter and carted him home.

The assassins were looking increasingly isolated and vulnerable. The expected support from the populace did not materialise: the right thing to do would have been to address the people and confirm the elimination of a tyrant, but instead they cowered in the Capitol. An impassioned and increasingly frenzied Mark Antony seized the initiative and systematically raised the crowd to fury, citing Caesar's achievements, displaying his bloody cloak and pointing out that a number of assassins had been shown mercy by Caesar. The verbal fireworks soon translated into real incendiaries when a macabre wax effigy of Caesar was erected in the Forum, graphically displaying the multiple stab wounds.[13] The Senate house was torched, badly damaging neighbouring buildings. A sort of poetic injustice was meted out when the poet Helvius Cinna was mistaken for the conspirator Cornelius Cinna and torn to pieces. Conspirators' houses were set alight and Caesar's funeral bier was ignited, piled high with looted furniture and mourners' clothing. The Temple of Caesar was built a few years later on the tragic site, at the east side of the main square of the Roman Forum; its altar still remains.

It fell then to Mark Antony to deal with the political repercussions and constitutional aftermath. Coming down on the side of compromise and conciliation, it was decided in a meeting he called on 17 March that the assassins would escape punishment, all of Caesar's appointments would be respected and that there would be a public funeral. In doing this, he cleverly undermined the conspirators, who, as *optimates*, were only intent on preserving the Republic. Antony ensured that their slaying of Caesar had the opposite effect.[14] Meanwhile, a flame was lit on an altar at the murder site by Caesar's ex-veterans waiting to be sent to new homes, and a cult of Caesar sprang up. The Jewish population of Rome, grateful to Caesar for exempting them from his ban on religious meetings, mounted an evening vigil.

Rome was thrown into unprecedented turmoil, but many aspects of life went on as normal with all its mundanities. For example, the Lex Ursonensis was passed in 44 BCE: the four surviving tablets (*CIL* 2, 5439) featuring the

Lex Ursonensis (official name Law of Colonia Genetiva Julia) comprise the foundation charter of the Caesarean *colonia* Iulia Genetiva at Urso in the modern province of Seville. As such, it provides a valuable record of legislation relating to the establishment of Roman colonies. The original law comprised nine tablets, each with three or five columns of text totalling over 140 sections (*rubricae*). The charter, in draft form written by Julius Caesar, was approved by the Roman assembly as a law under the auspices of Mark Antony after the assassination. The surviving four are in the National Archaeological Museum of Spain in Madrid.

The following are two samples of the type of subject covered in the legislation:

> '78. Respecting public roads and footpaths within the boundaries assigned to the colony, all such thoroughfares, roads, and footpaths that exist or shall exist or have existed in the said territories shall be public property.
>
> '79. Respecting all rivers, streams, fountains, lakes, springs, ponds, or marshes within the territory divided among the colonists of this colony: the holders and possessors of such land shall have the same rights of access, carriage, and drawing of water in respect to the said streams, fountains, lakes, springs, ponds, and marshes, as belonged to former holders and possessors. In like manner the persons who own or possess the said land shall have legal right of way to the said waters.'
>
> (trans.: Johnson, *Ancient Roman Statutes*, pp.97–104, n. 114)

Presumably the Acta Diurna, first published in 59 BCE, would have been published as normal, although the 16 March headline will have been more sensational than usual. It was a kind of daily gazette, a daily record, which recorded official events, ceremonies, speeches in the Senate, military developments and lawsuits. Public notices and significant births, marriages and deaths were included later. Its readership extended well beyond Rome into the provinces. The news they carried was carved on stone or metal and displayed on message boards in public and busy places such as the Forum Romanum: Rome's equivalent of billboards or outdoor digital screens. Just like yesterday's newspapers, they had a short life: the notices were taken down after a few days and, with a commendable anticipation of future needs, archived; scribes sometimes made copies to be despatched to provincial governors to keep them up to speed with events at the seat of government. *Publicare et propagare* – 'for publication and promulgation' – appeared at the end of the texts, identifying them as a kind of press release.

Within a month of the fateful Ides of March, the conspirators had fled Rome, counting amongst their number Cicero, who left Atticus on 7 April with the agreement (to our everlasting benefit) that they would keep in daily touch by letter, 'whatever happens, important or trivial'. Another highly respected friend of Cicero's, Matius, summed up the general mood when he predicted that Rome was doomed and that the Gauls would invade and take Rome.

We have already seen how superstition was an everyday part of Roman life; so it should come as no surprise that omens, prodigies and prophets of doom swirled in profusion around the Ides of March. We have Julius Obsequens, a Roman writer from the mid-fourth century CE, to thank for the precise detail surrounding supernatural events around 15 March 44 BCE, as published in his *Liber de Prodigiis*, an account of the wonders and portents that occurred in Rome between 249-12 BCE. According to Obsequens, things started to go bump in the night of the 14th and 15th when:

> 'the entrails were found to have no heart. His wife Calpurnia dreamt that the akroterion of the house, which had been added in accordance with a senatorial decree, fell down. At night when the doors of the bedroom were closed, they opened of their own accord, so that the light of the moon, which came inside awoke Calpurnia.'

But that was nothing compared to the shenanigans which took place on the day itself:

> 'At the games ofVenus Genetrix, which he performed for his colleague, at the eleventh hour a comet appeared from under the North Star and attracted everyone's attention. There were frequent earth tremors. The drydocks and many other places were struck by lightning. A violent whirlwind shattered the limbs and threw down a statue which M. Cicero had placed in front of the inner sanctum of Minerva, on

> the day before he went into exile in accordance with the plebiscite, and with its shoulders, arms and head broken portended dreadful things for Cicero himself. The bronze tablets from the temple of Fides were torn off by a whirlwind. At the temple of Ops the doors were broken. Trees were torn up by their roots and many buildings were demolished. A torch in the sky seemed to be born to the east. A star blazed conspicuously for seven days. Three suns gleamed, and around the lowest sun a crown similar to ears of grain in a circle gleamed out and afterwards when the sun had been reduced to one globe the light was limpid for months. In the temple of Castor some letters from the names of the consuls Antony and Dolabella were shaken out, which indicated that both of them would be exiled from their homeland. The baying of a dog was heard during the night in front of the home of the pontifex maximus, [Lepidus], from these things especially as the dog was mutilated by the others it portended scandalous disgrace to Lepidus. At Hostia a shoal of fish was left on dry land by the ebb and flow of the sea. The Po flooded and when it subsided below its banks left a large number of vipers.'

In addition, Servius (on *Georgics* 1, 472) reports an eruption of Mount Etna early in 44 BCE which may corroborate some of Obsequens' reports on the atmosphere, while a comet also reported for 44 BCE by Chinese astronomical sources may well be Obsequens' conspicuous seven-day star.

The year 43 BCE was just as volatile:

> 'The equestrian statue of the consul C. Pansa collapsed in the home of Antony. A decorated horse fell-down dead as it hurried into his sight. One of the people fell down in the blood of the sacrifices and offered him his hand spattered with blood as he set out. These funereal prodigies were for him, and then when he was fighting against Antony he was fatally wounded. An appearance of arms and weapons seemed to be borne from the land to the sky with a loud tumult. The standards of the legion, which had been left by Pansa as a garrison for the city, seemed to be cloaked in spiders' webs which had spun as though after they had remained stationery for too

long. Many places were struck by lightning. In the camp of Caesar [Octavian] at first light an eagle settled on top of the headquarters above the lintel, then after it was driven away by smaller birds which were flying around it disappeared from sight. A voice was heard from the oracle of Apollo: Madness to wolves in winter, a lack of grain in summer. … When Caesar led in his army down into the Campus Martius, six vultures appeared, then when he ascended the rostra after being created consul another six vultures were seen and they gave a sign for the new foundation of the city just like the auspices offered to Romulus.'

Things had not really settled down in 42 BCE:

'At Rome a mule gave birth by the Twelve Gates. A dead bitch belonging to a temple keeper was dragged away by a dog. Light so shone at night, that it seemed that people woke up for work as though it was daybreak. At Mutina the south facing standard of the Marian victory, of its own accord, turned northward at the fourth hour. When these things were being expiated by sacrificial victims, three suns were seen at around the third hour of the day, then they drew together as one globe. At Latinum on the Alban Mount when a sacrifice was taking place, blood flowed from the shoulder and thumb of Jupiter … It was designated as a prodigy that the praetor P. Titius had deposed a colleague because of dissension; and before the end of the year he was dead. It is agreed that no-one who had deposed a colleague had lived another year … As Brutus and Cassius were preparing their battle against Caesar and Antony a swarm of bees settled in the camp of Cassius … A vast multitude of vultures and other winged creatures which feed on the carnage of dead bodies, flew up to the army. When a boy was being carried in the procession of Victory in costume, he fell off the litter. When there was a ceremony of lustration the lictor placed the laurel wreath on the fasces when they were the wrong way round. As Brutus and his army were going out to battle an Ethiopian met them at the gate and was run through by the soldiers. Cassius and Brutus perished.'

The plebeians were outraged that a small clique of aristocrats had sacrificed Caesar on the altar of their own exclusive ambitions: Antony, who had never been totally committed to Caesar or his cause, nevertheless capitalized on this and set about harnessing their fury against the *optimates*. Any ambitions Antony may have harboured to take control of Rome himself were tempered by the unpalatable fact that Caesar, as noted above, had named his grandnephew Gaius Octavius his sole heir, bequeathing him land, money and the powerful name of Caesar itself.[15] Enter Octavian.

Octavian (63 BCE – 14 CE) was born Gaius Octavius into an old and wealthy equestrian branch of the plebeian gens Octavia. On assuming his adoption by Caesar, he took Caesar's name and was called Gaius Julius Caesar Octavianus. Octavian was born in Rome in a modest house on the Palatine Hill. From there he was taken to his father's home village at Velletri. His paternal great-grandfather, Gaius Octavius, was a military tribune in Sicily during the Second Punic War; his father, also Gaius Octavius, was governor of Macedonia. His mother, Atia, was the niece of Julius Caesar. Octavius was raised by his grandmother, Julia, the sister of Julius Caesar. He assumed the *toga virilis* around 47 BCE and was elected to the College of Pontiffs.[16] In 46 he took over the management of the Greek games that were staged in honour of the Temple of Venus Genetrix, built by Julius Caesar.

Chapter 12

The Second Triumvirate: Octavian, Mark Antony and Marcus Aemilius Lepidus (43–33 BCE)

When news of Caesar's death reached the 18-year-old Octavian, he was in Apollonia with Agrippa. Ignoring advice to take refuge in Macedonia, he ditched his studies and military training and crossed the Adriatic, landing at Lupiae near Brundisium. Here Octavian learned the full contents of Caesar's will and, at the same time, inherited the loyalty of most of the Roman populace and Caesar's former soldiers at Brundisium. Octavian needed money: he demanded some of the funds earmarked by Caesar for the war against Parthia, which amounted to 700 million sesterces and was banked at Brundisium. Octavian added to this when he appropriated the annual tribute sent from Rome's near eastern provinces. In his *The Roman Revolution* (p.3, n.2), Ronald Syme described the years 43-29 BCE as 'tangled, chaotic, hideous'. Few would argue, Octavian and Antony included.

Octavian's army so far consisted of Caesar's veterans and troops held in reserve for the Parthian war, Octavian milking all the while his status as heir to Caesar.[1] The march to Rome through Campania attracted more troops and funds. By June, he had assembled an army of 3,000 veterans, paying each of them a salary of 500 denarii.

Octavian arrived in Rome on 6 May 44 BCE, only to find Mark Antony embroiled in negotiations with the assassins regarding a general amnesty. However, many fled the city anyway, unnerved as they were by Antony's incendiary funeral eulogy, which had focussed public opinion against the assassins. Mark Antony did his cause no favours when he initially opposed the motion to elevate Caesar to divine status. Octavian, on the other hand, failed to persuade Antony to transfer Caesar's money to him, but he did succeed in ingratiating himself with the *optimates*, Caesar's tradtional enemies. Help came from an unexpected quarter when the leading *optimate,* Cicero, attacked

Antony in a series of speeches painting him as a threat to the Republic. Antony read the writing on the wall: public support was waning and his term as consul was drawing to a close, so he attempted to pass laws that would give him control over Cisalpine Gaul from the incumbent Decimus Junius Brutus Albinus. In the meantime, Octavian's recruitment campaign continued apace and Antony fled to Cisalpine Gaul.

But Antony had not taken into account an intransigent and stubborn Decimus Brutus. When Brutus refused to renounce Cisalpine Gaul, Antony blockaded him at Mutina. He was able to ignore the Senate's bleating and toothless resolutions to end the violence, as the Senate had no army to enforce their demands. Octavian saw a chance. Cicero helped again when he defended Octavian against Antony, saying, 'we have no more brilliant example of traditional piety among our youth'. Cicero went further when he urged the Senate to make Octavian a senator on 1 January 43 BCE with the the power to vote alongside the former consuls. Octavian was made *propraetor imperium*, legalizing his command of troops and allowing him to relieve the siege at Mutina along with Hirtius and Pansa, the consuls for 43 BCE. In April, Antony's armies were defeated at the battles of Forum Gallorum and Mutina, forcing Antony to retreat to Transalpine Gaul. Both consuls died in the battles, leaving Octavian in sole command.

The Senate rewarded Decimus Brutus more highly than it did Octavian, and went so far as to try to to give command of the consular legions to Brutus. Octavian, though, was a stumbling block when he stayed in the Po valley and refused to help in any further offensive against Antony. Octavian then sent an embassy of centurions to Rome, demanding that he be given the consulship left vacant by Hirtius and Pansa. Octavian went on to demand further that the decree declaring Antony a public enemy should be annulled. The Senate refused, so Octavian marched unopposed on Rome with eight legions. On 19 August 43 BCE, he was elected consul, with his relative Quintus Pedius as co-consul. Meanwhile, Antony allied with Marcus Aemilius Lepidus.

Mark Antony seriously underestimated Octavian, his political and his military skills. He even went so far as to allege that Octavian had secured his adoption through sexual favours shown to Caesar. Sexual slurring, particularly homophobic slurring, was a common political weapon used widely to discredit an opponent. Suetonius was not convinced, and discredits

Antony's accusation as mere political slander.[2] As we have seen, this was not the first time Caesar had been discredited: according to Suetonius, while staying at the Bithynian court of Nicomedes IV, 'he submitted to the king's pleasure'.[3] It was time well spent, however, as Nicomedes later bequeathed his entire kingdom to Rome.

Meanwhile, conspirators Brutus and Cassius were busy amassing a huge army in Greece. Antony was also recruiting to oppose this army: he needed soldiers, money from Caesar's war chests and to have his actions endorsed with Caesar's name. Octavian had a stake in all three and a role to play. The 'lex Titia' was passed on 27 November 43 BCE, legalizing, at a meeting near Bononia (modern Bolognia), the Second Triumvirate, a brand-new form of government, made up of Octavian, Mark Antony and Master of the Horse Marcus Aemilius Lepidus. The pact had a term of five years, and was renewed in 38 BCE.[4] Unlike its predecessor, the Second Triumvirate was a legal instrument which gave the three men dictatorial powers.

The Second Triumvirate was a 'three-man commission for restoring the constitution of the republic' (*triumviri rei publicae constituendae,* III VIR RPC). The three had the power to make or annul laws without involving the Senate or the people; their judicial decisions were not subject to appeal and allowed the Triumvirs to appoint magistrates uncontested, and manage government land. Their supreme power was accorded legal sanction; their *imperium maius* was greater than that of all other magistracies, including the consuls.

In 43 BCE, Lepidus handed over seven legions to Octavian and Antony to bolster their struggle against Brutus and Cassius to acquire eastern Roman territory. In so doing, Lepidus significantly reduced his own power. Antony kept Cisalpine Gaul and control of Gaul itself, while Octavian held Africa and nominal authority over Sicily and Sardinia – all rather paltry when compared with the territories Antony received.

The Triumvirs deified Caesar posthumously as '*Divus Iulius*' in 42 BCE, so making Octavian '*Divi filius*' ('Son of the Divine'). Remembering that Caesar had been repaid for his habitual clemency with his life, the Second Triumvirate reintroduced the terrifying proscription and proceeded to legally sanction the murder of numerous opponents, seizing their land and property to finance an army of forty-five legions gearing up to oppose Brutus and Cassius. By now, the pair had taken control of a number of Eastern provinces, including Greece,

Macedonia, Asia Minor and Syria. In 42 BCE, Octavian and Antony set out to war.

Their main objectives were to avenge Caesar's assassination, eliminate political enemies and, of course, acquire their valuable assets and properties. Conspirators such as Brutus and Cassius, and other individuals who had taken part in the Civil War on the wrong side – including wealthy people, senators, knights and republicans such as Sextus Pompey and Cicero – were all on the dreaded lists. A reward of 2,500 drachmae was offered for delivering the head of a free person on the list, while a proscribed slave's head brought in 1,000 drachmae. Anyone who informed on where someone on the list was hiding earned the same rewards. Most on the lists were killed, in some cases gruesomely.

According to Appian, 300 senators and 2,000 *equites* were proscribed and relieved of their property and, for those who did not manage to escape, their lives. Livy puts the number of senators butchered at 130. Notable victims of the proscriptions included Cicero, who had opposed Caesar and roasted Antony in his *Philippicae*, and Marcus Favonius, a follower of Cato and an opponent of both Triumvirates.[5] Quintus Tullius Cicero (Marcus Tullius Cicero's younger brother) appeared on the list because there was a desire to eliminate Cicero's entire family. Caesar's legate, Lucius Julius Caesar, and Lepidus' brother, Lucius Aemilius Lepidus Paullus, surprisingly also appeared because they had been amongst the first to condemn Antony and Lepidus after the two joined the Triumvirate; they both survived. Men and women, free and enslaved, whole towns and not just individuals throughout the Mediterranean, had to make the invidious decision to collaborate with the Triumvirs or risk opposing them.

The ambitious and assertive Fulvia Flacca Bambula (*c.* 83–40 BCE) is infamous for gleefully and sadistically pricking the decapitated Cicero's tongue with a hairpin: she took exception and revenge after Cicero had insinuated that Mark Antony, her third husband, only married her for her money.[6] Cicero's head was put on public display on the Rostra in the Forum after his proscription in 43 BCE.

In 42 BCE, Antony and Octavian despatched twenty-eight legions over the sea to the north of Greece to engage the armies of Brutus and Cassius, having left Lepidus behind in Italy. From there, the Triumvirs sent Gaius Norbanus Flaccus and Decidius Saxa with an eight-legion advance guard into Macedonia. Norbanus and Saxa met the combined armies of Cassius and Brutus near Philippi. Brutus and Cassius outflanked them, and they retreated toward Amphipolis, where Antony and his armies confronted the conspirators and found Amphipolis well defended. Norbanus was left in command of the town.

The Triumvirs brought nineteen legions to the battle, including the *Legio* VI, VII, VIII, X Equestris, XII, XIII, XXVI, XXVIII, XXIX and XXX, nearly all at full rank. They were supported by 13,000 cavalry under Octavian and 20,000 led by Antony.

Opposing them, Brutus and Cassius had seventeen legions (eight with Brutus and nine with Cassius), while two other legions were attached to the fleet. These, bar two, were somewhat depleted, but they were reinforced by levies from the Eastern allied kingdoms. Appian reports a total of about 80,000 infantry plus 17,000 horsemen, including 5,000 mounted bowmen. Loyalty and retention were issues assuaged in part with a gift of 1,500 denari for each legionary and 7,500 for each centurion.

In the first of two battles, Brutus clashed with Octavian, Antony with Cassius. Brutus initially pushed back Octavian and penetrated his legions' camp, while Antony defeated Cassius, who, hearing false news regarding Brutus' defeat, committed suicide. Brutus rallied the remnants of Cassius's forces and both sides retreated to their respective camps with their booty. While all this was going on, Antony and Octavian suffered a major reverse when the Republican fleet intercepted and wrecked their reinforcements – two legions and other troops and materiel under the command of Gnaeus Domitius Calvinus. This left Antony and Octavian in some jeopardy, particularly as Macedonia and Thessaly were unable to supply their armies for very long. The Triumvirs were forced to despatch a legion south to Achaia to collect more supplies. Morale was boosted by the promise of a further 5,000 denarii for each soldier and 25,000 for centurions.

Brutus had always been the brains behind the conspirators' armies and their strategy. Cassius had lacked the respect of his allies and his troops, he too resorted to incentives, offering 1,000 denarii for each soldier. Brutus was forced to attack on the afternoon of 23 October. The battle degenerated into close combat between the two armies, resulting in horrific slaughter.

Brutus's legions were extended so thinly in the centre that they could not defend the Triumvirs' initial charge. They were driven back gradually at first, but soon began to give ground more rapidly. Octavian's soldiers captured the gates of Brutus' camp, and Brutus retreated into the nearby hills with only four legions. Surrender and capture were inevitable; Brutus committed suicide.

Mark Antony later used these battles as a way to undermine Octavian, asserting that both were won using Antony's forces. Antony also called Octavian a coward for handing over direct military control to his close friend Marcus Vipsanius Agrippa.

Events in Greece triggered a reorganization within the Triumvirate. Octavian – who was now calling himself 'Imperator Caesar' – took the West, Antony the East. Cisalpine Gaul was absorbed into Italy, while Narbonese Gaul fell into Gallia Comata, creating a unified Gaul. Octavian took over Hispania from Lepidus, ever the poor relation, who came out of it all almost empty-handed, apart from the prospect of control over Africa. His treatment here was accounted for by a report that he had been secretly and treasonably negotiating with Sextus Pompey. The Italian peninsula was a free-for-all for the recruitment of troops, but in reality was not much practical use to Antony in the East.

Octavian delegated to Lepidus the defence of Rome against Lucius Antonius, who took the city with little trouble. Lepidus fled to Octavian. When Lucius withdrew from Rome soon after, Octavian retook the city. Lepidus was allocated six of Antony's legions to govern Africa and Numidia, leaving Octavian as the sole force in Italy. When Calenus, governor of Gaul and a supporter of Antony, died, Octavian merged his legions into his own armies, further reinforcing his power in the West. Antony took Egypt and allied himself with Cleopatra VII. The Treaty of Brundisium, signed in September 40 BCE, confirmed all these machinations. The meeting to sign the treaty was also notable for the degree of fraternization between the two armies – to them, the negotiations may have seemed pointless and of little consequence, for after all, they were all Romans and more concerned about surviving to collect their pay and, in due course, land.

Not for the first time did army veterans pose a problem for their commanders: where to settle them was the intractable question for both Octavian's own army veterans and those of Brutus and Cassius, who, if displeased, might sign up with potential political opponents. The invidious choice for Octavian lay between alienating countless Roman citizens by appropriating their land, or alienating thousands of Roman soldiers who had the potential to oppose him if he did not deliver land promised by Caesar for settlement. Octavian needed these soldiers – some 40,000 of them – to swell his armies, so he went for the former option, as government-controlled land to allot as settlements for veterans was exhausted. Eighteen of the richest towns in Italy consequently had their salubrious, fertile lands confiscated in the new land scheme, with entire populations expelled. Octavian had to ensure that the legionaries were kept on side; but in doing so he alienated tens of thousands of Italians, who flooded into Rome in desperate protest. There was to be no compensation.

The already fractious relationship between Octavian and Antony was starting to fall apart. Octavian's land settlement decision was never going to be popular with all those landowners and farmers dispossessed in favour of the soldiery. Antony's younger brother, Lucius Antonius, as consul, championed the farmers' cause and precipitated the Perusine War (41-40 BCE). Octavian faced Lucius Antonius and his fireball of a (third) wife, Fulvia Flacca Bambula. Velleius Paterculus records that she 'was creating general confusion by armed violence', and that Octavian's troops tied obscene messages to stones and fired them directly at Fulvia. Two were aimed at her clitoris with the unmistakeable suggestion that she was a tribade, a lesbian.

Fulvia and Antony's men traded such insults with those of Octavian about their leaders' sexual proclivities.[7] It is interesting to note that there was little point in such graffiti if the recipient could not read the message, as would be the case in many of Rome's other, foreign theatres of war, but since the combatants here mostly shared the same language, the messages made ideal weapons in the propaganda war raging between the two armies.

Martial[8] preserves for us a lascivious epigram which Octavian reputedly composed for Fulvia, in which she offered herself sexually to him but he turned her down. Martial's Octavian is implying that the ensuing civil war was caused because Fulvia was put out by his rebuffal.

Fulvia deserves to be remembered for more than her sadism and as an erotic military target: her military and political achievements are quite remarkable by any standards. Before her relationship with Antony, she had been married to two other powerful men. The first was the notorious Publius Clodius Pulcher in 62 BCE, then in 51 BCE Gaius Scribonius Curio, an ally of Julius Caesar's. Plutarch, in his *Life of Antony*, describes Fulvia as no wool-spinner or doer of housework, in effect no *matrona* at all; Fulvia's ambition was to rule over a powerful man, an ambition she was to realise as Mark Antony's third wife. Her marriage to three powerful politicians enabled her to influence, albeit indirectly, the course of Roman politics through the actions of her husbands. Plutarch continues: 'She did not think it worth anything to dominate an ordinary man, but she wanted to rule a ruler and command a commander.' Cleopatra was indebted to Fulvia for teaching Antony to obey a woman, since the Antony she inherited was used to and trained in listening to the rule of women. Plutarch calls her *polupragmon* and *thrasus* (interfering and bold); Appian calls her *philopragmonas* (meddlesome). In the second century CE, Florus describes what he believes to be the malicious influence she, masculinised, had over Antony: '*semper alias Antonii pessimum ingenium Fulvia tum gladio cincta virilis militiae uxor agitabat*' ('Antony was always evil minded, and his wife Fulvia, wearing the sword of manly military service, goaded him on'). This echoes Valerius Maximus' reference to the dagger (*pugio*), Fulvia wore on her *stola* (dress or robe).[9] Antony must have been impressed, and her influence must have been significant, because he struck coins bearing her image as a representation of Victory – the first time that Roman coinage had featured a woman. Another possible first was in city name-changing, when Antony's supporters renamed the city of Eumenia in Phrygia as Fulviana; subsequent mintings of the coins bear this name.

Fulvia exerted considerable influence on Mark Antony before and after the assassination of Julius Caesar, effectively harnessing the thuggish gangs of former husband Clodius to help Antony against Dolabella. She also took an enthusiastically active role in the subsequent bloody proscriptions, accompanying her husband to his military headquarters in Brundisium[10] and confounding Cicero's attempts to have Antony declared an enemy of the state in his absence.[11]

All the while, Antony was conducting an affair with Lycoris, the accomplished mime artist whom Cornelius Gallus celebrated in his elegies. Such was his attraction to Fulvia, though, that Antony renounced Lycoris for Fulvia. Fulvia's daughter, Clodia Pulcher, meanwhile, married the young, thrusting Octavian.

In 42 BCE, when Antony and Octavian left Rome to go after Brutus and Cassius, Fulvia was left behind to guard the fort, literally. Dio records that

Fulvia was in complete control: Publius Servilius and Lucius Antonius nominally were consuls, but in reality it was Antonius and Fulvia pulling all the strings. She, the mother-in-law of Octavian and wife of Antony, despised Lepidus, whom she considered lazy, and got on with things herself as she pleased. According to Dio,[12] Fulvia was one of the most powerful people in Rome at this time and proceeded to fight Antony's corner tirelessly, winning support from veterans when she toured Italy, children in tow.[13] And all of this despite the tensions caused by Antony's latest affair, this time with Cleopatra. Fulvia even helped raise eight legions for Antony to fight against Octavian in the Perusine War.[14]

When Octavian returned to Rome in 41 BCE to sort out the land settlement issues for Caesar's veterans, the acrimony between Octavian and Antony continued. Octavian took the opportunity to accuse Fulvia of megalomania and to divorce Fulvia's daughter, Clodia; the insult implicit in this was heightened when Octavian declared that he returned her still the virgin she was the day he married her.[15] Fulvia was also trying to delay the land settlements until Antony returned to Rome, so that he could share the credit with Octavian. Fulvia then struck an alliance with her brother-in-law, Lucius Antonius, and declared her endorsement of Mark Antony over Octavian.[16]

The eight legions she had raised around Italy occupied Rome for a short time while Lucius first mustered his troops at Praeneste, but then fell back to Perusia (modern Perugia), where he was besieged by Octavian. Lucius waited for Antony's legions in Gaul to come to his aid.[17] A serious communication breakdown meant that Antony remained unaware of Lucius' plight and so failed to help him. Appian records that Fulvia 'urged Ventidius, Asinius, and Calenus from Gaul to help Lucius, and having gathered another army, she sent it to Lucius under the command of Plancus'.[18]

After two months, in February 40 BCE, the siege of Perusia was ended when Lucius' forces were starved into surrender. Many of the inhabitants were slaughtered; they and others lost their land to veterans. Octavian posted Lucius into obscurity to Spain. Fulvia escaped death too, exiled to Greece with her children. She met with Antony, only to find that he was much displeased by her unwomanly prosecution of the war. Antony returned to Rome; Fulvia died in Sicyon, near Corinth.[19] She had been cynically scapegoated by the Triumvirs in an attempt to establish common ground between themselves. Antony married

Octavian's sister, Octavia Minor, in a further doomed attempt to cement the ailing alliance and a feeble public demonstration of his 'reconciliation' with Octavian. The only positive thing to come out of Fulvia's death was that Octavia adopted and cared for Fulvia's children.

Octavia was Mark Antony's fourth wife. The marriage made Antony and Octavian brothers-in-law, and as such was one of the most politically sensitive unions in a society where political marriages had almost become *de riguer* amongst elite families, where the desire for successful political advancement was sufficient grounds for casual divorce. The marriage was sanctioned by senatorial decree, necessary because it was within the *annus luctus* – the mourning period in which a widow could not remarry – and Octavia was pregnant with her late husband's third child, Claudia Marcella the Younger.

Things seem to have gone well at the start. Antony minted a coin bearing Octavia's portrait, making her the second Roman woman to feature on a coin after Fulvia, her immediate predecessor in Antony's affections. The couple travelled together, with Octavia happily residing with her husband in Athens during the winter of 39/38 BCE.[20] It was there that she was accorded the status of Athena Polias in Rome's eastern provinces.

Plutarch adds that 'there was even more opportunity for a reconciliation with Caesar [Octavian]. For when Antony reached Italy, and Caesar manifestly intended to make no charges against him, Antony himself was ready to put upon Fulvia the blame for whatever was charged against himself.'[21]

When it came to dealing with those loyal to Lucius, Octavian showed none of the clemency shown to Lucius or Fulvia. He chose 15 March, the anniversary of Julius Caesar's assassination, to have 300 Roman senators and equestrians executed. Perusia was plundered and razed as a warning for others contemplating defiance.

The Perusine War over, Octavian left for Gaul, tasking Agrippa as urban praetor in Rome to defend Italy against Sextus Pompeius (67–35 BCE), the other son of Pompey. In July 40 BCE, Sextus raided southern Italy while Agrippa was preoccupied with the Ludi Apollinares – games held in honour of Apollo. Agrippa attacked Sextus Pompeius forcing him to withdraw.[22] In August, both Sextus and Antony invaded Italy independently of each other. Agrippa retook Sipontum from Antony, bringing an end to the hostilities, and was one of the intermediaries through whom Antony and Octavian agreed on peace.[23]

Octavian, however, was informed that Salvidienus – still his chief general at this time - had offered to betray him to Antony: Salvidienus was prosecuted and either executed or committed suicide. Agrippa was now Octavian's leading general.

Meanwhile, Sextus was still acting the renegade and had to be dealt with. By agreement with the Triumvirate, in 39 BCE he was installed in Sicily and Sardinia. Antony and Octavian both coveted an alliance with Sextus, although Octavian had emerged as the favourite after he married Scribonia, a daughter of Lucius Scribonius Libo – a follower of Sextus as well as of his father-in-law. The previous year, Scribonia had been forced to divorce her second husband, Publius Cornelius Scipio, so that Octavian could marry her. The marriage may always have been doomed because Octavian, reputedly, was irritated by Scribonia's constant nagging over his infidelities. Scribonia bore Octavian's only natural child, the wayward Julia, who was born on the same day that he chose to divorce Scribonia little more than a year after their wedding. This was so that he could marry the redoubtable Livia Drusilla, who was six months pregnant with her second child by then husband, Tiberius Claudius Nero.

As if the social and economic problems ignited by the eviction of long-established farmers were not enough for Octavian to deal with, Sextus Pompey's piratical activities around Sicily, Corsica and Sardinia only served to exacerbate them. His frequent interceptions of Roman shipping was beginning to affect the grain supply. Antony and Octavian decided that things had gone far enough, and in 39 BCE negotiated an agreement with Sextus to stop the piracy. Appian says that Sextus entertained hopes of replacing Lepidus as the third Triumvir, but had to make do with an official confirmation that the three islands were rightfully his by the Pact of Misenum – in return for agreeing to stop his piracy. Sextus' admiral and second-in-command, the freedman Menas, took Sardinia from Octavian's governor, Marcus Lurius. Menas encouraged Sextus to kidnap and murder Antony and Octavian during their celebrations of the deal on Sextus' flagship, but Sextus declined.

If Octavian believed that the pact would see an end to the piracy, then he was to be disappointed. Octavian accused Sextus of breaching the pact when he started raiding Italian coastal towns; he attempted to take Sicily by force, but was defeated in two naval battles off Messina in 37 BCE. Octavian then turned for support to the experienced generals Marcus Vipsanius Agrippa and Titus Statilius Taurus. Agrippa wintered by training a navy on land and building a fleet near Lake Avernus. He then clashed with Sextus at Mylae in August 36 BCE, and again a month later, while Lepidus and Statilius Taurus invaded Sicily. Agrippa destroyed all but seventeen of Sextus' fleet in the Battle of Naulochus, while the survivors of his army surrendered. Sextus escaped by abandoning Sicily, losing his only base of support. He fled east with the remnants of his forces, but was captured and executed in Miletus without trial by Marcus Titius.

In the meantime, Antony was in need of troops to attack Parthia if he was to pass safely through Mesopotamia, Armenia and Parthia. He agreed to provide 120 ships, so that Octavian could resume his assault on Sextus, in exchange for 20,000 troops to fight the Parthians. Octavian was also able to bring Lepidus on board for a simultaneous joint attack on Sicily. When Octavian only provided 2,000 soldiers, Antony took this as a provocative slight.

Lepidus, who had raised a large army of fourteen legions and a not inconsiderable navy, naturally felt sidelined; even more so as he had initiated the first troop landings in Sicily and had taken several principal towns. Lepidus' sulky reaction gave Octavian the excuse he needed when, Sextus Pompey defeated, Lepidus stationed his legions in Sicily, arguing that he should take the island into his territories; alternatively, he naively suggested Octavian could have Sicily and Africa, if he agreed to give back his former provinces – Spain and Gaul – as stipulated by the lex Titia. Octavian was unimpressed, accusing Lepidus of usurping his power and fomenting rebellion. Things went from bad to worse when Lepidus' legions defected to Octavian, and Lepidus was obliged to submit. Octavian stripped Lepidus of all his offices except that of Pontifex Maximus, and exiled him to Cape Circeii, about 10km south-east of Rome

In the meantime, both Antony and Octavian needed military success to provide booty for their troops and augment their reputations as commanders. Octavian declared war in Illyricum to bring it under Roman sway, while Antony was girding up for his conflict with Parthia, taking advantage of schisms caused by the new Parthian king, Phraates IV (r. 37–2 BCE). Phraates is famous for murdering his father and all his thirty brothers. Antony made the mistake of overextending himself, and was forced to retreat with considerable losses.

As noted above, Antony married Octavia, Octavian's sister, in 40 BCE. She bore him to two daughters: Antonia the Elder and Antonia Minor. After

Antony's defeat in Parthia, Cleopatra had replenished his army, allowing him to invade Armenia in 34 BCE, seizing its king, Artavasdes, and occupying the country. Antony installed his son, Alexander Helios, as the ruler of Armenia, Media and Parthia; Cleopatra Selene II was crowned ruler of Cyrenaica and Libya, and Ptolemy Philadelphus was crowned ruler of Phoenicia, Syria and Cilicia. He also slyly conferred the title 'Queen of Kings' on Cleopatra, increasing fears in the Senate that Cleopatra 'was planning a war of revenge that was to array all the East against Rome, establish herself as empress of the world at Rome, cast justice from Capitolium, and inaugurate a new universal kingdom'.[24]

Octavian became consul again on 1 January 33 BCE, opening the session in the Senate with a vitriolic attack on Antony's nepotism, citing the titles and territories he had bestowed on his relatives and on Cleopatra, his queen.

Antony by now was living openly in Alexandria with Cleopatra; Octavia was unceremoniously packed off back to Rome. Antony minted coins to commemorate the Armenian victory, mimicked a Roman triumph in celebration and read out a declaration, known as the 'Donations of Alexandria', in which he parcelled out territories to Cleopatra's children. Cleopatra represented everything many Roman men loathed about ostentatious women: she was educated, politically astute, militarily powerful, somewhat promiscuous, she dominated powerful men and she was a monarch, a queen. Octavian saw his chance and, working with his friend and advisor Gaius Maecanas, used the humiliating dismissal of his sister to spread propaganda to the effect that Antony was losing his 'Romanitas' by rejecting a legitimate Roman spouse in favour of an 'Oriental paramour'. It was also suggested that Antony was planning to establish a second Senate in Alexandria.

In 32 BCE, the widening breach between Antony and Octavian led to about a third of senators, including both of that year's consuls, leaving Rome and defecting to Antony. Antony publicly and officially divorced Octavia, and went to Ephesus with Cleopatra to join their huge fleet, provided in large part by Cleopatra. Afterwards, Antony moved to Athens. His land forces came down from Armenia and set sail under L. Canidius Crassus.

However, the defections were not all one way. Octavian was able to take into his fold two key deserters from Antony in the autumn of 32 BCE: Munatius Plancus and Marcus Titius. The intelligence they brought with them was priceless, giving Octavian the ammunition he required to confirm to the Senate all his accusations against Antony.

Things got even more sordid when Octavian forced his way into the sacrosanct temple of the Vestal Virgins – a state archive amongst other things – and, with the help of the fickle Munatius Plancus, accessed Antony's confidential will, the details of which he publicly revealed. The will made substantial provision for his sons by Cleopatra to inherit Roman territories as kingdoms, designated Alexandria as the site for a tomb for him and his queen and named her son Caesarian as Caesar's legitimate heir. In late 32 BCE, the Senate revoked Antony's powers as consul and Octavian declared war on Cleopatra's regime in Egypt. It was obvious that Antony was going to support Egypt, so Antony and Octavian were effectively at war. Antony was declared an enemy of the state, and the two sides faced each other with roughly 200,000 troops apiece.

Chapter 13

Actium and Empire

The increasingly fragile relationship between the Triumvirates Octavian and Mark Antony finally shattered in 33 BCE. Octavian succeeded in having the Senate vote for a war against Egypt, culminating in 31 BCE in the decisive naval action off Actium, in which Cleopatra took flight with her fleet, soon to be followed by Antony. Octavian then invaded Egypt, and Antony's armies deserted to Octavian on 1 August 30 BCE.

Antony's plan was to invade Italy towards the end of 32 BCE. He got as far as Corcyra, where his way was blocked by a squadron of Octavian's ships. So he retired to winter at Patrae, while most of his fleet anchored in the Ambracian Gulf and his armies camped near the promontory of Actium. Marcus Vipsanius Agrippa defeated Antony's supporter Quintus Nasidius in a naval battle at Patrae.

By midsummer of 31 BC, Antony had manoeuvred his army into Greece; Octavian soon followed. Octavian brought with him his chief military advisor and closest friend, Marcus Vipsanius Agrippa, to command his naval forces. Although the ground forces were numerically comparable, Octavian's fleet was superior. Antony's fleet was made up of large vessels, but with inexperienced crews and commanders. Octavian's fleet comprised smaller, more agile vessels crewed with experienced sailors.

Octavian moved his soldiers across the Adriatic Sea to confront Antony near Actium. Meanwhile, Agrippa disrupted Antony's supply lines with his navy. The first action of the year was when Agrippa took the Greek city and naval port of Methone, previously loyal to Antony. Gaius Sosius, commanding a squadron in Mark Antony's fleet, managed to defeat a pro-Octavian flotilla led by Lucius Arruntius, but Dio tells us that when the latter was reinforced by Agrippa, Sosius' ally Tarcondimotus – the King of Cilicia – was killed and Sosius himself was forced to flee.[1]

Octavian's proposals for a conference were rejected by Antony. Agrippa then landed troops near Antony's camp on the north side of the strait, but Antony would not be tempted out: he was waiting for the rest of his forces to arrive. Cleopatra advised Antony that garrisons should be installed in strong towns, and that the main fleet should return to Alexandria. The fact that she was the provider of most of the fleet ensured that this was agreed.

So began the Battle of Actium, the largest naval battle in almost 200 years and one of the world's most decisive. The two fleets clashed outside the Gulf of Actium (modern Preveza) on the morning of 2 September 31 BCE. Antony had a fleet of 500 ships, of which 230 were large war galleys with towers brimming with armed men. He led these through the straits towards the open sea. Octavian had about 250 warships waiting beyond the straits and led by Agrippa from the left wing of the fleet, with Lucius Arruntius in the centre and Marcus Lurius on the right. Titus Statilius Taurus commanded Octavian's armies. Antony and Gellius Publicola commanded the right wing of Antony's fleet, while Marcus Octavius and Marcus Insteius led the centre, with Cleopatra's squadron positioned behind them. Gaius Sosius was in charge of the left wing of the fleet, while Antony's chief lieutenant, Publius Canidius Crassus, was in command of Antony's land armies.

Antony suffered a huge blow when one of his former generals, Quintus Dellius, defected to Octavian, taking with him Antony's battle plans.[2] According to Dio, this intelligence told Octavian that Antony and Cleopatra's plan was to burst through his naval blockade and flee. Initially, he was happy to allow this, confident that he could catch them and that the rest of the fleet would surrender when they saw their leaders' evident cowardice. Agrippa, however, argued that Antony's ships, although larger, could outsail Octavian's if they hoisted sails, and that Octavian should engage now. Octavian followed Agrippa's advice.[3]

Octavian's fleet, with its better-trained crews, soon saw off Antony's larger and less experienced navy. When Cleopatra saw how things were going, she retreated to open sea without entering the fray, leaving Antony to fend for himself. The commanders of Antony's land forces surrendered their legions without a fight. Antony managed to escape to Alexandria, but by the end of the day, much of his fleet was languishing at the bottom of the Ionian Sea.

The spring of 30 BCE saw Octavian attacking Alexandria. Antony, meanwhile, tried to raise an army in Cyrenaica with the help of Lucius Pinarius, but Pinarius had switched over to Octavian, who ordered him to move his four legions towards Alexandria while Octavian would advance from the west. All

Antony and Cleopatra could do now was wait for Octavian and Pinarius to arrive.

Before that, however, Antony attacked Pinarius with 10,000 soldiers, unaware that he was outnumbered two to one. Pinarius destroyed what was left of Antony's army. Antony then made his way back to Alexandria before Octavian arrived. As Octavian approached, the remnants of Antony's cavalry and fleet surrendered to Octavian. For Antony, the war was over.

The relationship, military and otherwise, between Antony and Cleopatra went back to 41 BCE. Before that, in 43 BCE, Cleopatra had allied with the leader of the Caesarian party in the east, the fickle Publius Cornelius Dolabella, who recognized her son by Caesar, Caesarion, as her co-ruler. But soon after, Dolabella was defeated in Laodicea by Cassius and committed suicide by proxy, by ordering one of his soldiers to kill him.[4]

Cleopatra and Antony ordered the execution of her sister Arsinoë, carried out sacrilegiously and scandalously on the steps of the Temple of Artemis; apart from her misguided, fatal defection, she was, it seems, a pretender to the Egyptian throne. Cleopatra also had Sarapion, her top general in Cyprus, killed for his collusion with Cassius. Appian concludes that Antony was now putty in Cleopatra's hands: 'Whatever Cleopatra wished it was done, regardless of the laws, human or divine.'[5] Cleopatra agreed the support Antony needed for his campaign against Parthia. The, possibly apocryphal, story where Antony tried to impress Cleopatra with his skills as a fisherman, shows how easily she could humour and dupe him, ever urging him to focus his foreign policy to the benefit of Egypt. Antony surreptitiously had fish attached to his line by divers; she retaliated the next day by replicating the prank, thus exposing his unsuccessful efforts to impress her, much to the mirth of his audience.

Cleopatra gave birth to twins by Antony on 25 December 40 BCE; the children were named Alexander Helios and Cleopatra Selene II. There then followed a hiatus in the relationship. In 36 BCE, Antony returned to Alexandria on his way to wage his war with the Parthians. The old acquaintance was rekindled and Antony remained in the Egyptian capital, marrying Cleopatra even though he was at the time still married to Octavia Minor, sister of Octavian. He and Cleopatra had another child, Ptolemy Philadelphus, during their stay in Antioch. Lucrative territories were signed over to Cleopatra to bolster the substantial natural resources and crops she already had access to:

Crete, Cyrene, Cilicia, Phoenicia and part of Arabia corresponding to modern Jordan were all ceded to Egypt, as were parts of Syria and troublesome Judaea, ruled by Herod the Great. Cedar from Lebanon for shipbuilding, the rare and priceless Balm of Gilead (*commiphora gileadensis* and *pistacia lentiscus*) from around Herod's Jericho – a key constituent in popular medicines and fine perfumes – Dead Sea bitumen (an essential ingredient in embalming fluid); all of this trade and produce came Cleopatra's way by the trireme load.

In 34 BCE, another opulent and dazzling ceremony – again with Cleopatra dressed up as Isis – celebrated the carving up of the Egyptian empire, the so-called 'Donations of Alexandria'. As noted, Cleopatra was Queen of Kings over Egypt while Caesarion took Cyprus as King of Kings; Alexander Helios and Philadelphus became kings east (Armenia, Media and Parthia) and west (Phoenicia, Syria and Cilicia) of the Euphrates, while Cleopatra Selene II was made queen of Cyrene and Libya. Cleopatra added Philopatris, 'lover of her country', to her titles. Caesarion was depicted as the Egyptian god Horus, while Cleopatra called herself *Nea Isis*.[6]

The 'Donations', reeking of monarchism as they did – not least with Caesarion elevated to 'King of the Kings' – must have unsettled the Senate. Antony, as we have seen, even tried to have Caesarion accepted as a true heir of Julius Caesar. All of this was perfect ammunition for Octavian, who was busy denouncing Antony as an enemy of Rome, asserting that he was seeking to establish a personal monarchy over Rome on behalf of Caesarion, bypassing the Senate.

While at Samos, Cleopatra sent Octavian a message with a gift of a gold crown and throne, offering to abdicate in favour of her sons. Octavian wanted to keep her on side as he had plans to parade her as a trophy in his triumph. Antony tried in vain to secure the army stationed near Paraetonium under Pinarius; he sent his eldest son Antyllus with money to Octavian and an offer to live his life out at Athens as a private citizen. Next spring, he was attacked on two sides: C. Cornelius Gallus advanced from Paraetonium while Octavian landed at Pelusium, assisted by Cleopatra. Antony was defeated by Gallus.

Even though Antony won a victory at Alexandria on 31 July 30 BCE, yet more of Antony's men deserted, leaving him with insufficient forces to fight Octavian. Antony had no choice but to take his own life. According to Plutarch, Cleopatra, fearing for her life from an Antony who believed that she had betrayed him, locked herself away in her mausoleum with her slave girls, sending messengers to Antony to inform him that she was dead. Antony ordered a slave, Eros, to kill him, but Eros elected to kill himself instead. Antony, following suit, stabbed himself in the stomach and lay down to die, but the wound proved not to be fatal. A further message arrived from Cleopatra with instructions to go to her; Antony agreed and was carried to the mausoleum. Cleopatra had already closed the massive, cumbersome doors so he had to be secured to a stretcher and unceremoniously hauled up through a window by Cleopatra's slave-women, with some considerable difficulty. This only served to exacerbate his wound and pain. Once inside, he was laid on a couch while an hysterical Cleopatra lamented at length. Antony calmed her down, drank a glass of wine and died.

Octavian, as noted, had wanted to take Cleopatra alive, to peacock her triumphantly in Rome along with her many luxuries and treasures, which were now perilously poised on a funeral pyre awaiting ignition. Proculeius was dispatched to the mausoleum to capture her, and managed to stop her from stabbing herself with a hidden knife. He then took the precaution of searching her for concealed poisons. Plutarch tells us that Cleopatra was known to carry poison in a hollow comb in her hair.[7] One of Octavian's freedmen, Epaphroditus, was left on suicide watch, and ordered to keep her comfortable.[8] After Antony's funeral, Cleopatra contracted a fever and depression; the concomitant loss of appetite led her to hope for death through starvation, but this was dispelled when Octavian made cruel threats regarding the possible fate of her children.

In the end, Cleopatra managed to deceive not only Epaphroditus but also Octavian, who thought he had finally persuaded her to live on. Her guards carelessly allowed a meal of succulent figs to be delivered to her and to two of her slave women; by the time the guards realised what they had done, Cleopatra was dead – 'upon a golden couch, arrayed in royal state' – and her maidservants, Iras and Charmian, were dying. Plutarch says that a venomous snake was hidden in the fig leaves or that it had been concealed in a water jar. Suetonius also says that an asp bite was responsible for her death.[9]

Octavian had relentlessly pursued a policy of denigrating Antony and Cleopatra and their relationship. He ridiculed and rubbished Antony and Cleopatra when he officially declared war on the queen, and officially relieved Antony of the powers he had feebly ceded to a woman. He alleged that Antony's mind was befuddled by drugs, insinuating that Cleopatra was a witch. He said the war would be fought against a motley force comprising Mardian the eunuch, Potheinus, Iras, Cleopatra's hairdresser, and Charmian, her lady-in-waiting, for they were in charge in the Antony and Cleopatra camp.[10] Octavian's propaganda machine was ruthlessly effective, painting Cleopatra as the enemy of the state before and after Actium. The vilification was to achieve mythic proportions in the nationalist poems of Virgil and Horace and in the politically independent Propertius. The more Octavian exaggerated Cleopatra and the threat she posed to a paranoid Roman state, then the greater his achievement when he eventually defeated her and extinguished that threat.

Following his mother's death, Caesarion was proclaimed pharaoh by the Egyptians but soon after was captured and killed, 'butchered without compunction'. Octavian had methodically exploited his position as Caesar's heir to further his own political career, and he was well aware of the dangers in allowing another person to do the same. He therefore followed the advice of Arius Didymus, one of Octavian's men, who neatly paraphrased Homer: 'It's no good thing to have too many Caesars.'[11]

Thus ended the Hellenistic, Ptolemaic line of Egyptian pharaohs, and with it all Egyptian pharaohs. Elder son apart, the children of Cleopatra and Antony were taken back to Rome to live with Antony's widow, Octavia Minor. Cleopatra Selene was later married by Octavian to Juba II of Mauretania.[12]

Within a month of Cleopatra's death, Octavian was named pharaoh and Egypt became his. In 27 BCE, the Senate bestowed upon Octavian the name of Augustus. Augustus was Rome's first emperor and would preside over the transition of the oligarchic, democratic Republic into the autocratic Roman Empire.

Chapter 14

The Cleopatra Effect

Cleopatra was, to some extent, scapegoated for the civil wars at the end of the first century BCE. The poets at the close of the Republic and in the early Principate were unanimous in their contempt and derision. Virgil is perhaps the most restrained but, by the same token, the most eloquent. In Book 4 of the *Aeneid*, Dido is betrayed by Aeneas, sidelined by his dedication to the mission to found Rome. Dido is incandescent with rage, and in a pit of misery and despair, 'she rages, out of her mind, and rushes through the city, mad as a Bacchant'. She confronts the treacherous Aeneas and promises to haunt him for ever:

> 'When I'm gone I'll follow you into the black fire of Hell, when icy death draws out the spirit from my limbs; my ghost will be everywhere; you'll pay the price, you traitor, and I will hear about it – the news will reach me deep down among the deadmen.'[1]

Virgil's audience would have recognized and appreciated the poignancy of Dido's threats: Rome did indeed pay the price for Aeneas' duplicity, with the devastating Punic Wars. Aeneas was indeed haunted by Dido, meeting again at arm's length in their frosty underworld encounter. The Dido episode resonated uncomfortably with the political upheaval caused so recently by Cleopatra, a foreign queen eerily reminiscent of Dido, whose facility for global power-play would be likened to the unnatural skills of Dido as sorceress.

More graphically, Cleopatra takes centre-stage on Aeneas' highly symbolic shield *ekphrasis*, which describes the armour given to him by Venus to fight for the establishment of Rome and the genesis of its proud history. She is twice called *regina* – 'the queen' – still a dirty six-letter word in Rome even so long after the fall of the monarchy. Her gods are monsters, *monstra*, which assume the shape of all manner of species and are ranged against the traditional Roman pantheon. Her defeat and her flight to Egypt are thrown into full relief.[2]

Horace excoriates the 'mad queen' – *regina demens* – in his famous poem celebrating her defeat at Actium: 'now the time has come to drink, get up and dance and feast!' Horace was sure that Cleopatra was plotting the death and destruction of Roman rule. Her retinue is made up of eunuchs: squalid, diseased and drunk, while she too is inebriated: she is a doom monster – *fatale monstrum*. Nevertherless, he concedes patronizingly that, in death, she does not act *muliebriter* – 'like a woman'. She has no terror of the sword and bravely brings on the snakes: no humiliating or undignified appearance in a Roman triumph for Cleopatra. The poem echoes sentiments first introduced in the *Epodes*. Written soon after Actium, Horace sneers at the effeminate Roman soldiers under Antony and Cleopatra: they are enslaved by a woman and answer to eunuchs, they have all gone soft, as evidenced by their decidedly un-Roman use of the *canopium*, the mosquito net.[3] Real Romans don't use mosquito nets.

Propertius is no less hostile. Cleopatra features in a poem in which she is compared with Cynthia. Cynthia is the poet's *domina*; she dominated him just as Cleopatra dominated Antony. Propertius is enslaved by a woman, just as Antony was. Calling a mistress *domina,* and calling their love for that *domina* '*servitium amoris*', were two of the outrageous ways in which the love poets controversially turned the usual man-woman relationship on its head: in the real world, the man was always the dominant partner, a real Roman would never be a slave to love. Insinuating Cleopatra into the poem embroils her in the decadent, erotic and exotic un-Roman world of the love poets, where women ruled and men were slaves, were love-sick or languished, '*exclusus*', locked-out on the doorstep, were cuckolded as pathetic lovers whose only combat experience was in the war of love, '*militia amoris*'.[4] Propertius, of course, was one of the champions of this roué lifestyle; his portrait of Cleopatra here is one of the first instances of her as an embodiment of woman's domination of men, a symbol which has endured down the years.

Cleopatra comes at the end of a list of powerful women Propertius uses to justify his Cynthia's domineering behaviour, but it is with Cleopatra that he piles on the invective when the poem turns into a celebration of Augustus. Chiming with Horace, we hear that she plotted to take over Rome, her marriage was sordid and Egypt was a place of deceit and disaster. She was a whore of a queen (*meretrix regina*), she tried to supplant Roman gods with Egyptian and to influence the Tiber with the Nile before her death. She had stained the reputation of the Macedonian house and was 'shagged out' (*trita*) by sex with her own slaves. To Romans, the latter was a cardinal sin and a crime which would have resonated with Propertius' audience: centuries before, at the dawn of Rome, the noblewoman Lucretia took her life at the mere prospect of such a heinous crime, while Verginia too died for her chastity. The triumphalist tone is resumed by Propertius in his celebratory poem exulting at the victory of the Battle of Actium and the defeat of Cleopatra.[5]

Significantly, Virgil, Horace and Propertius all studiously avoid naming Cleopatra: she is *illa, Aegyptia coniunx* ('the Egyptian wife'), *regina* ('queen'), *femina* or *mulier* ('woman'). Cleopatra's identity has been half erased, she has become a redacted opaque figure, to misquote Virgil, *horribile dictu* – 'too horrible to mention'. She is rendered halfway to *damnatio memoriae* ('condemnation of memory'). Cicero had also exhibited the same depersonalizing, cringing horror at the thought of her.

A century or so after her death, Cleopatra features in Juvenal's list of effeminate pathics – grieving after Actium, *maesta*;[6] Martial satirises her death.[7] In the epic *De Bello Civili*, Lucan's Cleopatra is evil: her beauty is sluttish (*incesta*) – a swipe at her marriage to her brother – her make-up is excessive and her jewels and clothing ostentatious. The banquet she lays on for Caesar is insufferably opulent, beyond anything then known at Rome, and is described at length as the last word in *luxus* ('luxury' or 'excess').[8] In the words of Pothinus, as he tries to foment war against Caesar, she is *inpia* – 'unholy' - devoid of that most Roman of Roman qualities, *pietas*, as she scuttles between husbands. She is selling off Rome and, witch-like, seduces Caesar with potions; their affair is *incestus* ('impure' or 'sinful'), their love *obscaena* and impious.

Unanimous as the poets are in their condemnation and vitriol, their opinions must, of course, be treated with caution. There was never going to be an objective picture, bearing in mind the exigencies of Augustan propaganda, patronage and nationalism, the universally held belief that women *per se* were inferior and should know their place, the demands of genre, particularly in satire, and the subjectivity, fear and loathing. Michael Grant called it all 'one of the most terrible outbursts of hatred in history'.[9]

As we know, the Romans were always unnerved by and uncomfortable with clever, educated, assertive women. Cleopatra, too, came to embody everything the Roman man suspected, feared or despised about difficult and flamboyant women.

She was certainly gifted, highly intelligent, assertive, ambitious and conspicuous: after all, she was a (successful) head of state, a (respected) military commander and a (capable) strategist. She infatuated and manipulated two of Rome's leading generals and most powerful politicians, although this may tell us as much about the innate weaknesses of even the strongest of men as it does about the strength of Cleopatra. And she convincingly assumed the guise of Isis, one of Egypt's most prominent deities. She restored the Egyptian empire to its original boundaries, rebuilt the ailing economy and made it a force to be reckoned with again within the Mediterranean. Quite simply, her actions indirectly helped shape the Roman constitution and the establishment of the Roman Empire after the Battle of Actium. There was a stark and vivid contrast between her and the typically silent, publicly invisible and politically insignificant Roman woman. No wonder then that government propaganda and innate Roman conservatism demanded that Cleopatra was commonly viewed as a *fatale monstrum* ('deadly monster').

Chapter 15

The Social and Literary Impact

What effect did all this civil unrest have on Roman society and culture? Many thousands of men fought and died in the wars, but, as in all wars, women and children were involved too and suffered in greater numbers, rendered widows or orphans, sentenced to a life as full-time carers for the homecoming injured, reduced to penury because the breadwinner was dead, disabled or proscribed. Rape may well have been a further destructive by-product, with its attendant life-changing, lifelong problems: trauma, sexually transmitted infections, unwanted pregnancies, dangerous abortions, abject shame and exile, divorced from home and family. What we know about war before the Roman civil wars and from conflicts since, right up to the present day, it would be surprising indeed if women were not violated.

Appian tells us that life for the Romans under the Second Triumvirate, for example, was so bad that the recent days of Caesar's dictatorship were viewed with some nostalgia, a golden age (47, 14, 4). Indeed, how could it be anything other than catastrophic? The Second Triumvirate regime was a new, *ad hoc* form of government in which the Triumvirates made it up as they went along, depending on events and outcomes. The Romans and Italian peoples were caught up in the middle of it all, and suffered accordingly. Historians since the classical period have by and large minimized or omitted altogether the social impact of the civil wars.

At the time, Roman society was changing, for men and for women: the ten-year military service stipulation was enforced less frequently; some women were enjoying a new-found independence, accelerated through a more forgiving and equal form of marriage. For men, alternative routes along the *cursus honorum* were increasingly popular, as a life in law or politics replaced soldiering as careers of choice or necessity; dissenting voices emerged from 'bohemian' poets and their hangers-on. We have noted how conservatives in earlier days, like Cato the Elder, firmly believed that war was good for you

– and good for the Roman people – in that it kept the traditionally belligerent Romans robust and resilient. On the other hand, all this new Greek stuff was making the Romans soft. Cato the Younger was of a similar opinion.

The impact of these changes on women was significant. Epigraphical evidence gives a very clear picture of what the Roman wife and mother was expected to be like and the qualities she was expected to exhibit. Although there is obviously a degree of cliché, idealization and stereotyping in the numerous epigraphs which have survived, we do get a good idea of what the Roman *matrona* was expected to be like. Certainly, much of this epigraphical evidence would suggest a high degree of subservience, compliance and unobtrusiveness amongst the women honoured and remembered.

Fairly typical is this funerary epigraph: 'Here lies Amymone, wife of Marcus, the best and most beautiful, wool spinner, dutiful, modest, careful with money, chaste, stay-at-home.'[1]

Amymone's virtues reflect the ideal Roman wife, the *matrona*. Many of the necessary qualifying epithets are here: *optima*, *pulcherrima*, *lanifica*, *pia*, *pudica*, *frugi*, *casta*, *domiseda*. Claudia, another dutiful wife and mother, was off the same block: beautiful, loving, mother of two children (one dead, one living), clever in conversation (*sermone lepida*), good bearing (*incessu commoda*), looked after the home and worked away at the wool (*lanam fecit*).[2]

As for the men, a number of poets were able to eschew the traditional *mos maiorum*, rejecting the *cursus honorum*, turning their backs on bar and battlefield for a life of *otium* ('leisure'), during which they would while away their time penning poetry and pursuing the objects of their affection. Horrified traditionalists regarded this otiose lifestyle as frivolous and decidedly un-Roman. The 'war of love' stood in direct and defiant contrast to traditional military service, *militia*; to the *cursus honorum*, the respectable ladder of civic and military service; to *virtus*, bravery and manhood – badges of Roman-ness – and to the *mores* of the day. To the conservative, the soldier of love (*miles amoris*) was something of a social misfit – what we might call, anachronistically, a bit of a Bohemian.

A brief survey of this literary and social revolution will clearly demonstrate how, in concert with the political turmoil and revolution of the day, Rome and the Romans were massively affected in every aspect of their lives. The civil wars and the Triumvirates were not just about political machinations, battles and power play; they had an incalculable human aspect as well. Not least they inculcated a kind of anti-war movement amongst côteries of what we might term middle class liberals.

Propertius, Tibullus, Ovid and others cliché and chorus 'make love not war' in direct opposition to what was expected of them as men and citizens of imperial, expansionist and bellicose Rome. Instead of donning greaves and shields and spending the best part of their lives guarding or acquiring far-flung foreign parts, they assumed the mantle of pacifist and poet, versifying in a life of *otium* in a cosmopolitan Rome. Anagrammatically, they had joined the army of *Amor*, not the army of *Roma*. The soldier of love was fighting endless battles with his mistress in a war of love, the objective of his pseudo-military service. She is the enemy, the other half of the conflict, the *sine qua non* of the poet's military service and of the battles he was fighting; she is his *causa belli*. The poets actually allowed themselves to be dominated by their women (their *dominae*), and even to be enslaved by them in *servitium amoris*; their *cursus honorum* and military career was *militia amoris*. They languished, locked-out, humiliated and rejected, on the doorstep of a capricious woman, *exclusus amator*. Good Roman *militia* was being supplanted by feeble, lovelorn 'soldiers', who were under the control of women rather than centurions.

Among the flourishing côteries anxious to imbibe and parade Hellenism and other exotic influences we can recognize such poets as Licinius Calvus, Varro of Atax, Valerius Cato, Furius Bibaculus, Helvius Cinna, Cornificius, Ticidas and, most famously, Catullus. Collectively, they went under the name of *poetae novi*, *neoteroi*, *delicata iuventus* or *Cantores Euphorionis*.[3]

To the conservative, traditional Roman, war was an unquestioned and unquestionable fact of life: it had been ever-present and a constant since the foundation of the city in 753 BCE, and was credited with getting the Romans to the place they were at in the first century BCE: a truly dominant power and successful expansionist civilization dominating the Mediterranean region, and further afield. Catullus, though, managed to dodge the military life and only had to endure two years on the staff of propraetor C. Memmius, governor of Bythinia in 57-56 BCE. No doubt others were equally successful draft dodgers.

This unconventional, un-Roman way of life pursued by the outré poets might have been expected to encourage not only outrage amongst conservatives, but also a pacifist, anti-war attitude amongst its adherents. And to some extent it did: Propertius (50-15 BCE) indignantly demanded to know: 'why should

I breed sons for Rome's triumphs? No blood of mine will ever produce a soldier.'[4] However, Catullus, thirty-five years or so earlier, as unconventional as any of the new poets, had, surprisingly perhaps, taken the establishment line that marriage and procreation was very much a duty: in his wedding hymn (*carmen* 61) he urges the happy couple to 'produce sentries for the borders'.[4] It was their duty to produce legitimate children to maintain the birth rate, to ensure the survival of a particular family, to supply the Roman Army and bureaucracy, the land and the law with a source of recruits. In Catullus' case here, the exigencies of genre seem to have overruled any pacifistic sentiments held by him.

Catullus' other flirtation with military was when C. Licinius Calvus persuaded him to compose some scurrilous lines about the first Triumvirs, particularly Julius Caesar, and Mamurra, one of Caesar's engineers. Caesar generously forgave him in the end. Poems 29, 41, 43 and 57 are the guilty ones; 29 sets the tone with Caesar and Pompey in the firing line:

> 'Who can see this, who can stand it, save the shameless, the glutton, and gambler, that Mamurra Mentula should possess what long-haired Gaul had and remotest Britain had before? You sodomite Romulus [Pompey], will you see this and bear it? Then you are shameless, a glutton and a gambler. And will he now, proud and overflowing, saunter over each one's bed, like a little white dove or an Adonis? … For such a name, General, have you been to the furthest island of the west, that this love-weary Mentula of yours should squander twenty or thirty million? … First he wasted his patrimony; second the loot from Pontus; then third the loot from Spain, which even the goldbearing Tagus knows. Now he is feared by Gauls and Britain. Why do you indulge this scoundrel? What can he do but devour well-fattened inheritances? Was it for such a name, most wealthy father-in-law and son-in-law, that you have destroyed everything?' (trans. Leonard C. Smithers, London, Smithers 1894)

In poem 41, Mamurra is in the firing line again as 'the indebted man of Formianus', friend of 'this girl with the ugly nose – Ameana, the well-worn prostitute'. He re-emerges in 43 as the 'spendthrift from Formiae',

> 'Hello, girl, neither with the smallest nose,
> Nor with pretty feet nor with black little eyes
> Nor with long fingers nor with dry lips
> Nor clearly with a very refined tongue.
> Girlfriend of the spendthrift from Formiae,
> Does the province report that you are beautiful?'
> (© Greg Drudy)

Poem 57 sums it up nicely:

> 'Everything is turning out well for those disgusting Cinaedii Caesar and Mamurra the pathicus. No wonder: the stains are equal for both of them, But one is from the city and the other is from Formia, And they are so ingrained that they cannot be washed out: they are diseased equally, and both are twins, Both are educated in one little bed, Nor is the latter a more gluttonous adulterer than the former; They are allied rivals even for little girls. Everything is turning out well for those disgusting Cinaedii.' (trans. Johnny Brezhnev, 2002)

The principal genre in which we identify pacifism is late first-century BCE elegy and lyric: Propertius, Tibullus and Ovid – pacifist, non-violent subversives who challenged the Roman military ideal. However, we should not forget contemporary philosophers and even some historians. Stoics, Cynics and Epicureans all preach pacifistic views central to their respective philosophies. More surprisingly, evidence of pacifistic views comes also with Sallust and Livy; later, in the late first century CE, Tacitus was to deplore Roman butchery. In the visual arts, Octavian's (by then Augustus) Ara Pacis (symbolizing civilizing or pacifying rather than peace *per se*) and the tragic Dying Gaul – which may even have featured in Julius Caesar's gardens, the Horti Caesaris – evoke pacifism, the complete opposite of the jingoistic belligerence of, for example, the column of Marcus Aurelius or the Arch of Constantine. Other civic projects constructed during the civil wars, redolent of civilizing, included a Temple of Apollo on the Palatine, a temple dedicated to Julius Caesar in the Forum, the theatre of Marcellus (Octavian's nephew), Agrippa's Pantheon and Octavian's mausoleum.

The motifs of *miles* and *militia amoris* (love expressed in militaristic terms) which we find in the elegists and in Horace and Ovid are themselves indicative of pacifism. For a Roman to fight in the war of love as a soldier of love was at once the abnegation and rejection of the conventional Roman way – namely, pursuing the *cursus honorum* according to the *mos maiorum* – and also a vocalization of the fact that the only war to be fought was the war of love – in short, pacifism. However, it is not a love poet but a comic playwright who introduces the motif to Latin literature. In the *Persa,* Plautus (*c.* 254–184 BCE) has Paegnium retort to Sophoclidisca, 'Still, that warfare is waged [*militia militatur*] much more successfully by spirit than by weight', when she suggests that he is not old, or even weighty enough, for love (line 231). In *Truculentus*, Astaphium asserts that he is a soldier under his mistress' command (229).

We can assume that the device was also used in literature of the third and second centuries that has not survived, but much later, a bitter Catullus (*c.* 84–54? BCE) describes Berenice's clothing as spoils (66, 13f); he also uses *militia amoris* language in *Carmen* 37: 'For my girl, who has fled from my embrace, she whom I loved as none will be loved, for whom I fought ferocious fights' (13).

The girl could not care less about Catullus' skirmishes: she is now being made love to by all the 'piddling back-alley fornicators', and in particular by one Egnatius, who brushes his teeth in Spanish urine. There are at least 100 extant examples of *militia amoris* in Roman elegy and lyric poetry, and three poems are devoted exclusively to it.

Propertius (47-14 BCE) has a problem with Cynthia and vows to 'pitch his camp [*castra*], somewhere else' (4, 8, 55) because of her infidelity. In the face of violent and hysterical protests from Cynthia, when he considers going off travelling with Tullus (1, 6, 29-30), Propertius could not be clearer about his position and his pacifistic leanings when he exclaims, 'I'm not naturally suited to glory or for arms; Love's is the only warfare which the Fates have planned for me.' Propertius must serve under Venus (4, 1, 37). A victory over Cynthia is likened to a triumph (2, 14, 23ff), complete with booty. In poem 3, 6 we find an incredulous Propertius demanding to know from Postumus just how he can leave Galla, his wife, crying her eyes out, 'and follow the soldier's trade, behind Caesar's flags'. 'What good is Parthian plunder', he asks, when his wife's tears go unheeded? He curses 'any man who prefers the arms of the camp to those awaiting him in his bed'.

Ovid (43 BCE – 17/18 CE) adopts the motif when he describes himself as booty (*Amores* 1, 2, 19f); the analogy is developed at *Amores* 1, 7, 35f with a lively, albeit mocking, description of Ovid parading as a conquering hero in glory behind his one humiliated captive, a dishevelled girl. It is, though, with *Amores* 1, 2, 19ff that the *militia amoris* motif is most extensively drawn, with numerous military references aimed at explaining the debilitating effects of unrequited love: surrender, military action, armistices, unarmed enemies, chariots, prisoners whipped into line, pomp, gold are all there.

Propertius introduces mythology into the device when he associates himself with such famous warriors as Achilles and wild Hector (2, 22, 34). Paris fought his biggest battles on Helen's knee (3, 8, 32). Sex episodes with Cynthia are lengthy *Iliads*, the ultimate war story in Propertius' day (2, 1, 13). Ovid redresses the balance between the sexes in the *Ars Amatoria* (3, 1-4) which, in Books 1-2, offered advice aimed at men chasing women. Women, he refers to mock-heroically, as Amazons and Penthesilea; these are the subject of his tuition in Book 3. By 'arming' women he, nevertheless, realises he is effectively betraying his own sex, his comrades in arms (3, 667f).

In the opening poem of his collection, Tibullus (*c.* 55–19 BCE) assures Delia that he has no care for glory in a few lines which manage to combine two other motifs related to *militia amoris* – the slave of love, *servitium amoris*, and the locked-out lover, *paraclausithyron* or *exclusus amator*:

> 'It's right for you, Messalla, to campaign by land and sea and that the front of your house exhibits the spoils of enemies: I am a captive bound in the chains of a lovely girl; I sit as a doorman before her unyielding doors. I care not for glory, Delia dear; I only want to be with you, and I will pray that people will call me slob and idler … here I am brave centurion and legionary. Go away, trumpets and ensigns! take wounds to the greedy men, and take them wealth.' (1, 1, 53; 75)

In the same poem he tells us that, like Propertius, his family lost land to Octavian in the 41-40 BCE proscriptions (41f) and now lives in very much reduced circumstances.

For a brief moment in 2, 6, Tibullus capitulates and tells Macer, a military friend whom he chastises for going off to war, that he too is off to do battle after all. If Amor looks after soldiers, Tibullus will be a soldier, *miles*, headed for the camps: so goodbye sex and goodbye girls! Tibullus is strong, *vires*, and he loves the sound of that trumpet. But the slamming of the door in his face brings him back to reality, and silences his bragging and boastful words (7-12). In 2, 3, 33, Cupid has set up camp in his house, a notion repeated by Ovid with *castra Cupido* (*Amores* 1, 9, 1).

With 1, 10, Tibullus concludes his first book by tackling the anti-war question head-on in a poem entirely devoted to the issue. He opens with a demand to know who it was who first 'forged the fearful sword', the iron man who invented slaughter and introduced war to men and, in so doing, facilitated dreaded death? Tibullus concedes, though, that it was his fellow man who started using for war what were intended to be hunting weapons. He laments the fact that once there was a war-free world but that now he is 'dragged to war, and some enemy has probably' got a spear with his name on it. In some desperation he implores his Lares to protect him, in return for which he will sacrifice a pig. Let someone else glory in war; war is madness. As for hell,

> 'There are no fields of corn down there, no tidy vineyards, only bold Cerberus, and the foul ferryman of Styx's stream. There, with eyeless sockets and scorched hair, a pallid crowd wanders by the lakes of darkness.'

Tibullus, however, wants a contented and long life, working the land with Peace in complete control. He concludes with a denunciation of domestic violence in the war of love: 'he whose hands are cruel, should carry shield and pike, and stay far away from gentle Venus.'

Ovid has the most elaborate use of the metaphor of lover as soldier in *Amores* 1, 9. Here, in over forty-six lines, he runs through the gamut of military life in the field and compares it with life as a soldier of love, trying to convince his readers that lovers are far from lazy: on the contrary, physically and psychologically, they really do compete with soldiers. Every lover is in arms and Cupid is camped out in the field: '*militat omnis amans, et habet sua castra Cupido*'. He reprises this in the *Ars Amatoria* (2, 233-42), where he asserts that love is a kind of warfare, *militia species amor est*, and that military skills are the same as those required to win over a woman. In *Amores* 2, 12, Ovid compares his conquest over Corinna to a military victory, reinforcing the metaphor by citing warring women who have shaped history – Helen of Troy, Lavinia and the Sabine women. Other allusions to the similarities between love and war include the following: lovers who betray and open up the gates to the enemy (*Ars Amatoria* 3, 577f); his once flaccid penis is now erect, keen to go on campaign and get on the job (*Amores* 3, 7, 68); Ovid is a war veteran (*Ars Amatoria* 3, 559f and *Remedia Amoris* 4), ready to retire from service (*Amores* 2, 9a, 23f) but happy to train new recruits (*Ars Amatoria* 1, 36). To Ovid, giving advice on the remedies for love is like supplying weapons, *arma*, to the combatants (*Remedia Amoris* 50).

Women themselves are portrayed as the victors in the war of love, reducing the poet to humiliating and abject defeat; but the poets, typically and masochistically, derive a perverse pleasure from this. We see it in Propertius (1, 6, 29f) and in Ovid at *Amores* 1, 9, 43f. Subservience in capitulation to the woman is vital (*Ars Amatoria* 2, 175; 2, 197; 2, 539f; 3, 565f and 3, 752f), thus bringing the lover's defeat in the war of love ever closer to slavery of love, *servitium amoris*. Just as in the real world of war, defeat in battle often leads to servitude.

So, the women pedastalised by the love poets, their *doctae puellae*, were the complete opposite to the typical *matrona*; they were anything but modest, discreet, *univira* (married only once), compliant or chaste, and it seems unlikely that between them they produced very much wool or did much housework.

A manifestation of the educated, professional and relatively liberated woman came in 42 BCE when the three members of the Second Triumvirate were casting round for funds to finance their wars with the assassins of Julius Caesar; the money procured from their proscriptions was quickly running out. An easy target was women's wealth. Accordingly they levied a super tax on the 1,400 richest women in Rome. The women were outraged and, in a rare example of public demonstration by *matronae*, they marched on the Forum where Hortensia, daughter of the celebrated orator Quintus Hortensius, delivered a passionate and eloquent speech at a *contio* before the Triumvirs. Hortensia questioned why women, who had no say in or benefit or glory from the wars, should be required to finance these wars. Attempts to disperse the women failed. Hortensia's passion won the day and the taxable quota was reduced to 400 women; men with over 100,000 sesterces had to make good the shortfall by loaning money to the Triumvirate. Appian[5] declared that the speech was so good that you would never know that it had been written and delivered by a woman. Valerius Maximus says that Hortensia's father 'breathed through the words of his daughter'.[6]

Mucia Tertia, daughter of Quintus Mucius Scaevola, earned something of a reputation as a diplomat. In 62 BCE, Cicero appealed to her to intercede with Metellus Nepos, her kinsman, who had vetoed Cicero's valedictory speech as consul. Later, she was sent to Sicily by Octavian to negotiate with Sextus Pompeius, her son, who was starving Italy with his grain blockade. Mucia was unsuccessful, but a later meeting with Pompey which included her daughter-in-law, Scribonia, Sextus' wife, was fruitful and led to the 39 BCE Treaty of Misenum. This ended the blockade. In 31 BCE, after Actium, she persuaded Octavian to spare Pompey.[7]

In an instance directly associated with the civil wars after the assassination of Julius Caesar, the pivotal family meeting (*consilium*) called by assassins Marcus Junius Brutus and Gaius Cassius Longinus at Antium included three powerful women: Servilia Caepionis (b. *c.*104 BCE, d. after 42 BCE), long-term mistress of Caesar, mother of Brutus and Cato the Younger's half-sister; Porcia Catonis, Brutus' wife and cousin; and Servilia's youngest daughter, Junia Tertia, or Tertulla (*c.* 60 BCE - 22 CE). Servilia actually chaired the *consilium* and was party to and influential in one of the most significant sequences of events in Roman history. Cicero tells that she made efforts to have the derisory *curatio frumanti*, the grain commission, removed from a senatorial decree outlining post-assassination appointments for Cassius and Brutus. In 63 BCE, Servilia had caused a scandal in the Senate during a debate on the Catiline conspirators. She sent a love letter to Julius Caesar; her half-brother Cato, who was on the opposite side to Caesar in the debate, accused Caesar of corresponding with the conspirators and, embarrassingly for all, demanded the letter be read out.

In 48 BCE, Servilia was still influencing Caesar when, after the Battle of Pharsalus, he gave orders for Brutus to be shown clemency even though he had defected to Pompey. Suetonius tells of the fabulously expensive (six million sesterces) pearl she received from Caesar and how, when she felt that Caesar's interest in her was waning, she offered Tertulla, her daughter, to him. This happened around the time of an auction at which Caesar sold a number of estates to Servilia at knock-down prices, causing Cicero to quip that they were an even bigger bargain as they had been further discounted by *tertia* – a third/Tertulla. In 43 BCE, Servilia chaired another crucial meeting which was convened to discuss how the conspirators should react to Cicero's plan to ask Brutus to bring his armies to Italy and what they should do about Marcus Aemilius Lepidus, Servilia's son-in-law, who had joined Mark Antony and was declared an outlaw. P. Servilius Casca (relative and assassin), Labeo (a lawyer), Scaptius (Brutus' agent) and Cicero were also present. In addition, Servilia acted as the eyes and ears in Rome for Cassius and Brutus when they fled the city. Cicero described her as 'a highly capable and dynamic woman'.[8]

The traditional form of marriage, *cum manu*, a relationship in which the wife entered a legal state of dependence on her husband who had legal control of her property, had more or less died out by the first century BCE, leaving women to marry in a much freer arrangement – but where love and affection were sometimes nothing more than a fortunate by-product.[9] Divorcing was easy and adultery was on the increase. Widowhood, free marriage and divorce often left women better off financially; certainly they could be more independent.[10] The social climate is well summed up by Horace, a fervent traditionalist. In *Odes* 3, 6, writing about Rome around 28 BCE, he describes how the traditional Roman *familia* and *matrona* were being corrupted at the end of the Republic: he talks of how 'generations rich in sin first sullied marriage, families and the home' and then focuses on the *matura virgo* who loses no time perfecting Greek dancing and other blandishments. She fantasises about *incesti amores* – illicit love - and at drinking parties indiscriminately and casually seeks out young adulterers. The lights are left lit so that her husband, who is taking payments for her services, can see it all, whether she's cavorting with a Spanish sailor or a door-to-door salesman: *dedecorum pretiosus emptor* – the buyer of her pricey shame.[11]

One of the catalysts of this increasing freedom for women – or, seen another, Horatian, way, the increasing permissiveness – was the very real impact of war on the lives of women and families. Many men were absent from home for increasingly long periods of time and for much of their careers, due to the demands of military service and provincial administration. This would have fostered a degree of independence amongst wives left behind at home. War widowhood could, paradoxically, have had a beneficial financial advantage for some women who were in a position to inherit the family business or fortune.

But such 'good fortune' could only ever benefit the lucky few middle-class families which had money. The vast majority had no such wealth to fall back on and were plunged by civil war widowhood into even more profound poverty. Women were often left to pick up the pieces during and after war, sometimes literally. For women, more often than not, their war was not over when Octavian emerged victorious at Actium: instead, women suffered often eternal widowhood. They had waited anxiously at home, always expecting the worst of bad news; when it came, as it did for tens of thousands of wives, sisters and mothers, they are left to grieve and mourn and to struggle on with their lives, often working their farms or businesses alone and bringing up young fatherless children. Where the husband-soldier is wounded, they may have to spend their lives as carers, tending limbless or otherwise traumatized ex-servicemen, coping with all the physical and psychological issues disabling injury brings.

The proscriptions too took a heavy toll on family life and relationships. Appian records a number of brave and devoted acts by women, often at great personal cost, following the proscriptions imposed by the Second Triumvirate after the assassination of Caesar:

> 'Acilius secretly fled from the city. His hiding-place was disclosed by a slave to the soldiers, but he prevailed upon them, in the hope of a larger reward, to send some of their number to his wife with a private token that he gave them. When they came she gave them all of her jewellery, saying that she gave it in return for what they had promised, although she did not know whether they would keep their agreement. But her fidelity to her husband was not disappointed, for the soldiers hired a ship for Acilius and saw him off to Sicily.
>
> 'The wife of Lentulus asked that she might accompany him in his flight and kept watch upon his movements for that purpose, but he was not willing that she should share his danger, and fled secretly to Sicily. Being appointed praetor there by Pompeius he sent word to her that he was saved and elevated to office. When she learned in what part of the earth her husband was she escaped with two slaves from her mother, who was keeping watch over her. With these she travelled in the guise of a slave, with great hardship and the meanest fare, until she was able to make the passage from Rhegium to Messana about

> nightfall. She learned without difficulty where the praetor's tent was, and there she found Lentulus, not in the attitude of a praetor, but on a low pallet with unkempt hair and wretched food, mourning for his wife.
>
> 'The wife of Apuleius threatened that if he should leave without her, she would inform against him. So unwillingly he took her with him, and he succeeded in avoiding suspicion in his flight by travelling with his wife and his male and female slaves quite openly. The wife of Antius wrapped him up in a clothes-bag and gave the bundle to some porters to carry from the house to the sea-shore, whence he made his escape to Sicily. Rheginus' wife hid him by night in a sewer, into which the soldiers were not willing to enter in the daytime, because of the foul stench. The next night she disguised him as a charcoal dealer, and brought him a donkey to drive, carrying coals. She led the way at a short distance, carried in a litter. One of the soldiers at the city gates suspected the litter and searched it. Rheginus was alarmed and walked faster, and, as if he were a passer-by, warned the soldier not to give trouble to women. The latter, who [at first] took him for a charcoal dealer, answered him angrily; but then he recognized him (for he had served under him in Syria), and said, "Go on your way rejoicing, general, because I still ought to call you that." The wife of Coponius purchased his safety from Antony; before this she had been chaste, but now she had resolved one evil with another.'[12]

In 43 BCE, Octavia the Younger (69-11 BCE) helped the proscribed Titus Vinius. He had been hidden in a chest by his wife, Tanusia, who concealed it in the house of a freedman, claiming that he was dead. Tanusia herself risked death for harbouring a proscribed person. Octavia agreed to help and arranged for Tanusia to deliver the chest to a festival attended by Octavian, where he was sprung from the chest. Octavian was so impressed by the couple's ingenuity and nerve that he pardoned Vinius and Tanusia and promoted Vinius to the equestrian order.[13]

The *Laudatio Turiae* celebrates, at some length, the life of a dutiful and exceptional wife (whose identity is mired in controversy) and gives a catalogue of those qualities expected of the good *matrona*: *pietas*, wool-working, looking after the household and its gods, modesty of dress and elegance, and financial generosity. Apart from furnishing the gold standard of wifely conduct erected in Rome by her grieving husband, Quintus Lucretius Vespillo, Turia had already endured the murder of her mother and father in the chaos which accompanied the conflict between Pompey and Caesar, a tragedy which galvanised Turia to seek revenge:

> 'You became an orphan suddenly before the day of our wedding, when both your parents were murdered together in the solitude of the countryside. It was mainly due to your efforts that the death of your parents was not left unavenged. For I had left for Macedonia [to join the Pompeians], and your sister's husband Cluvius had gone to the Province of Africa.
>
> 'So strenuously did you perform your filial duty by your insistent demands and your pursuit of justice that we could not have done more if we had been present. But these merits you have in common with that most virtuous lady your sister. While you were engaged in these things, you secured the punishment of the guilty.'

Turia's future husband was, of course, on the losing side at Pharsalus and went into exile. She petitioned Julius Caesar, a man not averse to clemency, and secured his freedom to return to Rome – which allowed the couple to marry.

When Vespillo was in exile, she moved in with her mother-in-law and valiantly defended the house against Milo, the renegade former owner who had not reckoned on Turia's bravery and fierce determination:

> 'Meanwhile when a troop of men collected by Milo, whose house I had acquired through purchase when he was in exile, tried to profit by the opportunities provided by the civil war and break into our house to plunder, you beat them back successfully and were able to defend our home.'[14]

The *laudatio* eloquently describes for us Turia's courage, loyalty and shrewdness in the face of her husband's enemy, Lepidus, in 43 BCE when his name appeared on the lists of the proscribed. The pretext for this calumny probably had more to do with the couple's easily extractable wealth rather than any offensive political affiliation. Valerius Maximus[15] adds that Turia had concealed Lucretius in their roof space – 'a safe hiding place' - and convincingly acted out the role of the bereft wife, dressing in rags, looking dishevelled and grieving over an apparently lost husband. What Turia did here went far beyond a requirement to work her wool and look after the housework. She agitated relentlessly to persuade Octavian to recall her husband, but Lepidus, his colleague in the Triumvirate, remained implacably against it. She begged him to think again, an act her husband labels 'The bitterest thing that happened to me in my life':

> 'You lay prostrate at his feet, and you were not only forced to stand up, but were dragged away and carried off brutally like a slave. But although your body was covered in bruises, your spirit was unbroken ... You provided abundantly for my needs during my flight and gave me the means for a dignified manner of living, when you took all the gold and jewellery from your own body and sent it to me and over and over again enriched me in my absence with servants, money and provisions, showing great ingenuity in deceiving the guards posted by our adversaries.'

As Appian shows, Turia may have been exceptional but she was not alone: the various depredations of the Civil War probably brought out the best in many women to some degree or other. Each of them faced a stark choice – hand over the husband and guarantee immunity from prosecution, or help him and become complicit.

As we can see, the proscriptions brought out the best and worst in those listed. Here are some other notable incidents mainly involving wives and slaves, as adapted from Samuel Clarke' description (1599-1682):

> 'Salvius Otho, a Tribune of the People, invited his Friends to his last Supper, and as they were sitting, in came a Centurion, and in the presence of them all, struck off his Head ... L. Villius Annalis, who had been Consul, flying from the murderers, hid himself in the Suburbs in a little House of one of his clients, but his own Son betrayed him to the murderers, who slew him there; but shortly after this Parricide

being drunk, quarrelling with the same Soldiers, was slain by them. C. Toranius also being betrayed by his own Son, was slain, who in a few days having consumed his Patrimony, was condemned for Theft, and banished into a place where he died miserably.

'Quintus Cicero was hid by his Son, whom they could never make to confess by any torments where his Father was; but the old man, not being able any longer to endure that they should torment so virtuous a Son, came and presented himself to the Murderers: whereupon the Son entreated them to kill him first, but they killed them both together. The Egnaces, the Father and Son, embracing one the other were both run through at once and slain. C. Hosidius Geta, was put into a grave by his Son as dead, who sustained and kept him till the danger was over. Aruntius, after he had comforted his Son, delivered up himself to the murderers, but his Son for grief starved himself.'

Some other children concealed and saved their parents:

'Q. Ligurius having been concealed by his Wife, was discovered by a slave, and killed, whereupon his Wife pined her self to death. Coponius was saved by his Wife, who lent her Body to Anthony for one night, to save him whom she preferred before her honour.

'But the Wife of Septimius, having shamefully given her Body to one of Anthonies Familiars, caused her Husband to be listed, that she might the more freely continue her Adulteries, and her Husband was slain by her means. Q. Vettius Salussus was hidden in a very secret place, but telling his Wife of it, she betrayed him to the murderers. Fulvius was discovered by one of his slaves and his Concubine, though he had made her free, and given her goods to maintain herself.

'P. Naso was betrayed by his slave, whom he had freed but with whom he had been too familiar; he revenged himself upon his slave, whom he killed, and then held forth his neck to the cut-throats. L. Lucceius had given his Freedmen as much as would have got him off the hook, but they ran away with it all, whereupon he delivered himself to the murderers. Haterius, who had hid himself in a very secret place, was sold and betrayed by his slave, and killed. Cassius Varus who was betrayed by a slave he had freed, had his Head struck off. Caius Plotius was hidden by his slaves, but being partial to Perfumes, the scent betrayed him; yet when the Soldiers could not find him, they cruelly tortured his Servants to make them confess where he was, which they would not do. So the Master pitying his faithful servants, came out of his hiding place, and delivered himself to the murderers.

'Appius Claudius exchanged his Gown with his slave, who in that habit presented himself to the murderers, and was slain by them instead of his Master. A slave of Menius did the same: he went into his Master's Litter, and offered his neck to the murderers, who cut off his Head, and so his Master escaped into Sicily. The slave of Urbinus Panopio, hearing that the murderers were coming to his Master's House, took off his Gown and his Ring, and gave him his own clothes, and put him out the back door: then he went upstairs and lay upon his Master's Bed, where he was bravely killed instead of Panopio. The slave of Antius Restio, though his Master had beaten him soundly a few days before for some knavish tricks, to save his Master, he decapitated an old man and showing that head along with his whippings to the murderers, made them believe that he had thereby revenged himself of his Master and he was dead; shortly after the two fled to Sicily.

'Statius Samnis, an honourable octagenarian Senator, made sure that no one would get their hands on his goods and set fire to his house and burnt himself in it. Cestius made his slaves make a great fire, threw himself into it and died: Sulpitus Rufus, who had been Consul, was murdered because he would not sell an island of his to Fulvia.

'Some valiantly defended themselves, for example Atteius Capito, who killed many Soldiers who ran towards him; but being finally overcome was slain. Sicilias Coranas hoping to escape, mingled with the Mourners following a dead Corpse, was discovered and slain.'

Exile had similar reponses and ramifications. Cicero relied heavily on the support of his wife, Terentia, during his exile in 58 and 57 BCE.[16] His letters to her reflect his isolation, homesickness and affection, both for her and for their daughter: Terentia is *fidissima atque optima uxor … mea lux*('most faithful and best of wives … light of my life'). Tullia and Terentia both interceded bravely on Cicero's behalf during his exile.[17] They also had to deal with his business affairs, the slaves and household, as well as the upbringing of their young son: Terentia remained the supportive wife, even though their marriage was annulled because of his exile. The two women demonstrated ostentatiously by wearing their hair unkempt and donning black mourning clothes, visiting friends in Rome in order to canvass support for Cicero's return. When their house on the Palatine was torched by Clodius' mob, Terentia sought sanctuary in the house of the Vestal Virgins. According to Plutarch, in earlier days Terentia seems to have been influential in her husband's handling of the Catilinarian conspiracy. In the same piece, he records how Cicero himself says that Terentia was more active in his political life than she ever was in domestic affairs.

To Suetonius, Porcia is brave because of an incident in her second marriage, to Brutus. Immediately before the assassination of Caesar, Porcia could see that her husband was unduly distracted and anxious. She made up her mind to share his concerns and proceeded to slash her thigh with a knife, causing substantial loss of blood. Brutus was understandably alarmed; Porcia explained the self harm, telling him that she was much more than just a sex partner in their marriage, indeed she was 'a partner in your joys and a partner in your sorrows' - for better or for worse. She, by virtue of her ancestry and her demonstrable bravery, claimed that she was above the usual weakness of women and was worthy of his confidence in anything that may be troubling him. Seeing Porcia's wound, Brutus told Porcia everything. Porcia had proved to him that she could conquer pain and would not, therefore, yield under an enemy's torture: Brutus could confide in her with absolute confidence. After Caesar's murder, Porcia and Brutus parted. Her husband showed how fully he appreciated Porcia's courage. Plutarch says that she was distraught on seeing a painting of Hector leaving Andromache for war; when Brutus heard this he, out of respect, declined to repeat Hector's parting words to Andromache but rephrased it as follows:

> 'Work at your loom and your distaff, and give your commands to your servants. She may not have the strength for the same exploits as are expected of a man, but she has the spirit to fight as nobly for her country as any of us.'

Plutarch's source is Bibulus, their son; it is remarkable because it represents the first example we have of an enlightened man enjoining his wife to renounce the traditional wool-working and fight for her country like a man. When Brutus was killed in 43 BCE, Porcia committed suicide by swallowing hot coals, an act which Valerius Maximus describes as 'her woman's spirit equal to her father's manly death'.[18]

We have seen how Catullus, Propertius, Tibullus and Ovid – and no doubt others whose work has not survived in any quantity - all sign up to the *militia amoris* school of life, fighting the war of love, pacifists in the ranks of the soldiers of love. Not for them the real battlefield, the *cursus honorum* and the *mos maiorum*. They had their hands more than full with their capricious, unfaithful, domineering *dominae*, their *doctae puellae*, their anti-*matronae*. But other poets, Virgil (70-19 BCE) and Horace (65-8 BCE) in particular, were much more establishment-minded, championing their emperor, cheerleaders for and champions of the nascent new regime, critical of the toxic years of the Republic.

Virgil's ten eclogues were published around 39 BCE, at the end of the turbulent Second Triumvirate (43-33 BCE). They may be seen, in part at least, as a metaphor for some of the unsavoury revolutionary changes of those years: rustic characters are depicted suffering, or embracing, those revolutionary changes, or alternatively experiencing happy or unrequited love. As a country boy himself, Virgil was appalled by the effects of veteran land distribution on the countryside and on its former tenants. According to Gregson Davis,

> 'the world of the Eclogues is permeated through and through with portrayals of human infelicity, catastrophic loss and emotional turbulence. The defining tenor of these poetic sketches is a profound anxiety about the human capacity to cope with misfortune.'[19]

All of this is a reflection of and informed by the deeply troubled times Virgil and Rome had just lived through. The *Eclogues* are clearly a highly vocal lament for the Rome that was – before the rapacious land reforms which accompanied the civil wars, and which wrecked the Italian agrarian economy and destroyed the lives of so many farmers, farming families and landowners.

Tityrus in the first eclogue may well be articulating Virgil's own opinion about the dispossession of farmers to accommodate discharged veterans. Meliboeus is one of these exiles, a refugee sullenly making his way toward a new home, be it in 'thirsty Africa', Scythia or Britannia, and leaving behind the land he has painstakingly cultivated, only to see it gifted to a war veteran:

> 'Shall a lawless soldier possess these trim fallows? A barbarian these cornfields? To what wretched pass has civil discord brought us! For whose profit we have sown our fields!'

He inquires how his friend Tityrus has managed to avoid being similarly dispossessed. Tityrus replies that he simply went to Rome to plead for his land and that a young boy, Octavian (?), granted his request: 'Pasture your oxen as of old, my children, rear your bulls.' All then was rosy in Tityrus' garden.

The fourth ecologue, the so-called Messianic eclogue dedicated to Asinius Pollio, looks forward to the birth of a child who will usher in a new golden age, a utopia in which peace will pervade the world; humanity and nature will become self-sufficient, there will be no more commerce and the land will need no ploughing and pruning. The identity of the expected child is hotly disputed: it may be Octavian, or it may, as many like to believe, be Jesus Christ.

The golden age presages the golden age described by Ovid in the context of a war-free world. Warfare, of course, was nothing new in ancient societies. Territorial defence or expansion, mineral deposits, naked aggression, trade protectionism and despotism all played their part, long before the Romans, in fuelling wars, conflict and confrontation. Ovid, in his *Metamorphoses*, writing at the dawn of the Empire, would have us believe that, once upon a time, men were ever true to their word, and that they inhabited a righteous, peaceful world in which laws, punishment, armies and fortifications were superfluous.[20] This golden age, this *aurea aetas*, never existed of course: violence, wars and the battles that constitute them have been as constant and ubiquitous as taxes and death.

The ninth eclogue introduces us to Moeris who, like Meliboeus, has lost his small farm in the land redistributions in the aftermath of the civil wars. The eclogue explores the efficacy of poetry as a mitigating agent in devastating loss. Lycidas asks Moeris to confirm that his lands had been preserved through

Menalcas' song: 'Surely I had heard that … your Menalcas had saved all the land by his songs.' Moeris replies: 'But songs of ours, Lycidas, have no more power among warring arms than Chaonian doves, as they say, when the eagle comes.'

In 29 BCE, Virgil published the *Georgics*, an agricutural didactic poem of 2,188 hexametres in four books. By now Virgil was well established in the côterie of Maecenas, Octavian's adjutant who worked tirelessly to discredit Antony in favour of Octavian.

It seems unlikely that the fractious and destabilizing effects of the civil wars would not have informed the *Georgics* to some extent. But while overt politics are absent, Virgil does address Octavian; moreover, the descriptions of the plague in Book 3 and bee society in Book 4 may well have political undertones. In any event, Donatus tells us that Octavian was obviously keen to hear the *Georgics*:

> 'When Augustus had returned after his victory at Actium and was staying at Atella to rest his throat, [Virgil] read the Georgics to him over four continuous days; Maecenas took up reading in turn whenever he himself broke off through weakness of voice.'[21]

In a poem that, from its publication in 19 BCE, has been described as 'the national epic of Rome', it is inevitable that the reader and listener of the *Aeneid* will have found it to be loaded with politics. Commissioned by Augustus, formerly Octavian, the politics in question revolve around the new constitution of Rome, the Empire – as led by Augustus – Actium, the civil wars and the Triumvirates.

In that sense, the *Aeneid* can be said to be a work of propaganda for the fledgling regime. On a personal level, Augustus is closely associated with Aeneas, the hero who delivered the Trojans out of burning chaos and annihilation at Troy, bringing them to the shores of Italy, from where they established Rome, the monarchy, the Republic and now the Principate. Augustus, similarly, was engaged in delivering the Romans out of the chaos, the internecine strife of the civil wars, securing Rome's position as dominant power in the known world, establishing the Pax Romana and delivering a momentous cultural renaissance.

Aeneas explains his mission and responsibility as leader of the displaced Trojans:

> 'New refugees in a great crowd: men and women
> Gathered for exile, young-pitiful people
> Coming from every quarter, minds made up,
> With their belongings, for whatever lands
> I'd lead them to by sea.'[22]

Augustus, and his place at the zenith of Roman history to date, is introduced in Book 1:

> 'From this noble stock there will be born a Trojan Caesar to bound his empire by Oceanus at the limits of the world, and his fame by the stars. He will be called Julius, a name passed down to him from the great Iulus. In time to come, have no fear, you will receive him in the sky, laden with the spoils of the East. He too will be called upon in prayer. Then wars will be laid aside and the years of bitterness will be over. Silver-haired Truth and Vesta, and Romulus Quirinus with his brother Remus, will sit dispensing justice. The dread Gates of War with their tight fastenings of steel will then be closed, and godless Strife will sit inside them on his murderous armour roaring hideously from bloody mouth, hands shackled behind his back with a hundred bands of bronze.'[23]

In the words of Sabine Grebe:[24]

> 'Vergil's Augustus represents the culmination of Roman history. Augustus is said to stand in one line with Aeneas, Ascanius, and Romulus, each of whom had founded a city: Aeneas founded Lavinium, Ascanius Alba Longa, Romulus Rome, and Augustus re-founded Rome through the establishment of peace, law and order after Rome had been dominated, for a century, by war, chaos,

and disorder. Each of the mythic figures ruled alone as king. His foundation of a city and the monarchic form of rule connect Augustus with his ancestors.'

But it is down in the underworld where the Aeneas-Augustus link is strongest. Here Aeneas is surveying the future:

'Turn your two eyes
This way and see this people, your own Romans.
Here is Caesar, and all the line of Iulus,
All who shall one day pass under the dome
Of the great sky: this is the man, this one,
Of whom so often you have heard the promise,
Caesar Augustus, son of the deified,
Who shall bring once again an Age of Gold
To Latium, to the land where Saturn reigned
In early times.'[25]

Virgil reinforces the link when he establishes a shared ancestry between Aeneas and Augustus. Julius Caesar (Augustus' great uncle) is in Virgil a descendant of Venus and Anchises (Aeneas' parents); Jupiter references a 'Trojan Caesar' as a descendant of Ascanius (as Iulus) and therefore of Venus.

To forge a direct connection between Caesar and Romulus, in the underworld Aeneas' father, Ascanius, describes his son's descendants through Augustus via Romulus, thus confirming the emperor's descent from Aeneas and Romulus, the founder of Rome.

Horace, a contemporary of Virgil, picks up the mantle of Augustan propagandist in his *Odes*, notably Book 4, published in 13 BCE when the Augustan regime was already well established. If anyone understood well the effects of civil war and Triumvirate politics, then it was Horace. His early adult life was enmeshed in the wars on and off the battlefield: in 44 BCE, Horace joined Brutus' army as a military tribune (*Satires* 1, 6, 47); in 41, when Brutus was defeated, Horace was allowed to return to Italy under the general amnesty, but the family property was confiscated (*Epistles* 2, 2, 46–51). Horace was lucky enough to find work as a quaestor's clerk (*Satires* 2, 6, 36f). Around 40 BCE, Virgil and Varius Rufus introduced him to Maecenas and are later accepted into Maecenas' côterie. In 33 BCE, Maecenas gifted him the Sabine farm which makes Horace socially and financially secure. Despite this beneficence, Horace, although ever a champion of the Augustan regime, was astute enough to remain politically independent when Maecenas and Augustus attempted to ingratiate themselves with him.

The *Epodes* were written around 30 BCE, earlier than the *Odes*. Horace alludes to Actium in the first poem, a tribute to Maecenas:

> 'Villains where are you rushing to? Why are your hands Grasping those swords that were sheathed? Hasn't enough Roman blood been shed over The fields, and Neptune's waves? Yet not so that Rome could burn the proud towers Of an envious Carthage, Nor that as-yet-unconquered Britons, might descend The Via Sacra in chains, But so that fulfilling the Parthians' prayers This city might destroy itself. That isn't the way of even the wolves or lions: They only fight other species. Does a blind frenzy drive you, or some fiercer power, Or some heinous crime? Answer me!' (trans. A. S. Kline, 2005; http://www.poetryintranslation.com/PITBR/Latin/HoraceEpodesAndCarmenSaeculare.php#anchor_Toc98670048)

Epode 9 is a much more detailed description of Actium and Octavian's military achievements before Actium:

> 'Dear Maecenas, when in your noble house, as is Jove's pleasure, shall I delight With you in Caesar's triumph, drinking Caecuban Cellared for festive banquets, While lyre and flutes sound, mingling their melodies, That Dorian, and these Italian? As lately, when Pompey, driven from the sea, Had fled, with his ships destroyed, Having threatened the city with shackles he'd taken From those faithless slaves, his friends. A Roman – you'll not credit it, posterity – Sadly, ups sticks and arms himself, For a woman's sake, and though a soldier, deigns To serve the withered eunuchs, While the sun looks down on her shameful pavilion, Among the warlike standards At this sight two thousand Gauls, chanting Caesar, Turned their snorting steeds aside, And the opposing fleet, when ordered to port, Remained there in the harbour. Hail, Triumph! Why

> delay the golden chariots And the unblemished steers? Hail, Triumph! In the war with Jugurtha, you never Returned such a general to us, Nor was Africanus, whose courage made a tomb For himself of Carthage, such. The enemy, beaten at sea and on land, Changes his scarlet cloak for black Against opposing winds, he either heads for Crete, Famed for her hundred cities, Or tries for Syrtes, blown by the northerlies, Or is borne over unknown seas. Bring more spacious bowls, lad, and pour the Chian, Lesbian, or Caecuban wine That's designed to prevent all seasick qualms. Let's delight in banishing fear and anxiety For Caesar's affairs, with sweet wine.' (trans. A.S. Kline, 2005)

In *Epode* 16, Horace shows how a whole series of first-century conflicts with barbarians had not achieved the destruction of Rome in the ways that the civil wars managed. To Horace, the solution to avoiding a repetition is to up sticks and leave:

> 'Another generation now's been ground down by civil war, And Rome herself's being ruined by her own power. What the neighbouring Marsians could not destroy, Nor the threat of Porsena's Etruscan armies, Nor Capua's rival strength, nor the fierceness of Spartacus, Nor the Gauls, who proved disloyal in changing times, Nor that savage Germany he conquered, with its blue-eyed youth, Nor Hannibal detested by our ancestors: Our impious generation, of cursed blood, will destroy, And the land will belong again to beasts of prey. A savage victor, alas, will stamp on our city's ashes. The horsemen will trample them with echoing hoof, And, vile to see, will insolently scatter Quirinus' bones, That are still sheltered, as yet, from the sun and winds! Perhaps, as would be wise, all, or the better part of you, Would prefer to escape this grievous suffering? Let no other plan be adopted but this, that just as The Phoceans fled into exile, having cursed Their fields and ancestral gods, leaving behind their temples To become the lairs of boars and ravening wolves, Let us go wherever our feet take us, wherever the Northern, Or the boisterous African gales, shall call us.
>
> Does that please you? Has anyone a better idea?'
>
> (trans. A.S. Kline, 2005)

In *Odes* Book 4, *Odes* 4 and 14 celebrate the military successes of Drusus and Tiberius. Number 4 praises Drusus on his victory over the Raeti and Vindelici. Drusus is likened to a young eagle and lion, while his stepfather, Augustus, gets the credit for having trained him to greatness. *Odes* 5 urges Augustus to return to Rome, and the peace and civil order prevailing under his reign. Augustus is 'Best guardian of Rome's people, dearest boon Of a kind Heaven'. Now no one need fear the barbarian threat:

> 'Who fears the Parthian or the Scythian horde,
> Or the rank growth that German forests yield,
> While Caesar lives? Who trembles at the sword
> The fierce Iberians wield?'

Horace honours the courage and exploits of Tiberius in 4, 14 and his victories over the tribes of the Raetian Alps. Augustus too is celebrated as the glory of the war, the defence of Roman and Italy, and as the undisputed ruler of the world. Horace records the *res gestae* of Augustus in 4, 15: peace, civil order, the re-establishment of public morals, the extended glory of the Roman name abroad, and security and happiness at home. Augustus, it seems, has solved all the domestic and foreign policy problems besetting Rome and her empire:

> 'Thy age, great Caesar, has restored
> To squalid fields the plenteous grain,
> Given back to Rome's almighty Lord
> Our standards, torn from Parthian fane,
> Has closed Quirinian Janus' gate,
> Wild passion's erring walk controll'd,
> Heal'd the foul plague-spot of the state …
> While Caesar rules, no civil strife
> Shall break our rest, nor violence rude,
> Nor rage, that whets the slaughtering knife
> And plunges wretched towns in feud.'[26]

In 1, 6, Horace asserts that he will not use his poetry as a vehicle to laud Augustus or Agrippa, but from 1, 37, where he excoriates Cleopatra, he repeatedly and explicitly praises Augustus, his regime and his policies. In 3, 1-6 and 24, he fully supports Augustus' attempts to restore some of Rome's old morals and ancient customs – the *mos maiorum*. *Odes* 2, 1 is dedicated to Gaius Asinius Pollio (76 BCE - 4 CE) and his history of the civil wars, the *Historiae*, which covers from 60-42 BCE. Now unfortunately lost, this history was an important source for both Appian's and Plutarch's work. The ode opens with Horace alluding to, and by association deploring, the political infighting, starting with the First Triumvirate established in the consulship of Metellus Celer in 60 BCE:

> 'Of all that civil unrest since Metellus, the phases, causes and the crimes of war, of Fortune's games, of great men's grave friendships, of weapons smeared with gore not yet atoned for – you are writing now a work where every turned phrase is a roll of dangerous dice. Let not the ash deceive: you tread on blazing coal.'

Horace makes no secret of the fact that the horrors of the Civil War are still fresh in the minds of many, that they still rankle and that they are still politically very sensitive. Horace warns Pollio that he is treading on thin ice, walking on hot coals. The emperor Claudius was later to be warned off from writing on the same subject for the same reasons. Claudius was a notable historian and student of Greek culture, who introduced three new letters into the Roman alphabet; his teachers included Livy and Sulpicius Flavus. When Claudius sat down to write his history of Rome, his mother, Antonia Augusta (36 BCE – 37 CE), astutely advised him not to reveal what he knew about the civil wars and the early days of the Empire.

Horace goes on to provide a roll call of Rome's military activity during the Civil War period:

> 'Even now I hear the war-horns' baleful roar in your raucous music, and the bugles' blare. I see the flash of swords strike panicked horses and the horsemen's eyes with fear. I see the great commanders filthy with war's not inglorious dirt, I hear the whole world fall at Rome's feet notwithstanding defiant Cato's dogged soul. The gods allied with Africa who, helpless to help, left unavenged that country's shores, now sacrifice to dead Jugurtha the grandsons of his conquerors. What

> field has Latin blood not fertilized, its graves attesting the unholiest of wars, and that the ears of Persia ring with the ruin of the West? What churning main, what river does not know those rueful wars' taste? What sea has the slaughter of Rome's own sons not dyed? What beach has our gushed blood not washed like water?'[27]

Odes 1, 2 sees Augustus saving the world after the Tiber floods brought about by the civil wars and the assassination of Julius Caesar. In 1, 12, Horace praises Augustus, linking him with gods and heroes, and distinguished Romans of old. In 1, 14, Horace describes the turbulence of an earlier time and cautions the Romans to ensure it is not allowed to recur. *Odes* 1, 35 shows Horace invoking Fortune to look after Augustus in his distant expeditions, and to save the state from ruinous civil wars. Jubilation, as we have seen, features in 1, 37, where we are encouraged to drink and dance to celebrate the death of Cleopatra. Horace encourages Maecenas to record Augustus' Civil War victories in prose, because his own lyric poetry is an unsuitable medium. In Book Three, *Odes* 2-5 celebrate Augustus and his achievements: 3, 2, extols the courage involved in fighting for one's country, and includes the famous lines '*Dulce et decorum est pro patria mori*' ('it is sweet and proper to die for the fatherland'); 3, 3, praises integrity, Pollux, Hercules and Romulus and the destiny of Rome. *Odes* 3, 4, describes how the Muses encourage Augustus to clemency and generosity as opposed to violence and arrogance, as promoted by the Titans and Giants. *Odes* 3, 5 recognises Augustus as a god on earth for his subjugation of the Britons and Parthians. The disgusting actions of the troops of Crassus who married Parthians after being taken prisoner are contrasted with the example of Marcus Atilius Regulus, who was released from Carthage to negotiate a peace, but dissuaded the Senate, and then returned to Carthage only to be tortured to death. Augustus will restore qualities like his. As we have seen, 3, 6 is one of many examples in which Horaces urges a return to the (good old) days of the *mos maiorum*, condemning contemporary immorality and the erosion of traditional religion, thus aligning himself with Augustus' legislative programme of moral reform. In 3, 14, Horace proclaims a festal day on the return of Augustus from Spain around 24 BCE, where he had vanquished the Cantabri. *Odes* 3, 26 is Horace's contribution to the *militia amoris* motif. Augustus' age is seen as a second golden age in the *Carmen Saeculare*, commissioned by Augustus in 17 BCE. The following is an extract:

> 'Now Faith and Peace, Honour, and ancient Modesty,
> Dare to return once more, with neglected Virtue,
> And blessed Plenty dares to appear again, now,
> With her flowing horn.' (trans. A.S. Kline, 2005)

We have already noted how Propertius' anti-war stance and political independence led him to assert that no son of his will ever join the military. His apparent pacifism stemmed, no doubt, from a childhood living in Asis (modern Assisi), a mere 15 miles from war-torn Perusia, where he will have witnessed the death and destruction caused by Octavian's siege of Perusia (41/40 BCE); his family suffered badly, with land confiscated by Octavian in 41-40 (4, 1, 27ff) and at least one relative killed. In the end, Octavian exterminated the Perusian senate, 300 or so innocent men whose only crime was that their city had been commandeered by external forces. According to Suetonius:

> 'After the fall of the city Augustus took vengeance on crowds of prisoners and returned the same answer to all who sued for pardon or tried to explain their presence among the rebels. It was simply: "You must die!" According to some historians, he chose 300 prisoners of equestrian or senatorial rank, and offered them on the Ides of March at the altar of the God Julius, as human sacrifices.'[28]

The town was then razed, according to Dio, except for the temple of Hephaistos and the statue of Hera.[29]

Propertius, then, had good reason to reject not just war but also Augustan moral and political values generally. The poet is much more interested in a *pax amoris* than any *pax Romana*. His main war poems comprise 1.21, 1.22, 2.7, 2.10 and 3.1-5. While there is praise for Augustus' achievements, there is always a suspicion that, for whatever reason, the poet was, on occasions, being somewhat disingenuous and that his true feelings were informed by his unhappy experience of Octavian's depredations in the Perusine War.

The two interrelated closing poems of the Monobiblos see Propertius suspend his treatment of things amatory to comment on the effects of war. In 1.21, we read of the tragic impact the death of Gallus has on his family; 1.22

opens with reference to the horrors of Octavian's actions at Perusia, where the words *Romana discordia* figure prominently:

> 'If the Perusine tombs of our country are known to you, funerals in Italy's hard times, when Roman discord hunted her citizens (This was especially painful for me, my Etruscan soil – you allowed my neighbour's limbs to go abandoned, no earth covers his poor bones) – neighbouring Umbria, below Perusia on the plain bore me, fertile Umbria, productive land.'

For Propertius the 'Roman discord' was clearly personal.

In 61 CE, just over a century after the Battle of Pharsalus, during the reign of Nero, Marcus Annaeus Lucanus – Lucan (39-65 CE) – started to write his epic poem, the *Bellum Civile*. Eight thousand lines later, the poem, in ten books, remained unfinished on Lucan's suicide, but by then Lucan and Nero had had a bitter falling out.

We have already noted how the sores inflicted by the civil wars of the first century BCE still pained and shamed the Roman people and psyche. The wars were still politically sensitive and controversial, and writing about them during the Principate was not without its hazards. Historians like Asinius Pollio and the emperor Claudius were warned off re-opening old wounds: Claudius jumped straight from Caesar's assassination to the peace effected by Augustus when he realized that he would not be able to speak openly and truthfully, *neque libere neque vere*, about the events. Seneca the Elder cites Labienus, who believed that the best way to deal with the civil wars in the public domain was to forget they ever happened: *optima ciuilis belli defensio obliuio est*. Moreover, Valerius Maximus, in his *exempla patientiae*, cites only two Roman examples before moving on lest he 'be forced to proceed into the accursed memory of civil wars'.[30]

Lucan, it seems, had no such qualms: in the proem to the poem (what may well be a later interpolation, and somewhat in contradiction to the tenor of the rest of the poem), Lucan even attributes the good state of affairs in Rome under Nero to the civil wars. Indeed, according to this, it was the civil wars that gave Rome Nero, and Rome is all the better for that: *multum Roma tamen debet ciuilibus armis quod tibi res acta est* ('But Rome is greater by these civil wars, because it resulted in you').[31]

Lucan's opening lines set the scene:

> 'We sing of wars worse than civil on Emathian plains,
> and crime let loose; how Rome's high race
> plunged her victorious sword into her innards;
> armies related to armies embattled, with the force
> of all the shaken earth bent on the fray;
> and burst asunder, to the common guilt,
> a kingdom's compact; eagle with eagle met,
> standard to standard, spear opposed to spear.'[32]

But, as we can see, the reality is that to Lucan the civil wars were responsible for the destruction of the Republic and a loss of liberty. *Virtus* equates to criminality, not least in the guise of Book 6's Scaeva.

Lucan's poem is notable for its exclusion of Olympian gods – characters which were central to Virgil's *Aeneid* and its action. The gods may be absent but the poem is replete with the supernatural; omens, prophecies, dreams, portents and eschatology are all there to add to the pervasive sensation of doom and gloom. Indeed, the supernatural serves to highlight and reflect 'Rome's turmoil on the supernatural plane' and 'contribute to the atmosphere of sinister foreboding'.[33] Such is the message Lucan wanted to convey about the Civil War years; they were terrible days. Nowhere else is this more evident than in Lucan's vivid and repellent portrayal of Erictho – perhaps the vilest witch in all literature. By taking her to the extremes, Lucan employs her as a vehicle to emphasize just how odious the civil wars were.

In first-century CE Rome, a witch was usually totally unscrupulous, devoid of any morals, and prepared to do whatever it took to get her way. That's why, by and large, witches are depicted as repellent creatures. In mythology, they are magical and scheming; in the real world, they were considered foul and repugnant, scuttling around in the deepest pits of depravity. In literature, witches plumb uncharted depths of obscene atrocity.

In Book 6, Sextus Pompey, driven by fear, wants to know the outcome of the impending battle; he rejects conventional forms of divination, electing instead to deploy the ungodly, 'the mysteries of the furious enchantress'.[34] Being in Thessally, he is local to the world's most dreadful witches and their *herbae nocentes*, 'pernicious herbs'. When the witches here cast their spells, even the gods above pause to take note, and can sometimes be persuaded to do the witches' will.

In some ways, although Lucan owed much to Virgil and the *Aeneid*, the *Bellum Civile* is an anti-*Aeneid*. Virgil's epic is a panegyric to Augustus and to the new Rome; it is optimistic and forward-looking. Lucan's poem looks back and is pessimistic, miring Rome in doom and disaster – the turbulent events of the end of the Republic mirrored in social and political events contemporary to Lucan. The repulsive picture of Erictho is one way Lucan achieves this. Another is the unremittingly bleak portrayal of historical characters: Caesar is always a volatile, fulminating and cruel man; Pompey is feeble and dull; only Cato escapes the gloomy characterization, a paragon of Stoicism facing up to a mad world. In Cato, Lucan presents Stoic and Republican principles in contrast to the brutal imperialism of Caesar, who becomes even more of a monster after Pharsalus.

Battle scenes in Virgil are certainly gory, but they are also indicative of glory, exuding *virtus*, heroism and honour. The battles were fought in a just war with honourable, patriotic aims. On the other hand, Lucan's war is morally bankrupt; his topology is a hell on earth where nature is utterly devastated and, for example, wild animals rive at the rotting flesh of the unburied dead. There is nothing heroic or honourable about Lucan's epic world; there is no *virtus* to be had here. To Lucan, a full century later, the civil wars were still remembered as positively craven, degenerate and shameful.

Endnotes

Chapter 1. How did it come to this?

1. *Divus Julius* 32. Suetonius gives the usually accepted Latin version, *iacta alea est*, although Plutarch, in his *Parallel Lives*, says that Caesar quoted a line from Menander: 'ἀνερρίφθω κύβος', 'let the die be cast'. Suetonius' translation is also quoted as *alea iacta est*. Alea was a game played with a die or dice rather than the dice themselves, so we could also translate as 'The game is on' or, in modern parlance perhaps, 'bring it on'.
2. Appian, *Civil Wars* 2, 35
3. Brunt (1971), pp.44–60
4. See G. Colin, *Rome et la Grece*; J. Griffin, *Augustan Poetry*, p.88ff and the Appendix, *Some Imperial Servants*. Various suggestions for the start and or cause of the decline have been made: Polybius, 31, 25, ascribes it to the victory over Macedonia; L. Calpurnius Piso (Pliny *NH* 17, 38, 244) goes with 154 BCE; Appian, *Bellum Civili* 1, 7, opts for the end of the war in Italy; Livy 39, 6, 7, prefers 186 BCE; Velleius Paterculus, *Historiae Romanae*, and Sallust, *Catilina* 10, 1, and *Jugurtha* 41, 1, prefer the end of the Third Punic War. See also Catullus 51.
5. See Cato, *On Agriculture*
6. By Alston, *Rome's Revolution*, p.11
7. Sallust, *Jugurtha* 101; Orosius 5, 15
8. Livy, *Epitome* 67; Orosius 5, 16; Dio 27 *fr*. 91; Eutropius 5, 1
9. Plutarch, *Sulla* 24–27; Livy, *op. cit.*; Orosius, *op. cit.*; Florus, *op. cit.*; Eutropius 5, 2

Chapter 2. The Social War (91–88 BCE)

1. Appian, *op.cit.* 1, 34, 152
2. Salmon (1958), *Notes on the Social War*

3. Appian, *op.cit.* 1, 41; Livy, *Epitome* 72, 73; Orosius 5, 18, 14–16
4. Appian, *op.cit.*
5. Appian, *op.cit.* 1, 42
6. Appian, *op.cit.* 1, 43; Orosius 5, 18, 1113; Livy, *Epitome* 73
7. Appian, *op.cit.* 1, 45; Orosius 5, 18, 11
8. Appian, *op.cit.* 1, 4748; Livy, *Epitome* 76; Orosius 5, 18, 18; Florus 3, 18
9. Orosius 5, 18, 24
10. Appian, *op.cit.* 1, 50; 1, 52; Orosius 5, 18, 23
11. Appian, *op.cit.* 1, 53; Livy, *Epitome* 76; Orosius 5, 18, 25
12. Matyszak, *Cataclysm 90 BC*, p.vii

Chapter 3. Sulla's First Civil War (88–87 BCE)

1. Appian, *Mithridatic Wars* 18, 21 – trans. Horace White, Loeb edition
2. Appian, *op.cit.* 19
3. Appian, *op.cit.* 22
4. Appian, *op.cit.* 23
5. Plutarch, *Sulla* 35 records that a mere three slaves took up the offer! Appian, *Civil Wars* 1, 57–58; Florus 2, 9, 68
6. Appian, *Mithridatic Wars* 18
7. Appian, *op.cit.* 19
8. Appian, *op.cit.* 18, 21 – trans. Horace White, Loeb edition
9. Plutarch, *op.cit.* 15–19; 20–21; Appian, *op.cit.* 41–45, 49. Frontinus, *Strategemata* 2, 3, 17
10. Plutarch, *op.cit.* 21
11. Plutarch, *Sulla* 14, 7. Appian, *op.cit.* 38
12. Appian, *Sicily fr.* 6; Appian, *op.cit.* 84–85; Plutarch, *Lucullus* 25–28, 6

Chapter 4. Sulla's Second Civil War (82–81 BCE)

1. Appian, *Civil War* 1, 84; Velleius Paterculus 2, 25, 2; Florus 2, 9, 20; Eutropius 5, 7
2. Plutarch, *Pompey* 7, 3; Appian, *op.cit.* 1, 87
3. Appian, *op.cit*; Florus 2, 9, 23; Livy, *Epitome* 87
4. Appian, *op.cit.* 1, 89
5. Appian, *op.cit.* 1, 90
6. Appian, *op.cit.* 1, 91; Velleius Paterculus 2, 28, 1; Livy, *Epitome* 88

7. Appian, *op.cit.* 1, 92; Livy, *op.cit.*
8. Plutarch, *Sulla* 3, 57–58
9. Livy, *Epitome* 88; Eutropius 5, 8; Appian, *op.cit.* 1, 93; Plutarch, *op.cit.*29–30; Velleius Paterculus 2, 27, 13; Orosius 5, 20, 9
10. See Lintott, *The Constitution of the Roman Republic*, p.110. Livy 22, 8, 56
11. Livy 3, 26–29. See Ward Fowler, *Passing Under the Yoke*
12. Plutarch, *op.cit.* 31
13. Eg: Anthony Everitt, *Cicero*, p.41
14. Velleius Paterculus 2, 22; 2, 41; Florus 2, 9; Suetonius, *Julius Caesar* 1; Plutarch, *Caesar* 1
15. Plutarch, *Sertorius* 12, 3
16. Plutarch, *op.cit.* 12, 34; 18, 36; *idem Pompey* 18, 3; Florus 2, 10, 67; Eutropius 6, 1; Orosius 5, 23, 34; 67; Livy, *Epitome* 90
17. Orosius 5, 23, 10; Livy, *Epitome* 91
18. Plutarch, *Pompey* 18, 3
19. Plutarch, *op.cit,* 19, 14; *idem Sertorius* 19; Appian, 1, 110 is suspect
20. Plutarch, *op.cit.*; Cicero, *Pro Balbo* 2, 5
21. Plutarch, *op.cit.* 21, 13; Appian, *op.cit.*
22. Appian, *op.cit.* 1, 112; Livy, *Epitome* 93
23. Appian, *op.cit.* 1, 107; Florus 2, 11
24. Plutarch, *Lucullus* 8; Appian, *Mithridatic Wars* 71; Livy, *op.cit.*
25. Plutarch, *op.cit.* 11, 13; Appian, *op.cit.* 75
26. Plutarch, *op.cit.* 11, 6; Appian, *op.cit.* 76
27. Plutarch, *op.cit.* 12; 15; 17, 12; Appian, *op.cit.* 77; 79–81
28. Appian, *Sicily fr.* 6; Appian, *Mithridatic Wars* 84–85; Plutarch, *Lucullus* 25; 28, 6
29. Appian, *op.cit.* 82
30. Appian, *op.cit.* 94
31. Plutarch, *Pompey* 28; Appian, *op.cit.* 96
32. Appian, *op.cit.* 111; a remedy with as many as sixty-five or so constituents, used as an antidote for poisoning. It was much in demand in the Middle Ages (against plague) and Renaissance, in Italy and France, for centuries. A revised recipe, theriac (*Theriacum Andromachi*), was prevalent in the nineteenth century.
33. Dio, 37, 13
34. Appian, *op.cit.* 112-113

Chapter 5. The Spartacus Revolt (73 71 BCE)

1. Plutarch, *Crassus* 8; trans. Rex Warner
2. Florus, *History of Rome*; Livy, *Epitome* 2, 8; trans. Edward Forster
3. Sallust, *Historiae* 3, 96; Frontinus, *Strategemata* 1, 5, 22
4. Appian, *Civil Wars*, estimates, or exaggerates, an army 70,000 strong.
5. Cf Plutarch, *op.cit.* 9, 6; Livy, *Periochae* 96. Sallust, *ibid.*, 3, 106
6. Appian, 1, 116–117
7. Florus, *ibid.* Orosius, *Histories* 5, 24, 18
8. Plutarch, *op.cit.* 9
9. Frontinus, 2, 4, 7. Plutarch, *op.cit.* 10, 13
10. Pirates: Plutarch, *ibid.* Barrels: Florus, *Epitome* 2, 8; Cicero, *Oratio Pro Sextio Roscio* 5, 2. Trench: cf Sallust, *op.cit.* 4, 25
11. Appian, 1, 119
12. Frontinus 2, 5, 34; Orosius 5, 24, 6; Plutarch, *op.cit.* 11, 23; Livy, *Epitome* 97
13. Crassus: Appian 1, 120. Plutarch, *op.cit.* 11, 45
14. Orosius 5, 24, 58; Livy, *ibid.*; Appian 1, 120; Plutarch, *op.cit.* 11, 67. Florus, *ibid.*
15. Plutarch, *Pompey* 21, 5. See Cicero, *In Pisonem* 58; Pliny, *NH* 15, 125; Plutarch, *Crassus* 11, 8; *Pompey* 22
16. Cicero, *Philippics* 3, 21; 4, 15; 13, 22. Horace, *Epodes* 16, 5; *Odes* 3, 14, 18–20
17. Cicero, *Ad Atticum* 7, 14, 2

Chapter 6. The Catiline Conspiracy (63–62 BCE)

1. Cicero, *Pro Caelio* 12
2. Cicero, In *Catilinam* 3, 9; Asconius 91c
3. Q. Cicero, *Commentariolum Petitionis* 3
4. Sallust, *Bellum Catilinae* 23, 51–4, 1; 21, 2
5. Sallust, *op.cit.* 26, 1; 26, 5
6. Sallust, *op.cit.* 27, 12; 30, 12; 27,3 28, 3; Cicero, *Pro Murena* 49
7. Cicero, *In Catilinam* 3, 46; Sallust, *op.cit.* 40; 45
8. Sallust, *op.cit.* 61, 4; Florus, *Epitome de Tito Livio* 2, 12; Cassius Dio 37; 39–40; Appian, *Civil Wars* 2, 7
9. Cicero, *Pro Caelio* 5; Sallust, *op.cit.* 34, 2; Cicero, *In Catilinam* 2, 13

Chapter 7. The Carrhae Disaster (53 BCE)

1. Dio 37; 48; Livy, *Epitome* 103
2. Josephus, *Jewish Antiquities* 14, 5, 2 (82–85); 14, 6, 3 (101–102); *Jewish Wars* 1, 8, 23 (160165); 1, 8, 7 (177)
3. Plutarch, *Crassus* 16, 5–6; translation in Sarah Iles Johnston, *Religions of the Ancient World* (Harvard University Press, 2004), p.510. See Cicero, *De Divinatione* 1, 29–30; Velleius Paterculus 2, 46, 3, the commentary by A.J. Woodman (Cambridge University Press, 2004); Appian, *op.cit.* 2, 18; Florus 1, 46, 3. For the departure, see Cicero, *Ad Atticum* 4, 13, 2, and *Ad Familiares* 1, 9, 20, and Lucan, *Bellum Civile* 3, 43ff and 3, 126–7
4. Cicero, *De Finibus Bonorum et Malorum* 3.22; 3, 75. Plutarch, *Lucullus*, 25ff.; Appian, *Mithridates* 87; Dio, 36, 1ff.; Sallust, *Histories* 4 fr. 69; Plutarch, *op.cit.* 30; Dio, 36; Cicero, *Oratio Pro Lege Manila* 23–24
5. Plutarch, *Pompey* 36; Pliny, *N.H.* 6,52; Dio, 37, 5, 2
6. Cicero, *De Domo Sua* 60, 124; Dio, 39, 56; Justin, 42.4.1; Appian, *Syriaca* 51, cf. Plutarch, *Crassus* 21
7. Plutarch, *op.cit.* 16
8. Translation by John Dryden. Dio 32.2; 40.20; cf. Plutarch, *op.cit.* 22
9. Plutarch, *op.cit.* 19
10. Mommsen, p.328. Tarn (1932), p.607
11. Plutarch, *op.cit.* 42, 10. Shakespeare, *Julius Caesar* 1, 2, 193
12. Gnaeus Pompeius Trogus a first-century BCE Roman historian of the Celtic tribe, the Vocontii in Gallia Narbonensis; a near contemporary to Livy. His *magnum opus* was the forty-four-book *Historiae Philippicae*, called that because the Macedonian Empire founded by Philip II forms the central theme of the narrative. This was a general history of lands ruled by Alexander and his successors. Justin wrote an *epitome* of Trogus' lost work, and in the manuscripts a series of anonymous *prologi* of the books by an unknown hand is extant. The last event recorded by Justin is the recovery of the Roman standards captured by the Parthians in 20 BCE.
13. Caesar, *Bellum Civile* 3, 31, 3; Velleius Paterculus, *History of Rome* 2, 46, 4; Appian, *Syriaca* 3, 9, 1. Tarn, *Greeks*, p.51.
14. Plutarch, *op.cit.* 25. From *Plutarch: Parallel Lives* (1916), trans. Bernadotte Perrin (Loeb Classical Library)

15. Dio, 40, 22–23. From *Dio* (1914), trans. Earnest Cary and Herbert B. Foster (Loeb Classical Library)
16. Plutarch, *op.cit.* 21, 6 21, 7
17. Tarn (1932), p.611. Dio 40, 26, 3
18. H. Bivar, *The Political History of Iran under the Arsacids*, pp.21–99
19. Cary, *A History of Rome*, pp.256–7
20. Ovid, *Fasti* 5, 583585; *Ars Amatoria* 1, 179180; Propertius 2, 10, 1314; 4, 7, 83–85

Chapter 8. The First Triumvirate: Julius Caesar, Pompey the Great and Marcus Licinius Crassus (59–53 BCE)

1. Suetonius, *Caesar* 16
2. Dio 37, 42
3. Plutarch, *Pompey* 49, 3
4. Dio 38, 4–7.6; Appian, *The Civil Wars* 2, 11–12; Plutarch, *Cato the Younger* 32, 2
5. Appian, *op.cit.* 2.12; Dio 38.9; Plutarch, *Lucullus* 42.7; Suetonius, *Julius Caesar* 20.5; Cicero, *Ad Atticum* 2.24
6. Cicero, *De Haruspicum Responsis* 17, 37 – 18, 38
7. Plutarch, *Cicero* 32
8. Dio, 39.64.1; Appian, *op.cit.* 2.19

Chapter 9. Caesar's Gallic Wars (58–50 BCE)

1. Caesar, *De Bello Gallica* 1, 3
2. *Idem,* 1, 4
3. *Idem,* 1, 56
4. *Idem,* 1, 78
5. *Idem,* 1, 89
6. *Idem,* 1,10
7. *Idem,* 1, 111
8. *Idem* 1, 13–24
9. *Idem,* 1, 31
10. *Idem,* 1, 1
11. *Idem, Bello Gallico* 2, 1 2, 5
12. *Idem*, 2, 6; 2, 12, 14–15
13. *Idem* 2, 4
14. *Idem,* 2, 4; 5; 12

15. *Idem*, 3, 8–9
16. Strabo, *Geography* 4, 4
17. Caesar, *De Bello Gallica* 4, 22
18. *Ibid*, 4, 23
19. *Ibid,* 4, 25
20. Strabo, 2:4.1, written soon after Caesar; Polybius, *Histories* 34, 5
21. *Idem,* 1, 31
22. Caesar, *De Bello Gallica* 7, 4; 7, 9; 7, 10. Trans. Loeb Classical Library, 1917
23. Polyaenus, *Strategemata* 8, 23, 5
24. Caesar, *De Bello Gallica* 7, 38
25. *Idem* 4, 33
26. *Idem* 1, 54
27. *Idem* 7, 47
28. *Idem* 7, 48
29. *Idem* 7, 53
30. *Idem* 7, 70
31. *Idem,* 7, 71–88

Chapter 10. Caesar's Civil War (49–45 BCE)

1. Plutarch, *Caesar* 23.5–6; *Pompey* 53.4–6
2. Florus 2, 13, 14
3. Plutarch, *Pompey* 54; *Cato Minor* 47–49
4. Suetonius, *Julius Caesar* 28
5. Plutarch, *Cato Minor* 49; *Pompey* 54.56, 57
6. Caesar, *op.cit.* 2, 4146
7. Caesar, *Commentarii de Bello Civili* 2, 2; trans. Loeb Classical Library
8. Caesar, *op.cit,* 3, 104; Livy, *Epitome* 104; Dio, *Historia Romanae* 42, 4
9. Dio 42, 34, 36. Caesar, *op.cit* 3, 109
10. Plutarch, *Caesar* 49.13; Lucan, *De Bello Civili* 10, 5658. Cf Dio 42.34.6–35.1. The translation is by Rex Warner, *Plutarch, the Fall of the Roman Republic*, p.290.
11. Lucan, *op.cit.* 10, 139–140
12. Suetonius, *Julius Caesar* 52, 1
13. Appian, *The Civil Wars*, 2, 90
14. Suetonius, *op.cit.* 76.3
15. Dio 43, 27, 3; Cicero, *Ad Atticum* 15, 15, 2

16. Appian, *Bellum Civile* 2, 102, 424; Dio, *op.cit.* 51.22.3
17. Cicero, *op.cit.* 15.15.2; 14, 8, 1
18. Dio, *op.cit.* 43.38; Caesar, *De Bello Hispaniensi* 31
19. Plutarch, *op.cit* 57

Chapter 11. Power Politics and Assassination (44–43 BCE)

1. Plutarch, *Caesar* 56, 7–56, 8
2. Dio 43,19, 23; Appian, *Civil Wars* 2, 101, 420
3. Caesar, *Commentarii de Bello Civili* 3, 109–112; *B. Alex.* 4; Dio 42, 3640; Lucan, *De Bello Civili* 10, 519–523
4. *De Bello Alexandrino* 23–24; cf Dio, 42, 42
5. Appian, *op.cit.* 2, 143, 1
6. Caesar, *De Bello Gallica* 2, 41–46
7. Plutarch, *op.cit.* 61
8. Suetonius, *Julius Caesar* 79, 2
9. Suetonius, *op.cit.* 82
10. Plutarch, *op.cit.* 66, 9
11. Lucan, *op. cit.* 72–89
12. Plutarch, *op.cit.* 67
13. Appian, *op.cit.* 2, 147
14. Florus, *Epitome* 2, 7, 1
15. Suetonius, *op.cit.* 83, 2; Appian, *op.cit.* 3, 9–11
16. Nicolaus of Damascus, *Augustus* 4

Chapter 12. The Second Triumvirate: Octavian, Mark Antony and Marcus Aemilius Lepidus,(43 33 BCE)

1. Appian, *Civil Wars* 3, 11–12
2. Suetonius, *Augustus* 61
3. Suetonius, *Caesar* 49
4. Suetonius, *Augustus* 13, 1; Florus, *Epitome* 2, 6
5. Dio Cassius, *Roman History* 47
6. Cicero, *Phillipics* 3, 16
7. See Hallet, *Perusinae Glandes*
8. Martial 11, 20.
9. Florus 2.16.2. Valerius Maximus 3, 5, 3

10. Cicero, *Phillipics* 13, 18
11. Appian, *op.cit.* 3, 8, 51
12. Dio 48, 4, 16.
13. Appian 5, 3, 19; 5, 2, 14
14. *ibid* 5, 4, 32
15. Dio 48, 5, 15
16. Appian 5, 3, 19; Dio 48, 10, 3
17. Appian 5, 4, 32. Dio 48, 15, 1
18. Appian 5, 4, 33
19. Plutarch, *Antony* 30, 3
20. Dio 48, 20
21. Dio 47, 7, 45
22. Dio 48, 28
23. Tacitus, *Annals* 11, 32, 5; *Histories* 3, 81. Suetonius, *Augustus* 101
24. Syme, *Roman Revolution* p.270

Chapter 13. Actium and Empire (31 BCE)

1. Dio 50, 14, 1–2; cf. Velleius Paterculus 2, 84, 2
2. Dio 50, 23, 13
3. Dio 50, 31, 1–3
4. Appian 4, 61, 262–263; Dio 47.30.4 and 47, 31, 5
5. Appian, *op.cit* 5, 9, 35
6. For the importance of balsam as a commodity, see Pliny *NH* 12, 111, and Josephus, *op.cit.* 15, 4, 2; bitumen, Diodorus Siculus 19, 98–99. Plutarch, *op.cit.* 54, 9
7. Plutarch, *op.cit.* 60
8. Plutarch, *op.cit.* 78–79
9. Suetonius, *Augustus* 17, 4
10. Plutarch, *op.cit* 82; 86
11. *Ibid* 81, 4 – 82, 1; Dio, *op.cit.* 51, 15, 5; Suetonius, *op.cit.* 17, 5
12. Plutarch, *op.cit* 87.1–2; Dio, *op. cit* 51, 15, 6; Suetonius, *op.cit.* and *Caligula* 26, 1

Chapter 14. The Cleopatra Effect

1. Virgil, *Aeneid* 4 300–301; 384–7; 450–473; 483ff
2. For Dido's curse, see O'Gorman, *Does Dido's Curse Work?; Virgil, op.cit.* 8, 696ff.

3. Horace, *Epodes* 9, 11–16
4. For themes used by the love poets and their significance, see Chrystal, *Differences.*
5. Propertius, *op.cit* 4, 6, 57–66
6. Juvenal 2, 109
7. Martial 4, 59
8. Lucan, *De Bello Civili* 10, 104–106; 107ff
9. *ibid.* 353ff. Grant, *Cleopatra* p.xvii

Chapter 15. The Social and Literary Impact

1. *CIL* 6, 11, 60–2
2. *CIL* 1, 107
3. All originally by Cicero: *De Oratore* 161; *Ad Atticum* 7, 2, 21; *Tusculanae Disputationes* 3, 45. See also Chrystal, *Investigation* p.15ff; Ross, *Backgrounds*; Tuplin, Cantores Euphorionis; *idem*, Cantores Euphorionis *Again*; Luck, *Latin Love Elegy* p.49ff; Crowther, *Valerius Cato;* see Lyne, *Latin Love Poets* pp.16974. For *otium* see Andre, *L'*Otium
4. Catullus 61, 71–73; Propertius 2,7,13f
5. Appian 4, 32–34
6. Valerius Maximus 8, 3
7. Cicero, *Ad Familiares* 5, 2, 6; Dio 48, 16, 3; 51, 2, 45
8. Suetonius, *Julius Caesar* 50; Plutarch, *Cato the Younger* 24, 1; *idem*, *Brutus* 5, 2; Appian, *Civil Wars*; Cicero, *Ad Familiares* 12, 7; *idem*, *Ad Atticum* 14, 21; 15, 11; 15, 12
9. See Pomeroy, *Relationship* p.222ff; del Castillo, *Position* p.171; Villers, *Statut* p.184f
10. Kiefer, *Sexual Life* p.24
11. See Horace, *Odes* 3, 6; Kajanto, *On Divorce*; Hamilton, *Society Women*. Pomeroy, *op.cit.*, argues that in Catullus' day women were enjoying a kind of *de facto* freedom on account of the disinterest shown by many *propinqui*. Decline in *patria potestas* is covered by Reinhold, *op.cit.* p.49; see also Fau p.30 and del Castillo, *op.cit.* pp.167–70; Richlin, *Approaches*
12. Appian 4, 39–40; trans. adapted from the Loeb Classical Library edition, 1913
13. Appian 5, 76; Plutarch, *Antony* 33, 3
14. *ILS* 8393. Tr. adapted from E. Wistrand

15. Valerius Maximus 7, 2
16. Cicero, Ad *Atticum* 15, 11
17. Cicero, *Ad Famiiares* 14, 46
18. Pliny, *Letters* 6, 24; Plutarch, *Brutus* 13; 23, 6; and Dio 44, 1314. See also Valerius Maximus 4.6 and 6, 7 on brave and faithful wives
19. Gregson Davis, in his *introduction to Virgil's Eclogues*, trans. by Len Krisak. Introduction by Gregson Davis, 2010
20. Ovid, *Metamorphoses* 1, 89–100
21. Donatus, *Vita Vergilii* 91–95
22. Virgil, *Aeneid* 2, 103640; trans. R. Fitzgerald, *The Aeneid* (1983)
23. *Ibid,* 1, 25796; trans. David West (ed.), *Virgil: The Aeneid: a New Prose Translation* (London 1991)
24. Grebe, *Augustus' Divine Authority and Vergil's 'Aeneid'*, p.48
25. Virgil 6, 789–794; trans. R. Fitzgerald, *The Aeneid*
26. John Conington trans. (London, George Bell and Sons, 1882)
27. Virgil, *Eclogues* 4, 8; Horace, *Odes* 2, 1
28. Appian 2.40; 2.45; 2.82
29. Suetonius, *Augustus* 14, 15, trans. Robert Graves
30. Dio 48, 14, 5
31. Suetonius, *Claudius* 41. Seneca the Elder, *Controversiae* 10.3.5; Valerius Maximus: 3.3.2: *ne…ad civilium bellorum detestendam memoriam progredi cogar*
32. Lucan, *De Bello Civili* 1, 44–45
33. Lucan, *op.cit.* 1, 17; trans. adapted from the 1896 Sir Edward Ridley translation
34. Braund (1992), pp.xxvii and xxviii

Timeline 133–27 BCE

133 BCE

Tiberius Gracchus tribune.

123–122 BCE

Gaius Gracchus tribune.

91–89 BCE

Social War between Rome and its Italian allies. Italians demand Roman citizenship and equal share in power.

88–87 BCE

First Civil War between Marius and Sulla. First march on Rome by Sulla.

88–63 BCE

Wars between Mithridates VI and Roman Republic.

86 BCE

Death of Marius.

83 BCE

Pompey fights under the Roman dictator Sulla.

83 BCE

Sulla's second march on Rome. Proscriptions.

80 BCE

Sulla is persuaded to give Pompey his first triumph in Rome.

71 BCE

Pompey is granted his second triumph for his victories in Spain.

Crassus crushes Spartacus.

Pompey defeats Sertorius' rebellion in Spain.

70 BCE
Pompey and Crassus are consuls.

67 BCE
The Gabinian Law is passed, giving Pompey power to deal with pirates.

66 BCE
The Manilian Law is passed, giving Pompey great power to deal with Mithridates VI of Pontus.

64 BCE
Pompey defeats the Seleucid Antiochus XIII and incorporates Syria as a province of Rome.

63 BCE
Cicero consul. Catiline conspiracy.

62 BCE
Pompey returns to Italy and disbands his army.

60–53 BCE
First Triumvirate between Caesar, Pompey and Crassus.

58–51 BCE
Julius Caesar's conquest of Gaul.

58–57 BCE
Cicero exiled from Rome.

58 BCE
Caesar attacks the Helvetii and defeats them.

55 BCE
Caesar invades Britain.

54–53 BCE
Ambiorix of the Eburones tribe destroys around 9,000 Roman soldiers at Atuatuca.

54 BCE
Caesar invades Britain for a second time.

53 BCE
Battle of Carrhae. Crassus is captured and executed by the Parthians. Standards lost.

52 BCE
Besieged at Alesia, Vercingetorix surrenders to Caesar.

Caesar defeated at Gergovia by Vercingetorix.

Pompey consul.

51 BCE
Caesar's siege and capture of Uxellodunum ends the Gallic War.

49 BCE
Caesar crosses the Rubicon. Civil war between Caesar and Pompey begins.

48 BCE
Caesar defeats Pompey at Battle of Pharsalus

44 BCE
The Allobroges unsuccessfully rise against Roman rule in southern Gaul.

Caesar becomes dictator for life. On the 'Ides of March' (15th) he is killed by conspirators including Brutus and Cassius. Octavian, son of Caesar's niece Atia, is adopted as his heir.

Mark Antony consul. Antony attacks Brutus.

43 BCE
Cicero killed in proscriptions.

Battles of Mutina.

Octavian marches on Rome. Octavian consul.

Lex Titia.

43–36 BCE
Second Roman Triumvirate: Antony, Octavian, and Lepidus. Mass proscriptions including Cicero.

42 BCE

Octavian and Antony defeat Republicans under Brutus and Cassius at the Battle of Philippi.

Death of Cassius.

Death of Brutus.

Lucius Antonius consul.

41 BCE

Antony meets Cleopatra.

Perusine War.

Peace of Brundisium.

39 BCE

Octavian marries Livia.

38 BCE

Octavian makes war with Sextus Pompeius.

36 BCE

Octavian strips Lepidus of all power except Pontifex Maximus.

Battle of Naulochus

34 BCE

Donations of Alexandria.

32 BCE

War between Antony and Octavian.

31 BCE

Octavian defeats Antony and Cleopatra at the Battle of Actium. Antony and Cleopatra commit suicide.

27 BCE

Octavian granted extraordinary powers by the Senate and assumes the name Augustus.

Bibliography

Abbott, F.F., *A History and Descriptions of Roman Political Institutions* (3rd ed.) (New York, 1963)

Abramson, E., *Roman Legionaries at the Time of Julius Caesar* (London, 1979)

Achaud, G., '*Bellum iustum, bellum sceleratum* Sous les Rois et Sous la Republique', *BStudLat* 24, 1994, pp.474-86

Adams, J.P., *Logistics of the Roman Army* (London, 1976)

Adcock, F.E., *The Roman Art of War Under the Republic* (Cambridge MA, 1940)

Adie, K., *Corsets to Camouflage: Women and War* (London, 2003)

Adler, E., *Valorizing the Barbarians: Enemy Speeches in Roman Historiography* (Austin TX, 2011)

Afflerbach, H. (ed.), *How Fighting Ends: A History Of Surrender* (Oxford, 2012)

Ahl, F., 'The Rider and the Horse: Politics and Power in Roman Poetry from Horace to Statius', *ANRW* 2.32.1, 1984, pp.40-110

Allison, P.M., *People and Spaces in Roman Military Bases* (Cambridge, 2013)

Alston R., 'Roman Military Pay from Caesar to Diocletian', *JRS* 84, 1994, pp.113-23

Alston, R., *Rome's Revolution: Death of the Republic and Birth of the Empire* (Oxford, 2015)

Aly, A.A., 'Cleopatra and Caesar at Alexandria and Rome', in Caratelli, G.P. (ed.), *Roma e l'Egitto* (Rome, 1992), pp.47-61

Anderson, A., *Roman Military Tombstones* (Oxford, 1983)

Anderson, J.G.C., 'Pompey's Campaign against Mithradates', *JRS* 12, 1922, p.99ff.

Anglim, S., *Fighting Techniques of the Ancient World 3000 BC–AD 500* (London, 2002)

Appels, A., *Roman Buckles and Military Fittings* (Witham, 2007)

Arieti, J.A., 'Rape and Livy´s View of Roman History', in Deacy, *Rape in Antiquity* (1997), pp.209-29

Askin, K.D., *War Crimes Against Women: Prosecution in International War Crimes Tribunal* (Amsterdam, 1997)

Austin, N.J.E., 'Ammianus on Warfare', *Latomus* 165, 1979

Babcock, C., 'The Early Career of Fulvia', *AJPh* 86, 1965, pp.1-32

Badian, Ernst, *Foreign* Clientelae (London, 1958)

Badian, E., *Roman Imperialism in the Late Republic* (Oxford, 1968)

Badian, E., 'Rome, Athens and Mithridates', AJAH 1, 1976, pp.105-28

Badian, E., 'The Early Historians', in Dorey, *Latin Historians*, 1966, pp.1-38

Badian, E., 'Waiting for Sulla', *Journal of Roman Studies* 52, 1962, pp.47-61

Bahmanyar, M., *Vanquished: Crushing Defeats from Ancient Rome to the 21st Century* (Oxford, 2009)

Baker, G.P., *Sulla the Fortunate: Roman General and Dictator* (1927)

Baldwin, B., 'Two Aspects of the Spartacus Slave Revolt', *CJ* 62, 1966, p.289ff.

Ball, W., *Rome in the East: The Transformation of an Empire* (London, 2001)

Balsdon, J.P.V.D., *Romans and Aliens* (London, 1979)

Balsdon, J.P.V.D., *Roman Women* (London, 1962)

Barnes, J., 'Ciceron et la Guerre Juste', *Bulletin de la Societe Francaise de Philosophie* 80, 1986, pp.41-81

Baronowski, D.W., *Polybius and Roman Imperialism* (London, 2013)

Barton, C.A., 'The Price of Peace in Ancient Rome', in Raaflaub, *War and Peace in the Ancient World*, pp.245-55 (Chichester, 2007)

Bauman, R.A., *Crime and Punishment in Ancient Rome* (London, 1996)

Bauman, R.A., *Women and Politics in Ancient Rome* (London, 1992)

Beard, M., *SPQR* (London, 2015)

Beard, M., *The Roman Triumph* (Harvard MA, 2009)

Beaver, J., *The Roman Military Punishments* (Cambridge MA, 2011)

Beck, H. (ed.) *Consuls and Res Publica: Holding High Office in the Roman Republic* (Cambridge, 2011)

Beesley, E.S., 'Cicero and Clodius', in *Fortnightly Review*, v.; G. Lacour-Gayet, De P. Clodio Pulchro (Paris, 1888), and in *Revue Historique* (Sept. 1889)

Bell, K.K., '"Translatio" and the Constructs of a Roman Nation in Virgil's "Aeneid"', *Rocky Mountain Review* 62, 2008, pp.11–24

Bell, M.J.V., 'Tactical Reform in the Roman Republican Army', *Historia* 14, 1965, pp.404-22

Bellemore, J., 'Cato the Younger in the East in 66 BC', *Historia* 44, 1995, pp.376-79

Benario, J., 'Book 4 of Horace's Odes: Augustan Propaganda', *Transactions and Proceedings of the American Philological Association* 91, 1960, pp.339-52

Berry, J., *The Complete Roman Legions* (London, 2012)

Bertrand, A.C., 'Stumbling Through Gaul: Intelligence and Caesar's *Bellum Gallicum*', *Ancient History Bulletin* 2, 4, 1997, pp.107-22

Best, E.E., 'Cicero, Livy and Educated Roman Women', *CJ* 65, 1970, pp.199-204

Billows, R.A., *Julius Caesar: The Colossus of Rome* (Routledge, 2009)

Bishop, M., *Roman Military Equipment* 2 (Oxford, 2005)

Bloch, R., *Combats Singuliers Entre Gaulois et Romans* (Paris, 1968)

Boissier, G., *Cicero and his Friends* (Eng. trans., 1897)

Boot, M., *Invisible Armies: An Epic History of Guerrilla Warfare from Ancient Times to the Present* (London, 2014)

Bordewich, F.M., 'The Ambush That Changed History', *Smithsonian Magazine*, September 2006

Börm, H. (ed.), *Civil War in Ancient Greece and Rome: Contexts of Disintegration and Reintegration* (Stuttgart, 2016)

Boudet, J., *The Ancient Art of Warfare* (London, 1966)

Bourriau, J. (ed.), *Understanding Catastrophe* (Cambridge, 1992)

Bowman, A.K., *The Roman Agricultural Economy* (Oxford, 2013)

Bradley, G. (ed), *Greek and Roman Colonization: Origins, Ideologies and Interactions* (Swansea, 2005)

Bradley, K.R., *Slavery and Rebellion in the Roman World (140 BC - 40 BC)* (London, 1989)

Bragg, E., 'Beyond the Battlefield: Caesar on Massacres, Executions and Mutilations', *Omnibus* 54, 2007, pp.15-18

Bragg, M. (presenter), *Spartacus. In Our Time* (BBC Radio 4, 6 March 2014)

Brand, C.E., *Roman Military Law* (Austin TX, 1968)

Braund, D.C., 'Piracy under the Principate and the ideology of imperial eradication', in Rich, J.R. (ed.), *War and Society in the Roman World* (London, 1993), pp.195-212

Braund, D.C., *Rome and the Friendly King: The Character of the Client Kingship* (London, 1984)

Braund, D.C., *Ruling Roman Britain: Kings, Queens, Governors, and Emperors from Julius Caesar to Agricola* (New York, 1996)

Braund, S. (ed.), *Ancient Anger: Perspectives from Homer to Galen* (Cambridge, 2003)

Braund, S. (ed.), 'Introduction', *Lucan: Civil War* (Oxford, 1992)

Breeze, D., 'The Organization of the Legion: The First Cohort and the Equites Legionis', *JRS* 59, 1980, pp.50-55

Brennan, T.C., 'Perception of Women's Power in the Late Republic: Terentia, Fulvia and the Generation of 63 BC', in James, *Companion* (2012), pp.354-66

Brewer, R., *Roman Legions and Their Fortresses* (London, 2000)

Broadhead, W., 'Colonisation, Land Distribution and Veteran Settlement', in Erdkamp, P., *A Companion to the Roman Army* (Chichester, 2007)

Broughton, T.R.S., *The Magistrates of the Roman Republic Vol 1: 509 BC – 100 BC* (Cleveland OH, 1951)

Brownmiller, S., *Against Our Will: Men, Women and Rape* (Harmondsworth, 1975)

Brunt, P.A., 'Conscription and Volunteering in the Roman Army', *Scripta Classica Israelica* 1, 1974, pp.90-115

Brunt, P.A, *Italian Manpower* (Oxford, 1987)

Brunt, P.A., 'The Army and the Land in the Roman Revolution', *JRS* 52, 1962, pp.69-86

Brunt, P.A., *The Fall of the Roman Republic and Related Essays* (Oxford, 1988)

Byrd, R., *The Senate of the Roman Republic*, U.S. Government Printing Office, 1995, Senate Document 103-23

Cadoux, T.J., 'Marcus Crassus: A Re-evaluation', *Greece & Rome* 3, 1956, pp.153–61

Cagniart, P., 'The Late Republican Army (146-30 BC)', in Erdkamp, P., *A Companion to the Roman Army* (Chichester, 2007)

Cairns, F., 'Propertius and the Battle of Actium (4, 6)', in Woodman, *Poetry and Politics in the Age of Augustus* (Cambridge, 1984), pp.129-68

Califf, David J., *Battle of Actium* (Philadelphia, Penn., 2004).

Campbell, B., *Ancient Siege Warfare: Persians, Greeks, Carthaginians* (Oxford, 2005)

Campbell, B., *Besieged: Siege Warfare in the Ancient World* (Oxford, 2006)

Campbell, B., *Greek & Roman Military Writers* (London, 2004)

Campbell, B. (ed.), *Oxford Handbook of Warfare in the Classical World* (Oxford, 2013)

Campbell, B., 'Teach Yourself How to be a General', *JRS* 77, 1987, pp.13-29

Campbell, B., 'The Marriage of Roman Soldiers Under the Empire', *JRS* 68, 1978, pp.153-66

Campbell, B., *The Roman Army, 31 BC–AD 337: A Sourcebook* (London, 1984)

Campbell, D.B., *Greek and Roman Siege Machinery 399 BC - AD 363* (Oxford, 2003)

Canfora, L., *Julius Caesar: The People's Dictator* (Edinburgh, 2006)

Carey, B.T., *Warfare in the Ancient World* (London, 2005)

Carney, T.F., *A Biography of C. Marius* (Chicago, 1970)

Carroll, M., *Celts and Germans: The German Provinces of Rome* (Stroud, 2001)

Carter, J., *The Battle of Actium: The Rise and Triumph of Augustus Caesar* (London, 1970)

Cary, M., *A History of Rome 3* (London, 1975)

Cary, M., 'The Lex Gabinia Once More', *Classical Review* 38, 1924

Casson, L., *Ships and Seamanship in the Ancient World* (Princeton, 1971)

Caston, V. (ed.), *Our Ancient Wars: Rethinking War through the Classics* (Ann Arbor, Michigan, 2016)

Chadwick, N., *The Celts* (London, 1970)

Champion, C.B., *Roman Imperialism: Readings and Sources* (Chichester, 2003)

Chaniotis, A. (ed.), *Army and Power in the Ancient World* (Stuttgart, 2002)

Chaplin, D. (ed.), *Livy: Oxford Readings in Classical Studies* (Oxford, 2009)

Chaplin, D., *Livy's Exemplary History* (Oxford, 2000)

Chavalas, M.V., *Women in the Ancient Near East* (London, 2013)

Cheeseman, G.L., *Auxilia of the Roman Army* (Oxford, 1914)

Chrystal, P., 'A Powerful Body of Women', *Minerva,* January-February 2014, pp.10-13

Chrystal, P., 'Differences in Attitude to Women as Reflected in the Work of Catullus, Propertius, the Corpus Tibullianum, Horace and Ovid' (diss, University of Southampton, 1982)

Chrystal, P., *How to be a Roman* (Stroud, 2017)

Chrystal, P., *In Bed with the Romans* (Stroud, 2015)

Chrystal, P., *Roman Military Disasters* (Barnsley, 2015)

Chrystal, P., *Roman Record Keeping and Communications* (Stroud, 2018)

Chrystal, P., 'Roman Women Go to War 1-4', *Omnibus* 68, October 2014

Chrystal, P., *Roman Women: The Women Who Influenced the History of Rome* (Stroud, 2015)

Chrystal, P., *Wars and Battles of the Roman Republic* (Stroud, 2015)

Chrystal, P., *When in Rome … A Social History of Rome* (Stroud, 2017)

Chrystal, P.,*Women at War in Ancient Greece & Rome* (Barnsley, 2017)

Chrystal, P., *Women in Ancient Rome* (Stroud, 2013)

Churchill, B., '*Ex Qua Quod Vellent Facerent*: Roman Magistrates' Authority over *Praeda* and *Manubiae*', *TAPhA* 129, 1999, pp.85-116

Cloud, D., 'Roman Poetry and Anti-Militarism', in J. Rich (ed.), *War and Society in the Ancient World* (1993), pp.113-38

Clutton-Brock, J., *Horse Power: A History of the Horse and the Donkey in Human Societies* (Harvard, 1992)

Cohen, E.A., *Military Misfortunes: The Anatomy of Failure in War* (New York, 1990)

Colin, G., '*Luxe Oriental et Parfums Masculins dans la Rome Alexandrine*', *RBPH* 33, 1935, pp.5-19

Colin, G., *Rome et la Grèce de 200 à 146 ans avant Jésus-Christ (Biblioth. des écoles franc. d'Athènes et de Rome, fasc. 94)* (Paris, 1905)

Collins, J.H., *Propaganda, Ethics and Psychological Assumptions in Caesar's Writing* (Frankfurt, 1952)

Connolly, P., *Greece and Rome at War* (London, 2006)

Cook, B.A. (ed.), *Women and War: A Historical Encyclopedia from Antiquity to the Present*, 2 Vols (Oxford, 2006)

Cooper, H.M. (ed.), *Arms and the Woman: War, Gender, and Literary Representation* (Chapel Hill NC, 1989)

Cotterell, A., *The Chariot: The Astounding Rise and Fall of the World's First War Machine* (London, 2004)

Coulston, J.C., *Roman Military Equipment from the Punic Wars to the Fall of Rome* (Oxford, 2005)

Courcelle, P., *Histoire Litteraire des Grandes Invasions Germaniques* (Paris, 1964)

Cowan, R., *For the Glory of Rome: A History of Warriors and Warfare* (London, 2007)

Cowan, R., *Roman Battle Tactics 109 BC-AD 313* (Oxford, 2007)

Cowan, R., *The Roman Conquests: Italy* (Barnsley, 2009)

Cowan, R., 'Wounds to the Front', *Ad Familiares* 33, 2007, pp.7-9

Crane, A.M., 'Roman Attitudes to Peace in the Late Republican and Early Imperial Periods: from Greek Origins to Contemporary Evidence' (PhD thesis, University of Kent, 2014)

Crawford, M., *The Roman Republic* (London, 1978)

Crawford, M.H., 'War and Finance', *JRS* 54, 1964, pp.29-32

Crump, G., *Ammianus Marcellinus as Military Historian* (Wiesbaden, 1975)

Crutchfield, M., A New Heroism: A Study of Battle Scenes in Lucan's *Bellum Civile* (diss., University of Missouri-Columbia, 2015)

Cuff, P.J., 'Caesar the Soldier', *G&R* 4, 1957, pp.29-35

Curchin, L.A., *Roman Spain: Conquest and Assimilation* (New York, 1995)

Curchin, L.A., *The Romanization of Central Spain: Complexity, Diversity and Change in a Provincial Hinterland* (London, 2004)

Dando-Collins, S., *Legions of Rome: The Definitive History of Every Roman Legion* (London, 2010)

Dart, C.J.,*The Social War, 91 to 88 BCE: A History of the Italian Insurgency against the Roman Republic* (London, 2014)

David, J.-M., *The Roman Conquest of Italy* (Oxford, 1997)

Davies, G., *Roman Siege Works* (Stroud, 2006)

Davies, R.W., *Service in the Roman Army* (Edinburgh, 1989)

Davies, R.W., 'The Roman Military Medical Service', *Sonderdruck aus dem Saalburg Jahrbuch*, 1970

Davis, P.K., *Besieged: 100 Great Sieges from Jericho to Sarajevo* (Oxford, 2001)

Davis, P.K., *100 Decisive Battles from Ancient Times to the Present: The World's Major Battles and How They Shaped History* (Oxford, 1999)

Dawson, D., *The Origins Of Western Warfare: Militarism And Morality In The Ancient World* (Boulder CO, 1997)

Deacy, S., (ed.), *Rape in Antiquity* (London, 1997)

de Blois, L., 'Army and General in the Late Roman Republic', in Erdkamp, P., *A Companion to the Roman Army* (Chichester, 2007)

de Brohun, 'The Gates of War (and Peace)', in Raaflaub, K.A., *War and Peace in the Ancient World* (Chichester, 2007), pp.256-78

Delbrück, H., *Warfare in Antiquity: History of the Art of War, Volume 1* (Lincoln NE, 1920) del Castillo, A., 'The Position of Women in the Augustan Age', *LCM* 2, 1977, pp.167-73

Delia, D., 'Fulvia Reconsidered', in Pomeroy, *Women's History and Ancient History*, pp.197-217

de Libero, L., 'Surrender in Ancient Rome', in Afflerbach, *How Fighting Ends*, pp.29-40

de Ligt, L., *Peasants, Citizens and Soldiers: Studies in the Demographic History of Roman Italy (2012)*

de Ligt, L., 'Roman Manpower and Recruitment During the Middle Republic' in Erdkamp, P., *A Companion to the Roman Army* (Chichester, 2007)

de Neeve, P.W., *Peasants in Peril: Location and Economy in 2nd Century BC Italy* (Amsterdam, 1984)

de Souza, P. (ed.), *War and Peace in Ancient and Medieval History* (Cambridge, 2011)

Dilke, O.A.W., 'Lucan's Political Views and the Caesars', in Dudley, D.R., *Neronians and Flavians: Silver Latin I* (London, 1972), pp.68-82

Dillon, S. (ed.), *Representations of War in Ancient Rome* (Cambridge, 2006)

Dixon, K., *The Roman Cavalry* (London, 1992)

Dixon, S., 'Family Finances: Tullia and Terentia', *Antichthon* 18, 1984, pp.78-101

Dixon, S., 'The Family Business: Women and Politics in the Late Republic', *C&M* 34, 1983, pp.91-112

Dodge, T.A., *Warfare in the Age of Gaius Julius Caesar - Volume 1: Arar & Bibracte to Uxellodunum, 110 BC to 50 BC* (New York, 2013)

Dodge, T.A., *Warfare in the Age of Gaius Julius Caesar - Volume 2: Brundisium & Massilia to Munda, 49 BC to 45 BC* (New York, 2013)

Dominik, W.J., 'Vergil's Geopolitics', in W.J. Dominik (ed.), *Writing Politics in Imperial Rome* (Leiden, 2009), pp.111–32

Donato, G., *The Fragrant Past: Perfumes of Cleopatra and Julius Caesar* (Rome, 1989)

Dorey, T.A. (ed.), *Livy* (London, 1971)

Dorey, T.A. (ed.), *Tacitus* (London, 1969)

Dorey, T.A. (ed.), *The Latin Historians* (London, 1966)

Dougherty, C., 'Sowing the Seeds of Violence: Rape, Women and the Land', in Wyke, *Parchments of Gender*, pp.267-84

Dowling, M.B., 'The Clemency of Sulla', *Historia* 49, 2000, pp.303-40

Dudley, D.R., *Neronians and Flavians: Silver Latin I* (London, 1972)

Dufallo, B., *The Ghosts of the Past: Latin Literature, the Dead, and Rome's Transition to a Principate* (Akron OH, 2007)

Duggan, A., *He Died Old: Mithradates Eupator, King of Pontus* (Michigan, 1958)

Earl, D.C., *The Political Thought of Sallust* (Cambridge, 1961)

Eckstein, A.M., 'Human Sacrifice and the Fear of Military Disaster in Republican Rome', *AJAH* 7, 1982, pp.69-95

Edwards, C., *The Politics of Immorality in Ancient Rome* (Cambridge, 1993)

Eggenberger, D., *Encyclopaedia of Battles: Accounts of Over 1,560 Battles from 1479 B.C. to the Present* (New York, 1986)

Ellis, P.B., *A Brief History of the Celts* (London, 2003)

Ellis, P.B., *Celt and Roman: The Celts in Italy* (London, 1998)

Elsner, J. (ed.), *Reflections on Nero: Culture, History, and Representation* (Chapel Hill NC, 1994))

Erdkamp, P. (ed.), *A Companion to the Roman Army* (Chichester, 2007)

Erdkamp, P., *Hunger and the Sword: Warfare and Food Supply in Roman Republican Warfare (264-30 BC)* (Amsterdam, 1998)

Erdkamp, P., 'War and State Formation in the Late Republic', in Erdkamp, *A Companion to the Roman Army*

Errington, R.M., *The Dawn of Empire* (Ithaca NY, 1972)

Erskine, A., *Roman Imperialism* (Edinburgh, 2008)

Evans, J.K., *War, Women and Children in Ancient Rome* (London, 1991)

Evans, R.F., *Soldiers of Rome: Praetorians & Legionnaires* (Washington DC, 1986)

Evans, R.J., *Gaius Marius: A Political Biography* (Pretoria, 1994)

Evans, R.J., *Roman Conquests: Asia Minor, Syria and Armenia* (Barnsley, 2011)

Everitt, A., *Cicero* (London, 2001)

Everitt, A., *Cicero: The Life and Times of Rome's Greatest Politician* (New York, 2003)

Fagan, G.G. (ed.), *New Perspectives on Ancient Warfare* (Leiden, 2010)

Fantham, E., 'Three Wise Men and the End of the Roman Republic', in Cairns, F., 'Caesar Against Liberty?', ARCA (43), 2003, pp.96-117

Fast, H., *Spartacus* (London, 1996)

Feldherr, A. (ed.), *Cambridge Companion to the Roman Historians* (Cambridge, 2009)

Feugere, M., *Weapons of the Romans* (Stroud, 2002)

Fields, N., *Spartacus and the Slave War* 73-71 BC (Oxford, 2009)

Finley, M., *Ancient History: Evidence and Models* (London, 1985)

Flory, M.B., 'The Integration of Women into the Roman Triumph', *Historia* 47, 1998, pp.489-94

Flower, H.I., 'Spectacle and Political Culture in The Roman Republic', in Flower (ed.), *The Cambridge Companion to the Roman Republic* (Cambridge, 2004), pp.322-43

Flower, H.I. (ed.), *The Cambridge Companion to the Roman Republic* (Cambridge, 2004)

Flower, H.I., 'The Tradition of the *Spolia Opima*: M. Claudius Marcellus and Augustus', *Cl Ant* 37, 2000

Frank, E., 'Marius and the Roman Nobility', *CJ* 50, 1955, pp.149–52

Frank, T., 'Roman Historiography Before Caesar', *American Historical Review* 32, 1927, pp.232-40

Frisch, H., *Cicero's Fight for the Republic* (Copenhagen, 1946)

Fuller, J.F.C., *Decisive Battles of the Western World and Their Influence Upon History: vol. 1* (London, 1970)

Fuller, J.F.C., *Julius Caesar: Man, Soldier and Tyrant* (London, 1965)

Gabba, E., *Republican Rome, the Army and the Allies* (Oxford, 1976)

Gabba, E., 'The Origins of the Professional Army at Rome: The *Proletarii* and Marius' Reforms', in Gabba, *Republican Rome*, pp.1-19

Gabba, E., 'The Perusine War and Triumviral Italy', *HSCP* 75, 1971, pp.139-60

Gabba, E., 'True History and False History in Classical Antiquity', *JRS* 61, 1981, pp.50-62

Gabriel, R.A., *A History of Military Medicine Vol. 1: From Ancient Times to the Middle Ages* (New York, 1992)

Gabriel, R.A., *Scipio Africanus: Rome's Greatest General* (Washington DC, 2008)

Gabriel, R.A., *The Great Armies of Antiquity* (London, 1992)

Gabriel, R.A., *The Great Battles of Antiquity: A Strategic and Tactical Guide to Great Battles That Shaped the Development of War* (London, 1994)

Gale, M., 'Propertius 2, 7: *Militia Amoris* and the Ironies of Elegy', *JRS* 87, 1997, pp.77-91

Garlan, Y., *War in the Ancient World* (London, 1975)

Garlick, B. (ed), *Stereotypes of Women in Power* (New York, 1992)

Gelzer, M., *Caesar: Politician and Statesman* (Cambridge MA, 1968)

Gentili, A., *The Wars of the Romans: A Critical Edition and Translation of* De Armis Romanis, ed. B. Kingsbury (Oxford, 2011)

Gera, D.L., *Warrior Women: The Anonymous* Tractatus De Mulieribus (Leiden, 1997)

Gilbert, C.D., 'Marius and Fortuna', *CQ* 23, 1973, pp.104–07

Gill, C. (ed.), *Lies and Fiction in the Ancient World* (Liverpool, 1993)

Gilliver, C.M., *Caesar's Gallic Wars 58-50 BC* (Oxford, 2002)

Gilliver, C.M., 'Combat in the Late Republic and Empire', in Sabin, *The Cambridge History of Greek and Roman Warfare Vol. 2,* (2007), pp.122-57

Gilliver, C.M., 'Display in Roman Warfare: The Appearance of Armies and Individuals on the Battlefield', *War in History* 14, 1, 2007, pp.1-21

Gilliver, C.M., 'The Roman Army and Morality in War', in Lloyd (ed.), *Battle in Antiquity* (Swansea, 1996)

Gilliver, C.M., *The Roman Art of War* (Stroud, 1999)

Goddard, E.H., 'Propertius, Cynthia, and Augustus', The Classical Review 37, 1923, pp.153-56

Goldsworthy, A., Pax Romana*: War, Peace and Conquest in the Roman World* (London, 2016)

Goldsworthy, A., *Augustus: From Revolutionary to Emperor* (London, 2015)

Goldsworthy, A., *Caesar: Life of a Colossus* (Yale, 2006)

Goldsworthy, A., '"Instinctive Genius" The Depiction of Caesar the General', in Welch, *Julius Caesar as Artful Reporter* (Swansea, 1998)

Goldsworthy, A., *In the Name of Rome* (London, 2003)

Goldsworthy, A., *Roman Warfare* (London, 2000)

Goldsworthy, A., *The Complete Roman Army* (London, 2003)

Goldsworthy, A. (ed.), 'The Roman Army as Community', *Jnl of Roman Archaeology* 34, 1999

Goldsworthy, A., *The Roman Army at War*, 3rd ed. (Oxford, 1996)

Gottlieb, G., 'Religion in the Politics of Augustus: Aeneid 1.278-91, 8.714-23, 12.791-842', in Hans-Peter Stahl (ed.), *Vergil's Aeneid: Augustan Epic and Political Context* (London, 1998), pp.21-36

Gowers, W., 'The African Elephant in Warfare', *African Affairs*, 46, 1947, pp.42-49

Gowing, A., *Epic and Memory: The Representation of the Roman Republic in Imperial Culture* (Cambridge, 2000)

Graf, F., 'Women, War and Warlike Divinities', *ZPE* 55, 1984, pp.245-54

Graham, F., *Dictionary of Roman Military Terms* (Morpeth, 1989)

Grainger, J.D., *Hellenistic and Roman Naval Wars 336-31 BC* (Barnsley, 2011)

Grant, M., *Greek and Roman Historians: Information and Misinformation* (London, 1995)

Grant, M., *Julius Caesar* (New York, 1969)

Grant de Pauw, L., *Battle Cries and Lullabies: Women in War from Prehistory to the Present* (Norman, OK, 2000)

Grebe, S., 'Augustus' Divine Authority and Vergil's "Aeneid"', *Vergilius* 50, 2004, pp.35-62

Green, P., *Alexander to Actium: The Historical Evolution of the Hellenistic Age* (Irvine CA, 1990)

Greenhalgh, P., *Pompey: The Republican Prince* (London, 1981)

Greenhalgh, P., *Pompey: The Roman Alexander* (London, 1980)

Griffin J., 'Augustan Poetry and the Life of Luxury', *JRS* 66, 1976, pp.87-105

Griffin, M. (ed.), *A Companion to Julius Caesar* (Chichester, 2009)

Groenman-van-Waateringe, W. (ed.), *Roman Frontier Studies 1995* (Oxford, 1997)

Gruen, E.S., *Culture and National Identity in Republican Rome* (Ithaca, 1992)

Gruen, E.S., 'M. Licinius Crassus: A Review Article', *American Journal of Ancient History* 2, 1977, p.125

Gruen, E.S., *The Last Generation of the Roman Republic* (Berkeley CA, 1974)

Gurval, R.A., *Actium and Augustus: The Politics and Emotions of Civil War* (Michigan, 1995)

Gwatkin, W.E. Jr, 'Some Reflections on the Battle of Pharsalus', *Transactions and Proceedings of the American Philological Association* 87, 1956

Gwynn, D.M., *The Roman Republic* (Oxford, 2012)

Haberling, W., 'Army, Prostitution and Its Control', in Robinson, *Morals,* 1943, pp.3-90

Hackett, J., *Warfare in the Ancient World* (London, 1989)

Haley, S.P., 'The Five Wives of Pompey the Great', *G&R* 32, 1985, pp.49-59

Hallet, J., '*Perusinae Glandes* and the Changing Image of Augustus', *AJAH* 2, 1977, pp.151-71

Halliday, W.R., 'Passing under the Yoke', *Folklore* 35, 1924, pp.93-95

Hammerton, J.A. (ed.), *Universal History of the World Vol. 3* (London, 1930)

Hansen, M.H., 'The Battle Exhortation in Ancient Historiography: Fact or Fiction?', *Historia* 42, 1993, pp.161-80

Hanson, V.D., 'The Status of Ancient Military History', *Journal of Military History* 6, 1999, pp.399-414

Hanson, V.D., *The Western Way of War: Infantry Battle in Ancient Greece*, 2nd ed. (Oxford, 2000)

Hanson, V.D., *Why the West Has Won: Carnage and Culture from Salamis to Vietnam* (Oxford, 2001)

Hanson, W.S. (ed.), *Roman Frontier Studies* (Oxford, 1979)

Harbottle, T., *Harbottle's Dictionary of Battles from 743 BC to the Present* (London, 1980)

Harkness, A., *The Military System of the Romans* (Miami, 2004)

Harl, K., 'The Roman Experience in Iraq', *Journal of the Historical Society* 7, 2007, pp.213-27

Harris, R., 'Independent Women in Ancient Mesopotamia', in B.S. Lesko, *Women's Earliest Records* (Atlanta, 1989), pp.145-56

Harris, R., 'Pirates of the Mediterranean', *The New York Times*, 30 Sept. 2006

Harris, W.V., 'Current Directions in the Study of Roman Imperialism', in Harris, *The Italians and the Empire* (1984), pp.89-113

Harris, W.V. (ed.), *The Italians and the Empire* (Rome, 1984)

Harris, W.V., *War and Imperialism in Republican Rome 327-70 BC* (Oxford, 1979)

Havell, H.L., *Republican Rome: Her Conquests, Manners and Institutions from the Earliest Times to the Death of Caesar* (London, 1914)

Hawkes, C. (ed.), *Greeks, Celts and Romans, Studies in Venture and Resistance* (London, 1973)

Henderson, J., *Fighting for Rome: Poets and Caesars, History and Civil War* (Cambridge, 1998)

Hengel, M., 'Crucifixion in the Ancient World', in L. Bove, *Labeo. Rassegna di Diritto Romano 1* (1955-1967).

Herwig, H. (ed.), *Cassell's World History of Warfare* (London, 2002)

Hildinger, E., *Swords Against the Senate: The Rise of the Roman Army and the Fall of the Republic* (New York, 2003)

Hinds, K., *Ancient Celts* (London, 2009)

Hogg, O.F., *Clubs to Cannon: Warfare and Weapons Before the Introduction of Gunpowder* (London, 1968)

Højte, J.M., *The Death and Burial of Mithridates VI* (Aarhus, 2009)

Holder, P.A., *Studies in the* Auxilia *of the Roman Army* (Oxford, 1980)

Holland, T., *Rubicon: The Last Years of the Roman Republic* (London, 2003)

Holmes, P., 'The "First" Catilinarian Conspiracy: A Further Re-examination of the Evidence', *Reinvention: a Journal of Undergraduate Research* (2011)

Holmes, R., *Acts of War: The Behaviour of Men in Battle* (London, 2004)

Holscher, T., 'Images of War in Greece and Rome', *JRS* 93, 2003, pp.1-17

Hooper, F., *Roman Realities* (Detroit, 1979)

Hopkins, M., *Conquerors and Slaves* (Cambridge, 1978)

Hopwood, K., *Death and Renewal: Sociological Studies in Roman History v. 2* (Cambridge, 1985)

Hopwood, K., *Organised Crime in the Ancient World* (Swansea, 1999)

Hornblower, S., 'The Age of Overseas Expansion (264-146 BC)', in Erdkamp, *A Companion to the Roman Army* (2007)

Hornblower, S. (ed.), *The Oxford Classical Dictionary*, 3rd edn (Oxford, 2003)

Hornblower, S., 'War and the Development of Ancient Historiography', in Sabin, *The Cambridge History of Greek and Roman Warfare* (2005)

Hoyos, B.D, *Roman Imperialism* (London, 2013)

Huzar, E.G., *Mark Antony: A Biography* (Minneapolis, 1978)

Hyden, M., *Gaius Marius: The Rise and Fall of Rome's Saviour* (Barnsley, 2017)

Hyland, A., *Equus: The Horse in the Roman World* (London, 1990)

Hyland, A., *Training the Roman Cavalry* (Stroud, 1993)

Jaeger, M., *Livy's Written Rome* (Ann Arbor TX, 1995)

James, S., 'Archaeological Evidence for Roman Incendiary Projectiles', *Saalburg Jahrbuch* 40, 1983, pp.142-43

James, S., *Rome and the Sword: How Warriors and Weapons Shaped Roman History* (London, 2011)

Jameson, M., 'Sacrifice Before Battle', in Hanson, V. (ed.), *Hoplites*, p.220

Janssen, L.F., 'Some Unexplored Aspects of *devotio* Deciana', *Mnemosyne*, 1981, pp.357-81

Jiménez, R.L., *Caesar Against Rome: The Great Roman Civil War* (New York, 2000)

Jiménez, R.L., *Caesar Against the Celts* (Stroud, 1996)

Johnson, A., *Roman Forts* (London, 1983)

Johnson, W.R., *Momentary Monsters: Lucan and His Heroes* (Ithaca NY, 1987)

Jones, D.E., *Women Warriors: A History* (Washington DC, 1997)

Jones, M.J., *Roman Fort Defences to AD 117* (Oxford, 1975)

Keaveney, A., *Lucullus: A Life* (London, 1992)

Keaveney, A., 'Sulla and Italy', *Critica Storica* 19, 1982, pp.499ff

Keaveney, A., *Sulla: The Last Republican,* 2nd edn (London, 2005)

Keaveney, A., *Rome and the Unification of Italy* (Liverpool, 1987)

Keaveney, A., *The Army in the Roman Revolution* (Abingdon, 2007)

Keegan, J., *A History of Warfare* (London, 1993)

Kelly, G.P., *A History of Exile in the Roman Republic* (Cambridge, 2012)

Kelly, R.C., 'The Evolution of Lethal Intergroup Violence', *PNAS* 102(43), 2005, 15,294–298,

Kennedy, D.L., *Settlement and Soldiers in the Roman Near East* (London, 2013)

Keppie, L., *Colonisation and Veteran Settlement in Italy 47-14 BC* (London, 1983)

Keppie, L., *The Making of the Roman Army* (London, 1984)

Kern, P.B., *Ancient Siege Warfare* (London, 1999)

Kingsbury, B. (ed.), *The Wars of the Romans: A Critical Edition and Translation of* De Armis Romanis (Oxford, 2011)

Kistler, J.M., *War Elephants* (Westport CT, 2006)

Kleiner, D.E.E., *Cleopatra and Rome* (Harvard, 2005)

Knapp, R., *The Invisible Romans* (London, 2011)

Koch, J.T. (ed.), *Celtic Culture: A Historical Encyclopedia* (Santa Barbara CA, 2006)

Kruebbe, A.D., 'Propertius and Augustus' (MA diss., The University of Texas at Austin, 2011)

Laqueur, W., *Guerrilla Warfare: A Historical & Critical Study* (London, 1977)

Leach, J., *Pompey the Great* (London, 1978)

Lee, A.B., 'Morale and the Roman Experience of Battle', in Lloyd (ed.), *Battle in Antiquity* (Swansea, 1996)

Lee, W.E., *Warfare and Culture in World History* (New York, 2011)

Leitao, D.D., 'Sexuality in Greek and Roman Military Contexts', in Hubbard, *Companion* (2014), pp.230-43

Lendon, J.E., *Soldiers and Ghosts: A History of Battles in Classical Antiquity* (New Haven CT, 2005)

Lendon, J.E., 'The Rhetoric of Combat: Greek Military Theory and Roman Culture in Julius Caesar's Battle Descriptions', *Cl.Ant* 18, 1999, pp.273-329

Levene, D.S. (ed.), *Clio and the Poets: Augustan Poetry and the Traditions of Ancient Historiography* (Leiden, 2002)

Levithan, J., *Roman Siege Warfare* (Ann Arbor TX, 2013)

Lewis, C.T., *A Latin Dictionary* (Oxford, 1969/1879)

Lewis, G.C., *An Inquiry Into the Credibility of the Early Roman History* (London, 2011 repr.)

L'Hoir, F.S., *The Rhetoric of Gender Terms: 'Man', 'Woman' and the Portrayal of Character in Latin Prose* (Leiden, 1992)

Lightman, M., *A to Z of Ancient Greek and Roman Women* (New York, 2008)

Lintott, A.W., 'Lucan and the History of the Civil War', in Charles Tesoriero (ed.), *Lucan. Oxford Readings in Classical Studies* (Oxford, 2010) pp.239–68

Lintott, A.W., 'Mithridatica', *Historia* 25, 1976, pp.489-91

Lintott, A.W., 'P. Clodius Pulcher – Felix Catilina?', *Greece & Rome* 14, 1967, pp.157-69

Lintott, A.W., *The Constitution of the Roman Republic* (Oxford, 2003)

Lintott, A.W., *Violence in Republican Rome* (Oxford, 1968)

Litchfield, H.W., 'National Examples of *virtus* in Roman Literature', *HSCPh* 25, 1914, pp.1-71

Lloyd, A.B. (ed.), *Battle in Antiquity* (Swansea, 1996)

Lomas, H.K., *Roman Italy 338 BC – AD 200: A Sourcebook* (London, 1996)

Lucas, F.L., 'The Battlefied of Pharsalia', *ABSA* 24, 1919-1921, pp.34-53

Luce, T.J., 'Marius and the Mithridatic Command', *Historia* 19, 1970, pp.161-94

Lyne, R.O.A.M., 'Virgil and the Politics of War', *CQ* 33, 1983, pp.193-203

Lynn, J.A., *Battle: A History of Combat from Ancient Greece to Modern America* (Boulder CO, 2003)

Mackay, C.S., *The Breakdown of the Roman Republic: From Oligarchy to Empire* (Cambridge, 2009)

Madsen, J.M., 'Mithradates VI: Rome's Perfect Enemy', *Proceedings of the Danish Institute in Athens* 6, 2010, pp.223-37

Magie, D., *Roman Rule in Asia Minor*, 2 vols (Princeton, 1950)

Marin, P., *Blood in the Forum: The Struggle for the Roman Republic* (London, 2009)

Marincola, J., 'Eros and Empire: Virgil and the Historians on Civil War', in Kraus, C.S. (ed.) *Ancient Historiography and its Contexts: Studies in Honour of A.J. Woodman* (Oxford, 2010)

Marincola, J., *Greek and Roman Historiography* (Oxford, 2011)

Majno, G., *The Healing Hand: Man and Wound in the Ancient World* (Cambridge MA, 1975)

Marsden, E.W., *Greek and Roman Artillery* (Oxford, 1969-1971)

Marshall, B.A., 'Crassus and the Command Against Spartacus', *Athenaeum* 51, 1973, pp.109ff

Marshall, B.A., *Crassus: A Political Biography* (Amsterdam, 1976)

Martin, S., 'Private Lives and Public Personae', www.dl.ket.org/latin2/mores/women/womenful.htm (1997)

Martindale, C., 'Deceiving the Reading: The Political Mission of Lucan's *Bellum Civile*', in Elsner, J., and Masters, J. (eds), *Reflections of Nero: Culture, History and Representation* (London, 1994), pp.151-78

Martindale, C., 'The Politician Lucan', *Greece and Rome* 31, 1993, pp.64-79

Masaoki, D., 'On the Negotiations Between the Roman State and the Spartacus Army', *Klio* 66, 1984, p.170ff

Maslen, M., 'Medical Theories on the Cause of Death in Crucifixion', *Journal of the Royal Society of Medicine* 99, 2006, p.185

Masters, J., *Poetry and Civil War in Lucan's* Bellum Civile (Cambridge, 1992)

Matyszak, P., *Cataclysm 90 BC: The Forgotten War that almost Destroyed Rome* (Barnsley, 2014)

Matyszak, P., *Mithridates the Great* (Barnsley, 2008)

Matyszak, P., *Sertorius and the Struggle for Spain* (Barnsley, 2013)

Matyszak, P., *The Enemies of Rome: From Hannibal to Attila the Hun* (London, 2004)

Maxfield, V., *The Military Decorations of the Roman Army* (Berkeley, 1981)

Mayor, A., *Greek Fire, Poison Arrows and Scorpion Bombs: Biological Warfare in the Ancient World* (London, 2009)

Mayor, A., *The Poison King: The Life and Legend of Mithradates, Rome's Deadliest Enemy* (Princeton, 2009)
McCall, J.B., *The Cavalry of the Roman Republic* (London, 2002)
McDonnell, M., *Roman Manliness:* Virtus *and the Roman Republic* (Cambridge, 2006)
McGing, B.C., 'The Date of the Outbreak of the Third Mithridatic War', *Phoenix* 38, 1984, pp.12-18
McGing, B.C., 'The Foreign Policy of Mithridates VI', *Mnemosyne* 89, 1986 (Leiden)
Meier, C., *Caesar: A Biography* (London, 1996)
Meijer, F., *A History of Seafaring in the Classical World* (London, 1986)
Mellersh, H.E.L., *Soldiers of Rome* (London, 1964)
Messer, W.S., 'Mutiny in the Roman Army: The Republic', *CPh* 15, 1920, pp.158-75
Millar, F., *Rome, the Greek World and the East Vol. 1: The Roman Republic and the Augustan Revolution* (Chapel Hill NC, 2001)
Miller, F., 'The Political Character of the Classical Roman Republic', *JRS* 74, 1984, pp.1-19
Milnor, K., 'Women in Roman Historiography', in Feldherr, *Cambridge Companion* (2009), pp.276-87
Mitchell, T.N., 'Cicero, Pompey, and the Rise of the First Triumvirate', *Traditio* Vol. 29, 1973, pp.1–26
Mommsen, T., *History of Rome* (London, 2014 repr.)
Mommsen, T., *Roman Constitutional Law* (1871-1888)
Montagu, J.D., *Battles of the Greek and Roman Worlds* (London, 2000)
Montagu, J.D., *Greek and Roman Warfare: Battles, Tactics and Trickery* (London, 2006)
Morgan, J.D., 'Palae-pharsalus – the Battle and the Town', *The American Journal of Archaeology* 87, 1983
Morrison, J.S., *Greek and Roman Oared Warships* (Oxford, 1996)
Murgatroyd, P., '*Militia amoris* and the Roman Elegists', *Latomus* 34, 1975, pp.59-79
Murray, W., *Hybrid Warfare: Fighting Complex Opponents from the Ancient World to the Present* (Cambridge, 2012)
Mustakallio, K., 'Legendary Women and Female Groups in Livy', in Setala, *Female Networks*, 1999, pp.53-64

Nefiodkin, A.K., 'On the Origin of the Scythed Chariots', *Historia* 53 (3), 2004, pp.369–78

Newark, T., *Women Warlords: An Illustrated History of Female Warriors* (London, 1989)

Nicolet, C., *The World of the Citizen in Republican Rome* (London, 1980)

Nilsson, M.P., 'The Introduction of Hoplite Tactics in Rome', *JRS* 19, 1929, pp.1-11

North, J.A., 'The Development of Roman Imperialism', *JRS* 71, 1981, pp.1-9

Northwood, S., *Early Roman Armies* (London, 1995)

Nossov, K.S., *Ancient and Medieval Siege Weapons: A Fully Illustrated Guide to Siege Weapons and Tactics* (London, 2006)

Nossov, K.S., *War Elephants* (Oxford, 2008)

Oakley, S.P., 'Single Combat and the Roman Republic', *CQ* 35, 1985, pp.39-410

O'Connor, C., *Roman Bridges* (Cambridge, 1994)

Osgood, J., *Caesar's Legacy: Civil War and the Emergence of the Roman Empire* (Cambridge, 2006)

Osgood, J., *Turia: a Roman Woman's Civil War* (Oxford, 2014)

Painter, K., 'The Politics of Art: The View of Actium in the Aeneid', *Undergraduate Review* 13, 2001,. https://digitalcommons.iwu.edu/rev/vol13/iss1/8

Paret, P., *Makers of Modern Strategy from Machiavelli to the Nuclear Age* (Princeton, 1986)

Parker, H., *The Roman Legions* (Oxford, 1928)

Patterson, J., 'Military Organization and Social Change in the Later Roman Republic', in

Rich, *War and Society in the Ancient World*, pp.92-112

Paul, G.M., 'A Historical Commentary on Sallust's *Bellum Jugurthinum*', *ARCA Classical & Medieval Texts* 13, 1984, pp.226-27

Payne-Gallwey, R., *The Projectile Throwing Engines of the Ancients* (London, 1907)

Peddie, J., *The Roman War Machine* (Gloucester, 1994)

Peel, M. (ed.), *Rape as a Method of Torture* (London, 2004)

Pelling, C.B.R., 'Pharsalus', *Historia* 22, 1973, pp.249-59

Pennington, R. (ed.), *Amazons to Fighter Pilots: A Biographical Dictionary of Military Women* (London, 2003)

Penrose, A. (ed.), *Rome and Her Enemies: An Empire Created and Destroyed by War* (Wellingborough, 2005)

Phang, S.E., 'Intimate Conquests: Roman Soldiers' Slavewomen and Freedwomen', *Anc. W.* 35, 2004, pp.207-37

Phang, S.E., *Marriage of Roman Soldiers (13 BC – AD 235)* (Leiden, 2001)

Phang, S.E., *Roman Military Service: Ideologies of Discipline in the Late Republic and Principate* (Cambridge, 2008)

Pitassi, M.P., *Roman Warships* (London, 2011)

Pitassi, M.P., *The Navies of Rome* (London, 2012)

Pitassi, M.P., *The Roman Navy: Ships, Men & Warfare 350 BC - AD 475* (Barnsley, 2012)

Potter, D.S., *Literary Texts and the Roman Historian* (London)

Potter, D.S., 'The Roman Army and Navy', in Flower (2004), pp.66-88

Powell, A. (ed.), *Hindsight in Greek and Roman History* (Swansea, 2013)

Powell, A., 'Julius Caesar and the Presentation of Massacre', in Welch, *Julius Caesar as Artful Reporter* (1998)

Powell, L., *Marcus Agrippa: Right-hand man of Caesar Augustus* (Barnsley, 2015)

Powers, D. (ed.), *Irregular Warfare in the Ancient World* (Chicago, 2013)

Quint, D., *Epic and Empire: Politics and Generic Form from Virgil to Milton* (Princeton, 1993)

Raaflaub, K.A., 'Born to be Wolves? Origins of Roman Imperialism', in Wallace, *Transitions* (1996), pp.273-314

Raaflaub, K.A., 'The Political Significance of Augustus' Military Reforms', in Hanson (1979), pp.1,005-25

Raaflaub, K.A., (ed.), *War and Peace in the Ancient World* (Chichester, 2007)

Raaflaub, K.A. (ed.), *War and Society in the Ancient and Medieval Worlds* (Harvard MA, 1999)

Rambaud, M., 'M. Le Soleil de Pharsale', *Historia* 3, 1955

Rankin, H.D., *The Celts and the Classical World* (London, 1987)

Rankov, B., Exploratio: *Military and Political Intelligence in the Roman World* (London, 1995)

Rauh, N.K., 'Caesar's Portrayals of Gauls as Warriors', in Welch, *Julius Caesar as Artful Reporter* (Swansea, 1998)

Rauh, N.K., *Merchants, Sailors and Pirates in the Ancient World* (Stroud, 2003)

Rawson, E., '*Crassorum funera*', *Latomus* 41, 1982, pp.540–49

Rawson, E., *Roman Culture & Society* (Oxford, 1991), pp.582-98

Rawson, E., 'The Antiquarian Tradition: Spoils and Representations of Foreign Armor' (1991)

Rawson, E., 'The First Latin Annalists', *Latomus* 35, 1976, pp.245-71

Rawson, E., 'The Literary Sources for the Pre-Marian Army', *PBSR* 39, 1971, pp.13-31

Regan, G., *Backfire: A History of Friendly Fire from Ancient Warfare to the 21st Century* (London, 2002)

Rehak, P., 'Rethinking the Meaning of the *Ara Pacis Augustae*', *The Art Bulletin* 83, 2001, pp.190-208

Reinhold, M., 'The Perusine War', *CW* 26, 1933, pp.180-82

Retief, F.P., 'The History and Pathology of Crucifixion', *South African Medical Journal* 93 (12), 2003, pp.938–41

Revell, L., *Roman Imperialism and Local Identities* (Cambridge, 2010)

Rice, J.W., 'Treaties, Allies and the Roman Conquest of Italy', in de Souza, *War and Peace in Ancient and Medieval History* (Cambridge, 2011), pp.51-75

Rice Holmes, T., *Caesar's Conquest of Gaul* (Oxford, 1911)

Rice Holmes, T., 'The War-craft of the Romans', in Hammerton, *Universal History of the World 3,* pp.1,717-33

Rich, J., 'Declaring War in the Roman Republic in the Period of Transmarine Expansion', *Latomus* 149, 1976

Rich, J., 'The Supposed Roman Manpower Shortage of the Later Second Century BC', *Historia* 32, 1983, pp.287-331

Rich, J. (ed.), *War and Society in the Ancient World* (London, 1993)

Richardson, J.S., *Appian, Wars of the Romans in Iberia* (Warminster, 2000)

Richardson, J.S., Hispaniae*: Spain and the Development of Roman Imperialism, 218-82 BC* (Cambridge, 2004)

Richardson, J.S., *The Romans in Spain* (Oxford, 1996)

Richardson, J.S., 'The Triumph, the Praetors and the Senate in the Early 2nd Century BC, *JRS*, 1975, pp.50-63

Ridley, F.A., *Spartacus – The Leader of the Roman Slaves* (London, 1961)

Ridley, R.T., 'The Dictator's Mistake: Caesar's Escape from Sulla', *Historia* 49, 2000

Riess, W. (ed.), *The Topography Of Violence In The Greco-Roman World* (Michigan, 2016)

Rihll, T., 'Ancient Military Technology', *Omnibus* 62, 2011, pp.28-30

Rivet, A.L.F., 'A Note on Scythed Chariots', *Antiquity* 53, 1979, pp.130–32

Robb, M.A., *Beyond* Populares *and* Optimates*: Political Language in the Late Republic* (Stuttgart, 2010)

Roberts, A. (ed), *Great Commanders of the Ancient World* (London, 2008)

Robinson, O.F., *Penal Practice and Penal Policy in Ancient Rome* (London, 2007)

Robinson, V. (ed.), *Morals In Wartime* (New York, 1943)

Rodgers, W., *Greek and Roman Naval Warfare* (Annapolis, 1937)

Rosen, K., '*Ad Glandes Perusinas* (*CIL* I 682 Sqq)', *Hermes* 104, 1976, pp.123-24

Rosenstein, N., Imperatores Victi: *Military Defeat and Aristocratic Competition in the Middle and Late Republic* (Berkeley CA, 1990)

Rosenstein, N., 'Military Command, Political Power, and the Republican Elite', in Erdkamp, *A Companion to the Roman Army* (Chichester, 2007)

Rosenstein, N., *Rome at War: Farms, Families and Death in the Middle Republic* (Chapel Hill NC, 2004)

Rosenstein, N. 'War and Peace: Fear and Reconciliation at Rome', in Raaflaub, *War and Peace in the Ancient World* (2007), pp.226-24

Roth, J.P., *Roman Warfare* (Cambridge, 2009)

Rowland, R.J., 'Rome's Earliest Imperialism', *Latomus* 42, 1983, pp.749-62

Roxan, M.M., *Roman Military Diplomas* (London, 1978)

Rubinsohn, Z.W., 'Mithradates VI Eupator Dionysos and Rome's Conquest of the Hellenistic East', *Mediterranean Historical Review* 8, 1993, pp.5-54

Runciman, S., *The Sicilian Vespers: A History of the Mediterranean World in the Later Thirteenth Century* (Cambridge, 1958)

Sabin, P., *Lost Battles: Reconstructing the Great Clashes of the Ancient World* (2008)

Sabin, P. (ed.), *The Cambridge History of Greek and Roman Warfare Vol. 1* (Cambridge, 2007)

Sabin, P. (ed.), *The Cambridge History of Greek and Roman Warfare Vol. 2* (Cambridge, 2007)

Sabin, P., 'The Face of Roman Battle', *JRS* 90, 2000, pp.1-17

Saddington, D.B., *The Development of the Roman Auxiliary Forces from Caesar to Vespasian* (Harare, 1982)

Sage, M.M., *Roman Conquests: Gaul* (Barnsley, 2008)

Salazar, C.F., *The Treatment of Wounds in Graeco-Roman Antiquity* (Leiden, 2000)

Salmon, E.T., 'Notes on the Social War', *Transactions and Proceedings of the American Philological Association* (89), 1958, pp.159–84

Salmon, E.T., *Roman Colonization under the Republic* (London, 1969)

Salmon, E.T., 'The Cause of the Social War', *Phoenix*,16, 1962, pp.107-19

Salmon, E.T., *The Making of Roman Italy* (London, 1982)

Sampson, G.C., *The Collapse of Rome: Marius, Sulla and the First Civil War* (Barnsley, 2013)

Sampson, G.C., *The Defeat of Rome: Crassus, Carrhae and the Invasion of the East* (Barnsley, 2014)

Santangelo, F., *Sulla, the Elites and the Empire: A Study of Roman Policies in Italy and the Greek East* (Leiden, 2007)

Santosuosso, A., *Soldiers, Citizens, and The Symbols Of War: From Classical Greece To Republican Rome, 500-67 BC* (Boulder CO, 1997)

Sartre, M., *The Middle East under Rome* (London, 2005)

Schatzmann, I., 'The Roman General's Authority over the Distribution of Booty', *Historia* 21, 1972, pp.17-28

Scott, K., 'The Political Propaganda 44-30 BC', *MAAR* 11, 1933, pp.7-49

Scott, W.C., 'Catullus and Caesar (C. 29)', *Classical Philology* 66, 1971, pp.17-25

Scott-Kilvert, I. (trans.), *Polybius: The Rise of the Roman Empire* (Harmondsworth, 1979)

Scullard, H.H., *Roman Politics: 220-150 BC* (Westport CT, 1981)

Scullard, H.H., *The Elephant in the Greek and Roman World* (London, 1974)

Seager, R., *Pompey the Great: A Political Biography* (Chichester, 2002)

Seager, R., 'The First Catilinarian Conspiracy', *Historia* 13, 1964, pp.338-47

Sekunda, N., 'Military Forces A: Land Forces', in Sabin, *The Cambridge History of Greek and Roman Warfare Vol. 1* (Cambridge, 2007), pp.325-56

Setala, P., *Female Networks and the Public Sphere in Roman Society* (Rome, 1999)

Shaw, B.D. (ed.), *Spartacus and the Slave Wars* (Boston, 2001)

Sheldon, R.M., *Ambush: Surprise Attack in Ancient Greek Warfare* (London, 2001)

Sheldon, R.M., *Intelligence Activities in Ancient Rome: Trust in the Gods But Verify* (London, 2007)

Sheldon, R.M., *Rome's Wars in Parthia: Blood in the Sand* (London, 2010)

Sheppard, S., *Pharsalus 48 BC: Caesar and Pompey - Clash of the Titans* (Oxford, 2006)

Sherk, R.K., *Rome and the Greek East to the Death of Augustus* (Cambridge, 1984)

Sherwin-White, A.N., 'Ariobarzanes, Mithridates, and Sulla', *Classical Quarterly* 27, 1977, pp.173-83

Sherwin-White, A.N., *Roman Foreign Policy in the East, 168 BC - AD1* (Oklahoma, 1983)

Sherwin-White, A.N., *The Roman Citizenship*, 2nd ed. (Oxford, 1973)

Shutt, R.H.J., 'Polybius, A Sketch', *G&R* 22, 1938, pp.50-57

Sidebottom, H., *Ancient Warfare: A Very Short Introduction* (Oxford, 2004)

Sidnell, P., *Warhorse: Cavalry in Ancient Warfare* (London, 2006)

Siefert, R., 'Rape in Wars: Analytical Approaches', *Minerva – Quarterly Report on Women and the Military* 11, 1992, pp.17-22

Sitwell, N.H.H., *Outside the Empire: The World the Romans Knew* (London, 1984)

Smethurst, S.E., 'Women in Livy's History', *G&R* 19, 1950, pp.80-87

Smith, F., *Service in the Post-Marian Roman Army* (Manchester, 1958)

Southern, P., *Antony and Cleopatra* (Stroud, 2011)

Southern, P., *Mark Antony* (Stroud, 1998)

Spaulding, O.A., 'The Ancient Military Writers', *CJ* 28, 1933, pp.657-69

Speidel, M.P., *Ancient Germanic Warriors* (London, 2004)

Spencer, D., *The Roman Alexander: Reading a Cultural Myth* (Exeter, 2002)

Stabryła, S., 'P. Clodius Pulcher: a Politician or a Terrorist', in J. Styka (ed.), *Violence and Aggression in the Ancient World* (Kraków, 2006)

Stadter, P.A., *Plutarch's Historical Methods: An Analysis of the* Mulierum Virtutes (Cambridge MA, 1965)

Stahl, H-P., *Propertius: 'Love' and 'War'* (Berkeley, 1985)

Stallibrass, S., *Feeding The Roman Army: The Archaeology of Production and Supply in NW Europe* (Oxford, 2008)

Starr, C.G., *The Influence of Sea Power on Ancient History* (Oxford, 1989)

Steel, C., *The End of the Roman Republic 146 to 44 BC: Conquest and Crisis* (Edinburgh, 2013)

Stephensen, I.P., *Roman Cavalry Equipment* (Stroud, 2003)

Strauss, B.S., *The Anatomy of Error: Ancient Military Disasters and their Lessons for Modern Strategists* (New York, 1990)

Strickland, J.M., *Rome, Regal and Republican: A Family History of Rome* (1854)

Sullivan, J.P., *Literature and Politics in the Age of Nero* (Ithaca NY, 1985)

Sumi, G.S., *Ceremony and Power: Performing Politics in Rome Between Republic and Empire* (Ann Arbor TX, 2005)

Sumner, G.V., 'The Legion and the Centuriate Organisation', *JRS* 60, 1970, pp.61-79

Sumner, G.V., 'Roman Policy in Spain Before the Hannibalic War', *HSCPh*, 1968

Suolahti, J., *The Junior Officers of the Roman Army in the Republican Period* (Helsinki, 1955)

Syme R., *A Roman Post-Mortem. An Inquest on the Fall of the Roman Republic* (Sydney, 1950)

Syme, R., *Sallust* (Berkeley, 1964)

Syme, R., *The Roman Revolution* (Oxford, 1939)

Tarn, W.W., *Octavian, Antony and Cleopatra* (Cambridge, 1965)

Tatum, W.J., 'Lucullus and Clodius at Nisibis (Plutarch, Lucullus 33-34)', *Athenaeum* 79, 1991

Tatum, W.J., *The Patrician Tribune: P. Clodius Pulcher. Studies in the History of Greece and Rome* (North Carolina, 1999)

Taylor, L., *Roman Voting Assemblies: From the Hannibalic War to the Dictatorship of Caesar* (Michigan, 1966)

Telford, L., *Sulla: A Dictator Reconsidered* (Barnsley, 2014)

Thein, A., 'Sulla the Weak Tyrant', in S. Lewis (ed.), *Ancient Tyranny* (Edinburgh, 2006), pp.238-49

Theodorakopoulos, E., *Ancient Rome at the Cinema* (Exeter, 2010)

Thiel, J.H., *A History of Roman Sea-Power Before the Second Punic War* (Amsterdam, 1954)

Thiel, J.H., *Studies on the History of Roman Sea-Power in Republican Times* (Amsterdam, 1946)

Toner, J., *Roman Disasters* (London, 2013)

Travis, H., *Roman Body Armour* (Stroud, 2012)

Trow, M.J., *Spartacus: The Myth and the Man* (Stroud, 2006)

Turner, B.A., *Military Defeats, Casualties of War and the Success of Rome* (London, 2011)

Turner, J., Pallas armata, *Military Essayes of the Ancient Grecian, Roman, and Modern Art of War* 1670-1 (New York, 2011 repr.)

Turney-High, H., *Primitive War: Its Practice and Concepts* (Columbia SC, 1949)

Urbainczyk, T., *Slave Revolts in Antiquity* (London, 2008)

Urbainczyk, T., *Spartacus* (Bristol, 2004)

Usher, S.F., 'Polybius and the Rise of Rome', *History Today* 13, 1963, pp.267-74

Van Creveld, M., *Men, Women and War: Do Women Belong on the Front Line?* (London, 2001)

Van Ooteghem, J., *Lucius Licinius Lucullus* (Brussels, 1959)

Versnel, H.S., Triumphus (Leiden, 1970)

Versnel, H.S., 'Two Types of Roman *devotio*', *Mnemosyne* 29, 1976, p.365-410

Vikman, E., 'Ancient Origins: Sexual Violence in Warfare, Part I', *Anthropology & Medicine* 12 (1), 2005, pp.21–31

Villers, R., '*Le Statut de la Femme a Rome jusqu'a la Fin de la Republique*', *Recueils de la Societe Jean Bodin II*, 1958, pp.177-89

Virlouvet, C., 'Fulvia the Woman of Passion', in Fraschetti, *Roman Women* (1993), pp.66-81

Wallace, R.W. (ed.), *Transitions to Empire* (Norman OK, 1996)

Wallinga, H.T., *The Boarding-bridge of the Romans* (Groningen, 1956)

Walsh, P.G., *Livy* (Oxford, 1974)

Walsh, P.G., *Livy: His Historical Aims and Methods* (Cambridge, 1961)

Ward, A., *Marcus Crassus and the Late Roman Republic* (London, 1977)

Warde Fowler, W., 'Passing Under the Yoke', *Classical Review* 27, 1913, pp.48-51

Warner, R. (trans.), *The Fall of the Roman Republic: Six Lives by Plutarch* (London, 1972)

Warry, J., *Warfare in the Classical World* (London, 1980)

Wasinski, V.M., 'Women, War and Rape: The Hidden Casualties of Conflict' (Diss. University of Leeds, 2004)

Watson, G.R., 'The Pay of the Roman Army: The Republic', *Historia* 7, 1958, pp.113-20

Watson, G.R., *The Roman Soldier* (London, 1969)

Weigall, A., *The Life and Times of Marc Antony* (New York, 1931)

Weigel, R.D., *Lepidus: the Tarnished Triumvir* (London, 2002)

Weinstock, S., Divus Julius (Oxford, 1971)

Weir, A.J., 'A Study of Fulvia' (Diss. Queen's University, Kingston, Ontario, 2007)

Welch, K.E., 'Antony, Fulvia and the Ghost of Clodius in 47 BC', *G&R* 42, 1995, pp.182-201

Welch, K.E., 'Caesar and His Officers in the Gallic War Commentaries', in Welch, *Julius Caesar as Artful Reporter* (1998)

Welch, K.E. (ed.), *Julius Caesar as Artful Reporter* (Swansea, 1998)

Wellesley, K., 'Tacitus as a Military Historian', in Dorey, *Tacitus* (1969), pp.63-97

Wells, C.M., 'The Daughters of the Regiment: Sisters and Wives in the Roman Army', in Groenman-van Waateringe, *Roman Frontier Studies 1995* (1997), pp.571-74

Wheeler, E.L., *Strategem and the Vocabulary of Military Trickery* (Leiden, 1998)

White, H., *Cicero, Clodius and Milo* (New York, 1900)

Whitehead, D., *Aineias the Tactician: How to Survive Under Siege*, 2nd edn (2002)

Wiedemann, T.E.J., 'Single Combat and Being Roman', *Anc Soc* 27, 1992, pp.91-103

Winkler, M.M., *Spartacus: Film and History* (Oxford, 2007)

Wirszubski, E.C., Libertas *as a Political Idea at Rome During the Latin Republic and Early Principate* (Cambridge, 1959)

Wiseman, T.P., 'Lying Historians–Seven Types of Mendacity', in Gill, *Lies and Fiction in the Ancient World* (1993)

Wiseman, T.P., *Remembering the Roman People: Essays on Late-Republican Politics and Literature* (Oxford, 2009)

Wiseman, T.P., 'The Credibility of the Roman Annalists', in *Roman Studies: Literary and Historical* (Liverpool, 1987), pp.293-96

Woods, M., *Ancient Warfare: From Clubs to Catapults* (Minneapolis, 2001)

Woolliscroft, D., *Roman Military Signalling* (Barnsley, 2001)

Wright, F.A., *Marcus Agrippa: Organizer of Victory* (London, 1937)

Zhomodikov, A., 'Roman Republican Heavy Infantrymen in Battle', *Historia* 49, 2000

Ziolkowski, A., *Credibility of Numbers of Battle Captives in Livy XXI-XXV* (1990)

Ziolkowski, A., '*Urbs Direpta* or How the Romans Sacked Cities', in Rich, J., *War and Society in the Ancient World* (1993), pp.69-91

Primary Sources

Appian, *Bellum Civili; Mithridatic Wars; Sicily; Syriaca*

Asconius

Aulus Gellius, *Attic Nights*

Caesar, *Bellum Civile; De Bello Gallico; De Bello Hispaniensi*

Cato, *On Agriculture*

Catullus

Celsus, *De Medicina*

Cicero, *Ad Familiares, Ad Atticum; Philippics; Tusculanae isputationes; De Finibus Bonorum et Malorum; Pro Balbo; Pro Rabirio Perduellionis Reo; Oratio Pro Sextio Roscio; In Pisonem; Pro Caelio; In Catilinam; De Divinatione; Oratio Pro Lege Manila; De Domo Sua; De Oratore*

Cicero, Q., *Commentariolum Petitionis; De Haruspicum Responsis*

Dio Cassius, *Historia Romana*

Diodorus Siculus, *Bibliotheca Historica*

Donatus, *Vita Vergilii*

Eutropius, *Abridgement of Roman History*

Florus, *Epitome of Roman History*

Frontinus, *Strategemata*

Horace, *Odes; Epodes*

Isidore, *Origines*

Josephus, *The Jewish War; The Life of Flavus Josephus; Jewish Antiquities*

Julius Obsequens, *Liber de Prodigiis*

Justinian, *Apologia*

Juvenal, *Satires*

Laudatio Turiae

Livy, *Ab Urbe Condita; Epitome*

Lucan, *De Bello Civili*

Macrobius, *Saturnalia*

Martial, *Epigrams*

K. Marx and F. Engels, *Collected Works*

Nicolaus of Damascus, *Augustus*

Orosius, *Historiae Adversus Paganos*

Ovid, *Metamorphoses; Fasti; Ars Amatoria; Amores; Remedia Amoris;Tristia*

Plautus, *Miles Gloriosus; Captivi; Persa; Truculentus*

Pliny the Elder, *Naturalis Historia*

Plutarch, *Antony; Julius Caesar; Sulla; Sertorius; Pompey; Lucullus; Crassus; Cato the Younger; Cicero; Brutus*

Polyaenus, *Stratagems*

Polybius, *Histories*

Propertius, *Elegies*

Sallust, *Catalina*; *Jugurtha; Histories*

Seneca the Elder, *Controversiae*

Seneca the Younger, *Consolatio ad Marciam*

Shakespeare, William, *Julius Caesar*

Strabo, *Geography*

Suetonius, *Augustus; Julius Caesar; Caligula*

Tacitus, *Annales; Histories*

Tertullian, *De Pallio*

Tibullus

Trogus, Gnaeus Pompeius, *Historiae Philippicae*

Valerius Maximus, *Factorum et Dictorum Memorabilium; Roman Exempla and Situation Ethics*

Velleius Paterculus, *Historiae Romanae*

Virgil, *Aeneid; Eclogues; Georgics*

Voltaire, *Correspondance General*

Websites

www.classicsforall.org.uk

www.perseus.org a fathomless source of Greek and Latin texts

www.romanarmy.net the website of the *Roman Military Research Society*

www.roman-empire.net/army/army/html

oxbow@oxbowbooks.com booksellers/publishers specializing in classics and archaeology

www.jrmes.org.uk website of the *Journal of Roman Medical Equipment Studies*

www.hellenicbookservice.com

www.fisher.library.utoronto.ca has some superb classical prints

www.jact.org Joint Association of Classical Teachers, publishers of *Omnibus*

www.friends-classics.demon.co.uk publishers of *Ad Familiares*

www.scholar.lib.vt.edu/stats/ejournals/ElAnt-current.html the website for Virginia Tech's *Electronic Antiquity*

www.womenforwomen.org.uk helping women survivors of war rebuild their lives

Some Latin Terms

aedile	public officer responsible for public works, entertainment and the distribution of grain, markets etc.
aerarium	the public treasury
ager publicus	Roman land in Italy; public land belonging to the Roman people
ager Romanus	Roman territory comprising *ager publicus* and *ager privatus*
ala (pl. alae)	wing of an army; usually a contingent of allies, about the size of a legion
amicitia	friendship without any further obligations; it could be concluded by a treaty, but also without
aristeia	epic poetry convention in which a hero in battle has his or her finest hour. An *aristeia* can result in the death of the hero
asses	bronze coins
auctoritas	influence, prestige
auxilia	troops provided by Rome's allies (*socii*)
capite censi	the head-count of *proletarii* of Roman citizens, who did not have sufficient property to qualify for military service and featured as numbers in the census. Marius changed all that and included the *proletarii* in his armies
Capitol	one of Rome's seven hills – the religious and symbolic centre of Rome
castra	military camp
centuria	a unit of the Roman legion; of varying size, around 80–100 men

centurio	commander of a century
civitas sine suffragio	citizenship without suffrage – form of citizenship granted to towns (eg Capua in 338 BCE) who were subject to Roman taxation and military service, but were denied the right to vote or hold political office
classis	fleet; also the Roman soldiers who made up the bulk of the armies. The *infra classem* were less wealthy, lightly armed skirmishers
cognomen	a man's third name; a woman's second. The name of a legion
cohors	one of ten sub-units of a legion
colonia	a town founded at a strategic place (e.g. a river crossing), populated with Romans and/or Latins
Comitia Centuriata	the assembly of citizens which legislated, elected magistrates, declared war, ratified treaties and judged capital offences
consul	the highest political office on the *cursus honorum*; two elected annually (usually). Consuls held *imperium*
corvus	bridge-shaped grappling/boarding device on warships. 'The raven'
cursus honorum	the sequence of public offices held by men of senatorial class
damnatio memoriae	the erasing of records, statuary and the memory of *persona non grata* after their death
decimation	the execution of every tenth man, chosen by lot from the ranks
deditio	surrender, with the assumption that the victor would extend *fides* and spare the lives of the defeated
devotio	an extreme act of bravery, in which a Roman gave himself up in battle in a suicidal attack against the enemy
dictator	temporary absolute leader, appointed for a limited period to resolve a crisis

dies nefasti	inauspicious days
dignitas	political dignity, related to tenure of offices in the *cursus honorum*
dilectus	the annual military levy
dona militaria	military decorations
dux	leader
equites	the equestrian order ranked below senators; the *equites* were middle-class businessmen and farmers; cavalry
exercitus	army
fetialis	war priest responsible for ensuring that Rome's wars were just in the eyes of the gods. Responsible for the rites performed for declaring war and concluding peace
fides	trustworthiness, good faith, loyalty – a quality the Romans were anxious to be seen to uphold, including respect for the law and *fides* in foreign relations
foederati	nations to which Rome provided benefits in exchange for military assistance
foedus	originally a sacred oath made by a fetial priest on behalf of the Roman people; a treaty
Foedus Latinum	Latin League; an association of communities in Latium, who were allied militarily
gens	family; clan, e.g. Claudii
gladius	short sword
glans	slingshot
haruspex	soothsayer
hasta	spear
hastati	soldiers of the second class, who stood in the front line; green, raw recruits
Hellenism	a culture of classical Greece, which percolated into Rome in the second century BCE
hoplite	heavily armed infantryman
imagines	portraits of ancestors

imperium	power, command, empire; power, particularly that power bestowed on consuls, generals and praetors
incestum	unchastity, particularly in Vestal Virgins; incest
indutia	cease-fire
latifundia	large estates in Italy
latrones	bandits; pirates
laudatio	eulogy
legio	legion; a levy of troops
lex	law
Libri Sibyllini	Sybilline Books. Three sacred scrolls, kept under guard. Only consulted when decreed by the Senate to give oracular advice in times of crisis, or to interpret portents and omens
magister equitum	Master of the Horse; second-in-command to the dictator; the master of the horse usually commanded the cavalry, as the dictator was forbidden to ride a horse
maiestas	power; authority; treason
manipulus	maniple; sub-unit of the legion, comprising two centuries
manubiae	the general's share of the booty
miles	soldier
naumachia	naval warfare
novus homo	a 'new man'; a man not of the aristocracy; a self-made man
onager	stone-throwing torsion catapult
otium	a lifestyle of ease and commercial, political or military inactivity
patricius	patrician; the dominant political class; aristocratic families
pax	peace
phalanx	close-knit body of heavily armed infantry
pietas	dutifulness – in all aspects of life
pilum	javelin
plebeian	non-patricians

polis	a Greek city-state
pontifex maximus	chief priest
praefectus	prefect, commander of an auxiliary force
preafectus urbi	prefect of the city
praetexta	white robe with a purple border, worn by a Roman boy before he was entitled to wear the *toga virilis*, and by girls until their marriage. Also worn by magistrates and priests
praetor	public office, responsible for justice; second-highest political and military office
Principate	the period of the emperors, from 27 BCE onwards
principes	troops in their twenties and thirties
proconsul	acting consul
proletarii	volunteer soldiers of the poorer orders, first recruited by Marius
raptus	seized, abducted, raped
res publica	the Republic; the period of Republican government in 509–43 BCE
res gestae	political and military achievements
rex	king
scutum	shield
secessio plebis	a general strike in which the plebeians downed tools, shut-up shop and deserted Rome, leaving the patricians to get on with running the city on their own. All business and services ground to a halt; there were five between 494-287 BCE
signifier	standard-bearer
societas	synonymous with *amicitia*. Peace and neutrality, with an obligation to military support
socius (pl. *socii*)	ally
spolia opima	the highest award for gallantry – won when a commander defeated an enemy leader in unarmed combat
testudo	tortoise-shaped formation in which shields are interlocked above the head

toga virilis	the plain white toga worn on formal occasions by Roman men between 14 and 18 years of age; also worn by senators. The first wearing of the *toga virilis* was one of the rites of passage of reaching maturity. See *praetexta*
triarii	veteran troops
tribuni plebei	officials responsible for protecting their fellow plebeians against injustices from the patricians; had a veto and sacrosanctity
tribunus militum	military tribune
trireme	standard warship, with three banks of oars
triumphator	a general who had been awarded a triumph
triumphus	triumph: the military procession along the Via Sacra, in Rome, for victorious generals. Spoils of war, prisoners and captured chieftains were paraded. The enemy chieftains were sometimes executed. The triumphator rode in a chariot, and was dressed as Jupiter
tumultus	crisis
vates	soothsayer; prophetess; priestess
velites	lightly armed skirmishing troops; 1,200 or so in a legion
via	road, as in Via Appia
virtus	manliness; courage; virtue
vis	force; rape; military strength

Appendix 1

Typical *cursus honorum* in the first century BCE

Ten years' military service in cavalry or on the political staff of a relative or friend.

Minimum Age	
30	***quaestor*** (eight to twelve in number): financial administration in Rome, or in a province, as second-in-command to the Governor. ***tribune of the plebs*** (ten): preside over the *concilium plebis*.
36	***aedile*** (four: two curule and two plebeian): administration role in Rome; responsible for the corn supply, festivals etc.; optional.
39	***praetor*** (six): judicial role in Rome; in charge of provinces not allocated to consuls; commanded one legion and allies.
40	***consul*** (two): governed larger provinces and held major commands in all wars; led two legions and two allied *alae*. Other roles included to preside over the Senate and assemblies. *censor*: magistracy held by most distinguished ex-consuls. Two in office for five years; their function was to carry out the census.

Appendix 2

Roman Assemblies

Senate

300 members regulated by the censors; members were from the eighteen senior centuries, i.e. they had property worth > 400,000 sestertii; role was to advise magistrates, especially the consuls.

Concilium Plebis

Made up of plebeians; divided into thirty-five tribes; membership based on ancestry; role was to elect the tribune and the *aedile*; passed laws.

Comitia Tributa

Made up of citizens, including patricians; role as above, but elected *curule aediles* and *quaestors*.

Comitia Centuriata

Comprised citizens divided into 193 voting centuries; originally formed from citizen militia, with membership based on possession of military equipment. Presided over by a consul or praetor. Functions: election of consuls, praetors and censors; declarations of war and ratification of peace treaties.

Index

CONTENTS

FOREWORD

Minnie Pearl remains one of country music's most important figures, and she never had a hit song. Offering readers a perceptive perspective on the groundbreaking career of a now overlooked comedic genius, this biography of a non-musician fits perfectly within the University of Tennessee Press's Charles K. Wolfe Music Series because it provides ample illustration of Minnie Pearl's many impactful interactions with prominent country musicians.

Howdy! The Minnie Pearl Story arrives in conjunction with the 100th anniversary of the Grand Ole Opry, and it is surprising that this character—so central to the story of that cultural institution and one of the major subjects of Opry legend and lore—had to wait until now to receive in-depth scholarly reassessment. A 1980 book—*Minnie Pearl: An Autobiography*, written by that character's creator Sarah Ophelia Colley Cannon (1912-1996)—offered self-reflection about Minnie Pearl's long existence in the limelight (from 1940 to 1991). Finally, *Howdy! The Minnie Pearl Story* offers a sustained, objective portrayal of that complex character, the result of painstaking research by biographers Mary Ellen Pethel and Don Cusic.

Throughout the last half of the twentieth century, Minnie Pearl was a litmus test of cultural identification among Americans. Three generations of Americans of a certain age and from a particular background identified with Minnie Pearl, who brilliantly embodied the archetype of a "hillbilly" woman from the upland South. Those fans were amused by her trademark greeting—*how-DEE!* (the emphasis was on the second syllable); her hat with its dangling price tag; and her perky personality, alternately daffy and sassy. They relished her good cheer, her humility, and her wisdom.

Minnie Pearl's homespun act was transmitted via the platforms provided by mainstream country music, which no doubt limited her exposure to those Americans who did not appreciate the genre. Without a connection to country music history, such people tended to view Minnie Pearl as somehow disingenuous, as offering a repertoire of stereotype-laden routines and cornpone raps. This book provides sufficient context to help the uninitiated better understand Cannon's comedy. Minnie Pearl was a humane comedic figure because Cannon was a humanitarian who employed her character in fundraising events to support a range of causes, including cancer research initiatives. Born and reared in Middle Tennessee and based throughout her adult life in Nashville, Cannon resisted the country music industry's sociopolitical culture and established aesthetic perimeters. While closely associated with such members of country music's old guard as Roy Acuff (who had been crowned within that world as the "King of Country Music"), she often pushed the establishment to acknowledge the brilliance of such upstart musicians as Elvis Presley, Johnny Cash, and Dwight Yoakam—musicians who were perceived initially as threatening to the genre.

Nashville and the country music community haven't always been open to newcomers who are a bit different. Three Grand Ole Opry anecdotes testify to this: in an apocryphal incident during the early 1950s, Chet Atkins unsuccessfully lobbied for an Opry appearance by East Tennessee-based country singer Buffalo Johnson, who was allegedly turned away backstage by Opry management because of a visible disability; in 1968, the Byrds, visiting Nashville to record the pioneering country rock album *Sweetheart of the Rodeo*, received boos and jeers during their Opry audience but consolation from country star Skeeter Davis, who told the rock group: "Don't worry about those people in there, they just don't get it yet"; while in 1981, Ernest Tubb literally and figuratively stood by a young John Anderson, who had been harassed for having long hair by Acuff, just before the young singer would perform on the Opry stage for the first time. At the time of their Opry experiences, Johnson, the Byrds, and Anderson, despite their obvious love for country music, had been seen as diverging from that show's norm.

In a profound and timely act of risk-taking, Cannon—not at the Opry but at one of country music's award shows—encouraged Yoakam, who had earlier castigated the country music establishment, to persist in the face of criticism. In a testimonial of Minnie Pearl's impact (transcribed in this book but first shared in the 2023 documentary film *Facing the Laughter: Minnie Pearl*), Yoakam divulged that

> Minnie embodied true inclusiveness. She wasn't part of the sanitized, modern version of inclusion—she lived it in a way that carried humanity with it. Her character made people feel seen and welcomed. That's the magic of Sarah Cannon. Sarah [literally] stopped me in my tracks at the first CMA Awards I went to . . . in 1986. Before the awards show, I'd been overly candid with the press about my opinions on country music. . . . At the time, I was

> grappling with the transition from the West Coast scene—Southern California and Bakersfield—into Nashville. I ran into backlash for speaking too freely. So, I show up at the awards knowing I'd caused some upset with my comments the year before. There were plenty of asides and private remarks from people saying, "You said exactly what I've wanted to say for five years," but those comments didn't erase the negativity around me that night. At the end of the show, after I didn't win, we were all leaving, and I felt a hand grab my arm. She spun me around, forcing me to look at her. There she was—Minnie Pearl—but not just Minnie; it was Sarah Cannon, serious and grinning all at once. She looked me dead in the eye and said, "Listen to me. We need you." I was stunned. I had never imagined that anyone in the industry needed me for anything. It was a moment of true humility.

By valuing the potential of Yoakam (and by extension several of Yoakam's contemporaries), Cannon encouraged a new generation (the country artists who became part of the so-called new traditionalist movement) to enter the fold of country music and thereby expand—and strengthen—the genre.

An indication of broad-based respect for her achievement as among the most recognized practitioners of comedy in US entertainment history, Minnie Pearl in 1986 was included in the initial offering of a recurring televised comedy event known as *Comic Relief*, which featured nationally prominent comedians sharing their talents to help achieve the goal of generating funds to grapple with the societal issue of homelessness.

Today, many Americans don't know much about Minnie Pearl or about the inspiring life and challenging times of Cannon. Retired from the public sphere after a 1991 stroke to her creator, Minnie Pearl has been out of the public eye for two generations. By telling the story of the legendary comedian and her brilliant comedic creation, a character who projected a feeling of genuine respect for everyday folks, *Howdy! The Minnie Pearl Story* is a gift to a twenty-first century society sorely in need of this sort of comic relief.

Ted Olson
East Tennessee State University

PREFACE

Mary Ellen Pethel: Howdy! In 2020, I worked as a consultant on a documentary about the life of Minnie Pearl, produced and directed by Barbara Hall and sponsored by Nashville PBS. *Facing the Laughter: Minnie Pearl* premiered in select theaters in February 2023, and the full-length film provided an in-depth examination of the life of Sarah Colley Cannon, better known as Minnie Pearl. Though Minnie Pearl has been honored and featured in many documentaries, articles, and books—this film was the first to examine her life and career specifically. In exchange for my consultation on the film, I was granted full access to the meticulous research conducted by the documentary team.

To my mind, this is a book long overdue. Minnie Pearl remains a singular figure in the history of the Grand Ole Opry, country music, and comedy. Moreover, Sarah/Minnie was a woman with deep ties to Nashville. Her Grand Ole Opry and *Hee Haw* career notwithstanding, she was an integral part of the local community for nearly sixty years. She first moved to Nashville in 1930 to attend the all-female Ward-Belmont School. While the school no longer exists, its legacy lives on through Belmont University, which occupies the same campus, and the all-girls college-preparatory Harpeth Hall School—two outstanding institutions where I've had the privilege to work. In fact, my first office at Belmont was in Fidelity Hall, one floor above Sarah's dormitory room.

However, as the book writing process began, I realized I needed a co-author—a historian with expertise in country music. I immediately knew who to ask—Dr. Don Cusic, a prolific author, friend, and Belmont University colleague. Joining forces in 2024, we began our work in earnest. The journey has been an absolute honor. Don, take it from here.

Don Cusic: I had written a musical, *Minnie Pearl: All the News From Grinder's Switch* and a coffee table book, *Nashville Sound: A Music*

On January 19, 2023, Belmont's Fisher Center for Performing Arts featured an event for the launch of the documentary *Facing the Laughter: Minnie Pearl*, which included a panel discussion. Co-author Mary Ellen Pethel (far left) was the moderator and panel members were (from left to right) the film's director and producer Barbara Hall, co-author Don Cusic, Minnie Pearl's longtime friend and agent JoAnn Bell, and award-winning singer and musician Kathy Mattea. Image courtesy of Sam Simpkins and Belmont University.

Timeline. So I was quite familiar with the story of Minnie Pearl. It was easy, when Mary Ellen Pethel asked me if I'd like to be a co-author of a book she was doing on Minnie Pearl, to say "yes." In fact, I jumped at the chance. I had worked as an "adviser" to Ken Burns for his country music documentary, and I distinctly remember Dayton Duncan—who did most of the writing for that documentary—saying that someone should do something on Minnie Pearl. There was so much there, and the documentary had only scratched the surface. That's another reason I wanted to co-author this book.

Minnie Pearl was two people—Minnie and Mrs. Henry Cannon—and I met Mrs. Cannon way back during the 1980s. She was the quintessential Southern Lady, full of warmth and charm. She treated a young man who had introduced himself to her with interest and kindness. And that's another reason I am happy and proud to be a co-author of this book.

We would like to offer a special thank you to the Johnny Cash Trust for allowing us to reprint the lyrics to "If I Told You Who It Was." We think you will agree it's the perfect way to end a chapter on Minnie Pearl and June and Johnny Cash. Of course, none of this would be possible without Barbara Hall and the documentary team, including Jessica Turk and Nashville PBS President and CEO Becky Magura. Our editor, Thomas Wells, was supportive of this book project from conception to publication, and we greatly appreciate his patience and steady hand.

Many friends, family, and colleagues also contributed to this project. Whether reading chapter drafts or offering words of encouragement, we'd like to acknowledge Dr. Stan and JoAnn Pethel, Dr. Krissie Rigsby, Dr. Pete Kuryla, Leigh Hitchcock, Polly Linden, Lynn Heath, Ali Hyrup, Nicola Bullard, Margie Martin, Jess and Moe Hill, Nichole Ritchie, Dr. Catherine Bass, Dr. Jennifer Duck, Kim Powell, Antionedra Maupin, Dr. Bonnie Smith-Whitehouse, Dean Jim McIntyre, Dr. John Gonas, Mike Curb, Dean Brittany Schaffer, Dr. Sarita Stewart, Chair Amy Smith, and Provost David Gregory. A special shout-out to the Dose crew.

The images in this book bring Minnie's story to life. To that end, we want to acknowledge Cameron Knowler at the Grand Ole Opry Archives, Mary Beth Pruett at the Hickman County Historical Society, Kelley Sirko and Laura Scott at the Nashville Public Library, Lauren Finney and Leigh Mantle at Harpeth Hall School, Molly Randolph at Belmont University, Kay Peterson at the National Museum of American History, the Country Music Association, Greg Burden, and especially Olivia Beaudry.

This book extends Minnie's story from the stage to the page and represents the first written biography of her life, career, and enduring legacy. Despite our best efforts, there are surely errors and omissions. Any mistakes are unintentionally ours. We hope you enjoy the incredible story of Sarah Cannon and Minnie Pearl. Throughout, we do our best to follow Minnie's advice: "Take the backroads not the highways." Buckle up and settle in for a scenic journey through time and place.

INTRODUCTION

The Person and Persona

The small-town thespian from Centerville yearned for the Shakespearean stage, but the applause Sarah Colley Cannon received did not come from polite society. Rather, the clapping and catcalls came from the audience at the Grand Ole Opry, and they were cheering for Minnie Pearl. It was an odd predicament for the daughter of an upper-middle-class family with a classical education. In Nashville, the tension between the powder-dry elites and beer-soaked entertainers was very real. The wealthy and well-connected in Belle Meade and Franklin loved to hate the country music industry. High-brow culture viewed the rough-and-tumble lifestyle of "bar musicians" as anything but respectable. After her Grand Ole Opry debut in 1940, Sarah found herself stuck in the middle.

From high tea to honky tonks—like going the wrong way on a one-way street—Sarah's career was going somewhere but not in the direction she envisioned. She wrote: "I won't pretend that I wanted to be on the Grand Ole Opry because I had been a fan all my life. I never thought about it one way or the other except that I didn't particularly like the music. . . . I had never even gone to see an Opry broadcast." And yet, author Robert K. Oermann noted, "Unwittingly, she emerged as the Opry's first solo female star."

Rare photo of Minnie Pearl with her clutch purse and showing her garter, which was used to hold up cotton stockings, c. 1942. Image courtesy of Harpeth Hall School Archives.

As time passed, Sarah embraced the duality and leaned into comedy and country music while maintaining her stature in Nashville society. Although she walked a tightrope, she managed to strike the right balance between the two worlds. Those who loved Minnie Pearl did not separate the character from the woman. Those who loved Sarah Cannon focused

A far cry from Minnie Pearl's knee socks, country dresses, and straw hat, the graceful and stylish Sarah Colley Cannon poses on the stairs of her home on Curtiswood Lane, next door to the Tennessee Governor's Mansion. Image courtesy of *Nashville Banner* Archives, Special Collections Division, Nashville Public Library.

on Minnie as an act, a caricature. In other words, her fans adored the hillbilly stereotype of Minnie Pearl, but her friends never doubted the artificiality of the character. After all, once the show was over, Sarah drove to her home on a sprawling estate next door to the Tennessee Governor's Mansion.

Sarah's comedy character was also a bit of a paradox. Minnie Pearl was a blend of brash and bashful. With her trademark straw hat and wide grin, she combined a bold, outspoken demeanor with self-deprecating simplicity. It worked. Live audiences, radio listeners, and television viewers saw her as lovable and laugh-out-loud funny. Oermann described her best: "Minnie Pearl was the man-hungry old maid, the homely wallflower with just enough pluck and grit to keep her chin up. She was a perpetually innocent, small-town gossip bubbling with the news of her neighbors."

Ann-Margret, Elvis Presley's co-star in *Viva Las Vegas*, performs with Minnie Pearl at the Opry, February 23, 1977. Ann-Margret was often called the Rhinestone Cowgirl. Also on the show that night were Bob Hope, Perry Como, and Chet Atkins. Image courtesy of *Nashville Banner* Archives, Special Collections Division, Nashville Public Library.

One of Minnie's favorite jokes went like this: "The robber said, 'Gimme your money.' I said, 'But I haven't got any money,' so he frisked me up and down and said, 'Are you sure you ain't got no money?' I said, 'No sir, but if you'll do that again, I'll write you a check.'" Her comedy would fall flat with many audiences today, but one can't help but admire Sarah's ability to simultaneously represent multiple perceptions related to gender. On

"Women of Country" laugh and listen to Minnie's advice, c. 1980. From left to right: Kitty Wells, Judy Harris, Dottie West, Gail Davies, Minnie Pearl, Dolly Parton, and Jeannie Pruett. Image courtesy of The Hope Powell Collection by Singleton/Curb.

the one hand, Minnie Pearl reinforced the role of the desperate female spinster in rural America even as Sarah pushed boundaries as a modern woman in a man's world, particularly after World War II.

Despite her theatrical training at the Ward-Belmont School and experience with the Sewell Theater Company, Sarah admitted she was unprepared for the realities of life on the road. During the 1940s and 1950s, traveling by car—or even hearse—with mostly male musicians presented unique challenges. Road trips were often marked by raunchy conversations, bad behavior, heavy drinking, and drug use. Still, Sarah found her niche and quickly earned respect. "There were about 50 members of the Opry cast. They were all very supportive . . . and accepted me into the 'family,'" she said, adding, "I represented no threat to any of them. I didn't sing, and I was a woman."

Like most Southern women, Sarah did not identify as a feminist, but she was acutely aware that the deck was stacked against her in an overwhelmingly male-dominated environment. Yet, Sarah subtly challenged cultural norms through her work as a performer, philanthropist, and partner—an ironic twist for a woman whose claim to fame was a character known for hollering "Howdy!"

For decades, the Grand Ole Opry's women primarily served as accompanists, backup singers, or small gospel groups performing between male headliners. Minnie Pearl was different; she had star power. Her rise coincided with WSM radio's growth into a fifty-thousand-watt radio powerhouse and the Opry's expansion to NBC's full network in 1943. Touring with Roy Acuff and Pee Wee King, Minnie's popularity soared, especially among servicemen during World War II. After the war, she married pilot Henry Cannon in 1947, who became her co-pilot in every sense of the word. For more than twenty years, he flew her to personal appearances in their plane, nicknamed "The White Poodle." By the 1950s, Minnie was a beloved veteran at the Opry, known for mentoring newcomers like Roger Miller, Mel Tillis, Patsy Cline, Kitty Wells, June Carter, Willie Nelson, Johnny Cash, Brenda Lee, Jean Shephard, Jeanne Pruett, and Loretta Lynn.

Throughout the 1950s and 1960s, Minnie appeared on numerous TV shows, including those hosted by Johnny Carson, Ed Sullivan and Carol Burnett, while also publishing cookbooks and "hillbilly humor" compilations. She met multiple U.S. Presidents, performed at Carnegie Hall, and shared the stage with Elvis Presley. But she also had to overcome difficult moments during her career. Sarah watched Opry colleagues, like Hank Williams, struggle with addiction. She mourned the death of Patsy Cline in 1963 and miraculously walked away after her own plane crashed in 1967. In business, her reputation was tested after the rise and sudden collapse of her restaurant chain, Minnie Pearl's Fried Chicken, in 1970.

After twenty-seven years of one-nighters on the road and weekly

An iconic silhouette of Minnie Pearl on stage at the Ryman Auditorium in 1974 before the Grand Ole Opry moved to the current Opry House located on Briley Parkway. Image courtesy of Grand Ole Opry Archives, Jim McGuire Collection.

Grand Ole Opry shows in Nashville, the fifty-eight-year-old joined the cast of *Hee Haw*, the most successful syndicated series in television history (1969–1993). While many stars of her generation faded, Minnie Pearl's popularity continued to grow as she successfully transitioned from radio to television. At the same time, Nashville evolved from a midsized Southern city into a globally recognized music mecca.

Remarkably, even at seventy-nine, she was still performing when she suffered a major stroke in 1991. In the five years that followed, Sarah rarely

Minnie and Dolly Parton sharing a laugh backstage of the Grand Ole Opry, c. 1986.
Image courtesy of The Hope Powell Collection by Singleton/Curb.

appeared in public, yet she continued to make her mark—establishing the Sarah Cannon Cancer Center in 1993. Three years later, Sarah Ophelia Colley Cannon passed away. Over the course of her life, her signature mix of humor and heart had endeared Minnie/Sarah to people from all walks of life. Country music stars, elected officials, and devoted fans flocked to her funeral. Even in death, she possessed the rare ability to bring people together.

This biography celebrates the life of Sarah Colley Cannon, best known as Minnie Pearl, whose story reflects the evolution of American culture and country music in the twentieth century. Thematic essays offer an intimate, behind-the-scenes view of life in Tennessee, the Grand Ole Opry, and significant moments connected to country music's biggest stars. Though some chapters overlap chronologically, the narrative focuses on key events and themes through the lens of Minnie Pearl. Her story is divided into three sections: *Before the Opry (1912–1940), On the Opry and the Road (1940–1970),* and *Beyond the Opry (1958–1996),* connecting her journey to the broader American cultural narrative.

Sarah Ophelia Colley Cannon was a woman who identified with multiple names that changed over time. Of course, Minnie Pearl also became a nickname—even in her personal life. As historian Kristine McCusker noted, "It is hard sometimes to say which person went where." For purposes of consistency and clarity, the first name Sarah is used for all chapters before Minnie Pearl's Opry debut in 1940. After 1940, she is identified as Minnie, with some exceptions.

It's been more than a century since the Grand Ole Opry debuted in 1925. It's been over eighty-five years since Minnie Pearl's first Opry performance. The Opry left its longtime home, the Ryman Auditorium, more than fifty years ago (1974). Three decades have passed since Sarah Cannon's death, but the memory of Minnie Pearl—and the $1.98 price tag that dangled from her hat—endures.

In the time since, the nation's collective sense of humor has evolved. Today, Minnie Pearl's act, rooted in the imaginary town of Grinder's Switch, feels less LOL and more OMG. However, this cultural shift prompts important questions for both older and younger generations to consider. Why did Minnie Pearl mean so much to so many? How did she use the simple stereotype of Minnie Pearl to her advantage? What were the highs and lows of her career? In what ways does the character of Minnie Pearl and the life of Sarah Cannon run parallel to themes in American history? How did she reconcile this dualism and the two worlds in which she operated? Why does she remain so popular?

Her signature salutation invites us to learn more: "Howdy! I'm just so proud to be here." Let's find out together.

NOTES

In the Colley family, she was called Ophelia, which was sometimes shortened to Phel. In college at Ward-Belmont, she was called Ophie. For the first seven years on the Grand Ole Opry, she was known as Sarah Colley. She married Henry

Cannon in 1947 at the age of thirty-four and became Sarah Cannon. In her philanthropic work, the names Sarah Cannon and Minnie Pearl were both used.

SOURCES

McCusker, Kristine M. "Sarah Colley Cannon (Minnie Pearl): Gossiping about Grinder's Switch—The Grand Ole Opry and the Modernization of Tennessee." In *Tennessee Women: Their Lives and Times*, edited by Sarah Wilkerson Freeman and Beverly Bond, 261–80. Athens: University of Georgia Press, 2009.

"Minnie Pearl—Comedy (Opry Live March 3, 1979)." Posted April 4, 2024, by Classic Country, YouTube video. https://youtu.be/lbtC15yhDlU?si=R7qBcxx_dlyEFQ50.

Oermann, Robert K. "Minnie Pearl Treatment_Version 1." *Facing the Laughter: Minnie Pearl.* Directed by Barbara J. Hall. American Public Television, 2023.

Pearl, Minnie, and Joan Dew. *Minnie Pearl: An Autobiography.* New York: Simon and Schuster, 1980.

ONE

Before the Opry, 1912–1940

CHAPTER ONE

Daddy's Girl, Mama's Charge

Growing up in Centerville, 1912–1929

Boundless energy. A vivid imagination. Big dreams. Born on October 25, 1912, Sarah Ophelia Colley's first word was "Howdy!" Well, not exactly, but figuratively it tracks. With a natural flair for performance, Sarah was destined to entertain, and Centerville was her first stage. The youngest of five, her parents set high standards—determined to raise a proper young lady. But Sarah remarked: "Nothing could have prepared . . . my proud, conventional southern parents . . . for the shock of a child determined to be in show business."

Sarah's parents, Frances (Fannie) Tate House Colley and Thomas (Tom) Kelley Colley, married in 1897. Fannie Tate's family had lived for generations in Franklin, Tennessee, just south of Nashville. Franklin was a small town known for its old money. Born in 1875, a decade after the Civil War, Fannie Tate grew up in a home built in 1873. Her father, William House, was a distinguished lawyer, while her mother, Ophelia Caroline Wood, was a socialite and an accomplished pianist. Years later, Fannie Tate passed down her musical talent by teaching her own daughters to play the piano—a skill that would prove essential to Sarah's evolution into Minnie Pearl.

As a teenager, Fannie Tate attended Nashville College for Young Ladies, a finishing school for affluent young White women. After graduation, Fannie Tate returned to Franklin as "quite the educated, elegant

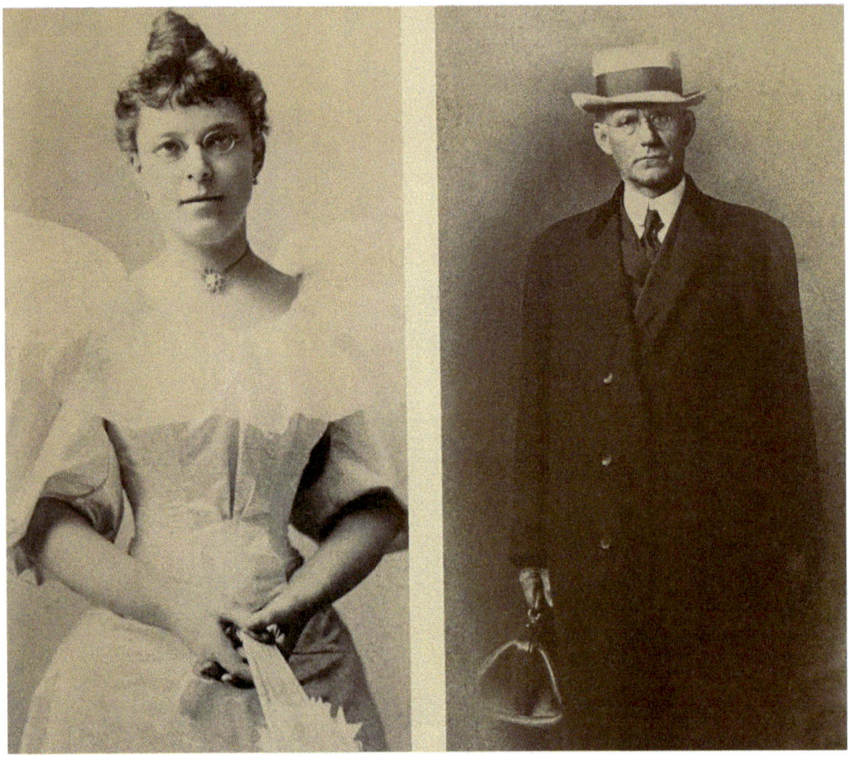

Frances "Fannie" Tate House Colley around the time of her wedding and Thomas "Tom" Kelley Colley. They were married in 1897 and moved from Franklin to Centerville. Fannie Tate was born in 1875 and passed away in 1963. Tom was born in 1857 and died in 1937 when Sarah/Minnie was twenty-five years old. Image in the public domain.

lady," and she and Tom Colley began their courtship. She was twenty; he was thirty-seven.

Thomas's family was less cultured and more country. The Colley family operated a lumber mill sixty miles west of Nashville in Centerville, Tennessee. He received some formal education, Sarah said, "But no one could ever tell how much." Tall and imposing at 6'4", Tom was known for his Stetson hat and custom-made clothes. Sarah said, "Daddy was quite the blade in his day, one of the most eligible men in Franklin. . . . And he always said 'Mama was the Belle of Franklin, and she never quit ringing.'" The newlyweds moved to Centerville so he could run the family business with his brother.

While Tom built their house in Centerville, he lived with his new bride at the only hotel in town, where the view "looked down on hogs

Tom and Fannie Tate Colley lived at the Centerville Hotel while they were building their home on the edge of town, 1897. Image courtesy of Mary Beth Pruett and Hickman County Historical Society.

wallowing in the streets." Their home was completed in 1898, just in time for the birth of their first child, Frances. Fifteen months after Frances, Virginia was born. Then, in 1902, the family welcomed Mary, and Dixie came along in 1905. With four daughters in less than eight years, Thomas and Fannie Tate settled into family life and Centerville's small-town culture.

Fannie Tate was active in the local Methodist church, the Women's Missionary Society, and other civic groups. She helped establish the local

The Centerville Train Depot was the main station for passengers and goods to travel to and from the small town, located about 60 miles west of Nashville, c. 1910. Grinder's Switch was nearby, which allowed Tom Colley to load his lumber and transport it to this station where it would be connected to a larger train for shipping. Image courtesy of the Hickman County Historical Society.

Tom Colley holds baby Sarah Ophelia, who he called "Phel," 1913. He was fifty-five years old when she was born. Image courtesy of Mary Beth Pruett and Hickman County Historical Society.

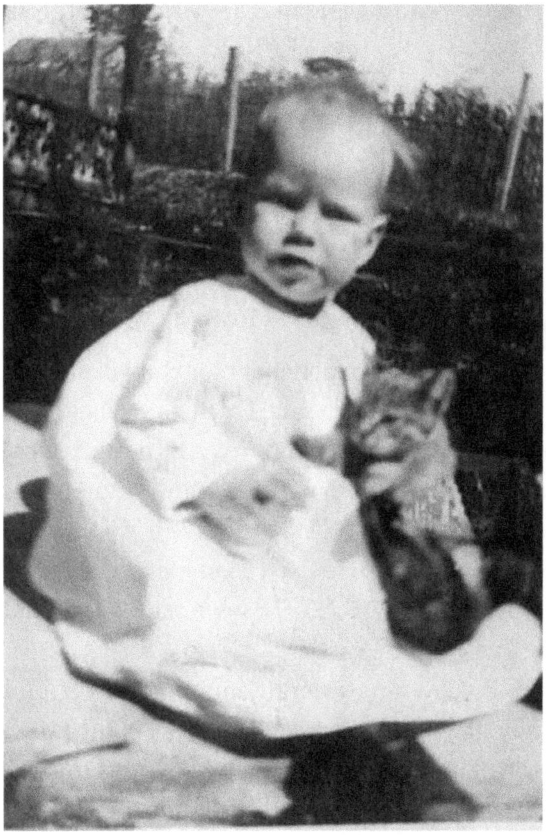

Sarah Ophelia Colley and her new kitten, 1913. Image courtesy of Mary Beth Pruett and Hickman County Historical Society.

chapter of the New York–based Chautauqua Literary and Scientific Circle (or Chautauqua Circle), which remains the oldest continuous book club in the US. Meanwhile, the Colley Brothers Lumber Company grew to accommodate the construction boom of the early 1900s. With the completion of Nashville's Union Station in 1901, and the railroad's extension to Centerville, the town emerged as a bustling mini-metropolis. The Colleys were primed to benefit from it all.

In 1912, with all the children in school, Fannie Tate surprised the family by announcing she was pregnant, giving Thomas one more chance for a son. He didn't get a boy, but by Sarah's own admission, he did get a "tomboy." Fannie Tate worked hard to instill ladylike behavior, but Sarah stood apart from her sisters—extroverted, curious, talkative, boisterous, and slapstick funny. Named Sarah Ophelia Colley after Thomas's sister and Fannie Tate's mother, she was known as Ophelia in Centerville. Her father's modification to "Phel" (pronounced "Feel") was a special term of endearment.

Sarah described her father as "a man of great integrity and a man of great dignity." He was also wrapped around "Phel's" finger. Tom whisked Sarah away on many adventures—riding down to the mill, encountering a "band of gypsies" in the woods, and even "honeysuckle hunting." When Sarah got in trouble, her mother handled the discipline, while Tom treated her to ice cream afterwards. Reflecting on her childhood, she asked, "Is it any wonder I was spoiled?"

Tom Colley was a great storyteller, with a penchant for embellishment. "Daddy was funny, he had great timing," Sarah said. From their Uncle Joe's death in a train robbery to the time a neighbor suffered a rattlesnake bite, each recitation produced a taller tale. If his daughters pointed out inconsistencies in his stories, he'd simply reply, "Well, of course it changed . . . Isn't it better that way?" Sarah recalled: "He used to say, 'Don't ever let the truth interfere with a good story,' which I always remembered and became a guiding principle for Minnie Pearl."

Just after Sarah's eighth birthday, a new family moved to town, and she was thrilled to learn they had a little girl her age. She couldn't wait to meet Monnette Thompson. Sarah tracked Monnette down on the way to school and introduced herself. Within days, they had become inseparable. "By the time we finished grammar school, there wasn't a nook in Centerville we hadn't investigated," Sarah reported, adding, "I had a best friend and someone to help me create and share the delightful fantasies of my childhood."

The town of Centerville was surrounded by the Duck River, and Sarah and Monnette loved to cross the bridge by her father's mill, climb the steep wooded hill, and explore the meadow on the other side. Sarah described their idyllic adventures:

> Everything around us was magic. We'd find a hollowed-out tree and pretend we were Alice in Wonderland. We'd pick wild violets . . . and pretend [the flower] was a king receiving his court. We spoke all the parts in dialogue that sounded like conversation from medieval times. . . . In the fall, when the trees released their leaves, we'd rake them into long rows as trenches for war games or secret passageways in a castle.

Back in 1898, Sarah's mother named the house "Gables," based on the gingerbread gable trim of the home's exterior. Perched on a hill overlooking the river, the white clapboard home featured a massive porch

Completed in 1898, the Colley home was the birthplace of Sarah Colley in 1912. Located in Centerville, Tennessee, the home tragically burned in 1940. Image courtesy of Mary Beth Pruett and Hickman County Historical Society. Sarah

that spanned nearly half the house. This porch would be one of the most important sources of creativity for Sarah as a child. Monnette and Sarah often imagined the porch as the bow of a grand ship, where they staged countless, epic dramas. In her words:

> We'd get all dressed up in my older sister's clothes—terrific Gatsby-type outfits with long-waisted dresses and headbands—and we'd pretend to be elegant ladies walking the deck of a romantic luxury liner . . . en route to some exotic port. We'd pause to speak to our imaginary suitors, all handsome and vying for our attention. What I couldn't dream up, Monnette could, and no two children ever inspired each other's imaginations more.

Another source of inspiration for Sarah was the family library, a formal room at the front of the house. All of her favorite things were in that library—books full of stories, a piano waiting to be played, and a window

Fannie Tate Colley and Sarah Opehlia ride through Centerville in a horse drawn carriage, c. 1914. Image courtesy of Mary Beth Pruett and Hickman County Historical Society.

seat that doubled as a stage. "All you had to do was remove the cushions and it became a perfect platform from which to perform," Sarah remembered. She continued, "My audience, usually composed of my sisters and their friends, would sit on the oriental rug as I stood on my stage to do my latest reading or dance. No wonder I was precocious . . . [with] them applauding and carrying on."

In addition to the library and front porch, the house also featured four bedrooms, a large kitchen, dining room, den, and bathroom. Before indoor plumbing, the bathroom was simply a room with a washbasin and a standalone tub. The household relied on a well for drinking and cooking, along with two non-flushing outhouses located behind the house. These "pit latrines" or "bucket toilets" were common for American households in rural areas. By 1920, the extension of electricity to Centerville brought

Sarah Ophelia and her mother Fannie Tate sit on the front porch of their home, c. 1916. Image courtesy of Mary Beth Pruett and Hickman County Historical Society.

indoor plumbing to the Colley household. Still, there was only one bathroom for the entire family. Outnumbered six to one, Tom Colley insisted that the reason he didn't go to church was that "Sunday morning was the only time he could get in the bathroom."

In truth, Sarah's father had a discordant relationship with organized religion. She described him as a "Godly man, a man of faith," though he rarely attended church services. Tom believed he could "communicate with God just as well at home" and chose to live out the Christian creed through his actions. Sarah said, "Daddy practiced the golden rule. He had a gun but never shot it... [And] he didn't drink, well, except for a decanter

Chautauqua Circle Club in Centerville, 1913. Infant Sarah Ophelia sits in her mother's lap with Mary, Virginia, and Dixie also seated in front of the group. Image courtesy of Mary Beth Pruett and Hickman County Historical Society.

on top of the wardrobe for special occasions." She concluded, "We had a saying in the country: 'There's two kinds of Christians, them that talks it, and them that lives it.' Daddy definitely fell into the second category."

In contrast, her mother was deeply pious and proper, taking it upon herself to instill those same values in her daughters. She was the pianist and organist at the Methodist church just down the road. And when she wasn't playing, she sang in the choir. She attended three services each week, led Bible studies, and was active in the Women's Missionary Society. Every time the church doors were open, Fannie Tate made sure her daughters were in the pews. Writing in 1979, Sarah recalled, "I felt like Mama did about church, even when I was little. I loved going to church, I still do." She recalled the weekly routine: "Sunday mornings brought a state of cheerful confusion to our house. . . .We wore button-up shoes, long white stockings, and sailor hats with our Sunday-go-to-meetin' dresses."

During the week, when they weren't in school, the girls completed household chores alongside their mother and two Black women whom Fannie Tate hired to "help manage the kids, cooking, cleaning, and laundry during the day." Their mother also regularly hosted club meetings at the house. Sarah attended more than her fair share of Chautauqua Circle book discussions, but she didn't mind—these meetings gave her an audience. Fannie Tate would let Sarah sing or play piano but with a caveat. Until it was her turn, Sarah had to sit still and be quiet—a tall order for the wild-eyed child of Tom and Fannie Tate.

Sarah noted their different approaches to parenting: "Mama was a loving woman and loved her children, but daddy was affectionate. . . . Every time he left, we kissed him and every time he came home, we kissed him." But Sarah maintained that her parents had a strong relationship. Though arguments may have occurred behind closed doors, she emphasized, "They always presented a united front and clearly loved each other." To illustrate her point, Sarah shared an endearing memory: "Back when the lumber business was booming, he'd go to Nashville to do business. . . . He'd always bring us a gift back and bring Mama Mitchell's Candy—that was her favorite."

While Tom showered the girls with gifts and affection, Fannie Tate was tasked with disciplining the children, and she maintained a "spare the rod and spoil the child" philosophy. There were no time-outs or empty threats. When Sarah acted up, her mother was quick to respond. Sarah exclaimed, "Oh, I got so many whippings. [Mama] could make you dance with a peach tree limb!" She continued, "Poor mama. She saw it as her charge to make me behave and act like a lady. Of course, I didn't—but they thought I would. Because I was apt to just jump right up in the middle of whatever was going on and say, 'Would you like to hear me sing?'"

Her sisters also ensured she received plenty of attention even before Sarah could get into trouble by her own volition. She wrote: "As a baby, Frances and Virginia paraded me around the town square in my carriage. . . . [And] the minute I could walk my sisters taught me little songs and dances so I could show off." At just eighteen months old, she made her public singing debut. By the age of four, she was playing the piano. Sarah laughed as she reminiscenced: "I could plunk out tunes by ear, sing at the top of my lungs, and dance a jig in front of the piano all at the same time. And I was ready to do it anytime, with very little encouragement. I must have been insufferable!"

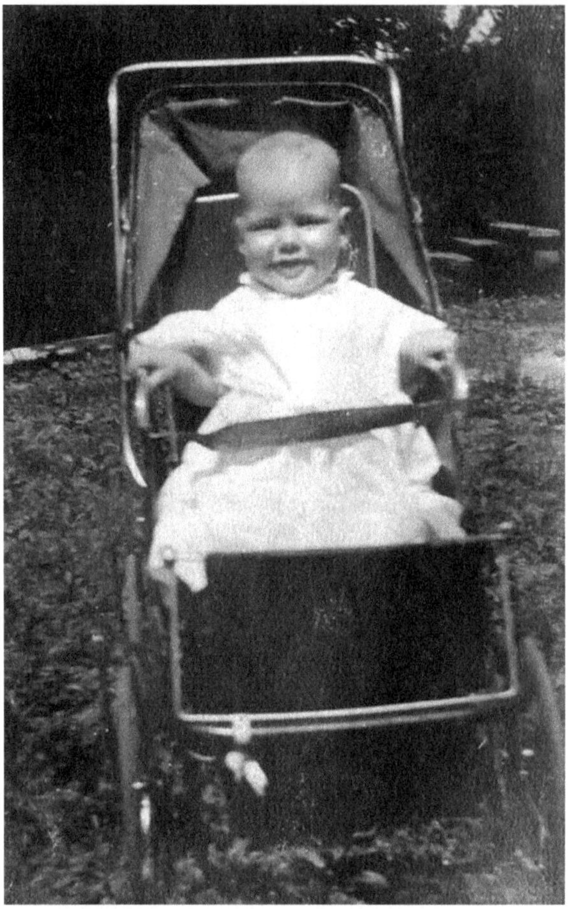

Sarah's sisters loved to "show her off" by pushing her through town and teaching her songs as a baby. Image courtesy of Mary Beth Pruett and Hickman County Historical Society.

Singing and dancing was one thing, but Sarah was also a talented musician. Her mother taught her to read music, and Sarah spent hours practicing the piano in the family library. At the age of ten, ever resourceful and clever, Sarah made a backroom deal with Mr. Rulander, who ran Centerville's movie theater. The 1920s marked the silent movie era, where storytelling depended heavily on the actors' physical expression. Intermittent screens of text (called inter-title cards) provided the necessary information for each scene. This isn't to say silent movies were truly silent: film reels arrived with sheet music, and pianists were hired to play the accompaniment, which served as the movie's soundtrack. These musicians controlled the emotional tone and helped advance the plot. The job required a skilled pianist and a quick learner. Sarah was both.

Mr. Rulander and Sarah came to an agreement. She provided piano accompaniment, and in exchange, she could watch any movie for free. Well, that was music—pun intended—to her ears. The movies also fueled her desire to be in show business. Sarah recalled, "I'd play romantic music during the love scenes and fast, exciting music during the action." But the gig didn't last long. Fannie Tate caught wind of Sarah's new job: "She suggested, very firmly, that I was much too young to be hanging out at the movie house playing piano. And that was that."

Sarah's brief stint at the theater had ended, but Fannie Tate and Tom decided to support her interests by allowing her to take "expression" lessons. No longer an academic discipline, "expression" has long since been replaced by performing arts and communications. For Sarah, "expression" included lessons in different types of performance from acting to dancing to reciting poems and monologues. She continued her study throughout high school, noting the significance:

> Of all my activities, none was more important than my expression lessons with Miss Inez Shipp. Twice a week I'd go to learn readings and scenes from plays, stage presence, voice inflection, timing—all the things that make up the study of acting. . . . My dream for my future by then was full-blown and as real to me as anything happening in my everyday life. *I was going to be one of the greatest dramatic actresses of my time.*

In a family with five girls, Sarah had the built-in advantage of learning from her big sisters. Like most teenage girls, they could all be quite expressive, or dramatic, depending on the circumstance. Sarah recalled: "Mary loved fantasy and romance and all the emotions. She would get her heart broken and teach me sad sonnets." One such poem was "Moods," by Angela Weld Grimké, a poet and author of the Harlem Renaissance in the 1910s/1920s. In an interview more than fifty years later, Sarah could still recall lines from the poem by heart: "I shall go quietly along this street and none shall know I am drunk with pain. Strange, strange that all at once happened and in one afternoon lain."

Sarah adored all of her sisters, but she idolized Dixie. Sarah reminisced: "Dixie was seven years older and started dating when I was eight, a very impressionable age. We slept in the same room in the same bed, and she always woke me up when she came in from a date and we'd talk and giggle." It was the 1920s, and Dixie embraced the image of the

Sisters Dixie and Mary "show off" their baby sister Sarah Ophelia, 1914. Sarah made her first public singing debut when she was eighteen months old in 1914. Image courtesy of Mary Beth Pruett and Hickman County Historical Society.

modern woman. Sarah wrote: "Those were the days of short dresses, flapper clothes, jazz, and the Charleston. . . . [Dixie] loved to date and dance and dart around in open-top cars with boys in raccoon coats." Dixie also played piano around town for social functions and regularly brought down the house with her rendition of Scott Joplin's "The Entertainer." All the while, little Sarah took mental notes: "I learned so much from my sisters because they were all so much older."

As Sarah came of age, Centerville's population was approximately 1200 people by the 1929. Centerville had a town square, four churches, a train station, two banks, and the Colley lumberyard and sawmill. The Hickman County Grammar and High Schools served grades K–12 in the same building. As the town's main industrial firm, the Colley Brothers Lumber Company was the largest employer in town. Tom ran the business side

A group of Centerville residents stand on the bridge that leads to Colley Town with the Colley Brothers Lumber Company sawmill in the background, c. 1920. Image courtesy of Mary Beth Pruett and Hickman County Historical Society.

of the company while his brother managed mill operations. Growing up, Sarah and her sisters "never wanted for anything," but she insisted they were not rich. She said, "We were one of the most prominent families, but that's like my [Minnie Pearl] gag where the emcee says to me, 'I hear you've been kissed by every man in Grinder's Switch, and I say, 'Well Grinder's Switch ain't such a big place.'"

Tom employed both Black and White men, and their families lived on a road down by the mill in what they called Colleytown. Sarah said,

"There were a dozen or so houses and no segregation, the White houses were right next to the Black houses. There didn't ever seem to be any problem. . . . I think my father had a lot to do with that and my Uncle John." Sarah often wandered down to Colleytown to play with children her age, but her favorite memories centered on Christmas:

> We'd rush in to open our presents, which Mama set out in stacks on the window. Our stockings, hanging from the mantle, were jammed full of nuts, sweets and fresh fruits. . . . After breakfast we bundled up in our overcoats and headed down to Colleytown to exchange Christmas presents with Daddy and Uncle John's workers. . . . [W]e went from house to house, exchanging store-bought presents for gifts of jams and jellies and other homemade things, and it was always a wonderful occasion.

"My lack of prejudice came from my parents," Sarah said, continuing, "They forbade us from using any slang words, and said that everyone deserved respect unless they proved otherwise. . . . We played with the children, Black and White, and there was never any question of difference." And yet, her father was a "Yellow Dog Democrat," which supported segregation and sought to disenfranchise Black voters. (This demographic was so named because supporters would vote for a "yellow dog" as long as it was a Democrat.)

In addition, their family remained deeply devoted to the "Lost Cause," bragging about the role of uncles and cousins who served in the Confederate Army. The default in their household was to call it the "War between the States." Sarah said her father refused to call it the Civil War because "[h]e said there wasn't anything civil about it."

This type of narrative is not uncommon in Southern history. Sarah's reflective sentiment remains sincere and authentic, but it also relies on contradiction and equivocation. For instance, many White Southerners saw themselves as unprejudiced due to positive interactions with Black individuals, even as they upheld beliefs that ignored historical injustices and reinforced second-class citizenship. Historian David W. Blight argued in *Race and Reunion: The Civil War in American Memory* that many Americans, particularly in the South, constructed memories of the Civil War that downplayed the central role of slavery and the racism that followed.

For all the complexity of Southern culture in the early twentieth century, Sarah viewed her childhood in simple terms. She was blessed with an affectionate father, a dutiful mother, four adoring sisters, a best friend, teachers, preachers, and a supportive community. She wrote in her autobiography: "I think one of the reasons Minnie Pearl has found so many fans is because she retains some of the childlike innocence that characterized my formative years. . . . The whole town was my playground. I ran and romped everywhere, investigated everything, visited anyone, and had a wonderful time doing it."

NOTES

"The Entertainer" is a 1902 classic piano rag written by Scott Joplin. It was sold first as sheet music by John Stark & Son of St. Louis, Missouri, and in the 1910s as piano rolls that would play on player pianos.

SOURCES

Baril, Buffie, and Brandon. "The Home of William and Ophelia House." *Lovely Franklin*, 2021, https://lovelyfranklin.com/the-home-of-william-and-ophelia-house-grandparents-of-sarah-colley-cannon-aka-minnie-pearl/.

Blight, David W. *Race and Reunion: The Civil War in American Memory.* Cambridge: Harvard University Press, 2001.

Pearl, Minnie. Tape recorded memoir by Sarah Colley Cannon, Nashville, Tennessee. Tape 1, Side A, Side B, 1979.

———. Tape recorded memoir by Sarah Colley Cannon, Nashville, Tennessee. Tape 2, Side A, Side B, 1979.

———. Tape recorded memoir by Sarah Colley Cannon, Nashville, Tennessee. Supplement to Tape 1, Side A/B, 1979.

Pearl, Minnie, and Joan Dew. *Minnie Pearl: An Autobiography.* New York: Simon and Schuster, 1980.

Villarreal, Rebecca. "Angelina Weld Grimké." *Beltway: A Poetry Quarterly*, August 2003. https://washingtonart.com/beltway/grimke.html.

CHAPTER 2

The Bells and Belles of Ward-Belmont

The Ward-Belmont School, 1930–1932

On a beautiful spring evening in April 1929, WSM radio's live broadcast caught the attention of listeners across the nation. It wasn't the Grand Ole Opry, which debuted as a "barn dance" on WSM in 1925. Instead, it was the first ever carillon concert at Ward-Belmont, an all-girls school in Nashville. What's a carillon, you ask? Typically housed in a belfry, a carillon is a set of twenty-three bells with broomstick-like keys. A gift from the school's alumnae, the bells were installed in the top of the estate's former water tower.

Percival Price, a world-renowned musician, christened the bells with *America the Beautiful*, *Ode to Joy* (Beethoven), *Andalle* (Schumann), and *The Harmonious Blacksmith* (Handel). The concert closed with the school's alma mater, *The Bells of Ward-Belmont*, with those in attendance singing along. This event reinforced Ward-Belmont's image as a school for Southern belles, quite literally. As the carillon's majestic peal echoed across campus, students stood under a canopy of oak and magnolia trees dressed in gowns and white gloves.

Meanwhile, also in 1929, Sarah Ophelia Colley started her senior year at Hickman County High School. As students at Ward-Belmont held tea parties, Sarah led the football cheerleading squad. She boasted: "If hollering had anything to do with [it] . . . I can personally take credit for

The Ward-Belmont Bell Tower prior to the installation of the carillon, 1914. The tower itself has stood since c.1850 and is today listed on the National Register of Historic Places. Image courtesy of Belmont University Special Collections.

quite a few touchdowns. I pranced up and down in front of the stands in my red plaid accordion-pleated skirt, white shirt, bobby sox, and white oxfords. . . . Half the time I'd go home from a game so hoarse I could barely speak." Sarah also played on the Hickman County basketball team and was active in the drama department, participating in every theater production while in high school.

Women attending traditional universities was far from the norm during the 1920s (only about 10 percent), but Tom and Fannie Tate Colley took pride in sending their daughters to the college of their choice. For example, Virginia attended Goucher College; Mary attended Agnes Scott College, and both went on to earn master's degrees.

Times were good for the Colley family, but two months into Sarah's senior year, everything changed. On October 29, 1929, the Stock Market crashed, leading to a massive financial crisis in the United States and triggering a global depression that lingered for more than a decade. Sarah recalled, "The first time money came into my life as a specter was

Aside from cheerleading, Sarah (standing far left, second row) was also active in athletics as a member of the girls' basketball team, 1927. Image courtesy of Mary Beth Pruett and Hickman County Historical Society.

in 1930. I was supposed to go to college; all of my sisters had gone. Just when I needed it, just when I wanted to go to college like the rest of my family, we were hard hit by the depression." Until 1929, business boomed for Tom Colley, but he operated without much of a safety net. Sarah noted, "The lumber business was one of the first to crash because all the new construction stopped." Six years later, the Colley Brothers Lumber Company closed its doors.

The economy severely limited Sarah's options for higher education. Her desire to attend an elite college, then train at the American Academy of Dramatic Arts was off the table. For the most part, Sarah took it in stride. "I felt as bad for mama and daddy as I did for myself," she said. Her parents could afford to send her to the University of Tennessee (UT) in Knoxville or the private Ward-Belmont School in Nashville. As the state's flagship university, UT was more affordable, but the more prestigious, all-female school known as Ward-Belmont featured a reputable theater

Sarah Ophelia Colley, who was called Ophelia in high school, is pictured here as a senior at Hickman County High School, Class of 1931. Her bobbed hair was all the rage for young women in the 1920s and early 1930s. Image courtesy of Harpeth Hall School Archives.

program and music conservatory. Led by Pauline Sherwood Townsend, the "School of Expression" at Ward-Belmont included alumnae such as Mary Martin, who later starred as Peter Pan on Broadway.

The tuition was $1,000, with $100 added for "expression" lessons and $100 for dancing. Sarah remembered clearly: "That was a big, big amount of money. I remember mama and daddy talking about it. So much of the decision came down to Ms. Townsend." Her high school teacher, Inez Shipp, wrote to Townsend and asked if she would accept Sarah as a student. In her letter, Shipp described Sarah as a young woman with "considerable talent." Townsend replied "yes." That sealed the deal. Sarah chose the two-year program at Ward-Belmont over a four-year degree at UT.

The school's campus was majestic—anchored by an Italianate mansion on one end and an elaborate brick water tower on the other. The Belmont Mansion was constructed between 1850 and 1860 by the Southern heiress Adelicia Acklen and her husband, Joseph Acklen. The estate was situated on a hill overlooking Nashville's downtown. Originally named Belle Monte, or "beautiful mountain" in Italian, the estate was ultimately sold to Susan Heron and Ida Hood in 1889. They opened Belmont College for

Pauline Sherwood Townsend was an iconic force at Ward-Belmont from 1903 to 1939. She taught dramatics and speech and served, for many years, as the School of Expression director. Townsend, pictured here in 1932, was instrumental in training Sarah Colley. One student noted: "Miss Townsend carried herself with an authority that demanded absolute respect. When she spoke, her own voice was a perfectly tuned instrument, which she played with virtuoso skill, so that even a slight inflection could create a mood or convey an idea." Image courtesy Harpeth Hall School Archives.

Young Women in 1890, which merged with Ward Seminary in 1913. The school was accredited as a junior college in 1925.

In the 1930s, Ward-Belmont was still regarded as a finishing school, preparing the "daughters of the rich" for marriage and high society. In reality, it upheld a rigorous academic curriculum that enabled many graduates to continue their education at traditional universities. While there, Sarah took classes in biology, Bible, English, art history, economics, chemistry, physiology, French, mathematics, expression, physical education, dancing, history, and home economics.

For those with means, an education at Ward-Belmont was meant for young White women who hoped to join Southern society's upper crust. For Sarah's part, she saw Ward-Belmont as a place where she could gain

Belmont Mansion was the summer home of Adelicia Acklen, completed in 1850. It served as the main administrative building for Ward-Belmont School. Fidelity Hall, Sarah's dormitory is to the left. Image courtesy of Belmont Mansion.

the skills needed to become a serious actor. She knew of the school's strict reputation but decided it was her best option. Surely, she thought, the all-girls school couldn't break her spirit.

Sarah was assigned to the dormitory known as Fidelity Hall, but upon her arrival she was directed to the Belmont Mansion to check-in with Emma Sisson, the Dean of Residence. With posture like a soldier at attention, Sisson greeted Sarah with hospitality but not enthusiasm. Sarah was immediately overwhelmed—not just by Sisson but also by the grandeur of her surroundings. In her words:

> I walked through the rooms that first day wide-eyed and open-mouthed. [It was] sumptuously beautiful: baroque gold-leaf moldings, 14-foot ceilings, Venetian glass, enormous crystal chandeliers . . . and magnificent oriental rugs. It looked more like a European palace than headquarters of an American girls' school.

Just a couple of miles down the road, men stood in bread lines amid the Great Depression. Yet, Ward-Belmont stood as an oasis of opulence. "I was struck immediately by the subtle, indefinable scent of wealth . . . substantial *old* money," Sarah said, adding, "I was terrified." Back in Centerville, the Colley home had been a hub of noisy activity with something always cooking in the kitchen. Belmont Mansion was deathly quiet and smelled of beeswax and eucalyptus. "I felt like I'd been dropped into a funeral home," she quipped.

Sarah's parents were wealthy by Centerville standards but not by the standards of Ward-Belmont. She noted, "Very few girls were there because their parents had scraped to send them, as mine had." Her insecurity was heightened after meeting her roommate from Texas who came from "oil money." Sarah watched her roommate unpack "outfit after outfit, all coordinated with different shoes, bags, and gloves." In contrast, Sarah's wardrobe consisted of the bare minimum. The only luxurious item in her trunk was a long black coat with a fox fur collar—a going away gift from her father. Sarah "nearly died" when her roommate pulled out two fur coats, including a full-length mink.

Things didn't get much better when she went to dinner. As Sarah ate on fine china with fancy silverware, she listened to the girls at her table. They gabbed about debutante balls, European vacations, and charge accounts for shopping. She said, "I sat like a lump, listening and feeling lower by the minute. I was a country bumpkin. I couldn't have felt more out of place if I'd been on Mars."

Intimidated and disoriented by her new surroundings, Sarah tried to recalibrate as she prepared for the first day of class. Though she often downplayed her intellect, Sarah was smart as a whip. At least she could shine in the classroom, right? Wrong. Back in high school, Sarah prided herself on her ability to lose herself in a dramatic role: "If the part called for tears to stream down my face, I could let them flow with no trouble at all." But her first session with Miss Townsend quickly shattered that confidence. That day, the tears didn't flow because she was acting.

Townsend asked Sarah to perform a monologue but was clearly unimpressed. She questioned why Sarah's voice sounded strained and harsh. Sarah confessed she'd done some yelling as a football cheerleader. Townsend exclaimed in disbelief: "Cheerleader! You've ruined the timbre of your voice, which is an essential tool for any dramatic actress." Townsend ended their session curtly: "We have a great deal of work to do." Sarah rushed out of the studio sobbing.

Then, in English, Sarah's professor, Dr. Rhea, "chopped her down to size." Asked to write an autobiographical essay, Sarah thought, "At last! Something I can do and do well!" But when the paper came back, it had so many red marks, it looked like a roadmap. Dr. Rhea's note read:

Sarah Ophelia Colley (left), nicknamed Ophie in college, walks with a friend on the campus of Ward-Belmont School in Nashville, 1932. Image courtesy of the Harpeth Hall School Archives.

> Miss Colley, someone has apparently misinformed you. From this paper I perceive you've been given the idea that you are funny. *You are not.* But even if you were, no amount of humor could cover up the fact that your carelessness and/or lack of knowledge in grammar, spelling, and sentence structure are inexcusable.

Belittled by Miss Townsend, demeaned by Dr. Rhea, and politely ignored by most of her classmates—Sarah spiraled into a deep depression. Withdrawn and homesick, Sarah managed to put on a brave face when she telephoned her parents. After all, the family lumber business was barely hanging on, and she knew the sacrifices they were making to pay for her schooling. In truth, she was the "lonely, sniffling, long-faced, sad-eyed girl" on campus who hid away in her dorm for several weeks.

Ward-Belmont didn't have national sororities, but the school did feature ten sorority-like clubs. Each club had a house on one end of campus known as Club Village. The "rush season" began in September, which served as a highlight for most first-year students. Not for Sarah—she was too embarrassed to attend parties or receptions wearing the same

Ward-Belmont students pose for a picture in between classes. "Ophie" Colley, as she was called, stands fifth from the right, just behind the first row. She stands to the right of the young woman with dark hair wearing a light, sleeveless dress. Image courtesy of Harpeth Hall School Archives.

outfit. Then, one day in late October, Sarah was wandering campus and came across one of the club cottages. She peeked in the door and caught a glimpse of a piano. The room was empty, so Sarah sat down and "let 'er rip."

Sarah was singing at the top of her lungs when she realized she wasn't alone anymore. She stopped and spun around to discover three girls sitting on the sofa. "Don't stop!" they screamed. One of the girls asked, "Why haven't we seen you playing at any of the rush parties?" Sarah answered

In 1932, Sarah Opehlia Colley, called Ophie at Ward-Belmont, was awarded "Most Humorous," a fitting superlative for the young woman who would later become one of most popular female comics of the twentieth century. Image courtesy of Harpeth Hall School Archives.

meekly, "No one ever asked me to play." They responded, "Well, how on earth could they ask if they didn't know you played?!"

The girls introduced themselves as Hot, Dot, and Annie—all seniors at Ward-Belmont. Sarah said, "Even their names were cute, and they were the liveliest threesome I'd seen since leaving Centerville . . . They were so relaxed, so casually confident." Hot, Dot, and Annie adopted Sarah Ophelia Colley and nicknamed her Ophie.

The trio of friends became a group of four, and they brought Sarah back from the depths of despair. They asked her to rush their club, Agora, invited her to parties, and introduced her around. By Thanksgiving, Sarah was back to her old self—spirited, engaged, and outgoing. Decades later,

In her second year, Sarah Ophelia Colley emerged as a leader, active in several organizations including the school newspaper, *The Ward-Belmont Hyphen*, the YWCA, year book, and other clubs on campus. Taken in 1932, the photo shows Sarah standing (second from right) with the newspaper staff. Image courtesy of Harpeth Hall School Archives.

Sarah wrote, “I couldn’t tell them at the time, but Hot, Dot, and Annie saved my life at Ward-Belmont.”

All the things that had once made Sarah feel out of place seemed to fade away. She simply needed to find her people and regain her perspective. Rather than avoiding awkward situations, she honed her sense of humor and leveraged her people skills to bridge the gap. She also discovered the power of self-deprecating laughter. “I soon forgot all about my sparse wardrobe,” Sarah quipped. While her classmates fretted over selecting dresses for special occasions, Sarah turned her limited options into a joke. “Well, I think I’m going to mix it up this time and wear my coral number,” she’d say with a grin.

“Once I got into the swing at Ward-Belmont, no one had more enthusiasm for campus life than I did,” said Sarah. She also emerged as a leader. She joined the YWCA club and was elected vice-president. She became a staff writer for the school newspaper, *The Hyphen*, and even won a coveted seat on the student council. When superlatives were given out in 1931, her peers voted her "Most Humorous."

Sarah also found her footing in the classroom. She majored in drama and minored in Shakespeare (yes, that was a minor) under the aegis of the English Department. After a brutal first semester with Dr. Rhea, Sarah redeemed herself with Theodora Scruggs—another member of the English faculty. Scruggs was a "marvelous instructor" and "a firm but beloved teacher." Even Miss Townsend warmed to Sarah, and she came to understand that Townsend's critical feedback was grounded in love. Townsend often said, "Colley if I didn't think you had talent, I wouldn't fuss about it. I only criticize people about whom I care, people who have potential."

In the spring of 1932, Sarah prepared for her senior recital—a rite of passage for all drama students. She worked for weeks on her one-woman show, a three-act play entitled *The Charm School.* On the night of her performance, the room was packed, with Tom and Fannie Tate Colley sitting proudly in the audience. As she took her final bow, she received a rousing ovation, which included Miss Pauline Townsend.

Sarah recalled, "It was a small triumph for me. I felt confident, prepared, effective. But most of all I had a strange presentiment of other nights to come, when I might make an audience forget for a while and go with me to a land of entertainment and happiness." Though she never became a Shakespearean actress, Sarah credited her classical training at Ward-Belmont as a key factor in Minnie Pearl's success on the Grand Ole Opry.

Sarah's time at Ward-Belmont was marked by individual achievements, but the camaraderie she shared with fellow students left an equally lasting impression. Reflecting on those days, she remarked, "Nothing surpassed the bonds we formed while living in close quarters under strict rules and by stern authority." With a hint of sarcasm, Sarah joked, "It was like living in a convent."

Decades later, Sarah Colley Cannon, Sarah Bryan Benedict, and Mary Elizabeth Cayce collaborated on an essay titled "Ward-Belmont: A Reminiscence." Published by the *Tennessee Historical Quarterly* in 1971, the following excerpt offers a glimpse into student life and dating during their time at the school.

Sarah returns to Ward-Belmont School as Minnie Pearl and has some fun as students sing while she plays the piano, c. 1944. Image courtesy of the Harpeth Hall School Archives.

> From 1912 when Ward-Belmont came into existence until the mid-1930s, the girls wore black, brown, or navy dresses and black, brown, or navy hats, shoes, and gloves as "uniform" to church or on chaperoned shopping tours. Violation of these regulations brought a student council penalty. Make-up and chewing gum were cardinal sins at any hour, and smoking and drinking were cause for immediate expulsion.

The controls for deportment were tough, clear cut, and detailed. Lesser infractions of the rules included: wearing high heels during the school day; wearing dresses of a fancy nature to classes; being tardy for classes or chapel services; whispering or talking in chapel; speaking to male acquaintances as they rode past our campus; making noise after lights out in the dormitory; having visitors (girls, of course!) in one's dormitory room during the study hour; having a radio or an electrical appliance or foodstuffs in one's room; playing one's victrola (wind up) too loud. Most unbecoming of all and quickly punishable was failure to have hose and underclothing properly connected so that bare skin (heaven forbid) be seen.

Endless detail governed and restricted the simplest activities. Cokes were offered for sale once a week and were suspiciously nicknamed "dopes." Shopping tours arranged in groups of five or six girls in Ward-Belmont uniform were chaperoned to the downtown stores, arriving by

Sarah Ophelia Colley Cannon returns to a later version of her alma mater, Ward-Belmont. After the school's closure in 1951, the high school division moved to Green Hills and reopened as the Harpeth Hall School. Here, Sarah (center) sits with Ellen Bowers Hofstead (left) and Mary Elizabeth Cayce (right) on February 20, 1986, to plan a Ward-Belmont reunion to be held at Harpeth Hall. They sit in the school's symbolic Ward-Belmont Room located in Souby Hall, the main administrative building. Image courtesy of *Nashville Banner* Archives, Special Collections Division, Nashville Public Library.

streetcar or taxi. Trips from distant points to and from Nashville were especially arranged for the girls on special trains to convey them to and from their homes to school. Security was the ever-present sentinel of every activity.

Truly, a faint heart never won a fair lady! Arranging for a date on the cloistered campus compared in process to getting behind the iron curtain. A gentleman wanting a date was screened by the home department; the girl's family was asked to file a written permission for the date. Once this process was accomplished; a pink permission slip was issued to the girl. The young gentleman called at Acklen Hall, gave his name to the distinguished butler, Whitaker, who invited the caller in with pomp and dignity, reported his arrival to the home department, and summoned the young lady of his choice to the reception rooms.

> One wonders if all this procedure was worth a two-hour (7:30 to 9:30) visit in a Victorian parlor equipped with full-length mirrors at strategic points, hard horse-hair sofas, and a gliding chaperone who somehow floated through the rooms continually making her presence known by clearing her throat! Should such an engagement prove successful and promising, and the girl and boy wanted to meet outside the school, restrictions tightened. Would you believe the parents supported such a system? They did, and with appreciation of the meticulous care being taken of their daughters!
>
> [T]he strict discipline and undisputed authority which governed our formative years was assuredly a good and powerful force in shaping our lives. Indeed, it did not stunt our growth. . . . The school was thought to produce graduates of the highest caliber equipped to meet life's trials with character, courage, and faith. To most of us, so has it been.

In May 1932, Sarah was awarded a General Diploma in Expression. She recounted: "When graduation day came . . . it would have been hard to imagine me as the same girl who had entered college two years earlier. Nobody cried louder or harder than I did as we stood on the steps at sunset and sang our Alma Mater, The Bells of Ward-Belmont. . . . I cried coming in, and I cried going out!"

Back in 1929, on the evening of the carillon concert, one student wrote, "Those bells! It's hard to believe they are real. It's like a fairy tale." Sarah's time at Ward-Belmont wasn't a fairy tale, but the innocent, insecure girl who stepped on campus in 1930 emerged as an educated, confident young woman in 1932. Moreover, WSM radio, which broadcast the carillon concert nationwide, was the same radio station that would launch Sarah's career on the Grand Ole Opry just a few years later.

Despite her transformation, the realities waiting for Sarah after graduation were far from ideal. With the nation still in the grip of an economic depression, she returned to Centerville. The American Academy of Dramatic Arts was no longer an option—her father was flat broke and in poor health. Lacking the opportunity for further education, Sarah needed to find another way to pursue her dream of acting. Luckily, the Sewell Theater Company would offer her that chance.

NOTES

The Ward-Belmont School emerged during the height of the Progressive Era, which produced the first significant number of female college graduates and witnessed the mass entrance of women into the workplace. In 1900, only 5 percent of middle-class White women worked outside the home and less than 3 percent attended college; but by 1925, approximately 20 percent participated in the workforce and 10 percent attended college.

Ward-Belmont's enrollment peaked in 1929 at 1,200 students, but the economic depression took its toll on the school. By 1938, the student body had been reduced to approximately seven hundred students. The school closed in 1951 after the campus was sold to the Tennessee Baptist Convention. In September 1951, Belmont College reopened on the Ward-Belmont campus as a four-year, co-educational college. In 1991, it became Belmont University. Also in September 1951, the Harpeth Hall School opened in Green Hills, 4.5 miles from Ward-Belmont's campus. It represented the high school division of Ward-Belmont, including all of its faculty and 161 students. It remains an all-girls school serving grades five to twelve.

Excerpt reprinted with permission from the *Tennessee Historical Quarterly,* published by the Tennessee Historical Society.

SOURCES

Benedict, Sarah Bryan, Ophelia Colley Cannon, and Mary Elizabeth Cayce. "The Bells of Ward-Belmont: A Reminiscence." *Tennessee Historical Quarterly* 30, no. 4 (Winter 1971): 379–82.

"History." *Belmont Mansion,* 2024. https://www.belmontmansion.com/history.

Holmes, Sydney C. "Belmont Mansion: A 19th Century Country Estate." *Belmont Mansion,* 2022. https://storymaps.arcgis.com/stories/6b03d1da03e44c3fa141a82d58036ca0.

Pearl, Minnie. Tape recorded memoir by Sarah Colley Cannon, Nashville, Tennessee. Tape 3, 1979.

Pearl, Minnie, and Joan Dew. *Minnie Pearl: An Autobiography.* New York: Simon and Schuster, 1980.

Pethel, Mary Ellen. *All-Girls Education from Ward Seminary to Harpeth Hall School, 1865–2015.* Mount Pleasant, SC: The History Press, 2015.

——. *Athens of the New South: College Life and the Making of Modern Nashville.* Knoxville: The University of Tennessee Press, 2018.

——. "'The Coming Woman': Ward Seminary, 1865–1913." *Tennessee Historical Quarterly* 72, no. 3 (Fall 2013): 183–204.

Ward-Belmont Hyphen, April 20, 1929, 1–3.

Yale University Guild of Carillonneurs. "What is a Carillon?" Yale University, 2021. http://yalecarillon.org/about-carillon.

CHAPTER 3

A Winsome Director

Wayne P. Sewell Production Company, 1934–1940

Picture it: Nashville, 1932. Sarah Ophelia Colley graduates from Ward-Belmont School. It's one of the worst years in American history to find a job, much less for a woman looking for work in the arts. People could live without theater and music; they couldn't live without food on the table. To complicate matters, Sarah's parents insisted she wait until she turned twenty-one before leaving home. Stymied and dispirited, she returned to Centerville, where she opened a small studio to teach piano, dance, and theater. "Centerville hadn't changed, but I had. . . . My fulfillment lay elsewhere," she lamented.

Although Sarah was glad to reunite with her family, times were tough. Her father's lumber business had been hard hit by the Great Depression, and money was tight. As she mulled over her future in 1932 and 1933, her thoughts drifted back to childhood memories of traveling shows that visited Centerville—particularly the Wayne P. Sewell Production Company, which brought "city culture" to "country folk."

Wayne Sewell was a prominent theater producer in Atlanta, and his wife Hetty Jane Dunaway rose to fame as a vaudeville actress, best known for her monologues (akin to today's one-man show) on the Chautauqua Circuit. Hetty Jane retired from acting just before 1920, and they

Part of Centerville's downtown square at the time Sarah returned from Ward-Belmont, c. 1932. Both Carothers Hardware and Bogle Black Motor Company were hit hard by the depression. Image courtesy of Mary Beth Pruett and Hickman County Historical Society.

moved to Wayne's family estate in rural Roscoe, Georgia—forty miles southwest of Atlanta. According to historian and author Rachel Louise Martin, Hetty Jane wrote ten musical comedies based in the vaudeville and minstrel traditions—including blackface, a practice in which actors wore dark makeup to mimic and mock the appearance, mannerisms, and speech of Black people. This form of entertainment was "popular with rural [White] audiences" in the Jim Crow South.

Business boomed for the Sewells throughout the Roaring Twenties, but everything changed with the Stock Market Crash of October 1929 and the ensuing Great Depression. To keep theater alive during such challenging times, creativity was essential—and Wayne Sewell rose to the occasion. He hit the road, booking plays in every small town and unincorporated village he could find on a map. One observer joked that some places were

Wayne P. Sewell featured in the *Atlanta Journal-Constitution*, "Sigma Nu Meets; Here Three Days," April 7, 1910.

"so small they were only there three days a week." Sponsoring organizations were often Exchange Clubs, American Legions, and Parent-Teacher Associations (PTA). Sewell sold the idea that the "coaches" would do all the work while the town reaped all the profits.

Wayne hired approximately 150 single women as coaches. To qualify for the job, candidates needed to be proficient in dancing, singing, teaching, directing, producing, and willing to sell advertisements and travel extensively. Oh, and by the way, the pay was only $30 a month, which translates to $700 (2025). For Wayne Sewell and his wife, this lucrative business model ensured a steady income even in the midst of an economic depression.

So, back to Sarah in Centerville. After turning twenty-one on October 25, 1933, she made up her mind: "I was determined to see the world and to try to get into show business. And the Sewell company seemed about the only avenue I had left in the early 1930s when we had no money and there were no jobs." She wrote to Mr. Sewell in Atlanta. To her delight, he replied with a job offer to begin in August 1934. Sarah saw this as

Sarah (far right) and the Colley family pose for a photograph, 1934. Her mother, Fannie Tate stands beside her holding one of the grandchildren. Her father, Thomas, is on the back row wearing a hat. Also pictured are her sisters, nieces, and nephews. This photo was taken shortly before leaving Centerville for her first job with the Sewell Theater Production Company. Image courtesy of Hickman Country Historical Society.

an opportunity not only to earn a living but also to gain the experience needed to pursue a career in professional acting.

Though her parents didn't approve, she stood by her decision, telling her mother and father: "I am of age, and I am going. That's all there is to it." Sarah didn't know it then, but her life was about to take a major detour. Far from the Broadway lights she desired, the character Minnie Pearl would be born on the road while working for the Sewell Company. Decades later, she reflected, "It was during these six years that I was to formulate and crystallize Minnie Pearl." (See Chapter 4: The Birth of Minnie Pearl.)

Typically, new coaches trained in Georgia during the summer, but Sarah had missed that window. Instead, Wayne Sewell directed her to meet a group of new coaches in Hendersonville, North Carolina. So, in August 1934, Sarah boarded her first Pullman train, waved goodbye, and headed to North Carolina. She checked into the Skyline Hotel in the town square and joined the rest of the Sewell crew. "I was out in the world, but I had no idea I was about to fall flat on my face," she said.

Sarah reminisced, "The play in Hendersonville went on very well and Sally Moore (the head coach) turned us all loose and pushed us out of the nest." From there, each Sewell coach was given a "route sheet," which included a list of towns, dates, a local point of contact ("committee man"), organizational sponsor, and train times. Sarah's first assignment was Valdosta, Georgia. A week and half later, Sarah directed her first production of "Dixie Blackbirds" and remarked that she "faked it good enough." She must have done something right because the Valdosta Lion's Club sent a telegram to Mr. Sewell to compliment Sarah's work in making the play a success.

For each production, the Sewell Company supplied a large trunk with the costumes, music, and scripts. These items were schlepped from town to town by, as the contract noted, "A Winsome Director" who oversaw rehearsals and directed the performance. The town was responsible for assembling the cast and securing an auditorium. Additionally, the sponsoring organization was required to provide the director with food and lodging and to help her sell advertisements to local businesses.

Most often Sarah stayed with local families. "I had plenty of food, but what I didn't have plenty of was money," she said. The Sewell coaches also received a great deal of attention. In Sarah's words: "We carried this ambiance and charisma of show business, and excitement. We brought the 'other world' to these little towns. The children followed us around, and the men went wild. I had 25 proposals in one year. Many 'passes' were made but very few ever forced themselves on me."

For the ten days she spent in each town, Sarah was the coach, director, producer, stage manager, make-up artist, costume seamstress, and the understudy. Jackie Smartt, a fellow Sewell coach, described the typical schedule in a joint interview:

> As soon as you got to a town, you had to get the cast together. On the first night, you'd read the book together and assign the parts. The second night we'd go through it, and everybody would read their parts. The third night, we'd do the first act by heart. The fourth night, we'd do the second act, and the fifth night we'd do the whole thing. Then that gave us two nights to practice it all together, dress rehearsal the night before, and then curtains up for the show. Nobody could do a halfway decent job, there's no way, but they did it.

Sarah added: "The best way to get people in the door was to put their children in the play. Mr. Sewell used to say, 'One on stage, three in the audience.'"

By day, Sarah ran around town selling ads to go in the play's program. By night, she did what she could to put together an amateur production in a week. Understandably, the local cast often forgot their lines. Sarah recalled "prompting them from the wings because I knew every line of every part." And sometimes, she had to step in at the last minute when a cast member didn't show up. She said: "So many times the men went out before the performance to get a little 'reinforcement' (liquor). In these small towns somebody was always a little drunk. You always had to be ready to jump in."

Every town and every show brought some level of stress to the Sewell coaches, but there were also moments of comic relief. In rural North Carolina, halfway between Raleigh and Wilmington, Sarah experienced one of those moments with an "ole boy named Jed." In Sarah's words:

> I had an ole boy in Pink Hill, North Carolina, and he was supposed to sneeze in [the play] Black-Eyed Susan. . . . The night I gave out the parts, somebody said, "Get Jed over there." I said, "Now all you have to do is sneeze." Everybody got kind of blank, and someone said, "He can't sneeze, he just squeaks." I asked, "C'mon Jed is that true?" He said it was. I told him, "Well, that won't work, they've got to hear you in the back of the auditorium." So, I said, "Ok, here's what you do . . . say: *'WHO IS SHE?'*" He did, then I told him to say it fast and loud. He yelled, "whoo-is-shhh!" And I said, "Close enough—that'll work." Every night in practice, he worked on his "sneeze."
>
> The night of the play he was scared out of his mind, absolutely scared to death. He walked out on stage for his big moment and yelled, *"WHO ARE WE?"* Well, that killed everybody. The cast on the stage laid down, they gave up, it was bedlam. The play was a comedy, but that night Black-Eyed Susan was funnier than it'd ever been.

As the company grew, Sewell hired a team of "bookers" who scoured phone books and pestered contacts in any town that had a church, school, or stop sign. Contracts were signed six or more months in advance; but as the date drew nearer, local organizations often had buyer's remorse. Two weeks out, the Sewell Company sent a reminder to the local committee that said, "Soon you will have the lovely opportunity to greet the 'Winsome Director' who is coming in to put on your play." A copy of the contract was included in case they tried to back out.

"It was pretty bad," Sarah recalled, adding, "When I got into those towns, many times they really didn't want me. But there I was, and I had to impress them fast." Her solution to this awkward situation was simple: "smile, smile, smile." Sarah wrote, "Even if you were sick or ready to drop

Hetty Jane Dunaway Sewell was an American actress, monologuist, and philanthropist in the 1890s and early 1900s. Dunaway is pictured here after her retirement from acting, c. 1920. In the 1920s, she created of the Dunaway Gardens resort near Newnan, Georgia along with her husband Wayne P. Sewell. Image in public domain.

from fatigue you had to *smile*—representing the Sewell Company at all times. For all those years I suffered from a chronic case of dry teeth!"

Sarah said, "I wasn't scared of the play or teaching the chorus girls, children, and townspeople how to sing and dance. What scared me was the business end—visiting merchants all over town and selling ads to fill up the space at the end of the program." Sewell's main slogan was: "Sell yourself first, and then sell your play." Sarah added, "He was teaching us the rudiments of salesmanship and remembering names." Sarah took the program template to a local printer the day before the show, and as people bought tickets for fifty cents apiece, they were handed a paper program with the title of the show, scenes, cast members' names, and local advertisements.

After each performance, profits were divided between Mr. Sewell (60 percent) and the sponsoring local organization (40 percent). The female directors, like Sarah, received a percentage of Sewell's 60 percent. "So, I didn't have much leftover, but I did have a lot of fun," she bantered. Paychecks were sent to the next town, which according to Sarah "was very

Patchwork Barn at Dunaway Gardens where Minnie Pearl trained other coaches and also performed, c.1925. Image in public domain.

Blue Bonnet Tea Room at Dunaway Gardens was a renowned restaurant. Today it serves as a suite for wedding ceremonies. Image courtesy of Dunaway Gardens, 2023.

The outdoor amphitheater at Dunaway Gardens. Image courtesy of Dunaway Gardens, 2023.

smart because it ensured that we kept going." She added: "I was good at it. I liked the attention, and I brought in a little bit of fresh air of the world outside."

From the start, Wayne Sewell recognized something special in Sarah. During her first week of training in Hendersonville, he took Sarah to dinner and revealed he had big plans for her. She recalled, "He was a very flashy, albeit unusual-looking man," often dressed in double-breasted plaid suits with long coattails. . . . He just looked like show business." With his niece set to marry, he asked if Sarah would be interested in taking over the training school for coaches. Sarah said, "He wanted to know if I was up for the challenge. I told him yes! Then again, I would have told him I could jump over the moon if it meant I could advance my career." Sarah finished her first year on the road and boarded a train to Newnan,

Georgia. She was picked up at the station and driven to Dunaway Gardens, located in a nearby village called Roscoe.

Dunaway Gardens was the ancestral home of Wayne Sewell, but it was his wife, Hetty Jane Dunaway, who made it a destination. In the 1920s and 1930s, the estate served as a theatrical training ground for aspiring actors, performers, and directors. It was also a popular retreat for those seeking refuge from Atlanta, and other visitors—like Walt Disney—came from across the country to find talent among those studying under the tutelage of Walter and Hetty. Even as the nation endured a severe economic depression, Dunaway Gardens created an exhilarating escape during the 1930s.

In its heyday, the gardens "played host to ballet troupes, indoor and outdoor theater performances, and a steady stream of fans who came to enjoy the spectacular shows." Hetty Jane brought her vision to life with extensive flower gardens, arrowhead-shaped pools, the Blue Bonnet Tea Room, an outdoor amphitheater, the Patchwork Barn indoor theater, the Shangri-La Honeymoon House, and the Wedding Tree—an ideal spot for nuptials.

When Sarah arrived, she was introduced to Walter's niece, Marjorie, who had directed the training program for several years. Sarah had just over a month to learn all the lines and melodies from every song, dance, and scene in each of the eight plays that were part of the Sewell production portfolio. Sarah reflected in 1979, "That was the hardest, concentrated work I've ever done in my life, and I've done some pretty hard work."

She was only twenty-two years old and was in charge of coaching the coaches—the "new girls" who came to Dunaway Gardens before going out on the road. Sarah was also in charge of the dormitory that was home to a dozen or so young women. They practiced dancing in the morning and worked on scripts in the afternoon. She recalled, "One week we'd learn Old Professor, then the next we'd learn Here Comes Arabella or Flapper Grandmother. At night, Mr. Sewell taught the business side of things."

Sarah embraced the challenge and balanced her role as a teacher and dorm mother. She also had the chance to save some money: "They paid me $25 a week . . . I thought I'd really made it to the top." During the week, Sarah was serious as she taught the "new girls" how to direct and produce Sewell's plays, but she loosened up on weekends. She said, "During those years I had access to a Model T Ford, and we'd get in that Model T and ride all over, hanging out like the Beverly Hillbillies."

The Sewell estate, Sarah said, was "an old-time, Gone-with-the-Wind, Georgia cotton plantation." Many formerly enslaved families remained on or near the property as sharecroppers, farming the land as tenants in exchange for a share of the crop. This practice incentivized sharecropping families to produce the biggest possible harvest to clear a profit, but it also ensured that Black communities in rural areas were perpetually in debt and tied to the land. In *Slavery by Another Name*, historian Douglas A. Blackmon argued that, during the Jim Crow era (1890s–1960s), sharecropping emerged as an "insidious new form of forced labor in the American South."

Thus, Dunaway Gardens wasn't merely a theater training school or an escape for White guests; it was also home to dozens of African American sharecroppers who worked the cotton fields. Sarah contended: "It was a very interesting relationship between the Sewells and their people [sharecroppers]. They were good to them, and the Black people who lived there were always so respectful, if not downright reverent." Such paternalistic commentary is common through the lens of White experience. Indeed, Black voices are largely absent from the historical record from this era.

Despite economic inequities and social injustices, moments of shared community did take place between the Sewells and local sharecroppers. Sarah recalled, "On Sunday nights, Wayne would say, 'Well, let's go down to the meeting.' And the three of us would drive over to the Black church and attend the Sunday night service." She fondly remembered these nights, "Every service Deacon Rowe would pray, and I always felt like he had a straight line to the Lord. He would ask God to bless Mr. Wayne, Mrs. Hetty Jane, and he'd bless me too. At the end he'd say, 'Oh Lord, bless us and prop us up on our leaning side.'" Sarah would end her prayers with this phrase for the rest of her life.

At the end of the summer, the Sewells closed their training camp and prepared for the new theater season. Decades later, Sarah summed up her time with The Sewell Company: "From 1935 to 1940, I went to the training school each May to teach the new girls, and then in October, we all set out on the road for the next several months. I worked myself to death, but that didn't matter. I loved it."

During these years Sarah experienced many highs and lows—endearing moments and difficult circumstances. Sarah was often scared, sometimes mistreated, and always broke. Yet, the lessons she learned and the experiences she gained proved invaluable as her career unfolded.

Reflecting in 1979, Sarah said: "I'm now so far removed in age and circumstance from that little girl in her 20s trying to make it in those little towns. . . My time with the Sewell Company was hard, and yet, when you consider the fact that something as great and valuable and fun to me as Minnie Pearl actually came out of the hardships—it makes it all worth it."

SOURCES

Blackmon, Douglas A. *Slavery by Another Name: The Re-Enslavement of Black Americans from the Civil War to World War II.* New York: Doubleday Books, 2009.

Dunaway Gardens. "History." Accessed May 2023. https://www.dunawaygardens.com/history/.

Martin, Rachel Louise. "Before the Howdy: Finding Minnie Pearl." *Oxford American* 121 (Summer 2023). https://oxfordamerican.org/magazine/issue-121-summer-2023/before-the-howdy-finding-minnie-pearl.

Oermann, Robert K. "Minnie Pearl Treatment Version 1." *Facing the Laughter: Minnie Pearl.* Directed by Barbara J. Hall. American Public Television, 2023.

Pearl, Minnie. Tape recorded memoir by Sarah Colley Cannon, Nashville, Tennessee. Tape 16, Side A, Side B, 1979.

———. Tape recorded memoir by Sarah Colley Cannon, Nashville, Tennessee. Tape 17, Side 1, Side 2, 1979.

———. Tape recorded memoir by Sarah Colley Cannon, Nashville, Tennessee. Tape 18, Side 1, Side 2, 1979.

———. Tape recorded memoir by Sarah Colley Cannon, Nashville, Tennessee. Tape 20, Side 1, Side 2, 1979.

Pearl, Minnie, and Joan Dew, *Minnie Pearl: An Autobiography.* New York: Simon and Schuster, 1980.

CHAPTER 4

The Birth of Minnie Pearl

Baileyton to Broadway (Nashville), 1936–1940

On a cold winter's day in 1936, a young Sarah Ophelia Colley stepped off a train in the snowy town of Baileyton, Alabama, unaware that the next ten days would change the trajectory of her life. What started as a difficult and lonely journey would end with the birth of Minnie Pearl, a country comedy character who would bring joy and laughter to millions.

In January 1936, Sarah was directing a play in La Crosse, Virginia, when she received her next assignment—a "little village in northern Alabama near Sand Mountain." After the show, she packed up the scripts and costumes and headed to the train station. Sarah had no idea she was headed into a blizzard. After the 650-mile journey, the train finally pulled into Cullman, Alabama. It was only 3:00 p.m., but the "swirling, frozen precipitation made it feel like dusk," according to historian Rachel Louise Martin.

The local school in Baileyton was sponsoring the play, so a school representative should have met Sarah at the station. But when she stepped onto the platform, not a single soul was in sight. She hurried, "half-frozen" into the depot, where the stationmaster was closing up for the day. Begrudgingly, he agreed to store her trunk of costumes overnight. Down to her last $7, Sarah found a local taxi and asked if the driver could get her to Baileyton. "The road's awful bad up there, don't know if'n I can make it," he told Sarah. She pressed, "How much would you charge to try?" He said $10; Sarah bargained him down to $5. "I had to keep a couple of dollars, and I was too proud to come right out and admit I was broke," Sarah recounted.

The "little old man" cranked the car, and they set off on the final fifteen-miles of the trip. For the next hour, Sarah sat white-knuckled, gripping the seat as the car lurched and the tires spun, skidding around one sharp curve after another. Sarah recalled: "We had to drive a narrow, winding mountain road that would have been scary even in clear weather." At last, they pulled up in front of the schoolhouse. Sarah paid the driver and watched the taxi vanish into the dark, drifting snow.

Sarah walked into the school, following the sound of voices coming from a classroom. As she stepped into the doorway, the principal looked up, and the other teachers fell silent. "I couldn't have been more unwelcome," she later lamented. The principal didn't say a word; she could tell he was annoyed. Sarah said assertively, "Well, I'm sorry, but I'm here to put on the play *Flapper Grandmother* for your school. You signed a contract, and I sent a letter last week." He acknowledged receiving the letter but assumed the weather would keep her away. Then, Sarah reminded him that she would need lodging. He responded with another moment of awkward silence. There wasn't a hotel in town and the boarding house was full. One of the teachers piped up, "What about Jim and Mattie Burden?" The principal sighed, still exasperated: "Yes, I bet they'd take-her in."

With the weather worsening by the minute, the principal threw Sarah's suitcase in his car. Given his foul mood, she was relieved the Burdens only lived a mile from the school. Sarah described the house as a typical rural log cabin with two sections separated by a "dog trot" or breezeway—a kitchen and bedroom on one side and a second bedroom on the other. The principal knocked and a "tall, thin lady in her seventies came to the door" wearing a "clean, faded print dress and an apron." It was Mattie Burden. "You could tell she'd worked hard all her life by the lines in her face and her worn hands," Sarah reminisced, adding, "Her gray hair was pulled up in a knot on the back of her head, like Granny in the Beverly Hillbillies."

The principal introduced Sarah to Mrs. Mattie Burden and explained, "She'll be here for ten days putting on the play at the school, and we want her to stay with you." Mattie seemed puzzled, "You mean live here?" Mattie thought for a second, then responded: "Well, we have Brother's room. I reckon he could sleep in the lean-to by the kitchen." The principal told Mattie that she'd be compensated. Sarah was deeply touched: "I could tell she had already decided to take me in whether he paid her or not. Her kindness had been apparent from the moment she opened the door."

Born in 1866, Martha Matilda Butler married Jim Burden when she was sixteen-years old. Shortly after their nuptials, they moved east of Baileyton, where they applied for land through the Federal Homestead Act of 1862. After approval, the couple purchased 160 acres and became homesteaders, farming cotton and tobacco. In 1892, they moved closer to town and built their modest cabin. There, over the next thirty years, Matilda (Mattie) and Jim (Pappy) Burden raised sixteen children, nine of whom survived to adulthood. By the time Sarah Ophelia Colley landed on their doorstep in 1936, only one (Brother) still lived at home.

Mattie led Sarah across the dogtrot to Brother's bedroom. There was a small dresser, a pipe stove, a bed, and clothes hanging from nails on the wall. Sarah later learned his name was Kyle, but no one ever (in his family or in town) called him anything but Brother. Sarah made small talk as Mattie started a fire. "Do you have any other children?" she asked. Mattie replied, "I've had 16 young-uns and never failed to make a crop." Mattie shared this not to brag or shock, but as a point of pride—timing her pregnancies to ensure she could still help with the harvest. Sarah asked what time they normally got up in the morning. Mattie said, "Well we get up at daylight, but we can get up earlier if you need." Sarah assured her, "No, no that's fine!"

Mattie, Pappy, Brother, and Sarah sat down to supper, a humble meal of cornbread, salt pork, and vegetables Mattie had canned in the fall. Reflecting on her time there, Sarah said, "She didn't have linens or silver or china, but I tell you right now, every time she put a meal on the table, it was the absolute best that she had in her house. She did the best she could, not because she was being paid, but because she wanted to treat me as a guest."

Over the next ten days, Sarah sold ads and rehearsed the play at school. Each evening, she returned to the Burden home, rejoining the family that had taken her in when she was cold and hungry. The warmth of their home wasn't just literal—she grew attached to Mattie, Pappy, and Brother. "They were country people, but they were also funny, witty people, who didn't know they were being funny, and didn't try to be," Sarah wrote.

One morning, Sarah and Brother stood in front of the fire in the kitchen. It was their first and only conversation. Sarah asked, "Why does

The Burden family in front of their cabin, c. 1904. They lived on the outskirts of Baileyton on Sand Mountain located in Cullman County, Alabama. Mattie Burden and her husband, James "Pappy" Burden, are on the far right. She stands with her hand on his shoulder while he sits, holding the reigns to the family's horses. Image courtesy of Greg Burden.

everyone call you Brother instead of Kyle?" He said, "Well, I never much did care for the name Kyle. I'd rather they'd named me Jim." Naturally, Sarah asked, "Then why don't you go by Jim?" He shot back, "I already got a brother named Jim." Sarah didn't laugh out loud, but she thought he was quite funny. Mattie may have been Sarah's muse for Minnie Pearl, but "Brother" was the character Minnie talked about most in her act. She later wrote: "I just loved it. . . . [t]he way these people expressed themselves had an innocence and a wit about it that charmed me."

The night of the play finally arrived, and it was a smashing success. Sarah said, "They called me out on stage when it was over and one of those lanky ole mountain boys walked up and handed me a huge bouquet of red roses." She was so moved she wept right there on the stage. The significance of the moment and the gesture was not lost on Sarah. She

Memorial marker for Mattie and James Burden located in Cullman County, Alabama, at the Corinth East Baptist Church Cemetery. Image courtesy of Greg Burden.

wrote: "Imagine the trouble and *expense* they had to go to in order to get a dozen roses up on that mountain in the dead of winter!"

Sarah Ophelia Colley had arrived to Baileyton broke, lonely, and feeling unwanted. She left with her pockets fuller, her heart lighter, and a newfound sense of belonging as beautiful as the red roses she held in her arms. As she departed, Mattie Burden paid her the highest compliment of all: "Lord have mercy child, I hate to see you go; you're just like one of us."

Over the course of Sarah's six years with the Sewell Theater Company, she'd seen and heard a lot of things as she traveled to small Southern towns. Along the way, she amassed a wealth of stories, tall tales, anecdotes, and rural legends. Mattie inspired Minnie, but it was Sarah's collective experience on the road that provided the vision for what would become the fictional town of Grinder's Switch.

After the trip to Baileyton, Sarah found herself thinking about "that cute old lady" more and more often. She developed an imitation that highlighted Mattie's dialect and mannerisms. In an interview in 1979, Sarah shared:

> I began using the character when I had to go into new towns to solicit ads or sell tickets to get a big turnout. Minnie Pearl would come out . . . and tell

> some stories before doing my spiel about the play we'd be putting on. It was a lot easier than standing up there as Sarah Ophelia Colley, and the people really seemed to enjoy her.

Sarah also started "doing Minnie Pearl" at the Sewell coaches' school to "loosen up the new girls." During one session at the Sewell training school in 1938, Sarah met a new recruit named Louise Smartt. Sarah bantered, "Her name was Louise, but her family called her Jack, I'm not sure anyone knows why."

Jack and Sarah became lifelong friends—both moving to Nashville in the early 1940s. Beyond the gift of friendship, Jack taught Minnie how to do "country corn," which was a parody of country music. Jack had been doing this act for friends and family for years in McMinnville, Tennessee. Jack showed Sarah how to sound like an "old country woman singing straight-faced and serious at the top of her voice, while also being off-key." It was a wild concept for Sarah, who had worked with Pauline Townsend at Ward-Belmont to classically train her voice. Decades later, Sarah noted the irony, "There I was practicing to sound like Edith Bunker on *All in the Family*."

Then, in 1939, it all came together. Sarah Colley Cannon was in Aiken, South Carolina, to direct a local play. There she met Carolyn McElveen. Carolyn took Sarah around to local businesses to sell ads for the play's program. In Sarah's words: "I began lapsing into Minnie Pearl's dialect, and she soon had me doing Minnie Pearl everywhere we went. . . . Carolyn didn't drop it when I left town. She began writing me letters. She'd say, 'Now, this Minnie Pearl character . . . is too good to let slip away. You've got to develop her, *use* her.'"

A month later, Carolyn invited Sarah back to Aiken to perform as Minnie Pearl at a Pilots Club Convention, offering $25 plus travel and hotel expenses. "I was thrilled to death! That was more than I made in two weeks," Sarah exclaimed. More importantly, it was the first time she would be paid to perform in front of an audience. Sarah had long hoped that her talent and training would lead to a serious acting role—this gig was far from that. Yet, in 1939, as work with the Sewell Company dwindled, Sarah was willing to try anything. She also had a new act—a self-deprecating spinster with a hillbilly accent. Embracing the chance to reinvent herself, Sarah decided to give Minnie Pearl a shot.

What she lacked was a costume that complemented her colorful character. Carolyn picked Sarah up from the hotel and took her shopping.

Sarah purchased an organdy dress with a collar and a straw hat. She grabbed and handful of plastic flowers on the way to the register and tucked them into the hat's band. It was just the pop of color the costume needed. At the convention, Sarah noted: "An incredible thing happened . . . For the first time, I *became* the character." She didn't know it then, but in that moment, Sarah Colley became Minnie Pearl—the "undisputed queen of country comedy" and one of America's most iconic entertainers.

In 1940, Sarah's time with the Sewell Company offically ended. Sarah Ophelia Colley limped home to Centerville. Moreover, the gingerbread-gabled home of Sarah's childhood burned to the ground in a tragic fire that same year. She wasn't sure of her next move, but she was sure of one thing: her dream of serious acting was dimming.

To help those suffering from the Great Depression, President Franklin D. Roosevelt's Works Progress Administration provided funding for local programs. One such government program included a new recreation center in Centerville. Sarah was hired as the center's director, which paid $50 a month, and she set up afterschool activities for kids in town. She was glad to have a job, but Sarah was in a full-blown slump: "My life was so dull, so boring. . . . I hated being tied down and trapped. My pride was hurt, and I was demoralized with no hope for my future. I could see myself ending up as Centerville's old-maid dramatics teacher."

In October 1940, a local banker and a family friend named Jim Walker threw Sarah a lifeline. There was a bankers' convention coming to Centerville, and he wanted Sarah to line up some acts with the kids from the recreation center. Sarah said she'd be glad to help. After they discussed the details, he stood up to leave. Just before he walked out the door, he turned back and said, "By the way, our speaker is flying in from Chicago, . . . and he might be late. If he is, do you think you could kill time by doing that character?"

On the night of the convention, Sarah's students performed their song and dance, earning generous applause from the audience. However, as Jim Walker predicted, the speaker's flight into Nashville was late. Walker asked, "Will you come out and do that thing?" Sarah walked onto the stage. "Howdy, I'm just so proud to be here. I'm Minnie Pearl, the mountain girl," she said bashfully. Minnie told stories and jokes; she even played piano and sang in the "country corn" style learned from Jack Smartt. Walker finally signaled that the speaker had arrived. She thanked them and bid goodnight.

When Sarah got home, her mother asked, "How was it?" Sarah replied,

Early promotional poster for a tent show sponsored by Jamboree Attractions. She is noted as the "Comedy Star of Prince Albert's Grand Ole Opry." This is representative of Minnie Pearl's many years doing one-night shows across the southeast before returning to Nashville for the Grand Ole Opry weekly broadcast and performance live each Saturday night. Image in public domain.

In the spring of 1942, Minnie earned a coveted spot in the elite cast of the Grand Ole Opry by joining The Prince Albert Show, a half-hour segment broadcast nationwide on the NBC radio network. This photograph marks her promotion, which catapulted her career. Also, in 1942, the William Esty advertising agency, which managed the show, suggested that Minnie replace her timid "Howdy" greeting with an exuberant "How-DEE!" The catchphrase, designed to elicit audience response, quickly became a signature trademark of her character. Image courtesy of the Grand Ole Opry Archives.

"Oh, alright I guess. It was fun." What she didn't know was that a man in the audience, Bob Turner, was a Nashville banker with connections to WSM radio. The following week, Turner called Harry Stone, the head of station programming, to tell him about "Minnie the mountain girl." The next day, Stone called Sarah: "Bob says you ought to be on the Opry. Would you like to come to Nashville and audition for us?"

On November 27, 1940, Sarah traveled to Nashville to audition for the Grand Ole Opry at the WSM radio studio. Obviously impressed, they booked her for that Saturday night at 11:05 p.m.—long after the NBC network portion wrapped at 8:30 p.m. The WSM producers were worried her comedy would come across as condescending, but her monologue was a hit. Her performance lasted three minutes and included some one-liners and a hillbilly serenade of "Maple on the Hill." Sarah said, "I asked mama how it went, and she said, 'Well, several people woke up.'"

Invited back the next week, Sarah arrived at the auditorium early. To her surprise, she was given a mail sack with more than three hundred letters addressed to Minnie Pearl. After her second appearance, she joined the Opry cast and quickly won the hearts of listeners with her pithy, unfiltered sense of humor. It was the start of a career in show business that spanned half a century.

Sarah's Opry debut in Nashville came nearly five years after her journey up Sand Mountain to Baileyton. Sarah never saw Mattie Burden again. "I only knew her for ten days," Sarah said, "but she had an impact on my life that has lasted ever since."

NOTES

The Homestead Act was passed by Congress and signed into law by President Abraham Lincoln in 1862 during the Civil War. The law allowed adult citizens or intended citizens who had not borne arms against the US government to claim 160 acres of public land. To obtain ownership, claimants had to (1) file an application, (2) improve the land by building a dwelling and cultivating crops, and (3) live on it continuously for at least five years. Once these requirements were met, they could file for a deed of ownership. The cost was minimal—making the land essentially free after the improvements and residency. The act incentivized rural development, settled remote areas, and discouraged support for the Confederacy.

For an in-depth essay about Sarah's visit to Baileyton, Alabama, and the family history of Mattie Burden, see Rachel Louise Martin, "Before the Howdy: Finding Minnie Pearl."

SOURCES

Crutchfield, Gail. "Genealogy Program Helps Writer Research Local Family That Influenced Minnie Pearl." *Wallace State News*, March 17, 2023. https://www.wallacestate.edu/news/2023/03/17/genealogy_minnie_pearl.html.

Kreps, Sharon Schuler. "Minnie Pearl – Straight Outta Baileyton." *The Cullman Tribune*, June 19, 2016. https://www.cullmantribune.com/2016/06/19/minnie-pearl-straight-outta-baileyton/.

Martin, Rachel Louise. "Before the Howdy: Finding Minnie Pearl." *Oxford American* 121 (Summer 2023). https://oxfordamerican.org/magazine/issue-121-summer-2023/before-the-howdy-finding-minnie-pearl.

Pearl, Minnie. Tape recorded memoir by Sarah Colley Cannon, Nashville, Tennessee. Tape 17, Side 2, 1979.

———. Tape recorded memoir by Sarah Colley Cannon, Nashville, Tennessee. Tape 18, Side 1, Side 2, 1979.

———. Tape recorded memoir by Sarah Colley Cannon, Nashville, Tennessee. Tape 19, Side 1, Side 2, 1979.

Pearl, Minnie, and Joan Dew. *Minnie Pearl: An Autobiography.* New York: Simon & Schuster, 1980.

CHAPTER 5

Grinder's Switch Comes to Life

Minnie Pearl's Imagined Community, 1936–1940

Let's go back four years and retrace a different part of Minnie Pearl's story—one that focuses not on the birth of her character but on the development of the imagined community of Grinder's Switch. In 1936, after leaving Baileyton, Sarah stopped in Centerville to visit her family. For the Colleys, it was a welcome surprise to see their youngest, prodigal daughter. Just months earlier, her father's lumber company had liquidated its assets. Another casualty of the Great Depression, the once-thriving mill was out of business. Tom and Fannie Tate were doing their best to stay afloat, and Sarah's visit undoubtedly lifted their spirits.

After two years of working and traveling, Sarah was back in her childhood home, and the memories flooded back. It was, after all, where her imaginative spirit and penchant for performance had been tolerated, if not encouraged. Sitting by the fire, she recounted her time in Baileyton and shared stories about the Burden family. As she spoke, she mimicked Mattie's voice and mannerisms. They were clearly entertained: "Mama said, 'Ophelia, you sound just like an old mountain woman!'" And what was Tom Colley's reaction? Sarah recalled, "He said, 'You'll make a fortune off that someday Phel, if you keep her kind.'"

The next year, 1937, Sarah was back on the road directing plays for the

Centerview town square in 1940 when Sarah Opehlia Colley returned home after her father's death and the end of her work for Sewell Theater Production Company. Image courtesy of Mary Beth Pruett and Hickman County Historical Society.

Sewell Production Company when she received word that there had been a death in the family. Her father had been in poor health, but his passing came as a shock. Heartbroken, she rushed to Centerville. Over the next few weeks, Sarah helped her mother and also dealt with her own grief. Tom wasn't just Sarah's father; he was her rock, her confidante, and her hero. She thought back to their final visit—the night she sat by the fire and told him about Minnie Pearl. Wistfully, Sarah acknowledged his prophetic words: "Daddy didn't live to see Minnie Pearl come into her own, but I've always tried to follow his advice and keep her kind."

Between the time of her father's death (1937) and her debut on the Grand Ole Opry (1940), Sarah honed her act. She grew more comfortable with Minnie Pearl as her alter ego, but what would be Minnie's setting? Drawing from memories of her hometown and her experiences on the road with Sewell, Sarah created the mythical town of Grinder's Switch.

The Colley family after the death of Tom Colley, 1953. From left to right: Fannie Tate, Frances, Virginia, Mary, Dixie, and Sarah Ophelia. Image courtesy of Mary Beth Pruett and Hickman County Historical Society.

To be fair, Grinder's Switch does exist. Located on the outskirts of Centerville, it's still marked by a small sign and depot platform. A "spur" or auxiliary railroad track, Grinder's Switch was used to load goods for shipment, including the lumber from Tom Colley's sawmill. The young Sarah spent many hours at Grinder's Switch playing in the woods while Tom and his workers stacked lumber onto train cars.

In Sarah's imagined Grinder's Switch, Minnie lived among a lively group of townsfolk. These characters were a compilation of her family, friends, and people she'd met on the road. But for Sarah, Grinder's Switch was more than a fictional community. After several years of hardship and loss, Minnie's innocent, timeless town provided a much-needed escape for Sarah.

Only once, at the very beginning, did Minnie Pearl share the stage with others to portray her cast of characters. After that, they existed entirely in

Centerville still hosts a radio program called "Grinder's Switch Live," in one of the buildings on the town square. Musicians come from near and far to participate in songs and jam sessions, 2023. Image courtesy of the author.

the vivid world she created, brought to life through her storytelling. Here are some of the most well-known personalities from Grinder's Switch:

Uncle Nabob was portrayed as somewhat lazy and prone to tall tales. Sarah said that her Uncle John was part of her inspiration for Uncle Nabob.

Aunt Ambrosia was the no-nonsense matriarch of Grinder's Switch. Her strong will, practicality, and commanding presence provided a contrast to Uncle Nabob's laid-back demeanor.

Lucifer Hucklehead was mischievous and always up to something. He often caused trouble in town, making him a source of humor and conflict.

Miss Lizzie Tinkum was the town gossip and old maid. She knew everyone's business and was the stereotypical "nosy neighbor" of Grinder's Switch.

Doc Payne was the town doctor but maintained quirks that made him more of a comedic figure than a reliable professional.

Brother represented the common man in rural America. In part, based on Kyle Burden from Baileyton, Brother was good-hearted but often made questionable decisions.

Cousin Jeb was referenced as the extended family member who was from the backwoods. He was often slow-witted with funny misunderstandings.

Handsome Peabody was a charming figure known for his good looks. He maintained an inflated ego and exaggerated sense of his own attractiveness.

Granpappy portrayed the town's cantankerous, stubborn old man. Granpappy always had strong opinions and was set in his ways.

Hezzie was, at times, Minnie Pearl's "feller." Simple and sometimes bumbling, Hezzie was in and out of love with Minnie.

The Grand Ole Opry primarily catered to White audiences. From 1927 to 1941, its performers were exclusively White, except for DeFord Bailey, a harmonica virtuoso. Like the Opry's audience, Minnie Pearl's small-town characters reflected a world devoid of people of color—a mirror of the segregated realities of the time. Meanwhile, just one mile from Ryman Auditorium on Jefferson Street, a thriving Black jazz and rhythm-and-blues district showcased stars like Ray Charles, Etta James, and Little Richard. These parallel musical worlds underscored the cultural divide while also reinforcing Nashville's reputation as Music City.

Back at Grinder's Switch, these fictional personas formed the basis for Minnie's world and shaped Sarah's comedic style. Writer Bobby Jean Sawyer noted, "She was famous for her lighthearted digs at the people of Grinder's Switch." Uncle Nabob was a regular target. "He ain't a failure," Minnie would say before delivering the punchline, "He just started at the bottom, and he liked it there." Another Minnie classic went like this: "We had so much fun celebrating July the 4th in Grinder's Switch, especially Uncle Nabob. Uncle Nabob always celebrates the fourth with a fifth."

Sawyer also pointed out: "Most often Pearl's humor was self-deprecating. She made jokes about her looks, her age, and her man-hungry ways." Minnie's quest for love included a great deal of ridicule, but her jokes were delivered with a twisted sense of pride. Pearl would say, "A feller

HEZZIE'S HOUSE
STORE
W
S
E
HEZZIE'S PATH
TO MY HOUS
MY PATH TO HEZZIE'S HOUSE
GRINDERS SWITCH
DEPOT
HOHENWALD
NO SWIMMING
SCALE OF WAGON

Cover of Minnie Pearl's Diary, which provided a tongue-and-cheek description of daily life in Grinder's Switch, 1953. Image courtesy of Harpeth Hall School Archives.

Minnie Pearl headshot in mid-1940s. Image courtesy of Harpeth Hall Archives.

told me I look like a breath of spring. Well, he didn't use them words. He said I look like the end of a hard winter."

George Lindsey, friend and future *Hee Haw* cast member, described Sarah's brand of gentle comedy: "She taught me that if you turn the joke on yourself then you're not hurting anybody. It's those jokes that always get a laugh." Lindsey followed her lead with his own self-deprecating character as Goober on *The Andy Griffith Show* and *Mayberry RFD.*

The final touch that completed the Minnie Pearl persona was her iconic costume. Her well-worn Mary Jane shoes, cotton stockings, flowered hat, and gingham dresses would become recognizable to millions. But it didn't start that way. Her first dress was a sleeveless yellow frock, paired with white sandals. She reflected, "I was thin as a rail then, and the dress made me look like Olive Oyl."

It's true that the original costume included a straw hat with flowers, but the hanging price tag was a happy accident that came later. Sarah wrote, "At first, I had on the straw hat and a cotton yellow dress. There

Pictured here in 1941, Minnie Pearl's persona is still in development. Initially, she performed while clutching a small purse, which was later dropped from her act. Also, notice her hat does not feature the signature $1.98 price tag. The price tag from the plastic flowers on top of her hat dropped down while she was on stage sometime between 1942 and 1944. Minnie claims that people thought it was funny, so she "just left it." Image courtesy of the Grand Ole Opry Archives.

wasn't a price tag yet." Months later, she purchased a new straw hat. That week on the Opry, she noticed the $1.98 price tag dangling from the brim. She quickly reached up to tuck it away but then paused. "No," she thought, "This is perfect." Sarah later recalled, "When the price tag fell down, people laughed, so I left it."

Albeit a stroke of marketing and branding genius, Sarah never dreamt that a price tag would become the longest-running joke of her career.

Bronze statue of Minnie Pearl presides over the Centerville town square, 2023. Centerville was the basis for the comedian's imaginary community of Grinder's Switch and rail switch located near the town. Image courtesy of the author.

Reflecting on its deeper meaning, she explained, "The price tag on my hat seemed to be symbolic of all human frailty." She elaborated, "There's old Minnie Pearl standing on stage night after night in her best dress, telling everyone how proud she is to be there. And yet, she's forgotten to take the $1.98 price tag off her hat." This simple, comedic detail transformed her down-to-earth charm into something more profound.

Last but not least, Sarah perfected her signature opening salutation. It took more than a year on the Opry before her subdued, "Howdy, I'm just so proud to be here," evolved into the familiar refrain: "How-DEEE! I'm jest so proud to be here!" Before long, it became a lively call-and-response. "How-DEEE!" they shouted back at the woman from Grinder's Switch, as she grinned from ear to ear with arms open wide. It was just as Opry founder, George D. Hay, told her before her debut: "Just love 'em, honey, and they'll love you back." Sarah recalled, "As far as the audience was concerned, I was one of them. And as the weeks went by, I felt more and more at home."

Red Foley, the legendary emcee of the Grand Ole Opry, captured the essence of Minnie Pearl in just a few words. On a sweltering night in Nashville's unairconditioned Ryman Auditorium, Foley stood in front of a packed house and introduced the next act: "She came up to WSM and asked if she could do a little talking, and she's been talking ever since. What she ain't got, she don't need. So, you just rare back and have fun. Now, here's Cousin Minnie Pearl!" The crowd welcomed their beloved Minnie Pearl with rapturous applause, waiting for her to greet them. Come to find out, they were proud to be there, too.

Today's Centerville features a park bench on the main square. A bronze statue of Minnie Pearl sits on the bench presiding over the imagined town she affectionately named Grinder's Switch. In 1980, she mused on the site that played such a central part of her act: "Grinder's Switch is a state of mind—a place where there is no illness, no war, no unhappiness, no political unrest, no tears. It's a place where there's only happiness—where all you worry about is what you are going to wear to the church social, and if your feller is going to kiss you in the moonlight on the way home. I wish for all of you a Grinder's Switch."

NOTES

Today, Centerville is part of what's called Nashville's Big Back Yard—a Tennessee natural watershed region anchored by the Natchez Trace made up of twelve connected communities of under five thousand people each. There is still a Grinder's Switch Radio Hour on Saturday mornings held in Centerville's historic former hardware store. It streams on WNKX FM (2023).

SOURCES

"Minnie Pearl: The Starday Years." *Starday*. CD set, 1998.

Pearl, Minnie. Tape recorded memoir by Sarah Colley Cannon, Nashville, Tennessee. Supplement to Tape 1, Side A, 1979.

———. Tape recorded memoir by Sarah Colley Cannon, Nashville, Tennessee. Tape 14, 1979.

Pearl, Minnie, and Joan Dew. *Minnie Pearl: An Autobiography.* New York: Simon and Schuster, 1980.

Sawyer, Bobby Jean. "Minnie Pearl: The Life and Legacy of the Queen of Country Comedy." *Wide Open Country*, October 2021. https://www.wideopencountry.com/just-proud-celebrating-life-legacy-minnie-pearl/.

TWO

On the Opry and the Road, 1940–1970

CHAPTER 6

WSM and the Grand Ole Opry

Golden Age of Radio, 1925–1941

The day after Minnie Pearl's first appearance on the Grand Ole Opry in 1940, she received a call from Ford Rush, the Opry's emcee. Rush asked if she'd come back the next Saturday and invited her to join the Opry's regular cast. Minnie hung up the phone and said, "Mama, you're not going to believe this; they want me to come back!"

The next week, Fannie Tate drove her daughter to WSM's studios in downtown Nashville. When they arrived, Margaret Frye, the receptionist, exclaimed, "Oh, am I ever glad to see you!" She handed Sarah a large mailbag and said, "This is all for you. Will you take it with you when you go home?" Inside were more than three hundred letters and cards from listeners. "I was flabbergasted! I didn't know much about show business yet, but I knew it was pretty good for an unknown to get that much response from a three-minute spot on the air at 11:05 at night," Minnie recounted.

Ford Rush's eagerness to invite her to join the Opry's cast of fifty musicians and performers now made perfect sense. Rush wanted to secure Minnie Pearl's act before anyone else could. He offered her $10 a week and told her to develop new material. Minnie knew she couldn't do it alone. "It became a family affair—sister Virginia wrote the gags; sister

Rod Brasfield and Minnie Pearl were a very popular comedy duo. Here, they use "corn scoops" to shovel fan mail, c. 1949. The Grand Ole Opry program originated on WSM, the radio station sponsored by National Life and Accident Insurance company, whose motto "We Shield Millions" made up the station's call name. Image courtesy of the Grand Ole Opry.

Dixie pitched in with office work; and Mama helped with costumes," author Robert K. Oermann explained.

Sarah wasn't sure she wanted to be Minnie Pearl—she still had dreams of the Shakespearean stage. She also worried about how her mother, Fannie Tate House Colley, might react. Coming from a "provincial, conventional, proper" family in Franklin, Sarah feared the character might be offensive. However, it quickly became clear that Fannie was just fine with "Minnie." Sarah recalled in an interview:

The Grand Ole Opry Cast is pictured here in Ryman Auditorium on June 5, 1943. This was the first performance at the Ryman, which served as the home of the Grand Ole Opry from 1943 to 1974. Previously, the Opry broadcast its live show from National Life and Accident Insurance Company's Studio C in Nashville (1925-1934), Belcourt Theater (1935–1936), Dixie Tabernacle (1936–1939), and War Memorial Auditorium (1939–1943). Image courtesy of the Grand Ole Opry Archives.

> Mama had changed a great deal living in Centerville. . . . And of course we were also desperate for money. During the week, I was working for the WPA (Works Progress Administration) rec center for $50 a month and supporting both mother and me. She always referred to Minnie Pearl as our salvation because if not for her, I don't know what we would have done. The money had run out.

Minnie settled into her new weekend gig, and the opening night jitters started to fade. As her nervousness subsided, she began to notice all of the other things going on backstage at the Opry. There was no rehearsal—in fact, the first thirty minutes were largely unscripted. The run-of-show list was taped to a board, and performers (and often their friends and family) wandered backstage to visit and catch up. The Opry had a laid-back, relaxed atmosphere, a stark contrast to Minnie's tightly scripted work at Ward-Belmont and the Sewell Theater Company. Initially, she found the Opry chaotic but soon realized there was a method to the madness. After fifteen years, everyone knew exactly what to do

On April 18, 1922, Dr. Crosland of Ward-Belmont School and 16-year-old radio enthusiast John "Jack" DeWitt Jr., made history with Nashville's first radio broadcast on WDAA. DeWitt later became WSM's chief engineer in 1932, spearheading its growth to a 50,000-watt powerhouse and was appointed president in 1947. This pioneering work in broadcasting set the stage for WSM's Grand Ole Opry, which began in 1925 and featured Sarah Ophelia Colley, a Ward-Belmont graduate, as Minnie Pearl. Image courtesy of the Grand Ole Opry Archives.

and when to do it. "Somehow it worked, and audiences were always entertained," Minnie said.

Although her family came from a relatively rural area, Sarah didn't see herself as "country." But Minnie had emerged, literally overnight, as a country comedy star. If she was going to join the Opry, she wanted to learn more about the radio station that broadcast the Opry and the insurance company behind it. Minnie was also curious about the women and comedians who had come before her.

The entity behind the Grand Ole Opry was the National Life and Accident Insurance Company, whose executives thought radio might be a good way to sell insurance. The radio boom began in the 1920s, quickly becoming indispensable for news and entertainment. As radios became more affordable for working- and middle-class families, audiences expanded, and businesses seized the opportunity to tap into this profitable industry. They did so through advertising and corporate sponsorship of programming—from music to lectures to dramatic shows. By 1939, nearly 80 percent of U.S. households owned a radio, and this era is remembered as the "Golden Age of Radio."

Back in 1925, Edwin Craig, the son of one of the National Life and Accident Insurance Company's founders, had a bold idea. Rather than paying to advertise or sponsor radio programming, why not *own* the station outright? Craig argued that cutting out the middleman would allow the company to control its content directly and maximize profits. He convinced his father and the other executives, who approved the plan to start a radio station. Next, they had to apply and get approval for the station's call sign, which were based on international letter designations. The United States was assigned AAA-ALZ, KAA-KZZ, NAA-NZZ, and WAA-WZZ. Given Nashville's location, Craig chose WSM, which was an acronym for the insurance company's motto: We Shield Millions.

With the radio frequency claimed, the call letters assigned, and a small staff and studios—WSM went on the air on October 5, 1925. National Life hired George D. Hay, known as "The Solemn Old Judge," to run WSM. Hay had been a top radio personality at WLS in Chicago, which featured the National Barn Dance, a music show aimed at rural Americans. Minnie attributed her early success to Judge Hay, who she described as "a Christian gentleman, [who] reminded us that the Opry was started and built on brotherly love." Minnie added, "He led by example. . . . and the country people in Nashville adored him."

George D. Hay, who was called the "Solemn Old Judge" was a radio personality who hosted a "barn dance" on a Chicago radio station. He accepted a position in Nashville in 1925 and founded what became the Grand Ole Opry, the longest running radio show in US history. George D. Hay is pictured here in the WSM studio with his signature cigar and wooden steam boat whistle tucked under his arm. Image courtesy of the Grand Ole Opry Archives.

On November 28, 1925, Hay hired Uncle Jimmy Thompson to play fiddle tunes on the air. This proved popular, and Hay developed the show with additional musical acts. Then, in December of that year, Judge Hay said during the live radio broadcast: "For the past half hour we have been listening to music largely from the Grand Opera but from now on we will present the Grand Ole Opry." And just like that, the Grand Ole Opry, an American institution, was born.

In many ways, the Opry's name was Hay's way of thumbing his nose at the high-cultured opera and theater crowd. Hay had long found Nashville's social elite irritating. Since the radio station's launch, Nashville's Upper Class complained about the station broadcasting country music—they wanted classical music and more sophisticated programming. Hay had a different goal in mind; and as the money rolled in, so did the executives at National Life.

As the Grand Ole Opry's popularity rose, WSM shifted the format from a studio radio show to a stage show with a live audience. The first Opry programs were broadcast from Studio A, on the fifth floor of the National Life Building. The room was about fifteen by twenty feet. People could watch from behind a glass wall as they stood outside in the hallway. Crowds soon filled the hall, so the show was moved to a larger studio that seated five hundred. But that wasn't big enough either. National Life executives began looking for a larger space in town. They jumped from the Hillsboro Theatre in West Nashville to the Dixie Tabernacle in East Nashville. In 1936, they moved back downtown to the War Memorial Building, which featured a 1,660-seat auditorium. This is the building where Minnie Pearl first stepped onto the Opry stage.

In the late 1930s, the William Esty Agency in New York was hired to find advertisers for the Opry. Account executive Dick Marvin convinced the R.J. Reynolds Company to sponsor the program. Their Prince Albert smoking tobacco was popular in the South, and Marvin thought it was a perfect fit. Although Marvin faced initial skepticism from his colleagues, he eventually won them over. Shortly after, twenty-six NBC stations agreed to air the Grand Ole Opry, expanding its reach through local NBC affiliates across nearly two thousand miles.

The first nationally broadcast show on October 14, 1939, began: "This program is brought to you by WSM, the station of the National Life and Accident Insurance Company in Nashville, Tennessee." Then, announcer David Stone said, "Prince Albert, the South's most popular tobacco, presents the South's most popular program, 'The Grand Ole Opry.'" As Roy Acuff played his fiddle in the background, Judge Hay stepped to the mic and said: "Friends, these are the same people you've been listening to for fourteen years; the only difference tonight is that they're coming to you from the Mexican border to the mountains of Virginia." He concluded

DeFord Bailey was the first Black performer on the Grand Ole Opry and continued with the show from 1927 to 1941. He was known as the "Harmonica Wizard" and was famous for songs such as "Pan American Blues." Despite his success and popularity, Bailey faced racism during the Jim Crow Era of segregation in the South. In 2005, DeFord Bailey was inducted into the Country Music Hall of Fame. In 2023, the city of Nashville named a street after DeFord Bailey in the Edgehill neighborhood. Bailey is pictured here in 1970. Image courtesy of Marilyn K. Morton and David C. Morton and in the public domain.

with an invitation, "Our show is ready to ride right down the middle of the road to our friends and neighbors throughout America. Join us."

Other performers that night included Uncle Dave and Dorris Macon, George Wilkerson, The Fruit Jar Drinkers Band, Brother Oswald, Bill Monroe, and DeFord Bailey. Not surprisingly, the cast was all White, except for DeFord Bailey. Historian Kristine McCusker synthesized the Opry's approach to race this way: "Rather than side with either integrationists (who wished for an interracial labor force) or segregationists (who wished strict divisions, usually unequal between Blacks and Whites), the Opry . . . opted for a third option: they embraced racially exclusive stages . . . on which Whites performed and Blacks were invisible."

DeFord Bailey was the exception—the first African American to join the Grand Ole Opry in 1928. Known as the "Harmonica Wizard," Bailey's performances of songs like "Pan American Blues" made him a beloved figure. Author and songwriter Alice Randall described DeFord as "the father of Country, and Country's first superstar." Randall explained his influence: "By 1932, WSM was broadcasting with 50,000 watts of power, which meant every Black person in America and some in Canada had a good chance of . . . listening to DeFord. And millions of White folk listened to him, too." DeFord Bailey was fired from the Grand Ole Opry in 1941 after a dispute between the Opry and ASCAP, a performing rights organization. McCusker noted, "After [DeFord's] departure, Blacks rarely . . . appeared on the air after 1941, until Charlie Pride broke the color barrier in the mid-1960s."

Another major event happened in 1941: the Federal Communications Commission passed a rule that a company couldn't own multiple radio networks. National Broadcasting Company (NBC) had two—the Red network and the Blue network. WSM executives worried that their station would be negatively impacted when NBC sold their Blue network, of which WSM was a part. Luckily, things turned out in the Opry's favor. NBC consolidated its affiliates before the sale, which actually increased the Opry's reach from 50 to 150 stations, turning Roy Acuff, Ernest Tubb, and Pee Wee King into household names. Minnie Pearl's timing was phenomenal. She had joined the Opry just months earlier, and these musical groups often wanted a comic to help warm up crowds and fill time during intermissions. As a woman, Minnie was a valued addition to the cast, bringing both variety and diversity to the lineup.

To be clear, Minnie wasn't the first comedian on the Grand Ole Opry. She wasn't even the first female comic. The first full-time comedian on the Opry was Lee Roy "Lasses" White, who performed as a Black-faced minstrel performer with his partner, Lee Davis "Honey" Wilds. White came to WSM in 1932 and the two performed as "Lasses and Honey." By 1934, "Lasses and Honey" were out and "Sarie and Sallie" were in. Played by Edna Wilson and her sister, Margaret Faith, Sarie and Sallie were the first female comedians on the Grand Ole Opry's cast—six years before Minnie Pearl's debut on November 30, 1940.

Edna developed the Sarie character while living in High Point, North Carolina. One night, while sitting around a campfire, she started "talking country" like an old mountain woman. Her humor relied on colorful phrases and a hillbilly dialect, blending a "country rube meets modern world" style. Word spread quickly, and soon people were paying her to perform at birthday parties and church socials. She asked her sister, Margaret, to join the act, and they became "Sarie and Sallie." The duo first aired on WSM radio in November 1934 and performed in long

Minnie signs autographs alongside her sisters Dixie Colley Shouse, Virginia Colley Burns, her mother, Fannie Tate Colley, and Dora Medearis who hosted the party for ladies from Nashville society, c. 1953. Image courtesy of Mary Beth Pruett and Hickman County Historical Society.

dresses, bonnets, and spectacles. Judge George D. Hay was so impressed that he paid each woman $20 per week—a huge sum during the Great Depression.

Sarie and Sallie performed frequently on the Opry between 1934 and 1938. Their success led to nationwide tours, although they returned to Nashville every Saturday for the Opry. After Margaret fell ill in 1938, Edna continued solo until her final performance in early 1941. Sarie and Sallie's departure from the Opry opened the door for another female comedian whose humor also centered on backwoods characters in the contemporary world. Once again, the timing was right for Minnie Pearl.

However, all was not right with Nashville's upper crust, who disliked country music and country humor. They felt it was an assault on good taste and an insult to the city. To the social elite, the Grand Ole Opry was an embarrassment, a blight on a city known as the "Athens of the

South" for its numerous institutions of higher education. The duality of Sarah Colley as a person and her persona as Minnie Pearl was crucial in bridging those two worlds.

In the 1930s, Sarah Colley was firmly part of the "Athens of the South" crowd, having graduated from the prestigious Ward-Belmont School. While her father liked and listened to the Grand Ole Opry, Sarah and her mother had more "refined" tastes. However, after joining the Opry and spending time with its performers, musicians, and WSM executives, the music began to grow on her. Reflecting on the experience, Sarah remarked, "If you're exposed to it long enough, it sneaks up on you, and I found myself as much a fan as the audiences who came to hear it."

From 1925 to 1941, the Grand Ole Opry's popularity and influence swept the nation—based in large part on the massive distribution of the show through NBC. Sarah joined the Opry's cast at an ascendant moment in 1940. Even as she warmed to country music, she maintained her reputation as a respectable member of the "old money" crowd connected to Ward-Belmont.

Something else happening in the world would play a major role in Minnie's transition from regional fame to national stardom. After briefly touring with Roy Acuff, she joined the "Camel Caravan" in 1941 to support US efforts in World War II (see Chapter 8: Camel Caravan and World War II). As part of this traveling entertainment group, Minnie performed at military bases throughout the United States and abroad. Her exposure to tens of thousands of troops would further catapult her career.

NOTES

Eventually, the National Broadcasting Company (NBC) sold its Blue radio network to Edward J. Noble, the owner of Life Savers candy, in 1943. Noble renamed it the American Broadcasting Company (ABC) later that same year. The sale was prompted by a 1941 FCC ruling that prohibited companies from owning multiple radio networks.

Listeners can still enjoy the Grand Ole Opry, the nation's longest-running radio broadcast, on WSM. In Middle Tennessee, tune in at 650 AM, stream it online via WSM's website, or listen on the go using the WSM mobile app.

Alice Randall tells the full story of DeFord Bailey's life and legacy in *My Black Country: A Journey Through Country Music's Black Past, Present, and Future.* Randall noted: "DeFord Bailey didn't vanish when he left the Opry. . . . In the wide Black world and in Black Nashville he continued to be part of the arts conversation. And he continued to be part of the political and legal conversation." Randall also connects DeFord to the conceptual "first family" of Country music. She posits, "What if DeFord Bailey is the papa, Lil Hardin Armstrong is the mama,

Ray Charles is their genius child, Charlie Pride is Deford's side child, and Herb Jeffries is Lil's stepson. You get a whole new way of looking at Country."

SOURCES

Anderson, Janna Quitney. *Imagining the Internet: Personalities, Predictions, Perspectives.* New York: Rowman & Littlefield, 2005.

Havighurst, Craig. *Air Castle of the South: WSM and the Making of Music City.* Champaign: University of Illinois Press, 2007.

McCusker, Kristine M. "Sarah Colley Cannon (Minnie Pearl): Gossiping about Grinder's Switch—The Grand Ole Opry and the Modernization of Tennessee." In *Tennessee Women: Their Lives and Times,* edited by Sarah Wilkerson Freeman and Beverly Bond, 261–80. Athens: University of Georgia Press, 2009.

National Association for Amateur Radio. "International Call Sign Series." http://www.arrl.org/international-call-sign-series.

Pearl, Minnie. Tape recorded memoir by Sarah Colley Cannon, Nashville, Tennessee. Tape 1, Side A, 1979.

Pearl, Minnie, and Joan Dew. *Minnie Pearl: An Autobiography.* New York: Simon and Schuster, 1980.

Randall, Alice. *My Black Country: A Journey Through Country Music's Black Past, Present, and Future.* New York: Black Privilege Publishing, 2024.

Rogers, Ricky. "Nashville Then Notes: Grand Ole Opry's Old Timers' Night." *Tennessean,* March 16, 2015. https://www.tennessean.com/story/news/local/2015/03/16/nashville-then-grand-ole-opry-municipal-auditorium-1975/24456097/.

Wolfe, Charles. *A Good-Natured Riot: The Birth of The Grand Ole Opry.* Nashville: The Country Music Foundation Press and Vanderbilt, 1999.

CHAPTER 7

Oh, Roy! The King of Country Music

Roy Acuff and Minnie Pearl, 1932–1941

In 1979, after forty years of friendship, Roy Acuff welcomed Minnie Pearl back onto the Grand Ole Opry stage. It was a reunion of sorts for two of the greatest legends associated with the longest-running radio broadcast in history. After her trademark "Howdy! I'm just so proud to be here," Minnie Pearl opened her monologue with a joke about her Opry debut four decades earlier:

> Miss Lizzie Timkum from Grinder's Switch told me, she said, "Now when you get up there at the Grand Ole Opry, you flirt with some of them fellers just for me." Well, I got up here on that first night, and I flirted with some of the fellers . . . just for Lizzie, not for me! And I seen some more handsome fellers, and I flirted with them too . . . just for Lizzie, not for me! *And then I saw that handsome Roy Acuff,* and that's when I decided to go into business for myself! Let Lizzie Timkum find her own fellers. . . . Oh, Roy!

Roy Acuff and Minnie Pearl shared a remarkable friendship that came to symbolize country music's golden era in the 1940s and 1950s. However, their relationship had a rocky start. Early on, Acuff hired—and later fired—Pearl from his traveling show. Yet, what began as a professional setback evolved into a lifelong bond that indeliby shaped both the Grand Ole Opry and country music for generations.

Roy Acuff in 1950. Image: Walden S. Fabry/Ross Photos, Public Domain.

It all started in December 1940. Country music's hottest star, Roy Acuff, invited Minnie to join him on the road and offered to pay her fifty dollars a week. Minnie said yes before he could finish the question. Combined with the ten dollars she earned for her Saturday night Opry performances, her weekly salary increased to sixty dollars—the most she'd ever earned.

Eight years earlier, Acuff's career in show business started unremarkably—playing fiddle for a snake-oil salesman in 1932. As part of the Doc Hauser Medicine Show, Acuff and other musicians performed to draw a crowd before Doc took the stage to promote Mocoton Tonic. Doc claimed the remedy could cure "dyspepsia, sick headaches, constipation, indigestion, pain . . . and other ailments." The tonic was 10 percent alcohol and sold for $1 a bottle. People lined up to buy it.

After Doc Hauser's grift ended, Acuff turned his attention to the Crazy Tennesseans—a band he formed in 1935. They hosted a daytime show on WROL and performed for school dances, county fairs, and other local events. During this time, Roy Acuff met fellow musician Charlie Swain, who had written a popular song called "The Great Speckled Bird." Acuff paid Swain fifty cents to make a copy of the song, and with Swain's permission, the Crazy Tennesseans added it to their act.

Several of the Grand Ole Opry's biggest legends gather to sing during rehearsal, c. 1947. From left to right: Roy Acuff known as the "King of Country Music," Red Foley who headlined and served as the Opry's emcee from 1946-1953, Minnie Pearl also called "Cousin Minnie Pearl," on the show, and Ernest Tubb known as the "Texas Troubadour." Image courtesy of the Grand Ole Opry Archives.

In 1936, a producer from the American Record Company heard "The Great Speckled Bird" and invited Acuff's band to Chicago for a recording session. There, they recorded twenty songs, including an expanded version of "The Great Speckled Bird," which became a breakout success. Acuff saw the record as a stepping-stone toward his ultimate goal: joining WSM's Grand Ole Opry. Eager to make his dream a reality, Acuff traveled to Nashville to meet with WSM executive Judge George Hay.

Sarah and Roy Acuff stand on the street with a young fan in downtown Nashville, c. 1941. It was during this time that Sarah toured with Roy Acuff and his band. Image courtesy of the Grand Ole Opry Archives.

Unfortunately for Acuff, Hay was dismissive of the audition, saying, "Sorry, boy, but the show is filled, and there are many applications ahead of you."

Meanwhile, Pee Wee King and his Golden West Cowboys were touring in Kentucky and Tennessee in 1937. While in Knoxville, Acuff crossed paths with King and his manager, J. L. Frank. Still determined to secure a spot on the Opry, Acuff used his connection with J. L. Frank to get a meeting with David Stone, the head of WSM's Artists' Bureau (and younger brother of WSM General Manager Harry Stone). After their meeting, Stone agreed to schedule Acuff and the Crazy Tennesseans to perform during a live broadcast in October 1937.

Eddy Arnold and Minnie as Mrs. Henry Cannon, c. 1975. Image courtesy of The Hope Powell Collection by Singleton/Curb.

The performance was a flop. Acuff sang *The Great Speckled Bird* in a "crooning" style that failed to connect with the Opry audience, and he was not invited back the following week. However, David Stone remained in touch and arranged another audition on February 5, 1938. On a rainy night at the Dixie Tabernacle in East Nashville, Acuff took the stage once again. This time, instead of "crooning," Acuff used his mountain voice to deliver a powerful rendition of "The Great Speckled Bird." The response was overwhelmingly positive. The next week, fan mail flooded WSM, and the band was offered a regular spot on the Opry. Roy Acuff had achieved his dream.

Not long after, WSM General Manager Harry Stone approached Acuff about changing the group's name. Stone felt that "Crazy Tennesseans" was demeaning and suggested instead "Roy Acuff and the Smoky Mountain Boys." Acuff acquiesced, but as a result, three band members quit. He quickly replaced them with Lonnie Wilson (guitar), Pete Kirby (dobro), Jess Easterday (bass, mandolin), and Jake Tindell (harmonica). With Roy Acuff on the fiddle, a new version of the Smoky Mountain Boys emerged.

Minnie with Roy Acuff and Ernest Tubb, c. 1975. Image courtesy of The Hope Powell Collection by Singleton/Curb.

There was one twist: the band wasn't all boys. Acuff believed having a female member would help to present a "family" image. So, in April 1939, he recruited Rachel Veach, a talented singer and banjo player from Nashville. During her audition, WSM's David Stone was unimpressed, but Acuff held his ground, saying, "If she can pick up her banjo and listen to me, she's what I want. She's country!" Rachel was well-received by audiences, but not everyone approved. Some questioned whether a young woman could travel with a group of men and still be considered a "lady." To address these concerns, Acuff changed the billing in a way that presented Rachel as Pete Kirby's sister. Not long after, the Smoky Mountain Boys welcomed another female performer—not a musician, but a young comic named Minnie Pearl.

On Tuesday, December 31, 1940, Acuff and his band, including Rachel and Minnie, piled into Acuff's long Cadillac. With their instruments tied to the roof, they set off for Evansville, Indiana. The group arrived early and Acuff went to find Pee Wee King and Eddy Arnold, who were also performing that day. Minnie was excited but anxious—this would be her first major public appearance as Minnie Pearl outside of Nashville.

To shake off her nerves before the show, Minnie put on her costume and made her way to the performance hall. She went over to the piano and cut loose. She belted out "Maple on the Hill" in her "country corn" style—purposefully loud and off-key. "It's a beautiful song, but I sung it like killing snakes," Minnie quipped. As she sang, Pee Wee King and Eddy Arnold walked in and spotted "an attractive young lady standing there straight-faced, going at it tooth and toenail at the top of her lungs." A look of horror crossed Eddy Arnold's face. "If he puts that girl on the show, they'll boo her off the stage. She can't sing!" Arnold exclaimed. King, amused, replied, "I think that's that new comic on the Opry, Minnie Pearl." Arnold laughed and let out a sigh of relief.

In Nashville, Minnie's act had been a hit, but in Evansville her routine fell flat. Unlike the Opry, where her act lasted three to four minutes, the stage show required twenty minutes of comedy. It was a significant leap for any comedian, and Minnie didn't have enough material to fill the time. There was another challenge as well. She later reflected: "I didn't have a full show, but that wasn't all. . . I was holding back. I still wasn't ready to divest myself completely of my own personality and become a silly character. I wasn't ready to give up sex appeal and a feminine image to be a clown."

From Evansville, the group traveled to multiple towns for more shows. Minnie's routine continued to underwhelm audiences. By the end of the week, she was exhausted and deflated. The group drove back to Nashville for the Opry's live Saturday night broadcast. That left Minnie with only Sunday to unpack, wash her hair, do laundry, pay bills, run errands, and repack. "The schedule was absolute madness," she wrote.

After each Opry performance, it was back on the road, where Minnie found herself "exposed to a new breed of people, both on stage and in the audiences." She was struck by the intensity, relentless pace, and long hours of the country music industry. Moreover, her fellow performers cussed like sailors, drank, and had "a jargon and lifestyle all their own." Minnie quickly came to terms with her new reality: "I had enough sense to know if I was going to be living in a man's world, *in their world*, I would have to accept it."

Despite the roughness of life on the road, Minnie saw Roy Acuff in a different light. "He was a professional . . . who gave his audiences everything he had every time he walked on stage," she said. "He was also a gentleman and a fine Christian. I was impressed by his consideration and his integrity." Minnie recalled a story that illustrated his character:

> One cold, winter night, we were running late to play in a schoolhouse back up in the hills. Because of the weather, the school's principal let the people go inside without paying. When we got there, the principal offered to make the crowd leave and re-enter so tickets could be sold. Acuff nixed that . . . He told the principal, 'Let them stay where they are. We'll put a cigar box out by the door, and they can drop their money in as they go out.' After the show, Roy said, 'I'll bet we didn't lose a dime.'"

As the months went by, Minnie Pearl continued to struggle on stage. Audiences just weren't laughing. Although Acuff never directly criticized her, he tried to offer suggestions. After one show, the group stopped at an empty truck stop to eat. Someone dropped coins into the jukebox, and Minnie began dancing, which she described as "sorta like old-time clogging." Roy watched for a moment then said, "Now why don't you do that on stage?"

She shot back, "Oh, that's too silly. I couldn't do that." He replied, "Minnie, you have to realize that you *must* be silly. . . . You can't feel embarrassed and be a comic. . . . [and] you can't be embarrassed about *being* a comic." With hindsight, Minnie said, "He was trying to help me, but I was too stupid to listen… I was 29 years old, and I just couldn't see

Minnie and Roy during rehearsal, c. 1982. Image courtesy of The Hope Powell Collection by Singleton/Curb.

my way clear to cut loose and act a fool. I had still not given up the other dream of being a dramatic actress."

Not long after, Minnie found herself backstage with Roy at the Opry. Acuff gently told her, "Minnie, you're just not fitting into our little act." Fighting back tears, she replied, "I know I'm not, and I'm so sorry. But I can't help it." He responded kindly, "I know you can't. It's going to take a little more experience. But I can't keep you because . . . I'm not making all that much money." With the benefit of hindsight and lived experience,

Roy Acuff and Minnie Pearl sculpture at the legendary Ryman Auditorium. Russ Faxon sculpted the commissioned piece, which was dedicated in 2001. Image courtesy of Library of Congress, Prints & Photographs Division, photograph by Carol M. Highsmith [LC-DIG-highsm-68736].

Minnie later admitted: "Roy was right. [He] couldn't have done a better thing for my career than fire me from my first job. It forced me to take a good long look at myself and my act."

Luckily for Minnie and Roy, their story didn't end there. They never toured on the road again, but they shared many appearances together on the Grand Ole Opry. Moreover, they remained close friends both on and off the stage. So, it came as no surprise when the Ryman Auditorium unveiled a new sculpture in their main lobby. Sculpted by Russ Raxon, "Oh, Roy!" immortalizes Roy and Minnie as they sit on a Ryman church pew. A fiddle tucked under one arm, Roy reaches out to Minnie with the other. With Minnie's hand on his elbow, price tag hanging from her hat, they turn to one another and smile.

Their significance to country music—and to each other—is hard to put into words, but the plaque beneath the sculpture captures it beautifully: "This is dedicated to the love and friendship that was shared with millions by two of country music's greatest performers. Roy Acuff, the King of Country Music, and Minnie Pearl, the Queen of Country Comedy, performed at the Ryman Auditorium from 1943 to 1974."

NOTES

The Opry broadcast its last Friday show from the Ryman on March 15, 1974. The next night, Roy Acuff opened the first Saturday night show in the new 4,440-seat Opry House off Briley Parkway. In 1999, the Grand Ole Opry returned to the Ryman for a residency and continues to hosts special broadcasts several times a year.

Roy Acuff passed away on November 23, 1992, at the age of eighty-nine. In addition to "The Great Speckled Bird," he was well known for songs including "Wabash Cannonball," "Fireball Mail," and "Night Train to Memphis.

SOURCES

Classic Country. "Minnie Pearl—Comedy (Opry Live March 3, 1979)." Posted April 4, 2024, by Classic Country, YouTube video. https://youtu.be/lbtC15yhDlU?si=R7qBcxx_dlyEFQ5o.

Pearl, Minnie, and Joan Dew. *Minnie Pearl: An Autobiography.* New York: Simon and Schuster, 1980.

Schlappi, Elizabeth. *Roy Acuff: The Smoky Mountain Boy.* Gretna, LA: Pelican Publishing Co., 1978, 1993.

Wolfe, Charles. *A Good-Natured Riot: The Birth of The Grand Ole Opry.* Nashville: The Country Music Foundation Press and Vanderbilt, 1999.

CHAPTER 8

Camel Caravan and World War II

On the Front Lines of Entertainment, 1941–1945

During the Battle of Okinawa, American troops reported hearing Japanese soldiers shout, "To hell with President Roosevelt, to hell with Babe Ruth, to hell with Roy Acuff!" The inclusion of Acuff in this unexpected trio confirmed his rise to prominence as the Grand Ole Opry's biggest star. By 1945, his influence was undeniable—a poll of soldiers stationed in Europe even ranked Acuff above Frank Sinatra as the most popular musical performer. Other Grand Ole Opry standouts, like Minnie Pearl and Pee Wee King, were also on the front lines of entertainment, bringing laughter and music to soldiers far from home.

Months before the United States declared war on Japan in December 1941, Opry entertainers began to mobilize. J. L. Frank, manager of Pee Wee King's Golden West Cowboys, and Esty Agency executive Dick Martin teamed up to create a traveling show called the Camel Caravan. Their concept became a reality when the Esty Agency secured sponsorship from R. J. Reynolds, the popular tobacco company behind Camel cigarettes.

Part business promotion and part patriotic goodwill, the Camel Caravan was a key part of the broader United Service Organizations (USO) war effort. While its primary mission was to entertain the troops, the tour also served to elevate the profiles of its performers and provided

Members of the Camel Caravan, led by Pee Wee King and Golden West Cowboys, pose in front of the full-size replica of the Greek Parthenon in Nashville's Centennial Park, 1942. Minnie stands second from the right. While on tour, Minnie chaperoned the "cigarette girls" who passed out free Camel cigarettes to U.S. soldiers. One of the "cigarette girls" stands on the end, next to Minnie. Image courtesy of the Grand Ole Opry Archives.

R. J. Reynolds with a platform to market their cigarettes. Pee Wee King's Golden West Cowboys and Minnie Pearl were among those recruited to join the Camel Caravan. Other tour hopefuls gathered in Nashville's Shelby Park to audition on a flatbed truck that doubled as a makeshift stage.

The Golden West Cowboys anchored the show and included King on accordion, Redd Stewart on fiddle, and Eve McColl, the singer and guitarist known as San Antonio Rose. In addition to King's group and Minnie Pearl, performers included pop vocalist Kay Carlisle, dancer Dollie Dearman, a trio of female singers (Mary Dinwiddie, Evelyn Wilson, Alcyon Bate Beasley), and the Camelettes—a group of four female dancers. Other musicians rounded out the tour: Chuck Wiggins (Cowboy Joe), Joe Zinkan, and Gene Widner. Master of Ceremonies was Opry regular Ford Rush, and Eddy Arnold was the emcee for the King portion of the show. Arnold opened each set with the song "I'll Be Back in a Year, Little Darlin"—a solace to those who had been drafted.

In July 1941, the Camel Caravan hit the road, packed into four long red cars emblazoned with the Camel logo. As they entered each military base, the lead car announced their entrance with electric bullhorns blaring: "The Camels are coming, Da DA, Da DA." The instruments traveled in a truck with fold-down sides that converted into a stage, while Pee Wee King's car pulled a trailer that doubled as a dressing room for outdoor shows. "As we passed, people would wave and blow their horns at us. People came up to thank us in hotels and restaurants," remembered King.

For the next nineteen months, the Camel Caravan visited four or five bases each week, with one or more shows each day. The tour allowed Minnie Pearl to further develop her comedic persona. After all, she'd only been on the Opry for eight months. Performing for soldiers forced her to sharpen her timing and delivery. Minnie recalled: "You had to be quick and punchy to get through to them, and that gave me the guts and brass to let Minnie kick up her heels and have fun."

The Camel Caravan also provided Minnie Pearl with a new level of financial success. Earning $50 per week for her performances and an extra $50 for chaperoning the Camelettes, she was making more money than ever before. Minnie quipped, "I would have agreed to chaperone King Kong for $50 a week. But I had no idea what I was getting into." In her words: "The (cigarette) girls would come running to me in tears, wanting to go home because some soldier pinched them as they passed down the aisles with their cigarette trays. The girls . . . wore cute, little majorette costumes with skirts so short they barely covered their blooms."

On Saturday night, December 6, 1941, the Camel Caravan finished their show and drove to San Antonio. Minnie was looking forward to a rare day off, but December 7 turned into a national nightmare. While visiting

Camel Caravan performance at an army base in Texas, 1941. This photo includes King on accordion, Redd Stewart on fiddle, and Eve McColl, the singer and guitarist known as San Antonio Rose. Also pictured, Minnie Pearl in the back and dancer Dollie Dearman at the microphone. Image courtesy of the Grand Ole Opry Archives.

with a friend, she heard the shocking news that the Japanese had bombed Pearl Harbor, a strategic U.S. naval base in Hawaii. The next afternoon, members of the Camel Caravan gathered to hear President Roosevelt's radio address. He declared that December 7 would "live in infamy" and announced that Congress had declared war on Japan. Reflecting on the sudden shift in atmosphere, Minnie later said, "We had no thought of war . . . until Pearl Harbor."

Minnie believed the tour might be canceled, but the troupe continued its performances, finding even more purpose as the war intensified.

Minnie described the uncertainty of the moment: "We were all frightened to death. We didn't know where the Japanese would strike next, and we were right in the middle of a prime target—Fort Sam Houston, Kelly Field, and Randolph Field. A precision bombing raid could have wiped out all three."

After Pearl Harbor, military bases tightened security. Minnie recalled, "After the attack, we got our first taste of what it was like to be at war.... We quickly realized that being entertainers didn't give us special privileges." Previously, the group had breezed onto bases, but that changed overnight. "We were not only stopped at the guard gate," she explained, "but also checked by Military Police, called MPs, for identification. Then, they searched our vehicles." Minnie found a way to turn the new protocols into a running gag: "I felt so at home when I got here.... Why, they even had fellers out there with my initials on their sleeve—M.P.—for Minnie Pearl!" The joke became a staple of her act, earning big laughs throughout the war.

More broadly, Minnie described the intensity of the tour as "absolutely invaluable." She reflected, "It helped me get Minnie Pearl in shape. There's only one thing that will season an act, and that's show hours—something I sorely lacked before the Camel Caravan." By "season an act," Minnie meant that she learned to deal with a wide range of audiences and their reactions. She explained, "Our shows aimed to entertain soldiers who were away from home and not happy about it." So, she developed new material, giving her humor a sharper, more suggestive edge. One joke from her show went something like this: "I heard that my friend Polly Petunia had been sick, so I called her. I said, 'Have you been bed-ridden?' 'Oh yes,' she said 'Hundreds of times. And twice in a haystack.'"

Despite her best efforts, Minnie still faced tough moments. One night, she was heckled by a drunk soldier. "This guy started hollering at me," she said and continued, "Every time I'd pull a gag, he'd step on my punch line.... The more they laughed, the louder he got. I began stumbling over my lines... and left the stage in shambles without finishing my act. I ran off the stage bawling my eyes out."

Backstage, Ford Rush, the show's host, found Minnie in tears and offered advice that would stick with her for the rest of her career. Decades later, she reflected on that night:

> Rush said, "If you are going to say, 'I'm funny, laugh at me,' you automatically become a target. The sooner you learn that the better.... If you're not

Minnie Pearl (center) sits with Gene Autry (right) and Pee Wee King (left), c. 1942. Image courtesy of the Grand Ole Opry Archives.

> experienced enough to handle a heckler, then ride over him. Get louder than he is. You've got a microphone, and he hasn't. He wants attention and if you don't notice him, he can't have any fun." And [Rush] was right! I can truthfully say I've never since let a heckler bother me . . . Sometimes I'd invite them on stage—that shuts them up fast.

In 1942, the Camel Caravan ventured overseas to boost the morale of US soldiers stationed in the Panama Canal Zone. The canal was a strategic place for ships to pass through, and the United States had heavily fortified military bases in the area. No one in the troupe had ever been out of the United States or experienced tropical heat. For the trip, Minnie purchased a "turquoise wool suit with a pink cashmere sweater." Meanwhile, Pee Wee King bought new outfits for his band—white wool pants and two shirts—heavy blue satin and heavy pink satin. "Nobody who actually lived in the tropics owned clothes like those," Minnie said with a laugh, adding, "The humidity was murder. It was like stepping into a furnace. And there I was in a wool suit!"

For many members of the Camel Caravan, it was their first time flying. "We were all terrified, especially when they loaded us onto an old DC-3 troop plane with bucket seats, and parachutes lined up in the middle of the aisle," Minnie recalled. After several shows in Panama, they traveled to perform for US troops in Guatemala City. Due to security concerns, they were ordered to remain in Guatemala for more than a week. Finally, the group caught a flight to Brownsville, Texas. Minnie reminisced, "When we got off that plane, we were so happy to be back on American soil that we kissed the ground!" From Texas they returned to Nashville, Tennessee, where they were welcomed as heroes. Minnie felt "an enormous sense of pride" and said, "We were greeted as if we'd come back from battle."

After nearly two years on the road, the Camel Caravan had traveled over 50,000 miles, performing 175 shows across 19 states at 68 military bases, hospitals, and airfields. But as World War II raged on in Europe and the Pacific, the tour became unsustainable due to logistics and gasoline rationing. Even so, the Camel Caravan left a lasting impact on both the performers and the troops they entertained.

By the time the war ended in 1945, Minnie Pearl had become a familiar and comforting presence for soldiers and civilians alike. Her performances during the war contributed to the growing popularity of country music and the Grand Ole Opry, solidifying her place in American entertainment history. She concluded: "The fact that these boys considered Minnie an old friend by the time they came home gave me a foundation for my career I might not have had otherwise."

SOURCES

Cusic, Don. *Eddie Arnold: I'll Hold You in My Heart.* Nashville: Rutledge Hill Press, 1997.

Oermann, Robert, and The Grand Ole Opry. *Behind the Curtain: Tales of Romance and Tragedy.* New York: Center Street, 2008.

Pearl, Minnie. Tape recorded memoir by Sarah Colley Cannon, Nashville, Tennessee. Tape 23, Side 2, 1979.

———. Tape recorded memoir by Sarah Colley Cannon, Nashville, Tennessee. Tape 24, Side 1, Side 2, 1979.

———. Tape recorded memoir by Sarah Colley Cannon, Nashville, Tennessee. Tape 26, Side 2, 1979.

Pearl, Minnie, and Joan Dew. *Minnie Pearl: An Autobiography.* New York: Simon and Schuster, 1980.

Quine, Katie. "Five Times Opry History Intersected with American History." *Grand Ole Opry,* April 6, 2020. https://www.opry.com/stories/5-times-opry-history-intersected-with-u-s-history.

CHAPTER 9

Road Life, Opry Life, and the Boys

Tent Shows, Pee Wee King, and Rod Brasfield, 1945–1958

From the mid-1940s through the 1950s, Minnie Pearl entered a transformative period in her career, navigating life on the road and at the Opry while sharing the stage with country music's most iconic performers. She toured with Pee Wee King and his Golden West Cowboys, enduring the challenges of the road while honing her comedic craft. At the same time, her decade-long partnership with Rod Brasfield amused audiences with their playful "double comedy." She also worked alongside other country legends like Ernest Tubb, Little Jimmy Dickens, and Chet Atkins. Country music and country comedy was evolving, too. Minnie transitioned from being the new, funny girl to a trusted confidante and mentor—offering advice, support, and sometimes a shoulder to cry on. It was an era full of laughter and hardship. It was also a defining chapter in Minnie Pearl's career.

Opry performers simply called it "The Road," but it represented a way of life. Countless towns, endless hours in a car, multiple shows a week—this was Minnie's world for more than ten years. She thought she was "road tested" from her years with the Sewell Theater Company and the Camel Caravan, but traveling with mostly male singers and musicians brought a whole new awakening. As she put it, "I didn't know nuthin. I didn't even suspect nuthin!"

Minnie Pearl and Ernest Tubb remained close friends for decades. Here, they pose for a picture in 1967. Image courtesy of The Hope Powell Collection by Singleton/Curb.

After World War II ended in 1945, Pee Wee King was eager to get back on the road. When his manager, J. L. Frank, offered Minnie a spot in their traveling show for $50 a week, she jumped at the chance. "I said yes so fast my head nearly spun," she later recalled. Minnie was particularly excited to work with King, whom she saw as the future of country music.

King's country music background was as unconventional as his approach to the genre. Born Julius Frank Anthony Kuczynski to a musical

Minnie Pearl in conversation with Gene Autry at an event, c. 1985. Image courtesy of The Hope Powell Collection by Singleton/Curb.

Polish family in Milwaukee, King didn't hail from the Appalachian hills or the cotton belt. He was an accomplished accordion player who got his start touring with Gene Autry in 1934. At their first rehearsal, Autry noticed that several men in the troupe were named Frank. Gesturing toward King, Autry quipped, "Let's call you Pee Wee." The nickname stuck, and so did King's reputation as a forward-thinking musician who pushed the boundaries of traditional country.

In 1937, Pee Wee and his band, the Golden West Cowboys, joined the Grand Ole Opry. According to the Country Music Hall of Fame: "King and his group were decidedly more polished. They could all read music and were American Federation of Musicians union members. They helped to modernize the Opry." King introduced an array of new instruments and sounds to the stage including trumpet, drums, and the electric guitar. Their "Big Band" model featured polkas, waltzes, and western songs. That wasn't all—King was the first to wear flashy cowboy attire on the Opry. He even hired a tailor in Hollywood to design costumes for his band.

So, back to Minnie and "The Road." In 1946, Pee Wee King purchased an old funeral hearse to serve as the band's transportation. The long station wagon–like vehicle had four rows of seats, but King removed the back row to store their instruments. "Gasoline and tires were our biggest problems," Minnie said, adding, "On one 500-mile trip we had 13 flat tires! I thought Pee Wee was going to explode." For those traveling in the hearse, the real struggle was the lack of space. Minnie Pearl vividly remembered, "There was absolutely no way to get comfortable. You could barely move. There were no headrests on the backs of the seats, so you sat straight up with your hands in your lap, stuffed in like sardines."

Their shows were mostly in small towns with populations under five thousand, often held in tents instead of indoor venues. Tent shows debuted in 1941 with the group "Jam-up and Honey," and soon Opry stars like Roy Acuff, Bill Monroe, and Pee Wee King followed with their own tent show tours. As bandleader, Pee Wee approached life on the road with a mix of discipline and dry humor. He had four rules for his troupe: "(1) Don't date in your wardrobe, (2) Don't take a girl across state lines, (3) Don't pick your nose on stage, and (4) Always laugh at Minnie when she's doing her act."

Minnie was captivated by the roustabouts, workers from circus backgrounds who set up and took down the tents. "The tent was called 'the rag,' and 'raising the rag' and 'striking the rag' meant putting it up and taking it down," she recalled. While performers traveled to the next town after the show, the roustabouts stayed behind to pack up, camping overnight on the grounds before moving on early the next morning. Minnie noted their biggest fears were "fire, hail, and a high wind," or a "blow," which could collapse the tent. Performers were trained to help lead the audience to safety in such emergencies. Minnie credited her "tent show days" with her development as a comedian. She explained: "[Tent shows] helped my professionalism, and it showed on my Opry network broadcasts. . . . [I]t was also becoming easier for me to let Minnie take over completely. I was beginning to feel comfortable and at home in her personality."

Despite her growth as a performer, life on the road with a bunch of men stuffed into a hearse was a far cry from the glamour associated with show business. From schoolhouse gymnasiums to tents to large city auditoriums—the towns blurred together. She described the conditions:

> There were countless drab, smelly hotel rooms, lumpy beds with chenille spreads and all-night diners. . . . And of course, the indescribable discomfort of riding all day in the hot summertime with no air conditioning. . . . Sometimes there'd be a bottle of whiskey passed around with a Coke chaser. . . . I'd arrive for a show with my clothes stuck to my back and every bone in my body aching.

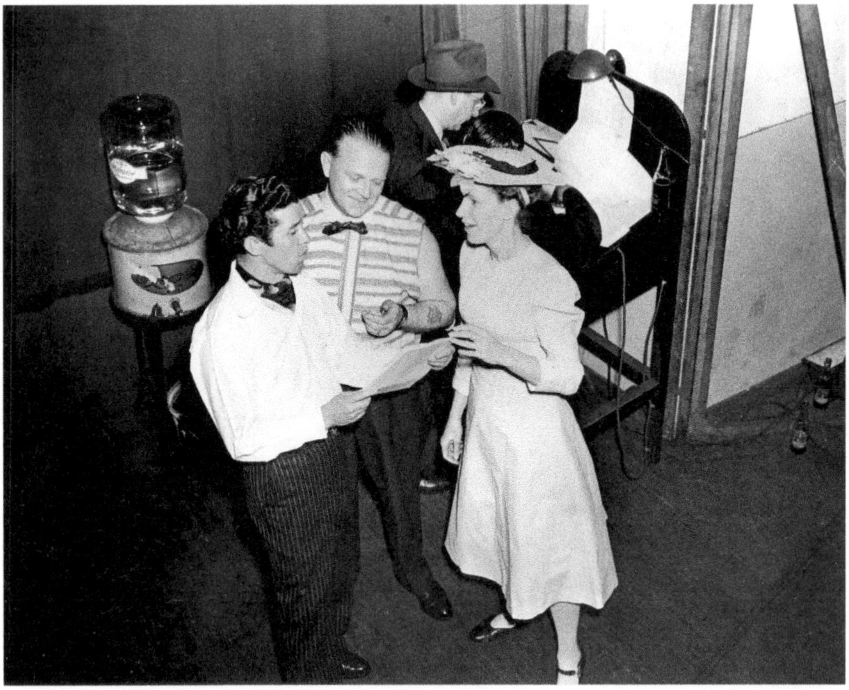

Even at the Grand Ole Opry, work included some watercooler-talk (water dispenser in the background). Pictured here in 1946, Roy Acuff (left), Jim Denny (center), and Cousin Minnie Pearl talk backstage at the Ryman. Behind the group, Fred Rose checks the run of show. Image courtesy of the Grand Ole Opry Archives.

Life on the road was physically taxing, but Minnie Pearl quickly earned the respect of "the boys." She said, "I didn't complain or whine or ask for any favors or special treatment because I was a woman. I took the rigors just like the men. I came from hardy stock." Though only in her thirties, Minnie became known as the "mother confessor," a trusted figure for advice. She recalled: "I was older than these boys . . . And without meaning to, I became involved in their lives. We traveled in such close quarters they just naturally shared their thoughts."

She became part of what she called "a very exclusive clique" of performers, sharing deep conversations in the quiet hours of the night as they traveled. She witnessed and wrote about the highs and lows of road life:

> I saw it break up marriages and increase the birth rate in small towns. . . . It could make poor men into millionaires and nice men into drug addicts. I saw fat men get skinny, skinny men get fat and young men get old before their time. Despite all the fame and attention, the effect for many was

Minnie and her comedy partner Rod Brasfield running their lines during a rehearsal break for the Grand Ole Opry's Prince Albert Show, 1950. Image courtesy of the Grand Ole Opry Archives.

> broken heads and broken hearts and men who were broken, period. . . . But I also saw some of the very best times of my life. . . . The camaraderie [was] strong and sweet.

After traveling all week, Pee Wee's troupe would return to Nashville in time for the Grand Ole Opry show on Saturday nights. The post–World War II era ushered in a new age for the Opry. Minnie was moved to the NBC network portion of the show, which allowed her to reach a larger radio audience. Even as music and media changed, Minnie benefitted from the boon in country music as a genre and a brand.

Roy Acuff left the Opry in 1946 to "strike out on his own." He wanted to tour the West Coast without having to return to Nashville every week. It was a great loss for the Opry family, including Minnie. Luckily, the Esty Agency scooped up Red Foley from Chicago. In March 1946, Foley made a guest appearance on the Opry as an audition of sorts. The Esty Agency was satisfied, and on April 13, 1946, Red Foley became the host

Minnie Pearl and Rod Brasfield on stage at the Ryman during a performance, c. 1952. The backdrop set represented Grinder's Switch, the imaginary community in which Minnie lived with friends and family. Image courtesy of the Grand Ole Opry Archives.

of the Prince Albert show. Known for his laid-back demeanor, Minnie quipped: "We used to laugh that Red Foley was so relaxed he'd fall asleep on stage if they dimmed the lights for a minute."

During Foley's tenure (1946–1954), the Opry experienced major changes. His smooth vocal style and ability to perform a variety of genres—from gospel to Western swing—attracted new audiences and performers. The show's music was still rooted in the old-time string band tradition with instruments like fiddles, banjos, and guitars. However, Minnie witnessed a significant shift when performers like Bob Wills and his Texas Playboys introduced amplified instruments, including electric guitars, horns, and drums. Guitarist Chet Atkins also brought his own

Minnie Pearl at Zibart's Book Store in Nashville, January 1954. This photo was taken for a book signing for "Minnie Pearl's Diary," which was self-published in 1953. Image courtesy of the Nashville Public Library Metro Nashville Archives.

style of playing guitar when he joined the Opry in 1950. These changes in sound reflected the broader evolution of country as it began incorporating elements of Western swing and honky-tonk.

A year after Red Foley joined the Opry, Minnie was backstage getting dressed. Suddenly, she heard the audience roar with laughter. "They were absolutely going wild over someone," she said. Minnie came out of her dressing room to see what was happening. When she looked on stage, she instantly recognized the performer. Minnie hadn't seen Rod Brasfield in twenty years, but as a teenager, she had idolized him. He was part of a traveling show called the Bisbee Comedians, which performed in her hometown of Centerville. Even as a young girl, Rod's comedic style caught her attention. She wrote, "He often wandered off script like when an actor was lying dead on the stage in a dramatic scene, and he turned to the audience and said, 'It ain't so serious. He'll be back tomorrow night.'"

Two decades later, there stood Rod Brasfield on the Opry stage—rail thin and wearing a suit big enough for a man twice his size, held up by suspenders. With his baggy suit, beat-up hat, and ill-fitting false teeth, he had audiences laughing before he even said a word.

In 1947, Rod Brasfield joined the Opry's weekly network show, which led to a ten-year partnership with Minnie Pearl. Although each held their own solo spot, they also performed "double comedy" together. As a "hap-

Minnie Pearl and Rod Brasfield, nicknamed the "Howenwald Flash," during a performance, c. 1948. His character was known for his hokey humor, baggy clothes, and ill-fitting false teeth. Image courtesy of the Grand Ole Opry Archives.

less, unlucky country boy," Brasfield's character was instantly relatable to rural audiences, and they couldn't help but root for him. Nicknamed "The Hohenwald Flash," after a Tennessee town, Rod and Minnie's exchanges were a hit not only with the Opry's live audience but also on NBC network television shows from 1948 to 1958.

Their performances featured spontaneity and playful banter—as when Rod quipped, "I bought myself a new car and the first thing I done was grease it all over," to which Minnie responded, "Grease it all over? Why'd you do that?" Brasfield would reply while clacking his false teeth, "So the finance company can't get a hold of it!" Minnie wrote, "His favorite expression was 'By Ned, buddy,' and it became his trademark, just as 'Howdee' became mine . . . The audiences loved him, and so did I."

Behind the laughs, Rod was battling his own demons. After years of heavy drinking, his health deteriorated. Minnie never confirmed whether he was tipsy during their double-comedy acts, but it's not hard to imagine that alcohol played a role in some of his erratic onstage mannerisms. Sadly, Rod Brasfield passed away in 1958 at the age of forty-eight. Reflecting on their time together, Minnie wrote, "He was one of the kindest men I ever knew."

From 1945 to 1958, country comedy found its place in the fabric of Southern folk culture while also attracting a more mainstream audience. Historian Bill Malone emphasized that country humor "asserted the humanity of working people's lives . . . [and] added the healing balm of laughter." Whether on the road or on the Opry, Minnie's comedy act was a reminder that "although often fraught with sorrow and pain, the world of country music is also a world of laughter." She showed that humor could be as vital to country music as the songs themselves.

Minnie's ability to navigate the evolving landscape of country music while preserving her signature humor made her one of the most endearing figures of the Opry's post–World War II era. However, there was another significant development during these years, which had nothing to do with comedy. It was far more serious—she had fallen in love.

NOTES

Pee Wee King's contributions to American music include "Slow Poke," "You Belong to Me," and "The Tennessee Waltz." King's "Tennessee Waltz" was named the state song of Tennessee and has been recorded by more than five hundred artists. After leaving the Opry in 1947, King helped pioneer country television. He was inducted into the Country Music Hall of Fame in 1974.

SOURCES

Jones, Loyal. *Country Music: Humorists and Comedians.* Chicago: University of Illinois Press, 2008.

Malone, Bill. *Don't Get Above Your Raisin': Country Music and the Southern Working Class.* Chicago: University of Illinois Press, 2006.

McCall, Michael, John Rumble, and Paul Kingsbury, eds. *The Encyclopedia of Country Music,* 2nd ed. Oxford: Oxford University Press, 2012.

Oermann, Robert, and The Grand Ole Opry. *Behind the Curtain: Tales of Romance and Tragedy*. New York: Center Street, 2008, 37.

Pearl, Minnie. Tape recorded memoir by Sarah Colley Cannon, Nashville, Tennessee. Tapes 28–32, 1979.

Pearl, Minnie, and Joan Dew. *Minnie Pearl: An Autobiography.* New York: Simon and Schuster, 1980.

CHAPTER 10

Minnie Pearl Finds Her Feller

Mr. and Mrs. Henry Cannon, 1946–1950

By 1946, at thirty-four, Sarah Colley/Minnie Pearl wasn't looking to get married. "After being on the road for nearly 13 years, I had seen too much or at least enough to make me very wary," she reflected. Despite going on plenty of double dates in Nashville with her roommate Orra Williams, Minnie remained apathetic. "I just didn't care," she admitted, adding, "Life on the road was more important to me than my life off the road." That all changed with Henry Cannon.

Minnie thought her dating days were over after Orra married Bill Pitner, but the newlyweds had other ideas. They set her up with Henry Cannon. Bill and Henry had grown up together in Franklin, Tennessee. Cannon was an accomplished pilot with combat experience in Japan during World War II. During the war, Henry listened to the Opry on the Armed Forces Network, so he told Bill he'd be glad to meet the woman known as Minnie Pearl.

Henry Cannon and Minnie Pearl were introduced in May 1946, but their initial date was a dud. They continued to socialize at parties hosted by Bill and Orra, but Henry and Minnie always showed up with other dates. Then, one Friday night in December, Minnie and a date were having dinner at Bill and Orra's when Henry called. He was with his cousin,

Minnie poses in a publicity photo, 1941. She picks petals in a game of "He loves me. He loves me not." This was a central part of her act—Minnie was always "looking for a fellar." Image courtesy of the Harpeth Hall School Archives.

Newt Cannon, and they were looking for a night cap. When they arrived at the apartment, Minnie thought to herself: "Henry Cannon without a woman! He looks very handsome tonight."

Newt, Bill, Orra, and Minnie's date went into the kitchen, which left Minnie and Henry alone in the den. Minnie exclaimed, "All of a sudden he put his hands on my shoulders and turned me around and kissed me very soundly." Then, Henry said, "Tell your date to take you home. I'll

Sarah returns to Centerville to introduce her mother to Henry Cannon, 1947. Image courtesy of Mary Beth Pruett and Hickman County Historical Society.

follow and pick you up and bring you back here." "I can't do that!" Minnie exclaimed. But that's exactly what she did. "It was uncharacteristic of me, but I just wanted to see Henry again," she confessed. Minnie returned with Henry to Bill and Orra's apartment. It was a chilly night in December with a full moon in the sky. Outside the apartment, Henry kissed her again. Then, he declared, "Baby, after the Lord made you, he sure must have buffed his nails." Minnie reminisced, "That did it. I was hooked!"

Engagement announcement for Sarah Ophelia Colley and Henry Rolffs Cannon in a local Nashville newspaper, February 16, 1947.

By the next evening, Henry and Minnie were already discussing marriage. Henry told her that she'd have to stop touring. Baffled, she asked, "What? What do you mean?" Henry replied plainly, "Well, if we're married, you can't be out there on the road." Minnie remembered the night clearly: "I looked at him like he was crazy, and he stared back at me as sober as a judge. Then he led me down the stairs, and when we walked into the apartment together, Bill and Orra both looked like the cat that swallowed the canary." Henry announced, "We just made up our minds—we're going to get married." Orra screamed with excitement; Bill jumped out of his chair.

Minnie was stunned: "I hadn't made up my mind about anything. I said, 'Wait a minute! This is all moving too fast for me.'" She even wondered if Henry was joking: "I had heard of being swept off your feet, but this was ridiculous. . . ." When Henry took her home that night, Minnie pumped the brakes. "Look, let's not kid around about this getting married business. I don't know what to think about it," she told him. They agreed to meet at 5:00 p.m. the next day to see if they still felt the same way. The following day, Henry arrived wearing his leather air-corps flying jacket and casual slacks, a far cry from the suit and tie she

Henry and Sarah pose for a picture after their wedding on February 23, 1947, at West End Methodist Church. Instead of a traditional wedding gown, Minnie opted for a beige gabardine suit with a three-quarters length, double-breasted jacket with a brown hat, gloves, alligator shoes, and a green orchid. Image courtesy of the Grand Ole Opry Archives.

was used to seeing him in. "He was a hundred times more glamorous," Minnie said and continued, "He looked like a real pilot . . . brave and steady in the air, rough and ready on the ground, sexy! I just melted, . . . that was it!"

Minnie went home to share the news with her mother. To her dismay, Fannie Tate Colley, was very unhappy to hear about the engagement.

"At home I have a relaxed and pleasant life," said Sarah Cannon in an interview. Most nights Henry and Sarah stayed in and avoided the cocktail party circuit. However, they remained active social figures in Nashville for special events, such as the one pictured here, c. 1978. Image courtesy of the Grand Ole Opry Archives.

Minnie said with a laugh, "She thought I had lost my mind!" Fannie Tate repeatedly voiced her disapproval, arguing it wasn't socially acceptable to rush into such things. In her world, couples were expected to be formally engaged for at least six months. Henry did have one thing going for him—he was from a well-to-do family in Franklin, Fannie Tate's hometown.

When Henry arrived the next evening, Mrs. Colley was regally positioned by the fireplace. She stood upright with her chin in the air, ready to set things straight. Minnie introduced them, and Henry, in the honeyed voice of a Southern gentleman, said: "Mrs. Colley, I have heard all my life that you were one of the most beautiful ladies who ever came out of

Franklin. I know now that they were right. I've heard my family speak of you often, and they always say you were one of the most popular belles in Franklin in your day." Fannie Tate had been ready to fight, but instead Henry won her over in ninety seconds. Minnie's mother disappeared into the dining room and emerged with one of her most prized possessions—pearl-handled knives. Fannie Tate presented the knives to the couple as a wedding gift.

Less than three months after Minnie and Henry's first kiss, they headed to the altar. On February 23, 1947, they married at the West End Methodist Church. Bill Pitney served as best man, and Orra was the matron of honor. Instead of a traditional wedding gown, Minnie opted for a "beige gabardine suit with a three-quarters length, double-breasted jacket," which was the height of fashion at the time. She completed the look with a green orchid and brown accessories—hat, gloves, alligator shoes and bag. After their vows, Henry kissed his bride, and Sarah Ophelia Colley became Mrs. Henry Cannon.

Years before their marriage, Henry had developed a passion for aviation. Captivated by the romance of flying, he earned his pilot's license before the attack on Pearl Harbor and later joined the Army Air Corps. After the war, Henry and his friend Vance Burke purchased a plane for $300 and started a small charter service. Eventually, Henry partnered with another pilot to establish Capitol Airways, a private charter company. He flew a variety of aircraft, including DC-3s. Minnie commented on his career: "I thought it was the most glamorous thing in the world."

Minnie wrote, "Any man I could override would not have held my interest for long." She admired Henry's strength and decisiveness, but she also loved that he was funny. Once, while backstage at the Opry, someone asked Henry how it felt to play second-fiddle to Minnie Pearl. "I don't play a musical instrument," he said without cracking a smile. Minnie described his sense of humor: "Henry is one of the funniest men I have ever met, and it makes him even more attractive. He has a dry wit, and his timing is absolutely perfect. . . . We'll be discussing something, and he'll make one of his wry observations, and I will absolutely *fall out*."

However, the honeymoon phase didn't last long. In the months that followed, Minnie struggled to balance two very different worlds: the social circles of the Southern elite and the down-home world of country music. She tried to embrace domestic life with house chores and social visits but quickly grew bored.

Minnie and her husband, Henry, celebrate their thirtieth anniversary with a cake, 1977. Image courtesy of The Hope Powell Collection by Singleton/Curb.

After twelve years of shows on the road, Minnie had sworn off one-night performances during the week. However, she continued to perform on the Grand Ole Opry every Saturday night. Minnie didn't think she would miss traveling. Besides, Henry and Minnie wanted to start a family. Time passed without a pregnancy—months turned into years. Minnie was heartbroken: "Every time I saw a pregnant woman, I envied her so much that it was an actual physical pain, a longing I could literally feel."

After two years of trying, Minnie finally broke down. She sobbed as she explained to Henry that she feared he would love her less if they didn't have a family. He responded calmly, "If God means for us to have children, we will have them. If He doesn't, we won't." His understanding and concern for her well-being, both physically and emotionally, helped Minnie accept their situation. Reflecting on those difficult years, she said, "His attitude and unwavering support saved me."

By late 1948, Minnie's contentment to sit at home shifted to an "itch" to get back on the road. She said in an interview: "I'd make out pretty well with the solid-citizen routine all week, but the time spent in that other atmosphere (Opry) on Saturday night destroyed me. I was hungry for the camaraderie of my buddies on the road, and I missed the transient life. I wanted to go!" Henry's job made it even harder. His aviation business began to cater to music celebrities, offering charter flights that allowed performers to travel longer distances in a shorter amount of time. Not only was Minnie sitting at home, but Henry was flying all over the country. Finally, she told Henry how she felt. As always, he was supportive. "Of course you miss it. Just as I would miss flying," Henry responded.

They settled on the perfect compromise: Minnie started performing again, and Henry flew her to her engagements. Air travel was a game changer. After an Opry performance, instead of performers squeezing into a car or bus, they boarded a plane to head for Sunday matinees out west. "It opened new vistas for all of us," said Minnie. Eventually, Henry sold his stake in Capitol Airways and focused solely on flying Opry performers, which included Minnie. (See Chapter 14: A Fatal Crash, A Near Miss)

In flying with Henry, Minnie came to realize that pilots and performers have many things in common. She explained:

> Unlike the 'normal' person, whose attention to the job is spread out over an eight-hour day, a pilot's work, like a performer's, is concentrated into a shorter period of time and demands *total* concentration. . . . Then when it's over . . . when the pressure and the responsibilities are off—they usually play with as much intensity as they work.

As a new decade dawned, life was good for the Cannons. By 1950, Minnie was back to performing multiple nights a week. Moreover, Henry's list of clientele was growing, and they were able to spend more time together. Henry also became her manager, which benefitted them both.

Sarah and Henry, her handsome husband, c. 1988. Image courtesy of The Hope Powell Collection by Singleton/Curb.

"I didn't know anything about money except that I could always spend a little more than I made," Minnie bantered.

He ensured they saved and invested wisely, leaving Minnie to focus on her performances. Their relationship—in business and in life—evolved into an equal partnership built on mutual respect, love, and trust. She wrote: "Business is as natural to [Henry] as it is unnatural to me. . . . We've had an agreement all these years that has worked beautifully—he doesn't tell me what to do on stage, and I don't tell him what to do in business."

In a sense, Henry had two women in his life, Sarah Ophelia Colley Cannon and Minnie Pearl. Sarah once accused Henry of loving Minnie Pearl (the character) more than he loved her. In typical fashion, Henry answered with a witty retort, "I love you more, but if I ever change my mind, I'll let you know." Minnie Pearl continued looking for a feller, but Mrs. Sarah Colley Cannon found hers in 1947.

NOTES

Henry and Sarah Cannon were married forty-nine years before her death in 1996. Henry Cannon passed away a year and a half later, on November 8, 1997.

SOURCES

Facing the Laughter: Minnie Pearl. Directed by Barbara J. Hall. American Public Television, 2023.

Pearl, Minnie. Tape recorded memoir by Sarah Colley Cannon, Nashville, Tennessee. Tape 33, Side 1, 1979.

———. Tape recorded memoir by Sarah Colley Cannon, Nashville, Tennessee. Tape 34, Side 1, 1979.

———. Tape recorded memoir by Sarah Colley Cannon, Nashville, Tennessee. Tape 35, Side 1, 1979.

Pearl, Minnie, and Joan Dew. *Minnie Pearl: An Autobiography.* New York: Simon and Schuster, 1980.

CHAPTER 11

I'm So Lonesome I Could Cry

Hank Williams Sr. and Elvis Presley, 1944–1964

Hank Williams and Elvis Presley never met, but they are forever linked as two of the most influential performers in music history. Minnie Pearl, who knew them both, often remarked on their similarities—from their humble beginnings to the heavy burdens of fame.

Both men were born into poverty—Hank in Alabama and Elvis in Mississippi—and raised by strong-willed mothers. On stage, their natural charisma captivated audiences: Hank with his rocking movements and Elvis with his iconic hip-shaking. Raised in the South, they were deeply influenced by the region's rich musical heritage—Hank's sorrowful ballads and Elvis's electrifying mix of gospel and country. They also shared a deep appreciation for Black music, weaving the blues into their performances to create new styles and genres. Hank became the Father of Country and Western Music, while Elvis ascended as the King of Rock 'n' Roll. Yet, their paths never crossed: Hank died in 1953, and Elvis didn't perform on the Opry until 1954.

The song "I'm So Lonesome I Could Cry" is one of the strongest musical and symbolic connections between these two men. Written and recorded by Hank in 1949, the song was one of his biggest hits. Elvis, a longtime admirer of Hank, often covered "I'm So Lonesome I Could Cry"

Hank Williams in a 1948 promotional photo for WSM before his Opry debut in 1949. He received six encores after his first performance. Heath issues and substance abuse led to his untimely and early death just five years later in 1953. Williams was only twenty-nine years old. Image courtesy of the Grand Ole Opry Archives.

and eventually recorded it in 1973. The haunting melody and themes of loneliness and sorrow reflected the struggles both men endured offstage.

Minnie Pearl, who met Hank in 1944 and performed with Elvis in 1961, saw these struggles firsthand. She witnessed Hank's downward spiral on the road as his addiction worsened, and years later, she observed similar warning signs in Elvis. As someone who straddled both worlds—country music and early rock 'n' roll—Minnie's perspective offers a unique lens into the lives of these two legends, their shared fate, and the enduring legacy of their music.

Minnie Pearl's lasting fame is partly due to her connection with Hank Williams, whom she met in 1944 at a radio station in Dothan, Alabama. Minnie was with Pee Wee King for a radio promotion, and when they arrived, they found Hank and Audrey Williams waiting. Minnie remembered: "He was wearing a tan suit, boots, and a cowboy hat that was slightly soiled. He was tall, terribly thin, and hollow-eyed. He appeared to be in his early twenties." Audrey, on the other hand, was "a very attractive blonde with beautiful skin and a good figure." Hank didn't make a big impression on Minnie. "I didn't sense any greatness," she quipped. That was all about to change. Minnie said, "It wasn't long before we were all hearing about Hank Williams. When he hit, he exploded." He was the biggest thing country music had ever seen, and the fans adored his music and his charisma.

Hank signed with Acuff-Rose Publishing. His first big hit came in 1947 with "Move It On Over." A string of releases followed, culminating in "Lovesick Blues," which held the top spot on the country charts for sixteen weeks. Minnie first saw Hank Williams perform on the Louisiana Hayride tour in 1948. Henry, her husband, had flown the band out west, and Minnie tagged along. "I recognized him as the man I'd met in Dothan, but Hank was a different person," she said, continuing, "He was alert and bright-eyed, with an immaculate wardrobe and a clean white hat. He was on his way."

The following year, Hank joined the Grand Ole Opry, and Minnie watched his Opry debut from the wings. In that moment, she understood the difference between stars and superstars. She wrote:

> An excitement seemed to spread through the crowd, growing with each song. By the time he reached his last number, the excitement had grown to a fever pitch. The crowd wouldn't let him leave the stage. The rest of us might as well have stayed at the airport—especially me, who had to follow him. It was not one of my better shows. They still wanted more of Hank!

Minnie performed with Hank frequently after he joined the Opry, even touring Europe together in late 1949. The trip to Europe was organized by the William Esty Agency. Hank and Minnie were joined by other Opry stars including Red Foley, Roy Acuff, Little Jimmy Dickens, and

Time to take flight, 1949. A group of Grand Ole Opry stars prepare to travel to Europe to visit military bases in the aftermath of World War II. Little Jimmy Dickens stands in the middle with Sarah/Minnie Pearl and Hank Williams, in a white hat, on the right. Image courtesy of the Grand Ole Opry Archives.

Rod Brasfield. It was Minnie's first and only trip to Europe and included multiple stops in Germany and Austria to entertain troops stationed in US-occupied zones after World War II.

By 1949, Minnie had given up her dream of being a serious actor, but in an ironic twist, the trip gave Minnie a glimpse into that world. The Grand

Ole Opry performed at the Vienna Opera House, best known as a symbol of classical music and cultural refinement. While in Europe, they dined in restaurants "full of old-world charm" and attended elegant parties where "Strauss waltzes filled the air." It was a stark contrast to the honky-tonk tunes that emanated from the Ryman Auditorium in Nashville.

The European tour was both uplifting and exciting for Minnie, who reminisced: "I'll never forget Hank at his peak with a twinkle in his eyes . . . and his unforgettable songs." Their time abroad also confirmed for Minnie, and the rest of the group, what many at the Opry suspected—Hank had a substance abuse problem. The trip would mark the beginning of Hank's drastic descent.

Just two years later, Minnie experienced a night with Hank that she would never forget. Minnie, Hank, and Ernest Tubb were booked to play in San Diego. Tubb was running late because of car trouble, and Hank was there but in "bad shape." The promoter asked Minnie to open the show. She agreed, walked to the mic, and told jokes to stall for time. Twenty minutes later, Tubb and his band arrived and began the show, and Minnie gladly headed backstage. She recounted: "I got off just in time to see this pathetic, emaciated, haunted-looking, tragic figure of a man being assisted through the side door." Minnie couldn't believe it was Hank; she was heartbroken. In her words:

> By this time, he was killing himself with drugs and alcohol. He was a pitiful lost child to me, and I had never seen him in such bad shape as he was that day. I ran to him and hugged him. Hank threw his arms around me and clung to me, crying. I tried to comfort him, to tell him that everything was going to be all right. . . . No one will ever know what tortured dreams he had. Perhaps all of life was a bad dream to Hank.

The promoter of the show insisted that Hank perform. They gave him coffee, dunked his face in cold water, and steered him onstage. "It tore me apart to see Hank out there trying to sing . . . hanging on to the microphone for dear life. [It was] a sickening caricature of the superb, magnetic performer he was at the height of his career," Minnie lamented. After the show, the promoter asked Minnie and Audrey, Hank's wife, to drive him around "to keep an eye on him and help him sober up."

"That was the longest automobile ride I've ever had. We drove around for a couple of hours, and Hank was really hurting, his body craving help," Minnie remembered. Rocking back and forth, Hank sat in the car—hunched over with his arms crossed tightly over his stomach. Minnie tried

Elvis Presley with his longtime backup group The Jordanaires, March 1957. The Jordanaires recorded, toured, and made television appearances with Elvis, which included the Pearl Harbor Memorial concert in 1961. Press Department, Capitol Records. Public domain, via Wikimedia Commons.

to lift his spirits, saying, "Come on, Hank. Let's sing." She started singing "I Saw the Light." Hank joined in, but his voice cracked and faltered. Suddenly, he stopped, put his hand on hers, and said, "That's just it, Minnie. There ain't no light. It's all dark." Hank Williams died six months later, on January 1, 1953, at the age of twenty-nine. "His body was just worn out from whiskey and pills," Minnie said with a sigh.

A year and a half later, in 1954, Elvis made his first and only appearance on the Grand Ole Opry. Despite having a breakout hit with "That's Alright Mama," the emcee couldn't even remember his name—introducing him to the stage as "a young man from Memphis." Alongside his bandmates, guitarist Scotty Moore, and bass player Bill Black, Elvis played just one song—Bill Monroe's "Blue Moon of Kentucky." Sam Phillips, owner of Sun Records, had lobbied Jim Denny, the Opry's manager, to get Elvis on the show. Elvis had hoped to join the Opry, but Denny wasn't a fan

Elvis Presley and a roomful of other young men being sworn into the US Army as part of their induction at Fort Chaffee, Arkansas, March 24, 1958. His army service later inspired Elvis to commit to raising funds for the memorial at Pearl Harbor. Associated Press/Standard-Sentinel March 25, 1958, page 1, Public domain, via Wikimedia Commons.

of his music or performance style. After a brief but tense conversation, Elvis returned home.

Months later, Elvis joined the Louisiana Hayride show (another common link with Hank), based in Shreveport. The show was similar to the Grand Ole Opry: live radio broadcasts every Saturday and performances on the road during the week. For Elvis, those two years were instrumental in developing his sound—a fusion of rhythm and blues with country and western influences that evolved into rockabilly and, eventually, rock 'n' roll. His music featured a driving rhythm with a strong backbeat and raw, dynamic vocals. The electric guitar and upright bass enhanced the energy, while his sexual charisma helped transform rock 'n' roll into a cultural movement.

Raised in Memphis, Elvis grew up listening to country music on the radio, including Hank Williams and the Grand Ole Opry. Like Hank,

Elvis Presley (center), Minnie Pearl (far left) are transported from the Honolulu airport to the Naval Airbase at Pearl Harbor, March 25, 1961. Photo courtesy of Flickr.

Elvis had a powerful connection with fans, though his musical style and physicality on stage set him apart. In 1956, the Opry dismissed several members who failed to meet the required twenty-six performances per year. As a result of this controversial decision, Minnie chose to take a "temporary leave of absence" from the Opry. That same year, Elvis "exploded onto the scene," selling ten million records.

By 1961, Elvis was the biggest celebrity in the United States, if not the world. That same year, Minnie received an unexpected phone call from Colonel Tom Parker, Elvis's manager. Parker, who had booked Minnie during the 1950s, invited her to accompany Elvis to Hawaii for a charity event aimed at raising $50,000 to construct a memorial over the sunken USS Arizona. The cause was particularly meaningful to Elvis, who had served in the US Army from 1958 to 1960. It was also close to Minnie's heart due to her time with the Camel Caravan. The troupe had performed for US troops after the bombing of Pearl Harbor.

The fundraiser was set for March 25, 1961. Minnie and Henry flew to Los Angeles to join Elvis and the other performers before flying to Ho-

Fans at the airport bury Elvis in Hawaiian lays, Colonel Parker stands behind him on the right, March 25, 1961. Photo courtesy of Flickr.

nolulu. Minnie was impressed: "He had such good manners. Elvis said 'Yes, sir' and 'Yes, ma'am' to everyone, even if they were just a few years older, and he treated Henry and me with the greatest respect. I remember marveling that his wealth and status as a worldwide superstar had not gone to his head." She also couldn't help but notice how different he seemed from the man she had seen on stage. "He had a quiet, almost shy, personality," Minnie recalled.

Upon landing, the flight attendant asked Elvis to stay behind while the other passengers deplaned. Elvis looked out to see five thousand fans screaming at the runway fence. Minnie asked, "How do you stand it?" Elvis replied, "Oh, I'm used to it now." As she watched him gaze out the plane window, Minnie thought back to Hank Williams and the pressures both men endured. "How could anyone live with it?" she wondered.

Before the show, Colonel Parker asked Minnie to "stay close to Elvis" for the publicity shots. She noticed Elvis seemed nervous: "He looked like a zombie—resigned, deadpan, expressionless." She saw something else in Elvis on the trip—the same weary eyes she had seen in Hank Williams.

Concert flyer for the March 25, 1961 benefit concert at Bloch Arena, Pearl Harbor. The show featured Elvis but opening acts included Minnie Pearl, "The Pride of Grinder's Switch," as well as The Jordanaires, D.J. Fontana, and Scotty Moore. With 4,000 people in attendance, Elvis opened the show with "Heartbreak Hotel." The concert raised over $60,000 with a $5,000 personal contribution from Elvis. This was his first show in three years after serving in the US Army from 1958 to 1960. He stayed in Hawaii after the concert to film *Blue Hawaii*. Image courtesy of the US Naval Institute News.

Elvis Presley at the press conference before his benefit concert in Honolulu on March 25, 1961. Minnie Pearl sits behind him at the table. Photo courtesy of Flickr.

In fact, by this time, Elvis was addicted to a cocktail mix of narcotics—amphetamines to keep him awake and sedatives and painkillers to help him sleep. Unlike Hank, however, Elvis managed to keep performing, his addiction largely hidden from the public for much of his career.

On the night of the concert, Honolulu's Bloch Arena was packed with over 4,000 fans. Minnie performed her comedy act before Elvis took the stage. As she headed backstage, the standing-room-only crowd erupted, and she witnessed the "Presley charisma" in full force. Laughing, she said, "The rest of us might as well have stayed home."

The concert exceeded its $50,000 goal, raising more than $60,000. For once, Minnie was glad not to be the center of attention. She was famous, but Elvis was on a another level. She admired him but also felt sorry for

Carter Family promotional portrait, 1927. From left to right: Maybelle, A. P., and Sara Carter. By 1929, Victor had sold over a hundred thousand copies of "Wildwood Flowers" and "Keep on the Sunny Side." Victor Talking Machine Company.

Originating from southwest Virginia, the trio included A. P. Carter, his wife Sara, and his sister-in-law Maybelle Carter. Their first recording, "Bury Me Under the Weeping Willow," was made for Victor Records in 1927, two years before June was born. Throughout the 1930s, June and her sisters often accompanied the family on tour. Reflecting on her childhood, June later wrote, "As a child, I didn't realize the Carters were special people. To me, they were always plain Mother, Aunt Sara, and Uncle Doc (A. P.)."

In 1940, the original Carter Family trio disbanded, and Maybelle turned to her daughters—June, Helen, and Anita—to form a new group, "The Carter Sisters and Mother Maybelle." Anita had a beautiful voice, could yodel, and stood on a chair to play the upright bass, while Helen harmonized and played guitar and accordion. Though not as musically gifted

From left to right, Minnie Pearl, Ernest Tubb, and June Carter pose for "Classic Country: Grand Ole Opry Stars of the Fifties," 1997. Image courtesy of the author.

as her sisters, June's mother taught her to play the autoharp. June wrote: "There was no way I could play like my mother. I flung the picks hard at those strings—plucked, jumped, tore into that autoharp like I was driving a truck. But Mother was always gentle, always kind."

June looked for other ways to contribute, noting, "When you don't have much of a voice . . . you pick something you can use. In my case, it was just plain guts. I talked a lot and tried to cover up all the bad notes with laughter." Audiences were receptive to June as the "funny girl," and she began dreaming of a professional career as a comedian. It was, in fact, her ambition to be the "funny girl" that led her to Minnie Pearl.

In 1940, while on tour, the Carters performed in Birmingham as part of a showcase that also featured Minnie Pearl. Before their rehearsal,

June Carter and Minnie Pearl enjoy a playful moment backstage as June helps Minnie with her hat before a show at the Ryman Auditorium. Minnie was invited to join the Opry cast in 1940, and June joined the Opry a decade later in 1950. These two women were friends, leading figures on the Grand Ole Opry, and fellow comedians, c. 1953. Image courtesy of the Grand Ole Opry Archives.

Maybelle sought out Minnie to introduce her eleven-year-old daughter, June. Minnie recalled the encounter vividly:

> I was in the dressing room before a show in Birmingham, and this lovely, beautiful lady came in. It was Mother Maybelle, and she had brought June who was cute as she could be. Maybelle said, "I want you to hear this child, she can imitate you exactly." And June started in, "Howdy! I'm just so proud to be here." Maybelle asked, "Do you think I oughta . . . let her imitate you?" I said, "No, let her get an entirely different act. She's too good to do an imitation, . . . and I want her to have her own career." I looked at June and said, "Always be yourself. Be an individual."

June Carter, a celebrated member of the Carter Family and regular performer at the Grand Ole Opry, shared the stage and a deep camaraderie with Minnie Pearl. Both iconic women brought humor and heart to the Opry, cementing their legacies as beloved entertainers in country music history. Image courtesy of the Grand Ole Opry Archives.

Later that afternoon, Minnie watched June rehearse and immediately recognized her potential: "[June] was a born actress, a born performer. It didn't take any great insight to see that this girl had enormous talent as a comic." From June's perspective, she deeply valued Minnie's opinion and took her advice to heart: "After our meeting, I went home to the

Johnny Cash and June Carter Cash were married in 1968. Pictured here in *LOOK Magazine*, April 29, 1969. Joel Baldwin, Public domain, via Wikimedia Commons.

valley and started dreaming new dreams." But Minnie's mentorship was far from over. June later wrote:

> The week after I talked with her, Cousin Minnie sent me a letter. That was the most wonderful thing that could happen to a little girl who had dreams of being a great entertainer. . . . I felt very special because she had taken the time to write to me when she was such a big Opry star.

By 1946, June had developed her own original comedy routine as the hilarious "Aunt Polly." Four years later, the Carter Sisters and Mother Maybelle officially joined the Grand Ole Opry. At the time, June was twenty-one, and Minnie Pearl was thirty-eight. Despite the shared spotlight, there was no rivalry between them. Minnie reflected, "We never had any problems about being jealous or envious . . . And yet, at the same time, June challenged me in a way."

Minnie Pearl with Johnny Cash on stage as part of the 50th anniversary of the Grand Ole Opry celebration in 1975. Image courtesy of The Hope Powell Collection by Singleton/Curb.

A little healthy competition was just what Minnie needed. She admitted, "At that time, in the early 50s . . . I thought I was doing great and had the country comedian thing all tied up." Then, one night, Minnie was in Nebraska on tour, which meant she had to miss the live Opry broadcast. It served as a wakeup call. Minnie recalled vividly:

> We were way out in Stockton, Nebraska, and I heard June come on. We had the radio turned on in the car . . . I said, "Uh-oh, I'd better get home. That

Minnie Pearl with June Carter Cash delight the audience with two "Minnie Pearl" acts, c. 1975. It was reminiscent of the way they met in 1950. When June was eleven-years old, Maybelle Carter introduced June to Minnie who did a "perfect imitation" of Minnie Pearl. Image courtesy of The Hope Powell Collection by Singleton/Curb.

> girl is going to take it away from me, and I mean soon!" Cause she was really good. She was hilarious, and the audience obviously loved her. She had that audience rolled. When that happened, I was reminded of my father when he used to say, "Don't ever think you can't be replaced."

June Carter didn't replace Minnie Pearl as the reigning country comic, but Minnie admitted, "[June] kept me on my toes without knowing it."

Minnie on stage with June Carter Cash at the Country Music Awards, c. 1977.
Image courtesy of The Hope Powell Collection by Singleton/Curb.

Throughout the 1950s, the two women often shared the Opry stage and toured together extensively, forging a relationship built on affection and collaboration. June often spoke about the joy of "clowning around" with Minnie during spontaneous onstage moments and admired her kind-hearted humor. "She could make people laugh without ever being mean-spirited," June said.

Five years after Minnie and June joined forces, Johnny Cash made his breakthrough in 1955 with the release of his first single, "Cry! Cry! Cry!"

The following year, Minnie met Johnny after his debut performance on the Opry. She was instantly drawn to his voice and unique style. By that time, Minnie had been an Opry fixture for sixteen years, but she welcomed Johnny like "he was kin." Johnny's serious, brooding image sometimes intimidated other performers—but not Minnie. During one live broadcast, she teased: "Why don't you ever wear anything but black?" Cash, with a grin, replied, "I'm saving all the color for your jokes, Minnie!"

By the 1960s, Johnny Cash was battling the demons of drugs and alcohol. During one Opry rehearsal, Minnie noticed he seemed distant and withdrawn. Hoping to lighten the mood, she tugged at his coat and quipped, "Johnny, I think if you wore a brighter suit, we might be able to see you without a flashlight!" Cash couldn't help but laugh.

Meanwhile, Johnny and June's story began on that same fateful Opry night in 1956. Their connection was instant, but their relationship faced a significant obstacle—both were married to others at the time. Complicating matters further, Johnny's drug use was spiraling. After leaving the Opry in 1965, he hit rock bottom. During this dark period, June stood by him, helping Johnny overcome his addiction. Their love story culminated in their 1968 marriage, and they remained deeply devoted to one another for the next 35 years. Decades later, Johnny wrote to June: "You still fascinate and inspire me. You influence me for the better. You're the object of my desire, the #1 Earthly reason for my existence."

Though his bond with June defined his personal life, Johnny's friendship with Minnie Pearl was another source of camaraderie throughout his career. In 1972, Johnny appeared on *The Glen Campbell Goodtime Hour*, where Campbell delighted him with a surprise guest: Minnie Pearl. Cash responded, "You mean the Nashville sexpot is here?"

As Minnie walked out on stage, an all-male dance troupe, dressed in tuxedos, serenaded her with a song: "From the top of her bonnet to the tip of her boot, there's only one description, the lady is cute. She's eager and willing and loaded with class. If you'll pardon the expression, the lady's a gas! Now, it's time to introduce you to our favorite girl—here from Nashville—Miss Minnie Pearl!" After her routine, which included a joke about loving New York subways because "that's where a girl could get a feller to carry her purse," even Johnny couldn't stop chuckling.

Minnie, June, and Johnny were truly kindred spirits who, individually and collectively, shaped generations through their storytelling and music. Minnie passed away in 1996, while Johnny and June died just months apart in 2003. Yet, in a fitting twist, these two beloved female comedians let Johnny Cash get the last laugh.

In 2014, Cash posthumously released *Out Among the Stars*, often referred to as the "Lost Album." One of its tracks, recorded in the mid-1980s, is a playful tribute delivered in the "Talking Blues" style about meeting a girl in Nashville. The lyrics unfold like an inside joke about Johnny's love for the "funny woman" at the Opry. At first, the audience assumes the song is about June—but keep listening. (Lyrics courtesy of the Johnny Cash Trust.)

"IF I TOLD YOU WHO IT WAS"

I was down in Music City 'bout a week ago
I wanted to see the Grand Ole Opry show,
So I hailed a cab and I headed down to Opryland
They said they sold their last ticket the day before,
So I kinda just hung around the backstage door
And down the steps she came, man oh man

My favorite female country star,
She waved to her fans and headed for her car
Her tire, unlike her body, was very flat
She said, "Could you change my tire?"
I said, "Your wish is my desire."
As she raised the lid, I grabbed her bumper jack
She said, "I sure do appreciate ya changing my tire."

Chorus:
If I told you who it was, if I told you who it was
You'd say I was making it up
You've seen her on the screen and in country magazines
You'd think I was making it up
She said it was our little secret and by golly, I'm gonna keep it
Anyway you wouldn't believe it if I told you who it was

She said, "You need a lift?" and I said, "Well,
You can drop me off at the York Motel,"
So we headed down Briley Parkway into town
I told her, "I got all your records, ma'am,"
She smiled and said, "Well I'll be damned.
Say, you're kind of cute, fella, wanna mess around?"

When we got to my room, just to be polite
I said, "Sure wish I could've heard you sing tonight."
She smiled at me and said, "Whatcha wanna hear?"
Now if I was one of them country music folks

I tell you, she'd sure get my vote
For the best performance of the year

Chorus:
If I told you who it was, if I told you who it was
You'd say I was making it up
You've seen her on the screen and in country magazines
You'd think I was making it up
She said it was our little secret and by golly, I'm gonna keep it
Anyway you wouldn't believe it if I told you who it was

Well, I'll tell you this much:
When I put my arms around her and squeezed her real tight
She looked up at me with those big, beautiful eyes,
Took a deep breath, and then sighed, and said . . .
[Minnie Pearl in her own voice] "Howdy! I'm just so proud to be here!"

Chorus:
If I told you who it was, if I told you who it was
You'd say I was making it up
You've seen her on the screen and in country magazines
You'd think I was making it up
She said it was our little secret and by golly, I'm gonna keep it
Anyway you wouldn't believe it if I told you who it was.

NOTES

Listen to the song on the @johnnycash YouTube channel using the search term, "Johnny Cash—If I Told You Who It Was."

During *The Johnny Cash Show's* three-year run (1969–1971), Minnie Pearl made several memorable appearances.

In the 1970s and 1980s, Minnie took several female performers under her wing. These women, and more, were mentored by Pearl and formed lasting friendships with the comic icon. See the last chapter, "Star-Studded Memories."

In 1988, Johnny Cash, alongside Roy Acuff, presented Minnie Pearl with the American Academy of Achievement's Golden Plate Award in 1988.

SOURCES

Cash, John Carter. *Anchored in Love: An Intimate Portrait of June Carter Cash.* Nashville, TN: Thomas Nelson, 2007.

Cash, Johnny. "If I Told You Who It Was." Posted *March 20, 2016, by Johnny Cash Official, YouTube video. https://youtu.be/MUxQI1PNrD8?si=u92voQgoUG_JiOdy*

Cash, June Carter. *Among My Klediments.* Grand Rapids, MI: Zondervan Publishing House, 1979.

Cooper, Peter. "Johnny Cash Album Makes Writers Thank 'Stars.'" *Tennessean,* March 27, 2014. https://www.tennessean.com/story/entertainment/music/peter-cooper/2014/03/26/johnny-cash-lost-album-bobby-braddock/6926445/.

Duncan, Dayton, Julie Dunfey, Peter Coyote, Buddy Squires, Florentine Films, and WETA-TV (Washington, DC). *Country Music*. Edited by Erik Ewers, Craig Mellish, Ryan Gifford, and Margaret Shepardson-Legere. Directed by Ken Burns. PBS, 2019.

"Johnny Cash, Minnie Pearl, & Glen Campbell." *The Glen Campbell Goodtime Hour*, January 11, 1972.

Pearl, Minnie. Tape recorded memoir by Sarah Colley Cannon, Nashville, Tennessee. Tape 2, Side A, 1979.

Pearl, Minnie, and Joan Dew. *Minnie Pearl: An Autobiography.* New York: Simon & Schuster, 1980.

THREE

Beyond the Opry, 1958–1996

CHAPTER 13

Country Music and Southern Politics

Jim Crow, Music Row, and Civil Rights, 1958–1974

Country music has long had a complicated relationship with race, class, and politics. Even before the genre emerged, the term "Jim Crow" originated in the 1820s from a blackface minstrel character performed by Thomas Dartmouth Rice. This racist portrayal became the namesake for Jim Crow laws.

It's no coincidence, then, that the first major country music hit—Fiddlin' John Carson's 1923 recording of "Little Old Log Cabin Down the Lane"—romanticized the antebellum South. A Georgia native, Carson performed at political events with Tom Carter and Eugene Talmadge as well as at Ku Klux Klan rallies. His popularity grew in tandem with the rise of Southern populism, which codified segregation and disenfranchised Black voters in the twentieth century.

The country music audience was predominantly White and working-class, which historian Nancy Isenberg described as "a group long aggrieved." After the Civil War and the passage of the 13th, 14th, and 15th Amendments, Isenberg argues, working-class Whites viewed newly freed Black laborers as a threat to their social status and economic opportunity. Both groups were mostly uneducated and lacked access to capital, leading poor Whites to tie their identity more closely to race as a means of leveraging socioeconomic and political power.

Advertisement for George Wallace rally on April 12, 1958, in his bid for the Democratic party nomination for Alabama governor. Minnie Pearl warmed up the crowd before Wallace delivered his campaign stump speech. Wallace was defeated by Democrat John Patterson who went on to become Alabama's 44th governor, serving from 1959 to 1963. Source: *Advertiser-Gleam*.

In particular, Southern states used Jim Crow laws to reinforce this racial hierarchy, bolstered by the US Supreme Court's 1896 decision in *Plessy v. Ferguson*, which established the doctrine of "separate but equal." This ruling legitimized the Southern states' efforts to circumvent constitutional amendments and federal legislation, including the Civil Rights Act of 1866. During the Jim Crow era, a combination of legal statutes and extralegal practices systematically denied African Americans their basic human and civil rights.

Even after World War II, advocating for civil rights was a losing proposition for White politicians in the South. In Alabama, George Wallace, initially a "moderate" on racial issues, learned this hard truth when he lost the 1958 primary to John Patterson. Patterson's openly racist platform outmatched Wallace's more "restrained" stance. Renowned civil rights attorney Arthur Shores explained: "[Wallace] was viewed as somewhat liberal at that time. When he ran against Patterson, there were relatively no Black votes that amounted to anything, and the candidate who could holler 'n-----' the loudest was elected. Patterson just outdid Wallace on that score." After the 1958 primary defeat, Wallace declared he had been "out-segged" (out-segregated) and vowed it would not happen again.

This political and cultural landscape helps explain why Minnie Pearl, despite her apolitical comedic persona, chose to work for Wallace's campaign in 1958 and later supported his presidential bid. Her involvement was unsurprising given her predominantly White, blue-collar fan base. Yet, her participation wasn't purely ideological—it was also financially motivated. Earning $12,000 for personal appearances ($135,000 in 2025), Minnie opened Wallace's rallies with her signature humor and began each performance with her famous line, "Howdy! I'm just so proud to be here!" Her act was light-hearted and largely avoided Wallace's platform, as shown in this excerpt:

> I'm having a big time here with Judge Wallace and all of his fine folks. You know up at Grinder's Switch . . . my Uncle Nabob, I saw him run for several things. In fact, the last time I seen him he was running for the edge of town—had the whole town behind him! Well, I'll tell you this, he run for office of constable just last year. He was talking to a friend and said, "I'd like mighty well for you to vote for me." The friend told him, "Why listen to me, I wouldn't vote for you if you were St. Peter hisself!" Uncle Nabob said, "If I was St. Peter, you couldn't vote for me 'cause you wouldn't be in my district!"

Using country music celebrities to attract voters was not unique to the Wallace campaign. In Arkansas, Thomas Barton hired Minnie Pearl, Eddy Arnold, and Uncle Dave Macon to appear at five rallies when he ran for the US Senate. (He lost.) In Tennessee, Estes Kefauver's campaign for the US Senate hired Minnie Pearl, George Morgan, and Hank Fort to perform at rallies in Tennessee. (He won.) In Alabama, Big Jim Folsom formed a country group, the Strawberry Pickers, to perform during his campaign rallies.

Whether Pearl's support for Wallace was driven by personal belief, political expediency, or financial gain is difficult to untangle. Likely, it was a combination of all three. Historian Dan T. Carter remarked, "George Wallace believed what he believed at the moment and believed it vehemently." Like Wallace, Pearl may have been motivated by pragmatism, but there were also real-life consequences. Moreover, there was nothing light-hearted about the violence taking place in Alabama.

Martin Luther King, Jr. delivering his "How Long, Not Long" speech in Montgomery, Alabama on March 25, 1965. Image: Social Studies for Kids.

In 1962, Wallace won the governorship, having embraced racist rhetoric. In his inaugural address he infamously declared: "Segregation now! Segregation tomorrow! Segregation forever!" Months later, Governor Wallace physically blocked the entrance to the University of Alabama to prevent the enrollment of two Black students. Martin Luther King Jr. said of Wallace: "I am not sure that he believes all the poison that he preaches, but he is artful enough to convince others that he does." Wallace's biographer, Dan Carter, concurred, writing: "Wallace was a political demagogue who manipulated the fears and racial anxieties of working-class Whites, not to improve their condition, but to gain personal power and influence."

Historian Taylor Branch described the emotional fervor Wallace harnessed in *Parting the Waters: America in the King Years 1954–1963*, noting:

> The lines had been drawn, and segregation now meant more than separate facilities. It was a personal and political creed, a fierce line of demarcation between old Southern customs and the threat of Federal intrusion and Black demands for equality. Politicians like George Wallace tapped into this raw current of resentment, promising to . . . defy all challenges to white supremacy, no matter the cost to national unity or common decency.

In stark contrast to Wallace's defiant stand at the University of Alabama in 1963, Dr. King delivered his historic "I Have a Dream" speech that same year in Washington DC. King envisioned a future of racial harmony, where his children would be judged "not by the color of their skin, but by the content of their character." As the epicenter of the civil rights struggle, Alabama became the stage for these opposing forces. Montgomery, the state capital, was not only the birthplace of the bus boycott but also home to the Dexter Avenue Baptist Church, where King served as pastor. This ideological clash between Wallace and King reached a breaking point in 1965 during the events of Bloody Sunday.

On March 7, civil rights activists, including John Lewis, attempted to march peacefully from Selma to Montgomery to demand voting rights. As they crossed the Edmund Pettus Bridge in Selma, marchers were met with brutal violence from state troopers. Bloody Sunday sparked national outrage, with images and footage of the violence dominating news coverage. Despite Wallace's efforts to stop the march, the activists regrouped and returned. On their third attempt, they successfully completed the fifty-four-mile walk to Montgomery.

They arrived in Montgomery on March 25, 1965. The Reverend Martin Luther King Junior addressed a crowd of approximately 25,000 gathered on Dexter Avenue just steps away from the State Capitol building. He said, in part:

> They told us we wouldn't get here. And there were those who said that we would get here only over their dead bodies, but all the world today knows that we are here, and we are standing before the forces of power in the state of Alabama saying, "We ain't goin' let nobody turn us around." . . . If the worst in American life lurked in [Selma's] dark streets, the best of American instincts arose passionately from across the nation to overcome it.

Less than five months after the march from Selma to Montgomery, on August 6, 1965, President Johnson signed the Voting Rights Act. The bill was meant to address a "clear and simple wrong," Johnson asserted, and its purpose was "to right that wrong" following the "outrage of Selma."

Following an assassination attempt in May 1972, George Wallace was visited in the hospital by Congresswoman Shirley Chisholm, despite their ideological differences. She also ran in the Democratic primary for the 1972 presidential election. Though Wallace won two state primaries after the shooting, the attack effectively ended his campaign. He later addressed the Democratic National Convention from his wheelchair in July 1972 in Miami Beach, Florida. Visible at convention were signs for both Chisholm and Wallace. He remained paralyzed from the waist down for the remainder of his life. Image courtesy of Library of Congress, U.S. News & World Report Magazine Photograph Collection.

Wallace complained that the legislation was an overreach by the federal government and a threat to states' rights. However, rather than stepping away from politics, he shifted his ambitions from the state level to the national stage.

In 1968, George Wallace ran for President of the United States as the nominee of the American Independent Party. His appeal reached beyond the South, as noted by historian Howard Zinn. In *The People's History of the United States*, Zinn wrote: "George Wallace expressed the deepest reactionary sentiments of millions of White Americans, denouncing the federal government . . . and appealing to working-class Whites' fear of losing their status in a rapidly changing society."

"Reactionary sentiments" were ripe for the picking in Nashville. As author Paul Hemphill noted in *The Nashville Sound*, "Music Row was practically a battlefield command post for George Wallace in 1968." Supporters included Hank Snow, Grandpa Jones, Ferlin Huskey, George Morgan, Hank Thompson, the Wilburn Brothers, Billy Walker, and Minnie Pearl. (Roy Acuff endorsed Richard Nixon.) Wallace's populist promise to "throw the briefcases of Washington bureaucrats into the Potomac River," resonated with those in the country music world who felt overlooked by the political establishment and dismissed by cultural elites.

Wallace was also part of a broader shift in party politics as the South switched from solidly Democratic to Republican in the 1960s and 1970s (except for Democrat Jimmy Carter). Historian Alvin Impson wrote:

> George Wallace was not the only candidate willing to resort to demagoguery in the 1968 presidential election. In some ways Wallace might well be compared to Richard Nixon, whose meteoric rise through California politics mirrors Wallace's in Alabama. Wallace staked his career on the race issue; Richard Nixon built his on communism. The views of both changed over time to fit with political expediency. . . . Neither would let ideology stand in the way of winning an election.

As the votes in the 1968 presidential election were counted, Wallace's anti-establishment message garnered him 13.5 percent of the popular vote. He also won the electoral college in five states (GA, AL, MS, LA, AR). However, in the end, Republican Richard Nixon's "Southern Strategy" attracted enough White voters to win the election over Democrat Hubert Humphrey.

George Wallace returned to Alabama and was reelected governor in 1970. Grover Hall Jr., former editor of the *Montgomery Advertiser*, was once asked why Wallace continued running for office despite the changing mood of the country. Hall responded: "What makes the mockingbird fly? The mockingbird is the brassiest, sassiest, fightingest bird in the garden. He'll take on anything twice his size. He'll drive a bluejay crazy just for the hell of it. Nothing scares him . . . God made the mockingbird. And

Shirley Chisholm, a New York Congresswoman, was the first Black woman in Congress (1968–1972) and the first African American woman to run for president, declaring her candidacy on January 25, 1972. Her campaign slogan was "Unbought and Unbossed." After rival George Wallace survived an assassination attempt, Chisholm visited him in the hospital. Pictured here, she speaks at the 1972 Democratic National Convention in Miami Beach, where George McGovern became the Democratic nominee but lost to Richard Nixon. Image courtesy of the Library of Congress, U.S. News & World Report Magazine Photograph Collection.

God made George Wallace." Historian Alvin Impson offered a similar perspective, describing Wallace as a political survivor: "Wallace was not overly concerned about pursuing a particular agenda. . . . [He] focused his attention on how to exploit a problem rather than on realistic, concrete solutions."

In 1972, while serving as governor, Wallace launched another bid for the presidency. His campaign, however, took a surprising turn in May at a rally in Laurel, Maryland. While speaking, he was shot and severely wounded. During his recovery, Wallace was visited by an unlikely rival, Congresswoman Shirley Chisholm—the first Black woman to serve in Congress. Chisholm was also running in the Democratic primary in an attempt to shake up national politics. The visit lasted for fifteen minutes. Chisholm told Wallace that she, too, had survived an attack and believed God had spared her for a higher purpose. As author Adam Nicholas Phillips observed, "With profound empathy, she urged Wallace to see his survival as an opportunity to 'be more than what you were.'"

Permanently paralyzed from the waist down, Wallace's injury marked a turning point in his career. His daughter later called the assassination attempt a "real awakening." This event also marked a shift in Wallace's career, which coincided with another political reality: Black voters had become a crucial part of Alabama's electorate.

In 1974, he ran for a third term (and a fourth term in 1982). In these campaigns, Wallace began reaching out to Black voters and toned down his segregationist message. He also expressed regret for past actions, eventually stating: "I was wrong. Those days are over. . . . I've learned what pain is, and I'm sorry for any pain that I've caused." In his final two terms, Wallace publicly asked for forgiveness and appointed 160+ African Americans to state governing boards and commissions. Despite his contrition, Wallace remains one of the most despised antagonists of the Civil Rights era.

Meanwhile, 1974 also marked a pivotal moment for country music. That year, the Grand Ole Opry relocated from the historic Ryman Auditorium in downtown Nashville to a state-of-the-art venue off Briley Parkway. The move addressed longstanding issues at the Ryman, including cramped dressing rooms, a leaky roof, and the lack of central heating and air conditioning. It was uncomfortable for both audiences and entertainers. The new auditorium debuted on March 16, 1974, with a show attended by President Richard Nixon and Governor George Wallace.

THE TENNESSEAN

Second Class Postage Paid at Nashville, Tenn.

NASHVILLE, TENN., MONDAY, MARCH 11, 1974

10 CENTS

Arab Meet Flounders, Postponed

From Wire Reports

CAIRO — A meeting of Arab oil ministers called by Egypt to consider lifting the oil embargo on the United States floundered here yesterday and was postponed until Wednesday in Tripoli, Libya.

The representatives of only six of the nine Arab countries that originally imposed the embargo last Oct. 17 showed up here, and they decided that nothing could be done without the other three.

THE THREE absentees were Algeria, Libya and Syria, which have indicated resistance to a lifting of the embargo and oil production cutbacks before more evidence of progress is seen on Israeli withdrawal from the occupied Golan Heights.

President Anwar el-Sadat of Egypt has said that the embargo should be lifted in view of the U.S. efforts that brought about military disengagement of Israeli and Egyptian forces on the Sinai front.

Ahmed Zaki Yamani, the Saudi Arabian oil minister, who came here for the meeting, has been quoted in recent press interviews as saying that the embargo no longer served a useful purpose and should be ended.

HOWEVER, YAMANI told reporters here yesterday that "there cannot be a meeting of the Arab oil ministers without the Algerians."

The change of the site to Libya restored the conference to where it was to have been held originally, according to an invitation that had been

(Turn to Page 6, Column 3)

—Staff photo by Jerry Bailey

Like Leaving an Old Friend

Minnie Pearl tries to cover the tears she sheds for the "ghosts" of Ryman Auditorium while Roy Acuff offers words of explanation to the audience during the last Saturday night Grand Ole Opry in the old building.

It Was Nearly Routine...'Til Minnie Cried

Nixon I
Fraud H
—News

NEW YORK (AP) — President Nixon's 1969 income tax return is the subject of a criminal fraud investigation by the Internal Revenue Service, Newsweek magazine reported yesterday.

Quoting unnamed sources, the magazine said that "in recent weeks, IRS special intelligence agents, who do only criminal investigations, have interviewed Edward L. Morgan, a onetime White House aide; Arthur Blech, Mr. Nixon's personal accountant, and Frank DeMarco, the President's former tax lawyer."

"THE KEY question," Newsweek said, "is whether a fraudulent deed to Mr. Nixon's vice presidential papers was drawn up in the spring of 1970 to make it appear that he had actually given the papers to the archives one year earlier—before congressional legislation outlawed deductions for such gifts."

Nixon claimed a $576,000 deduction for donating the papers to the National Archives.

The magazine said DeMarco has testified "he had a new deed typed up and had Morgan sign it on the President's behalf in April 1970, but he insists that the new version was only a copy of an original he drew up the year before."

THE 1969 document has not been produced, however,

After forty-three years at Ryman Auditorium, the Grand Ole Opry's last night at the Ryman was an emotional affair for many. The article shows Roy Acuff and Minnie Pearl, in tears, onstage. The headline reads: "It Was Nearly Routine . . . 'Til Minnie Cried." In 1974, the Grand Ole Opry moved to a new complex near Nashville's airport, *Tennessean*, March 11, 1974.

Nixon even joined Roy Acuff on stage to sing "Happy Birthday" to the First Lady, Pat Nixon. George Wallace sat in the front row. Seated right beside him was Minnie Pearl.

Minnie Pearl's association with Wallace in the 1950s and 1960s reflects and highlights the complex interplay of politics, race, class, and country

Minnie Pearl bowls with Nashville Mayor Ben West at an event, 1956. West served as Nashville's mayor during a pivotal period from 1951 to 1963. He was in office during the Civil Rights Sit-Ins in 1960 and helped to make Nashville's downtown the first southern city to desegregate lunch counters. He also led the effort to combine city and county governments into a single Metro government, which began in 1963. Image courtesy of the Nashville Public Library Metro Nashville Archives.

music in mid-century America. For Wallace, Minnie's support helped him connect with Southern White voters, many of whom were fans of the Grand Ole Opry. For Minnie, her complicity and involvement with Wallace, placed in context, reveals the power of money and the pressure to remain relevant in a region with deeply ingrained social and cultural dynamics.

NOTES

In 1965, activists made three attempts to march from Selma to Montgomery:

MARCH 7, 1965 (BLOODY SUNDAY): The first attempt was met with brutal violence by state troopers and local law enforcement as marchers crossed the Edmund Pettus Bridge. This day became known as Bloody Sunday.

MARCH 9, 1965 (TURNAROUND TUESDAY): The second attempt, led by Martin Luther King Jr., was a symbolic march that stopped at the bridge after King decided to turn the marchers back, waiting for federal court approval to proceed.

MARCH 21-25, 1965: The third and final march, protected by federalized National Guard troops, successfully reached Montgomery. On March 25, Martin Luther King Jr. delivered his famous speech on the steps of the Alabama State Capitol.

Martin Luther King Jr. was assassinated on April 4, 1968. He was shot while standing on the balcony of the Lorraine Motel in Memphis, Tennessee, by James Earl Ray, a fugitive who had escaped from prison the year before. King was in Memphis to support a sanitation workers' strike. Rushed to the hospital, Dr. King was pronounced dead an hour later at the age of thirty-nine.

George Wallace died on September 13, 1998, at the age of seventy-nine. He passed away in Montgomery, Alabama, due to complications from septic shock, which resulted from a bacterial infection. Wallace had been in poor health for years, due to the lasting effects of the assassination attempt on him in 1972, which left him paralyzed from the waist down and using a wheelchair for the remainder of his life.

SOURCES

Branch, Taylor. *Parting the Waters: America in the King Years 1954–1963*. New York: Simon & Schuster, 1988.

Carter, Dan T. *The Politics of Rage: George Wallace, the Origins of the New Conservatism, and the Transformation of American Politics*. New York: Simon & Schuster, 1995.

Hartman, Andrew. *A War for the Soul of America: A History of the Culture Wars*. Chicago: University of Chicago Press, 2015.

Impson, Alvin John. "*George Wallace and the Politics of Race*." PhD diss., Texas A&M University, 1994 (9520394). ProQuest Dissertations & Theses Global.

Isenberg, Nancy. *White Trash: The 400-Year Untold History of Class in America*. New York: Penguin Books, 2016.

Jones, Ray. "Minnie Pearl Stand-Up While Opening for George Wallace in the 1958 Campaign for Governor of Alabama." Posted June 10, 2011, by Ray Jones, *YouTube video*. https://www.youtube.com/watch?v=aH8jCaLhU-k.

Phillips, Adam Nicholas. "When Shirley Chisholm Visited George Wallace." *Interfaith America*, July 19, 2024. https://www.interfaithamerica.org/article/shirley-chisholm-visit-george-wallace/.

Polenberg, Richard. *One Nation Divisible*. New York: Penguin Books, 1981.

Shores, Arthur. "Oral History Interview with Arthur Shores, July 17, 1974." Interview by Jack Bass and Walter DeVries. Southern Oral History Program Collection (#4007). Documenting the American South, University of North

Carolina at Chapel Hill. https://docsouth.unc.edu/sohp/A-0021/excerpts/excerpt_1087.html.

United States Senate. "The Senate Passes the Voting Rights Act, August 4, 1965." https://www.senate.gov/artandhistory/history/minute/Senate_Passes_Voting_Rights_Act.htm.

"Wallace Rally Booked in Troy, Minnie Pearl, Too." *The Andalusia Star-News* (Andalusia, Alabama), February 27, 1958.

Zinn, Howard. *A People's History of the United States*. New York: Harper & Row, 1980.

CHAPTER 14

A Fatal Crash, A Near Miss

Airplane Travel and Patsy Cline, 1960–1967

Country music may be about hard luck and pickup trucks, but by the 1960s, Opry performers had traded long roads and late nights for airplanes soaring through the skies. For Minnie and her husband, Henry Cannon, flying wasn't just a convenience—it was their livelihood. Minnie's job depended on her ability to travel, and Henry piloted a private charter service, making for the perfect partnership. However, air travel came with its own risks—something Minnie understood all too well after losing her friend Patsy Cline in a tragic plane crash. Just a few years later, Minnie experienced her own terrifying near-miss after an emergency landing near Knoxville.

Air travel in the 1960s revolutionized the country music industry, and Henry's charter service became a valuable asset. His Beechcraft DC-3 was also small enough to land at rural airfields near concert venues, bypassing the limitations of commercial flights. Minnie described him as an "innovator," adding, "The stars who flew with Henry admired his calm demeanor, honesty, and kindness. Plus, he wasn't impressed by celebrities. And that impressed THEM!"

On Saturday nights after the Opry, performers would board Henry's plane and wake up in cities like Las Vegas or Phoenix, ready for a Sunday

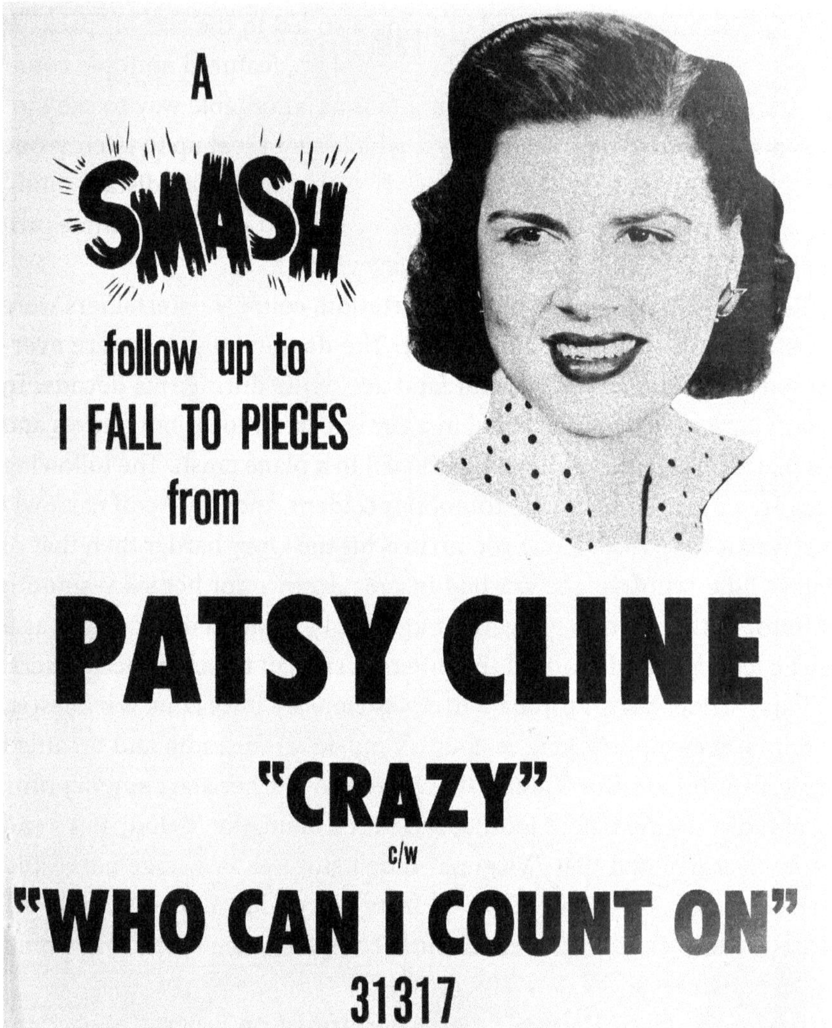

Advertisement published on Cashbox magazine promoting the release of Patsy Cline's single "Crazy," October 7, 1961. Public domain, via Wikimedia Commons.

powerful ballads. Twenty years her senior, Minnie supported and nurtured Patsy, offering advice and encouragement. They also performed together on multiple occasions, both in Nashville and on the road. A particularly memorable night came in 1959 in Springfield, Missouri, at the Jewell Theater. There, they shared the stage with Pee Wee King, Redd Stewart, and Leroy Van Dyke. Minnie brought down the house with laughter; Patsy brought down the house with "Walkin' After Midnight."

In 1961, Patsy's career skyrocketed with the release of "I Fall to Pieces." This instant classic topped the *Billboard* country charts and crossed over into the Hot 100 for pop music. Later that year, she was involved in a horrific automobile accident. Her injuries were severe: a dislocated hip, a fractured arm, and a gash stretching across her face from her right eyebrow. Despite her injuries, Patsy soon returned to the Grand Ole Opry stage, performing on crutches. She'd say to the audience: "I recorded a song called 'I Fall to Pieces,' and I was in a car wreck. Now I'm really worried, because I have a brand-new record, and it's called 'Crazy.'"

The story behind this iconic song is, well, you guessed it—crazy. Written by Willie Nelson, a little-known songwriter in Nashville at the time, the track was originally titled "Stupid." In 1961, Nelson tried to sell the song to executives on Music Row but couldn't find any takers. In addition to songwriting, Nelson also played gigs around town, often singing at Tootsie's Orchid Lounge, the famed Honky Tonk bar across a back ally from the Ryman. When Nelson sang 'Stupid' for the regulars at Tootsie's, they loved the melody but balked at the title and chorus. So, Nelson wisely renamed the song "Crazy." Patsy's husband, Charlie, who often spent Saturday nights at Tootsie's while she was on the Opry, heard Nelson sing the song one night. He loved it.

Charlie asked Willie to play the song for Patsy. She didn't like it at first, but Charlie convinced her to record it. Still on crutches and suffering from a broken rib and arm, Patsy recorded Willie Nelson's song. "Crazy" went on to become one of her biggest hits. According to *American Songwriter*'s Alex Hopper, Patsy's musical execution and crooning chorus, made "her claims of 'feeling so lonely' cut right to the bone." The song reached number two on the charts, followed by her number one hit, "She's Got You." Patsy was named "Favorite Female Vocalist" by *Billboard* magazine in 1961.

As if Patsy Cline's star couldn't shine any brighter, the end of 1961 brought another major milestone. Alongside fellow Grand Ole Opry members, including Minnie Pearl, she traveled to New York City for a special performance at Carnegie Hall. The packed lineup featured Opry stars Jim Reeves, Marty Robbins, Faron Young, and Bill Monroe. Before the event, New York columnist Dorothy Kilgallen scoffed at the performers, calling them "hicks from the sticks."

Once in New York, however, it was clear that Kilgallen had misjudged country music's widespread appeal. The show sold out, and Patsy Cline

Promotional flyer for November 29, 1961, performance of Grand Ole Opry members at Carnegie Hall. Carnegie Hall Rose Archives.

Members of the Grand Ole Opry traveled to New York City for a performance at Carnegie Hall on November 29, 1961. The concert was sold out and symbolized the growing popularity of country and bluegrass music across the nation. From left to right: Louis "Grandpa" Jones, Sarah Cannon/Minnie Pearl, Faron Young, Bill Monroe, and Patsy Cline. They are holding keys to the city presented to them by New York City Mayor Robert F. Wagner Jr. Image courtesy of the Grand Ole Opry Archives.

made history by becoming the first female country singer to grace the Carnegie Hall stage. As for Minnie? As usual, she was the "cultural bridge" between the city slickers and the country folk. Mayor Robert Wagner presented Minnie and the group with a key to the city. By all accounts, the trip to New York City and Carnegie Hall was a smashing success and served to legitimize country music. The visit also confirmed what the Opry already knew—their music was popular everywhere.

After the Carnegie Hall performance, Patsy was indisputably one of the most popular singers in the nation. Patsy was also a new mother—having given birth to her second child. She was in high demand, but the pressures

This promotional poster was for a show in Baltimore, Maryland with Red Foley, Webb Pierce, Minnie Pearl, and others on March 16, 1963. Eleven days prior, Patsy Cline died in a plane crash on March 5, 1963, along with fellow country music stars Cowboy Copas and Hawkshaw Hawkins, and the pilot, Randy Hughes. Image courtesy of Belmont University Archives and Special Collections.

The Grand Ole Opry held a moment of silence at the March 9, 1963 show to honor Patsy Cline and others killed in a plane crash four days earlier. Minnie Pearl managed to get through her act, but there were many tears on and offstage that evening. Image courtesy of Grand Ole Opry Archives.

of touring took a mental and physical toll. Even so, she continued pumping out hits. The next year, Patsy released "When I Get Thru With You" and "So Wrong." In January 1963, the single "Leavin' on Your Mind" was released—reaching number eight on the *Billboard*'s Hot Country chart.

Two months later, on March 5, 1963, the unthinkable happened. Patsy Cline was killed instantly in a fiery plane crash, along with Cowboy Copas, Hawkshaw Hawkins, and their manager Randy Hughes. Months earlier, Hughes had purchased a Piper PA-24 Comanche. He had a pilot's license but lacked the necessary instrument training for flying in poor conditions. After a benefit show in Kansas City, the group was grounded overnight due to storms and turbulence. Despite continued weather warnings the next day, Hughes decided to fly the group back to Nashville. About ninety miles from their destination, the plane went down near Camden, Tennessee, killing everyone on board.

The following morning, Roger Miller, a friend and fellow country artist, set out to search for the missing plane based on its last known communication. He was the first to discover the wreckage and confirmed the fatal crash. Shockwaves of grief rippled throughout the nation. Patsy Cline, the country music star who helped pioneer the "Nashville Sound," was dead.

Cline's body was brought back to Middle Tennessee. Her wake was held in the Goodlettsville home she and her husband had recently purchased. That weekend, the Grand Ole Opry debated whether to cancel its show but ultimately decided to go on. The Jordanaires sang a gospel song in her honor as the audience wept. Then, it was time for Minnie Pearl's act. She courageously took the stage and made it through her routine. Though Minnie got the crowd to stop crying, she was visibly emotional. She walked off the stage, tears streaming down her face.

Four years later, Minnie would have her own brush with death in an airplane. She and her husband, Henry, had been flying together for years. Henry had sold his half-interest in Capital Airways but kept his small plane, eventually focusing exclusively on Minnie's travel. They affectionately named the plane "The White Poodle" after their dog, Sam, who accompanied them on most trips. Flights on "The White Poodle" were joyful times as they traveled across the country for Minnie's performances.

Minnie described a typical flight: "We didn't talk much. Henry would be checking the weather and his maps while I read, and Sam slept." For her, flying felt like being "suspended in a safe, euphoric world devoid of problems and pressures." Minnie usually sat in the back seat with her papers and books, which Henry jokingly called the "turkey nest." In April 1967, after a show in Baltimore, Minnie and Henry boarded their single-engine Beech Bonanza to fly home to Nashville. The weather was perfect—clear blue skies and full visibility. Everything seemed fine as they passed Knoxville at 8,700 feet. Then the engine stopped.

Neither Minnie nor Henry spoke as he tried to restart the engine. There was plenty of fuel, enough for five hours, so that wasn't the issue. He worked through various controls to no avail. The silence in the cockpit was deafening. Minnie later recalled, "It was very disconcerting to look out the window of a single-engine plane and see the prop[eller] just sitting there motionless." Henry shifted all controls to manual operations—still nothing. With the engine unresponsive and their altitude dropping rapidly, Henry looked at his wife and said calmly, "Fasten your seatbelt, honey. I'm going to set this thing down." Minnie buckled up and braced herself.

The *Knoxville News-Sentinel* documented the plane, known as the White Poodle, after Henry Cannon's emergency landing. The caption reads: OPRY STAR GROUNDED— This Beechcraft Bonaza, with Grand Ole Opry star Minnie Pearl aboard, used this plowed field beside I-40 just west of Cedar Bluff Road as a landing strip, April 19, 1967.

They were flying directly above Interstate 40, the highway that runs between Knoxville and Nashville. Henry spotted a small field and prepared for an emergency landing. Minnie remembered, "In order to get us down safely he had to keep our wings up because the gasoline was stored there, and the plane would have exploded if those gas tanks had been ripped open." Thanks to Henry's skill and expertise, they landed safely. The propeller dug into the ground, but the wings never touched, allowing them to walk away, completely unharmed.

Minnie later said, "Everything happened so fast I didn't really have time to think, but I do remember that it never occurred to me to doubt whether Henry could land the plane. I just knew he would." She also believed it was a moment of divine intervention: "God had planned to let us live. God was the pilot, and Henry was his co-pilot." Later, they learned that the problem wasn't due to a mechanical defect or pilot error. It was just a simple freak accident—a piece of metal had lodged in the fuel line and choked the engine. A friend offered to lend Henry a plane to fly back to Nashville later that day, but Henry insisted, "I'd be more comfortable on a commercial flight." Henry Cannon never piloted another plane.

Surviving that close call in 1967 marked the end of a significant chapter in Minnie's life. The memory of Patsy Cline, whose star had burned out far too soon, served as a poignant reminder of how fragile life could be. Determined to keep her feet firmly on the ground from that point forward, Minnie resolved to make the most out of life. At fifty-five years old, she still had many things she wanted to accomplish, and she'd been given a second chance.

Of course, over time, Minnie Pearl found a way to joke about her near-death experience: "I've been grounded by a lot of things in my life—bad weather, broken hearts, and busted tires—but nothing grounds you like an engine that quits mid-air!"

NOTES

The package show circuit used a "cash and carry" system. In other words, concert promoters collected money from ticket sales and paid performers in cash. It was not unusual for a performer to carry paper bags full of money as they traveled. After the Great Depression, most were cynical about banks anyway. For example, Roy Acuff, was known to pin bags of money behind hotel room curtains to "keep it safe while he performed."

Posthumously, Patsy Cline's record label released "Sweet Dreams" and "Faded Love," which also topped the charts. Additional collections and live performances released after her death have only added to her legacy and iconic status.

Patsy Cline was the first solo female artist elected to the Country Music Hall of Fame (CMHOF) and inspired scores of women in country and pop music including k. d. lang, Loretta Lynn, Linda Ronstadt, Trisha Yearwood, and Wynonna Judd. According to the CMHOF, "Her unique, crying style and vocal impeccability established her reputation as the quintessential torch singer."

SOURCES

Hopper, Alex. "Behind the Meaning of the Patsy Cline Classic 'Crazy.'" *American Songwriter*, September 8, 2022. https://americansongwriter.com/the-meaning-behind-the-lyrics-of-the-patsy-cline-classic-crazy/.

Nassour, Ellis. *Honky Tonk Angel: The Intimate Story of Patsy Cline.* New York: St. Martin's Press, 1981, 1993

"Patsy Cline." *Country Music Hall of Fame*, 2024. https://www.countrymusichalloffame.org/hall-of-fame/patsy-cline.

Pearl, Minnie, and Joan Dew. *Minnie Pearl: An Autobiography.* New York: Simon & Schuster, 1980.

CHAPTER 15

A Tale of Two Fried Chicken Chains

KFC, Jack C. Massey, and John Jay Hooker, 1960–1970

The first edition of *Minnie Pearl Cooks* was published in 1970, the same year Minnie testified before a US Senate committee about the collapse of the restaurant franchise that bore her name. Just two years earlier, Minnie Pearl's Fried Chicken (MPFC) had gone public with stock prices soaring and hopes high. Minnie believed her success in the fast-food industry would rival her fame in entertainment. Instead, this business venture turned into a cautionary tale marked by speculation, rapid expansion, mismanagement, and lackluster food.

"When Minnie Pearl's Chicken System Inc. went public in May 1968, many thought it would be the greatest business success story of the twentieth century," wrote historian E. Thomas Wood. The chain symbolized Nashville's enterprising spirit, fueled by the folksy charm of Sarah Cannon, known to millions as Minnie Pearl. John Jay and Henry Hooker, Minnie's business partners, forecasted five hundred restaurants by 1970. It was a bold claim for a company that "had not yet sold a drumstick."

Investors eagerly jumped on the bandwagon, hoping to replicate the success of Kentucky Fried Chicken (KFC), co-owned by Nashvillian Jack C. Massey. As journalist Bill Carey explained in *Fortunes, Fiddles & Fried Chicken: A Nashville Business History*, the Hooker brothers believed KFC's success had paved the way "much like Coke paved the way for

Early advertisement in June 1968 for Minnie Pearl's Chicken. Note John Jay Hooker is listed as the president and board chair. This advertisement ran roughly a month after the company went public on the stock market on May 2, 1968. Image in public domain.

Kentucky Fried Chicken founder Harland Sanders as a young man, circa 1914. Public domain, via Wikimedia Commons.

Pepsi." John Jay declared, "It's about time KFC had some competition." But what started as an effort to capitalize on the fried chicken frenzy ended in financial failure, resulting in a big slice of humble pie and a hefty serving of mea culpa for those involved.

In the 1960s, franchising experienced a boom across the United States, especially in the fast-food industry. Companies expanded rapidly without the high costs of owning each location, while franchise operators benefitted from running businesses under established brands. The Interstate Highway System fueled this growth by connecting previously isolated markets. Unlike mom-and-pop restaurants, chains like McDonald's offered the consistency and speed sought by interstate travelers. Attorney and author William L. Killion noted that revenues from these businesses "grew 3,600 percent from 1955 to 1970, with 670,000 franchise-operated locations generating $90 billion annually by 1970."

Historian John T. Edge observed, "Fried chicken is more than sustenance in the South. It is a totem of identity and a symbol of pride." So, it's no surprise that multiple fried chicken franchises emerged during this period, with Kentucky Fried Chicken leading the pack. The "franchise bubble" of 1955–1969 eventually burst in 1970, and unfortunately for the

Hookers and their investors, Minnie Pearl's Fried Chicken was part of that collapse. To understand why MPFC failed, one must first understand how KFC succeeded—after all, this is a tale of two chicken chains.

Harlan Sanders, better known as Colonel Sanders, had humble beginnings. With only a sixth-grade education, Sanders dropped out of school. He held various jobs until 1930, when he opened a service station in Corbin, Kentucky. Realizing he could make extra money by selling Southern-style food, including fried chicken, Sanders turned his service station into a restaurant. His pressure-cooked chicken, seasoned with a blend of eleven herbs and spices, was a hit with customers. Unfortunately, the restaurant was seven miles from I-75, and the drop in customers forced him to close.

In the early 1950s, desperate and relying on a monthly $105 Social Security check, Sanders traveled to Indiana and Ohio to franchise his recipe. His model was simple but effective: he leased pressure cookers and sold his secret blend of spices to restaurants, along with napkins and buckets bearing his image. The approach worked, and by 1960, he had laid the foundation for what would become the Kentucky Fried Chicken empire. Marvin Hopper, a Nashville entrepreneur, heard about Sanders and negotiated a one-page contract granting him exclusive rights to serve Sanders's fried chicken in Nashville in exchange for five cents per chicken sold. Despite a rocky start, Hopper opened a successful location on Gallatin Road. Over the next three years KFC exploded, with more than five hundred franchised outlets across the United States by 1963.

Harlan Sanders needed legal help and reached out to John Y. Brown Jr., a young lawyer from Louisville, Kentucky. Brown saw the potential in KFC and teamed up with Jack C. Massey, a Nashville businessman in pharmaceuticals, to purchase the entire company. In 1964, Massey and Brown acquired KFC for two million dollars, gaining control of all franchise contracts, patents, trademarks, and the rights to Sanders's name, image, and likeness. As part of the deal, Sanders stayed on as a goodwill ambassador, earning $40,000 annually for life.

In March 1966, Kentucky Fried Chicken entered the stock market for a mere fifteen dollars per share. Over the next two years, KFC opened six hundred new outlets, and in 1968, another six hundred stores were added. The company's rapid expansion during these years was "unparalleled in the history of restaurants," and KFC emerged as a dominant force in the fast-food industry. One notable franchisee, Dave Thomas, used his

John Jay Hooker (far left) on November 30, 1968, stands with Democratic state leaders before announcing his bid to run for governor. From left to right: John Jay Hooker, Charles Worley (Treasurer), William R. Snodgrass (Comptroller), Joe C. Carr (Secretary of State), and Tennessee Governor Buford Ellington. Image courtesy of *Nashville Banner* Archives, Special Collections Division, Nashville Public Library.

earnings to establish a new chain called Wendy's. Thomas quickly became a multi-millionaire in his own right. Eight years after KFC went public, in 1972, Jack Massey and John Brown sold the company to a firm called Heublein for $239 million ($1.8 billion in 2025). The sale represented one of the largest profit margins in American business history.

Back in Nashville in 1966, John Jay Hooker watched the skyrocketing success of Kentucky Fried Chicken and wanted a piece of the action. Hooker was a wealthy and well-connected man with deep family ties in Nashville. Journalist R. W. Apple Jr. noted: "He [was] a dark haired Nashville lawyer. . . with that kind of easy charm that marked him as a member of the Southern aristocracy. He was a friend of both John F. Kennedy and Robert F. Kennedy." Only thirty-six-years old at the time,

Hooker had run and lost the 1966 Tennessee gubernatorial race but fully intended to run again. Hooker recounted in an interview:

> The day after I lost the [1966] election, it was raining cats and dogs but when I drove past a Kentucky Fried Chicken restaurant, people were getting out of their cars to pick up chicken. I got to the office and Henry (brother) was on the phone, talking to his stockbroker about price/earnings ratios. I asked him what PE ratios were, and he explained that Wall Street was selling Kentucky Fried Chicken at 40 times its earnings.

John Jay asked his younger brother: "You mean while we're working here night and day, Massey's making money while he sleeps? . . . How long have you known about this Henry and why ain't we in it, too?"

With the success of so many fast-food restaurants like McDonald's, Wendy's, and Dairy Queen, it seemed like a no-brainer. With ambitions for financial success and his sights set on the Governor's Mansion, John Jay (and Henry) jumped into the franchising business in 1967. All they needed was a face and a name. Enter Minnie Pearl. She was a nationally recognized figure, a Tennessee native, and a comedian of Grand Ole Opry fame. The Hooker brothers approached Henry and Sarah Cannon/ Minnie Pearl. Minnie was instantly interested. "I think it's about time I went into some sort of business," she said. Her husband and business manager, Henry, needed more coaxing, but he finally agreed. The contracts were signed, and Minnie Pearl's Chicken System, Inc., (MPFC) was born.

The difference between KFC and MPFC was apparent from the start. KFC was franchised after Colonel Sanders sold an already thriving business to Brown and Massey. Even so, Sanders remained fiercely protective of his recipes. Journalist Bill Carey noted: "Harlan Sanders wasn't about to let the company serve bad food in his name. . . . Franchisees were required to attend a school where Sanders's cooking methods were the curriculum." Sanders was also a one-man quality control team. Franchisee Ray Danner recalled a surprise visit: "The Colonel came in and said, 'The ginger's wrong. They're using domestic ginger not imported Jamaican ginger.' From then on, we added four ounces of Jamaican ginger to our spice pack. And the next thing you know our sales went up."

In contrast, Minnie Pearl's Fried Chicken was built on an "idea and money." The old saying goes, "Don't count your chickens before they hatch." Well, Minnie Pearl's Fried Chicken counted everything—in speculative and spectacular fashion. The Hooker brothers were excellent salesmen, but they had no experience in food service or operations. MPFC

Minnie Pearl's chicken supplies the food for members of the Billy Graham Committee, July 19, 1969. From left to right: Howard Hooper, Minnie Pearl, Frances Thompson Gunn, Reverend James Gregg. Image courtesy of *Nashville Banner* Archives, Special Collections Division, Nashville Public Library.

sold franchises before ever frying a chicken or opening a restaurant. Journalist Lyndsay Cordell wrote, "There was no chicken recipe in this chicken business. . . . Every store had their own menu."

On June 18, 1967, the *Nashville Tennessean* announced the launch of Minnie Pearl's Fried Chicken. Two months later, on August 20, University of Tennessee Head Football Coach Doug Dickey became the first franchise holder. Just eleven days later, construction began on the first location at 2807 Franklin Road in Nashville.

The Hookers were eager to take the company public and sell stock. John Jay and Henry owned a combined 650,000 shares and Minnie Pearl owned 96,000 shares. Other major stockholders included prominent Nashvillians such as US Congressman Richard H. Fulton, publisher Amon Carter Evans, newspaper editor John Seigenthaler, and Ingram Corp. President Bronson Ingram. Ingram was skeptical of the business model but said John Jay Hooker had persuaded him. Years later, his wife, Martha Ingram said, "In Bronson's mind, it was money he had kissed goodbye forever." However, most people who could afford to invest were eager. Jimmy Bradford Jr., a well-known Nashville businessman, said: "People just went hog-wild."

Author Bill Carey captured the excitement surrounding Minnie Pearl's Fried Chicken: "Hooker's idea caught fire, thanks to his personal magnetism and the free publicity from Nashville's newspapers." The fact that two local newspaper editors were investors didn't hurt either. On its opening day, the stock surged from twenty dollars to over forty dollars. On paper, the company's value shot up to $64 million. An article in the *New York Times* noted, "Early on, they did so well for themselves and their friends, they became the darlings of the rich and powerful of Nashville."

Despite the hype, the company made more money selling franchises than actual chicken. To start, the lack of infrastructure delayed store openings. By 1968, over three hundred franchises had been sold, but only forty restaurants were up and running. Those that were open were not profitable. Still, the Hooker brothers took home 49 percent of each franchise sale. Of the $13.4 million in total revenue that year, only $144,810 came from chicken sales, while over $8 million was tied up in promissory notes. To make matters worse, the tightening money market made it harder to secure bank loans, which hindered the expansion of stores in key markets. The company was running out of time to position itself as a legitimate contender to KFC.

In an effort to mitigate the rocky roll out, the Hooker brothers rebranded the company as Performance Systems Inc. (PSI) and diversified their assets. However, the real problem persisted: customers who tried the fried chicken didn't come back. Jimmy Bradford recalled, "I told Henry Hooker that no one at the company knows a damn thing about cooking chicken." Hooker agreed but pushed back: "You're right. But the easiest thing to do is fix the chicken. We'll call up General Mills . . . and they'll get us someone who knows." PSI executive, Richard L. Fulton also provided insight: "The company issued recipe books, but many of the managers, especially retired military cooks, insisted on using their own recipes, leading to inconsistency across locations." The unpredictable, and often mediocre, food only exacerbated the other structural issues facing PSI and MPFC.

In an interview, John Jay Hooker reflected, "The wind was at our back

Minnie Pearl Chicken closes in Donelson on Lebanon Road on May 8, 1970. This was the second restaurant closure for Minnie Pearl's Chicken in Nashville, the first was on Gallatin Road. Image courtesy of *Nashville Banner* Archives, Special Collections Division, Nashville Public Library.

in 1968. In 1969, it turned around." Indeed, by 1969, Performance Systems Inc. was in serious trouble. Hooker had promised 500 franchises by 1970, but fewer than 50 restaurants had opened. The stock price plummeted, dropping from forty dollars to ten dollars within weeks. Amid this turmoil, Hooker announced a second bid to run for governor and reassigned most of PSI's staff to work on his campaign. With limited resources and manpower to address its mounting problems, the company struggled to stay afloat. Minnie Pearl's Fried Chicken was a flop; KFC would remain the fried chicken king.

The downfall of Minnie Pearl's Fried Chicken also implicated media executives who had invested in the company and provided favorable coverage, even as clear warning signs emerged. The involvement of the *Nashville Banner* and *Nashville Tennessean* turned into a scandal of its own when the national media revealed their conflicted interests.

Sarah Cannon, better known as Minnie Pearl, prepares her famous chicken tetrazzini. This was one of her signature dishes, originally published in *Minnie Pearl Cooks* (1970). The full recipe can be found at the end of this chapter. Image courtesy of *Nashville Banner* Archives, Special Collections Division, Nashville Public Library.

Minnie Pearl didn't lose any money, but her pride and reputation took a hit. In fact, she earned a significant sum by selling her stock before the company's failure was apparent. Though she played no direct role in business decisions and served primarily as a marketing figurehead, the company's downfall still weighed heavily on Minnie. As Bill Carey noted, "[The] Ward-Belmont graduate who managed to walk in both country music and Nashville society circles . . . was embarrassed about the failure of the company that carried her stage name." Buddy Killen, an executive at Tree Publishing and a close friend of Minnie, added, "She was deeply bothered by all the negativity and by being associated with something so stigmatized."

On January 21, 1970, Minnie Pearl and John Jay Hooker were called to testify before a US Senate committee about the downfall of MPFC. Their testimony was part of a larger investigation into food franchises, especially the risks of rapid expansion without proper oversight. Although no immediate legislative action followed, their appearance helped inform future regulations aimed at protecting investors and small business owners.

A subsequent SEC investigation into Minnie Pearl's Fried Chicken uncovered financial mismanagement but did not lead to any formal charges. The Hooker brothers had overstated the number of franchises and exaggerated growth projections. However, the contract signed by investors noted the founders' limited business experience and explicitly warned: "These are speculative securities." It also stated that the company's income came "primarily from the sale of franchises" rather than operations. John Jay and Henry Hooker did not maliciously deceive investors, franchisees, or customers, and their risky business practices were common at the time. Unfortunately, their actions led to financial instability and inflated stock prices.

Days after Minnie Pearl and John Jay Hooker's testimony, the *Chicago Tribune* published an editorial titled "The Southern Fried Chicken Bubble," which summed up MPFC this way: "The company sold more stock than franchises and more franchises than chicken." By September 1970, Minnie Pearl's Fried Chicken hit rock bottom with stocks trading for only forty-four cents per share. A final report revealed that the company had lost $31 million. The magnitude of PSI's losses became a primary talking point in the gubernatorial race of 1970. Author E. Thomas Wood concluded: "Hooker won the Democratic nomination but was defeated by Republican Winfield Dunn, who criticized Hooker's business failure using Minnie Pearl's good name to sell bad chicken."

When Minnie Pearl published *Minnie Pearl Cooks* in 1970, it must have been a cathartic experience, especially as the last remaining franchises closed their doors. The cookbook, filled with recipes for Southern "comfort food," showcased Minnie's personal favorites, including her mother's famous "Corn Pudding" and her aunt's "Southern Chicken Tetrazzini." (See Notes.) Known for her love of cooking, Minnie Pearl's Fried Chicken might have fared better if Minnie had crafted the menu herself. But as journalist Jennifer Justus reminds us: "While her restaurants didn't last, her recipes still do."

As she put the restaurant debacle behind her, she channeled her energy into a new venture—television. The show? A little program called *Hee Haw*.

NOTES

Recipes courtesy of Minnie Pearl Cooks. Nashville, TN: Aurora Publishing, 1970.

MAMA'S CORN PUDDING

This corn pudding is comparable to a souffle. It is not a hold over dish. If brought to the table and served directly from the oven, it is light and beautiful, but if allowed to sit any length of time, it loses its lightness. . . . The secret of this recipe is the way you take the corn off the cob. Scraping the cob makes all the difference.

4 large ears fresh corn
2 eggs, well beaten
1 tablespoon melted butter
½ teaspoon of salt
¼ teaspoon of pepper
1 teaspoon sugar
1 cup milk

Preheat oven to 400° F. Butter 2-quart casserole dish. Cut top kernels off corn. Scrape cob. Add remaining ingredients to corn. Pour into prepared casserole dish. Bake in oven about 30 minutes or until corn pudding has risen and is lightly brown on top. Makes 4 to 6 servings.

MINNIE'S CHICKEN TETRAZZINI

2 cups chopped celery
1½ cups chopped onion
3 tablespoons butter
2 cups chicken broth
1 tablespoon Worcestershire sauce
A pinch each of salt and pepper
½ cup sliced stuffed olives
1 cup chopped pecans
1 10½ oz. can condensed cream of mushroom soup
½ cup milk
1 cup grated sharp cheddar cheese
½ pound spaghetti, cooked and drained
6 cups chopped, cooked chicken

In a saucepan, cook celery and onion in butter until tender. Add chicken broth. Worcestershire sauce, salt, and pepper. Simmer about 15 minutes. Slowly stir in mushroom soup, milk, and cheese. Mix thoroughly. Remove from heat. Add cooked spaghetti. Let stand for 1 hour.

Preheat oven to 350° F. Grease a 9x13-inch baking dish. Add chicken and olives to spaghetti. Place in prepared dish. Sprinkle with chopped pecans. Bake 20 to 25 minutes or until hot and bubbly. Makes 12 servings.

This tale of two chicken franchises ended very differently for the businessmen associated with KFC and MPFC. John Brown became the honorary chairman of the National Democratic Party in 1972, and in 1979 became the fifty-fifth governor of Kentucky. Jack C. Massey co-founded Hospital Corporation of America with Thomas F. Frist Sr. and Thomas Frist Jr. in Nashville. HCA became the largest chain of for-profit hospitals in the nation, and Massey left active management in 1978. Massey also transformed Volunteer Capital (holding company for Wendy's) to make yet another fast-food restaurant a mass success. Massey was the first American businessman to take three different companies public on the New York Stock Exchange. KFC has more than thirty thousand locations in 150 countries worldwide with $5.16 billion (2023) in annual sales.

John Jay Hooker hadn't broken any laws, but he had broken the trust of many Tennesseans. Hooker survived the Democratic Primary and faced a little-known Memphis dentist, Winfield Dunn, in the 1970 gubernatorial election. No Republican had won the state's highest office since the 1920s, but that November, Dunn was swept into office. Hooker later became the publisher of the *Nashville Banner*. With limited success, Hooker ventured into the restaurant business again and later became chairman of United Press International. John Jay Hooker was a perennial politician with multiple unsuccessful bids for public office but remained a major advocate for campaign finance reform. Though his career was marked by both triumphs and failures, he was remembered for his charm, idealism, and relentless pursuit of justice.

Minnie Pearl Cooks published several new editions between 1970 and 1984, but that wasn't Minnie Pearl's first foray into food and recipes. She first published recipes in the 1940s in a short-lived publication called the *Grinder's Switch Gazette*. Brenda Colladay, former archivist at the Country Music Hall of Fame, said, "It's the earliest instance I've seen of a country star and recipes together."

SOURCES

Apple, R. W. Jr. "Chicken and Tennessee Politics." *New York Times*, January 27, 1970.

Bennett, Julie. "What Really Happened to Minnie Pearl Fried Chicken?" *Franchise Times*, November 5, 2020. https://www.franchisetimes.com/article_archive/what-really-happened-to-minnie-pearl-fried-chicken/article_8093c591-b894-58f7-a8fa-b63089a3d459.html.

Carey, Bill. *Fortunes, Fiddles and Fried Chicken: A Nashville Business History.* Franklin, TN: Hillsboro Press, 2000.

Cordell, Lyndsay. "What Ever Happened To Minnie Pearl's Fried Chicken?" *Wide*

Minnie Pearl (far left), Lulu Roman (center), and the Hee Haw Honeys on the set of *Hee Haw*, c. 1979. Image courtesy of the Grand Ole Opry Archives.

Grandpa Jones, disapproved of her boyfriend, "Loverboy." The show delivered quick punchlines and one-liners, with a barn-themed set where the cast lounged on hay bales and barrels. During a recurring segment, a string band performed a parody song, "May the Bird of Paradise Fly Up Your Nose." Grandpa Jones followed the song with a joke: "Twenty years ago the girls wore bathing suits that looked like Mother Hubbard's; now they wear ones that look more like her cupboard." After filming wrapped, Minnie and Grandpa returned to Nashville.

Minnie Pearl and Grandpa Jones sit on the front porch of the *Hee Haw* set, 1977. They worked together on several recurring segments called "The Cooking Spot" and "The Post Office." Grandpa Jones was best known for his trademark reply, "What'd ya say?" Image courtesy of the Grand Ole Opry Archives.

Minnie Pearl (left), Roy Acuff (center), Buck Owens with *Hee Haw* cast, 1979. Grandpa Jones stands behind Minnie's right shoulder, Archie Campbell stands in the center between Minnie and Roy as he laughs with Gordie Tapp and Junior Samples, seated on the far right in a baseball cap. Image courtesy of the Grand Ole Opry Archives.

Around this time, CBS was exploring new opportunities in rural-themed programming. Inspired by the success of sitcoms like *The Beverly Hillbillies* and *Green Acres,* the network saw potential in a country music variety show. Producers John Aylesworth and Frank Peppiatt pitched the concept, leading CBS to greenlight a one-hour special. What began as a single broadcast became the foundation for *Hee Haw,* which evolved into a syndicated program with a remarkable twenty-eight-year run.

Recognizing the show's potential, the producers sought talent who could bring authentic country charm and humor to the screen. In 1969,

Minnie on stage with Roy Clark, c. 1975. Image courtesy of The Hope Powell Collection by Singleton/Curb.

Minnie Pearl and Grandpa Jones were invited to join the cast of *Hee Haw*. When Grandpa Jones told his wife about the offer, she skeptically remarked, "Hee Haw? Whoever heard of a name like that for a show? That'll be enough to kill it right there." Jones reached out to other potential cast members to get their thoughts. Jones recalled: "We all agreed that our acts were getting a little stale, and our records weren't getting much play on the radio. Maybe a little TV exposure was what we needed, so we agreed to sign on."

The show's creators, John Aylesworth and Frank Peppiatt, designed *Hee Haw* as a mix of live country music performances and comedic sketches based on rural stereotypes, featuring slapstick humor and corny

Co-presenters Minnie Pearl (center right) and Kitty Wells (far right) look on as Charley Pride gives an acceptance speech for one of his two awards at the "5th Annual CMA Awards" on Oct. 10, 1971, at the Grand Ole Opry House, live telecast on the CBS Television Network. Pride won awards for both Entertainer and Male Vocalist of the year (1971). His career as a Black star in country music in the 1960s and 1970s helped break racial barriers in the country music industry. Image courtesy of The Hope Powell Collection by Singleton/Curb.

characters. Debuting in 1969, the show was co-hosted by country stars Roy Clark and Buck Owens and included a cast of recurring characters including Minnie Pearl, Grandpa Jones, George "Goober" Lindsey, Lulu Roman, Dale Evans, and Roy Rogers. Minnie Pearl's widespread recognition made her an easy choice. As producer Sam Lovullo noted, "We quickly discovered there were remarkably few country acts with any prior national exposure. Among the few was Minnie Pearl, a bona fide country legend whose long association with the Grand Ole Opry had earned her a national following."

Hee Haw was a product of its time and, like many shows of the era, reflected the cultural landscape and media norms of the 1960s and 1970s.

Miss Minnie, as she was often called on set, quilting with the "girls" on Hee Haw, 1983. Image courtesy of the Grand Ole Opry Archives.

Charley Pride, one of the few prominent Black country musicians, broke racial barriers as the first guest star, alongside Loretta Lynn on June 15, 1969. However, beyond guest appearances, African American characters were largely absent from *Hee Haw*'s regular programming. That said, there were several notable African American men who performed on the show including Ray Charles, Sammy Davis Jr., Dizzy Dean, and Joe Frazier.

On the show, Minnie played several roles—the house mother in a girls' dormitory, editor of the *Grinder's Switch Gazette*, and the cantankerous passenger in "Driving Miss Minnie." She shared recurring segments with Grandpa Jones, such as "Grandpa's and Minnie's Kitchen," a spoof on cooking shows, and "The Post Office," which featured

Hee Haw's cast in the famous "kornfield" giving the weekly "Salute!" to a town or city in the United States, c. 1980. Image courtesy of Fandom, CC BY-SA.

unhappy customers reading their mail. But her most famous sketch was "Minnie Pearl's Schoolhouse," where she played the teacher to "students" like Roy Clark, Junior Samples, and other cast members, all dressed as kids licking oversized lollipops. Minnie also appeared as a honky-tonk piano player, singing along with young, attractive cast members known as the "Hee Haw Honeys."

One of the show's most memorable sketches on *Hee Haw* was the beloved song "PFFT! You Was Gone!" When chosen for this segment, Minnie sang in the loud, off-key "country corn" style alongside a male counterpart like Grandpa Jones, Goober, or Kenny Price. As they wailed their way through the song, guest stars often joined in on the last chorus:

From left to right: Minnie Pearl and music icons Ray Charles and Willie Nelson smile together at an awards ceremony, 1980s. Ray Charles pioneered the genre of soul music during the 1950s, and Willie Nelson was one of the main figures of the original country music "Outlaws," a subgenre that developed in the late 1960s. Photo by Hulton Archive/Getty Images.

Where, oh where, are you tonight?
Why did you leave me here all alone?
I searched the world over and thought I'd found true love,
But you met another and PFFT! You was gone!

Other regular spots included "KORN News," where Minnie spoofed local news with Don Harron and "Gloom, Despair and Agony on Me," where cast members lamented their misfortunes surrounded by moonshine jugs. Other audience favorites included "Lulu's Truckstop," "Sample's Sales," "Archie's Barber Shop," "The Joke Fence," and "The Empty Arms Motel." The highlight each week was "Hee Haw Salutes," where the guest star stood in a cornfield with the show's cast and called out the name of his/her hometown. Then, the entire cast would rise from the cornfield and yell "SAA-LUTE!"

The guest list for *Hee Haw* represented all American musical genres. Some included established celebrities like Jerry Lee Lewis, Johnny Cash,

Sarah/Minnie presents the legendary Barbara Mandrell with the Minnie Pearl Humanitarian Award at the CMA Awards, 1991. Minnie was a trusted mentor and friend to Barbara Mandrell, and the two shared a close relationship for many years. Image courtesy of the Grand Ole Opry Archives.

Roger Miller, Ernie Ford, Doc Severinson, Ernest Tubb, Willie Nelson, Ray Charles, Waylon Jennings, and Garth Brooks. For others, the show helped launch their career. For example, Barbara Mandrell made her first national appearance on *Hee Haw* in 1972. According to Lovullo: "Full of energy and hardworking . . . Barbara's appearance gave her the opportunity to demonstrate her versatility. She sang a song while also playing the steel guitar, horns, and saxophone. At the end . . . she pretended to be exhausted and 'collapsed' out of the camera shot." The audience loved it.

Another musician whose time on *Hee Haw* helped make him a star was Ronnie Milsap. Lovullo first discovered Milsap at Roger Miller's King of the Road Lounge. Milsap was a talented musician who, like Ray Charles, was blind. But that didn't stop him from taking part in sketches. Milsap especially enjoyed the "Kornfield Salute."

Minnie Pearl with Dolly Parton at the Country Music Awards in 1975. Image courtesy of The Hope Powell Collection by Singleton/Curb.

Finally, most people don't realize that Reba McEntire's first nationwide exposure was on *Hee Haw* in 1981. Lovullo booked her on the recommendation of a friend, Red Steagall. Reba was "a little nervous during rehearsals," but afterward she went to Lovullo and said, "Sam, I'm country and if I make it in this business, I'm going to stay country."

Many of *Hee Haw*'s female guests, including Barbara Mandrell, Reba McEntire, Loretta Lynn, Tammy Wynette, Dolly Parton, Tanya Tucker, and Amy Grant, were mentored and befriended by Minnie Pearl. Tammy Wynette appeared on the show over 20 times between 1969 and 1980, while Loretta Lynn, who credited Minnie as a trusted mentor, made 24 guest appearances—the most of any artist. Tanya Tucker described Minnie as "another mother," and Amy Grant often sought her guidance. Dolly Parton, who appeared twice, summed it up: "Everybody loved Minnie Pearl, and she was like our big sister—all of us girls would go to her for advice. She was always there for me in my times of need."

Minnie Pearl's warm, yet sharp-witted humor fit perfectly with *Hee Haw*'s aim of celebrating rural America with a mix of comedy sketches and musical performances. Minnie compared the atmosphere on set to her early years on the Grand Ole Opry. "There is a free-swinging informality that catches you up in a 'let's laugh and have fun mood.' I liked working on tape because if you mess up, you immediately do it again. But sometimes on Hee Haw our 'mess-ups' are so good they keep them."

With *Hee Haw*'s focus on both country music and rural humor, Minnie bridged the gap between her live performances and radio broadcasts with the broader world of television. Though she wasn't the show's creator, producer, or director—*Hee Haw* was made for Minnie Pearl. In many ways her comedic style, coupled with her decades-long success, served as the show's template. After all, *Hee Haw* was based on character-driven comedy, with cast members playing exaggerated stereotypes and wearing costumes to match.

Not everyone loved *Hee Haw.* Initially, the weekly show was panned by TV critics. "There were so many negative articles about the show that people began tuning in just to see how bad we were," Lovullo recalled, continuing, "Once they found us, people were surprised that they liked what they saw." One commentator noted that the show's humor was "cornball, but hilarious cornball." Others remarked that *Hee Haw* had made old-fashioned country humor that felt fresh, especially to audiences in New York, Los Angeles, and other big cities. By its fifth broadcast, *Hee Haw* was a bona fide hit, attracting twenty million viewers and often ranking among the top ten TV shows.

Despite *Hee Haw*'s initial success, CBS canceled the show in 1971. *Hee Haw* was seen as the country counterpart to the more urban and "hip" *Laugh-In,* but ultimately the show didn't appeal to enough advertisers. However, the *Hee Haw* team wasn't ready to give up and found a creative

Ralph Emery, Minnie Pearl, Chet Atkins and Grandpa Jones on TNN production set, c. 1983. Image courtesy of The Hope Powell Collection by Singleton/Curb.

way to keep the show going. They formed a new company, continued taping the show, and sold it as a syndicate to other cable television networks. Their gamble paid off. Incredibly, *Hee Haw* stayed on the air for another twenty-four years. The last show, number 585, aired on June 30, 1992. After the syndication run ended, reruns were broadcast on The Nashville Network (TNN) from 1993 to 1995.

Minnie said that her work on *Hee Haw* was a "great professional pleasure." She also believed in the show's concept, despite criticism: "Some folks said it was a caricature of country music and they put it down as such. I didn't agree. I loved it from the first." *Hee Haw* producer, Sam Lovullo, wrote about Minnie's influence: "I've often said that one of the keys to *Hee Haw*'s success was her authentic legendary Nashville presence. At first, we were hesitant to oversimplify her 'hat lady' character, but she didn't seem to mind . . . And as a comedienne, her timing was the greatest."

Hee Haw preceded The Nashville Network (TNN) by ten years, but both enterprises played important roles in Minnie Pearl's career, which shifted to an emphasis on TV appearances as she grew older. The network debuted on March 7, 1983. As the cameras rolled for the first time, Ralph Emery, longtime country legend, said, "Welcome to the Nashville Network. It's a coast-to-coast party and we've invited twenty million people to join us."

Programming for TNN featured a variety of shows, all connected in some way to country music and Southern culture. Early shows included *Bobby Bare and Friends* (focused on songwriters), *I-40 Paradise* (sitcom), *Dancin' USA* (similar to *American Bandstand*), *Fandango* (game show), *Yesteryear in Nashville* (a music history show hosted by Archie Campbell), and a fishing show called *Country Sportsman. Grand Ole Opry Live* and *Nashville Now*, hosted by Ralph Emery, emerged as the network's two flagship programs.

As *Nashville Now* settled into its format, "Let Minnie Steal Your Joke" became one of the most popular spots. "People sent in jokes—not all of them clean, I might add—and Minnie Pearl picked her favorites to read over the air," said Ralph Emery, the show's host. On one episode, neither Minnie nor Emery could stop laughing. Emery said, "The joke was too corny to be funny, but for some reason that made it hilarious." Here it is:

> Two nuns were traveling when their van ran out of gas. They walked down the road to a gas station to buy a gallon or two, but the station had no container. So, the nuns went down the road to a hospital and asked if they could borrow a container. "Certainly, Sisters," said the attendant. "But the only container available is a bed pan. The nuns accepted the loan, went back to the station and got their gas. As they were pouring it into the tank a car drove by and a guy yelled out the window: "Now that's real faith!"

Arguably, Ralph Emery and Minnie Pearl were TNN's biggest stars, which provided them with the opportunity to participate in high-profile events. One such event came in 1990 when Dick Clark invited them to present at the ACE Cable Awards. Ralph recalled that they almost missed their flight because of "Minnie's penchant for stopping to talk with anyone and everyone." Luckily, they made their flight and safely landed in Los Angeles.

In the Green Room before the show, Minnie was in deep conversation with Emmy-winner Cicely Tyson. Ralph described the scene that

Minnie with TNN star and show host Ralph Emery, 1983. Image courtesy of The Hope Powell Collection by Singleton/Curb.

followed: "All of a sudden, a group of boxers arrived to participate in a James Earl Jones segment. Evander Holyfield walked in, followed by several others. Then came the magic moment—the legendary Muhammad Ali walked in."

Emery noticed a shift in the room: "The waters parted, as it were." On one side stood Muhammad Ali, and on the other, Minnie Pearl. Emery sat back and absorbed the moment: "When Ali saw Minnie his face broke into a broad smile. Despite his struggles with Parkinson's, he raised his arm and waved. Minnie was thrilled and waved back. . . . It was clear Ali was delighted to see her."

Later, after their spot as presenters, Minnie and Ralph were walking back to the Green Room when they encountered Whoopi Goldberg. Whoopi threw her arms around Minnie in a big hug, visibly excited to see her. On the flight home, Emery reflected on the beauty of a person like Minnie: "In just one night, Muhammad Ali, Cicely Tyson, and Whoopi Goldberg had singled her out as someone special."

The establishment of two television networks in Nashville—The Nashville Network (TNN) and later Country Music Television (CMT)—had a

Minnie presents the Vocal Group of the Year to the Oak Ridge Boys at the 1978 CMA Awards. Image courtesy of The Hope Powell Collection by Singleton/Curb.

significant impact on country music and on Minnie Pearl's career. These networks provided a local outlet for television exposure, which meant that country music performers could avoid long flights to New York and Los Angeles. Moreover, shows like *Nashville Now* presented a fresh, contemporary image of country music, blending "down-home sophistication" with modern appeal. This offered a counterbalance to the more condescending depiction of hillbilly culture on *Hee Haw*. By the 1980s, the country music industry had evolved to embrace both styles—much like Minnie Pearl and Sarah Cannon, two distinct personas that complemented one other.

In 1975, country music was transitioning with new sounds and styles. Minnie Pearl (far left), Roy Clark (with guitar), and Mel Tillis (right of Clark) embraced the younger generation of musicians like Tanya Tucker (right of Minnie) and Juan Raoul Davis "Johnny" Rodriguez (right of Mel Tillis). Image courtesy of The Hope Powell Collection by Singleton/Curb.

From the late 1950s through the 1980s, Minnie Pearl successfully transitioned from radio to television—one of only a few Opry performers to do so. Her versatility and talent allowed her to transcend multiple mediums, which not only kept Minnie Pearl relevant but also introduced her to new audiences. From longtime fans to younger viewers who watched *Hee Haw* with their grandparents—Minnie Pearl's name recognition spanned generations.

NOTES

During her career, Colley recorded a half-dozen albums and about twice as many singles with such labels as Bullet, King, RCA, Everest, and Starday. Most of her records were monologues. When she did sing, she exaggerated the flaws in her voice. She had only one hit, "Giddyup Go–Answer," a maudlin recitation that "answered" a similarly maudlin recitation by Red Sovine. It did not reflect her usual comedic style, and, although the song made the top 100 chart for country music in 1966, she rarely mentioned it.

SOURCES

Cusic, Don. *Eddy Arnold: I'll Hold You In My Heart.* Nashville, Rutledge Hill, 1997.

Emery, Ralph, with Patsi Bale Cox. *50 Years Down a Country Road.* New York: William Morrow and Company, 2000.

Emery, Ralph, with Patsi Bale Cox. *The View From Nashville.* New York: William Morrow and Company, 1998.

Havighurst, Craig. *Air Castle of the South: WSM: The Making of Music City.* Chicago: University of Illinois Press, 2007.

Jones, Louis M. *Everybody's Grandpa: Fifty Years Behind the Mike.* Knoxville: University of Tennessee Press, 1984.

Lovullo, Sam, and Marc Eliot. *Life in the Kornfield: My 25 Years at Hee Haw.* New York: Boulevard Books, 1996.

Pearl, Minnie, and Joan Dew. *Minnie Pearl: An Autobiography.* New York: Simon and Schuster, 1980.

CHAPTER 17

Life at Home in Nashville

"At Home, I Have a Relaxed, Pleasant Life," 1970–1996

One day, Minnie Pearl's husband, Henry Cannon, was planting flowers in their front yard when a tourist approached and asked if he worked there. Henry simply replied, "I do." When the woman inquired how long he had been employed, he said, "As long as Minnie Pearl has lived here." Curious, the woman then asked if the job paid well. With a grin, Henry answered, "No, but if I do a good job, she lets me sleep with her."

As Sarah Cannon/Minnie Pearl approached her sixtieth birthday in 1982, she left behind the relentless pace of touring to embrace life with Henry in Nashville. "At home, I have a relaxed, pleasant life," Minnie wrote.

Twelve years earlier, in 1970, Minnie and Henry purchased a house at 874 Curtiswood Lane, surrounded by notable neighbors like Governor Winfield Dunn, Ray Stevens, and Opry legends Webb Pierce and Tex Ritter. Minnie and Henry's social life revolved around simple pleasures, deliberately avoiding the city's glitzy cocktail circuit. "At night, we're old home bodies," Minnie explained, continuing, "We have an early dinner, then read or watch television unless there's some function we are absolutely obligated to attend."

The couple paid $200,000 for the house, and renovations gave it a feel of both warmth and elegance. One of the standout features was the tennis court they added to the backyard. "Our home became a tennis

Sarah and Henry enjoyed playing cards at home, c. 1985. Image courtesy of the Grand Ole Opry Archives.

hangout," Minnie recalled, as friends regularly joined them for matches. Every Monday night, Minnie and Henry played doubles—though, as Minnie joked, "never as partners." If spotted in her light-blue sweatsuit and sneakers, it was a sure sign she was either headed to—or returning from—the court.

While Minnie Pearl's onstage persona was known for her gaudy gingham dresses and signature $1.98 flowered hat, Sarah Cannon's personal style told a different story. She preferred classically Southern attire but with a touch of business sophistication. Her go-to outfit was "a silk

—Staff photo by Robert Johnson

High Bidders: The Cookeville Women's Symphony Guild auctioned a day of tennis with Minnie Pearl and the high bidders were Mrs. Phillip Webb, right, Mrs. Robert Lowe Jr., second from left, and Mrs. Bob Langley with Minnie (Mrs. Henry Cannon), left, at Belle Meade Club's indoor courts. They played tennis and had lunch at the club with Minnie.

The Cookeville Women's Symphony Guild auctioned a day of tennis with Minnie Pearl as part of a fundraising event. Minnie played doubles with the winners, pictured here, at the Belle Meade Club's indoor courts, October 13, 1976.

blouse, slacks, and a well-tailored blazer." Her main accessory? A string of pearls—a fitting choice given her stage name.

Even as Minnie's performance pace slowed down, she remained busy as ever. She spent countless hours in her home office, the walls painted her favorite shade of yellow and adorned with pictures, awards, and stacks of books. "I'm about halfway through most of them," she quipped. Despite her warm and welcoming demeanor, Minnie was all-business when it came to daily communication. Her phone rang constantly, and she often answered without a greeting, diving straight into the details: "Where do I need to be? What time? Full costume or just the hat? Okay." When the conversation was over, Minnie hung up without a goodbye—just a decisive click of the phone.

Sarah Cannon and Minnie Pearl were opposites of one another. While Minnie paraded on stage in the simple dress of a country girl, Sarah was more comfortable in the plush surroundings of her estate on Curtiswood Lane. An avid tennis player, Sarah had a court built in her backyard, 1976. Image courtesy of *Nashville Banner* Archives, Special Collections Division, Nashville Public Library.

Minnie's typical weekday was a whirlwind of activity. Mornings were spent working at home, followed by lunch with friends in Green Hills and afternoons filled with meetings at organizations like the Grand Ole Opry and the Country Music Association (CMA). During one visit to the CMA, she overheard a conversation among staff members about a woman's husband who had recently grown a beard. One colleague mused, "I don't think I could kiss a man with a beard." Minnie entered the room just in time to reply, "I don't mind going through the bushes to get to a picnic!"

With fewer live performances, Minnie turned her focus to new creative outlets. Following the release of her autobiography in 1980, she began writing a weekly column for the *Nashville Banner* called "Minnie's Memories." She collaborated with writer Susan Quick, who visited her home two or three mornings a week. While working on a story, Minnie often called old friends like Roy Acuff and Eddy Arnold to help fill in forgotten details. Quick fondly remembered a visit with Minnie as they worked through a column: "We were writing about her time with the

Minnie Pearl was active in the local Middle Tennessee community. Here she speaks to an event in Dixon on December 14, 1977. Image courtesy of *Nashville Banner* Archives, Special Collections Division, Nashville Public Library.

Sewell Company in the 1930s. All the sudden, [Minnie] sprang to her feet, grabbed an umbrella, and performed a song-and-dance she still remembered perfectly. As she danced and twirled the umbrella, years slipped away—Minnie became a young girl again."

Though Minnie embraced life at home, she remained a vital link between the country music world and Nashville's elite social circles. She and Henry joined the exclusive Belle Meade Country Club, a place where few other Opry stars were welcomed. Bill Denny noted the tension: "During the 1950s and '60s, there was a continuing conflict. . . . The business community was happy to sell you a car if you were in the music industry, but they didn't want their daughter to marry your son." The tide had shifted by the 1980s as the business class began to recognize the economic potential of Music Row's recording industry and the Grand Ole Opry's growing influence on tourism.

President Ronald Reagan presents Sarah Colley Cannon, better known as Minnie Pearl, with Cancer Society Award in the Oval Office at the White House, April 2, 1987. Image courtesy of the National Archives, RR-WHTV Collection.

> two ladies, but we know they won't mind sharing it because they've been inseparable for almost 50 years. This TNN award goes to Mrs. Henry Cannon and Miss Minnie Pearl!

Sitting between her husband and Roy Acuff, Minnie shot out of her seat with surprise, genuinely surprised and deeply moved. She became the very first recipient of the Minnie Pearl Humanitarian Award, an honor that would later be awarded to distinguished artists such as Dolly Parton, Amy Grant, Reba McEntire, Vince Gill, Barbara Mandrell, Emmylou Harris, Ernie Ford, Kathy Mattea, Alabama, Martina McBride, and Diamond Rio.

Although Minnie's dedication to service was far-reaching, she found her

—AP Laserphoto

'So Proud To Be Here'

WASHINGTON — First lady Rosalyn Carter chats with Mrs. Henry Cannon prior to the start of c congessional wives luncheon where Mrs. Carter was the guest of honor. Mrs. Cannon is better known as "Minnie Pearl," to millions of Grand Ole Opry fans.

Sarah Cannon speaks with First Lady Rosalyn Carter in Washington DC, 1979. Newspaper clipping, Harpeth Hall Archives.

greatest fulfillment in supporting causes closest to home. Whether supporting the Humane Shelter, Vanderbilt Children's Hospital, or the Heart Association, Minnie invested her time and energy in improving her community. She served as state chair for Easter Seals and led Tennessee's Toys for Tots program, while contributing to national efforts through Nashville chapters of the Red Cross, Salvation Army, and Boys' and Girls' Clubs. Minnie also championed the arts and history through her advocacy for the Tennessee Performing Arts Center and the Tennessee State Museum.

Without a doubt, Minnie's deepest passion was working with the American Cancer Society. She had already lost her mother, Fannie Tate, in 1963—a loss she described as "devastating." But it was the death of her sister, Dixie, that filled her with anger. Minnie said in an interview:

Sarah (far left) stands in the kitchen of her home with (from left to right) Mary Cannon, Virginia Colley Burns, and Mary Colley Kershaw, 1959. Image courtesy of the Hickman County Historical Society.

> I was angry at the [breast] cancer that killed her. . . . It was my first experience of seeing the ravages of that disease close at hand, and it is a devastating monster. I wanted to cling to her. I depended on Dixie so much. Even in all her pain towards the end, her eyes would light up when we talked about our old days and our idyllic childhood.

After Dixie's passing, Minnie channeled her grief into work with the American Cancer Society. She even co-chaired the organization's national campaign in 1972–1973. Little did she know that she would face her own battle with cancer just a few years later. In 1985, Minnie publicly announced her breast cancer diagnosis. She underwent aggressive radiation treatments and had a double mastectomy.

A year after her diagnosis, Minnie's cancer was declared in remission. In a press conference she said, "The toll that cancer takes is enormous, but I've been given a second chance, and I intend to use it." True to her word, Minnie dedicated herself to fundraising efforts that led to the establishment of the Sarah Cannon Cancer Research Institute, which opened in 1987. This leading center for cancer research would expand to more than

APRIL SHOWER—Amy Grant and Minnie Pearl headline April Evening '88 Thursday at 7:30 p.m. at the Grand Ole Opry House. The "Shower of Stars" also features Robin Williams, James Taylor and other entertainers.

Sarah Cannon (left) and Amy Grant (right) promote a benefit concert for the American Cancer Society, 1988. *Tennessean*, April 3, 1988, 133.

twenty hospitals across five US states and the United Kingdom. Fittingly, the center where Minnie received her own treatment was later named the Sarah Cannon Cancer Center in her honor. Five years later, she launched the Minnie Pearl Cancer Foundation, which provided grants to programs offering direct services to patients, such as counseling and retreats.

Amy Grant, Grammy Award–winning singer and songwriter, shared two memorable moments that highlighted both Minnie's humanity and their shared commitment to cancer work and philanthropy. In one story, the two found themselves squeezed into a tiny hall bathroom, changing clothes for a charity event. Grant recalled: "I had my back to her, and all of a sudden, Minnie said, 'Well, would you look at this?' I turned around, and she had everything off. She said [pointing to her face and then her chest], 'Over 70 up here, look like a teenager right here!'" Grant admired Minnie's unfiltered humor: "Even in such an intimate setting, she just invited you in."

Amy Grant and Minnie Pearl shared more than a connection through show business—they had a personal bond through Amy's father, Dr. Burton Grant, a radiation oncologist at Vanderbilt Hospital. Dr. Grant had played a key role in Minnie's cancer treatment and later contributed to the establishment of the Sarah Cannon Cancer Research Institute.

In 1988, Amy organized a fundraiser in honor of her father, who had received the American Cancer Society's John Seaton Award. When it came time to find a co-host, Amy immediately called Minnie. Amy said, "I felt like with her, I had firepower. And she brought it." Minnie reached out to James Taylor, Art Garfunkel, and Robin Williams who agreed to perform. "I know they said yes because of Minnie," Amy said with a smile.

Even after her battle with cancer, Minnie continued entertaining. She said in an interview, "When I work now, it's for the sheer fun of it. That marvelous sound of laughter is like a drug, and "I'm totally addicted." In 1986, Minnie participated in Comic Relief's inaugural televised fundraiser, aimed at raising money for the homeless. Robin Williams, Billy Crystal, and Whoopi Goldberg co-hosted the four-hour special on HBO. Minnie joined an impressive lineup that included George Carlin, Michael Keaton, Richard Dreyfuss, Penny Marshall, and Howie Mandel. The event was wildly successful—raising $2.5 million.

As Minnie approached her eightieth birthday, she often reflected on life in spiritual terms. She and Henry regularly attended Brentwood Methodist Church, and her faith deeply influenced her perspective. She wrote:

> I used to think I'd failed because I never became a dramatic actress. What I didn't see at the time was that God had another plan for me—Minnie Pearl was the role I was meant to play all along. God wouldn't have given me Minnie Pearl if He hadn't intended me to use her to make people smile or laugh. I know many people scoff at the idea of God having some divine plan for our lives, but I believe it.

On June 15, 1991, Minnie performed what would be her final show in Joliet, Illinois. Two nights later, Henry heard Minnie fall in the bathroom. She was taken to the hospital, where doctors determined she had suffered a stroke. The physical effects were so severe that she was bedridden for the remainder of her life. To receive full-time care, Minnie was moved from her home on Curtiswood Lane to a local residential facility.

After decades of Minnie Pearl being seemingly everywhere, she vanished from public life. For the next five years, only close friends and family

Minnie and Henry Cannon at a TNN Awards Ceremony. This photo was taken months before Minnie suffered a debilitating stroke in 1991. Image courtesy of The Hope Powell Collection by Singleton/Curb.

were allowed to visit. Through it all, Henry rarely left her side. On March 4, 1996, Sarah Ophelia Colley Cannon, better known as Minnie Pearl, passed away at the age of eighty-three.

"Not every country song has to end in heartbreak," Minnie once said—and neither did her story. Minnie Pearl's life was over, but her legacy in the public and popular imagination would continue.

NOTES

The Sarah Cannon Cancer Research Institute became part of HCA Healthcare in 2012. This partnership allowed the institute to expand its reach and integrate cancer care into HCA's network of hospitals and healthcare facilities across the United States and internationally. Since joining HCA, the Sarah Cannon Cancer Research Institute has grown into a global leader in cancer research, known for pioneering clinical trials and contributing to several FDA-approved therapies. The Sarah Cannon Cancer Network now operates through more than twenty hospitals and research centers in the United States and the UK, continuing to deliver innovative care and support to cancer patients worldwide.

The Minnie Pearl Humanitarian Award was discontinued in 2005 after TNN's interests were sold to various channels, including Spike (2006–2018) and Paramount (2018–present).

SOURCES

"Amy Grant Wins the Minnie Pearl Award, 1996." Posted June 22, 2011, by Zane Storey, YouTube video. https://www.youtube.com/watch?v=5JO8rEgGYoc.

"Burton Paine Grant of Nashville, Tennessee." *The Tennessean*, July 1, 2018. https://www.legacy.com/us/obituaries/tennessean/name/burton-grant-obituary?id=7222357.

Goldsmith, Thomas. "Minnie Getting Roy Acuff Award Discussing Importance of Volunteerism." *Tennessean*, November 14, 1987. https://www.newspapers.com/article/the-tennessean-minnie-getting-roy-acuff/94859385/.

Havighurst, Craig. *Air Castle of the South: WSM: The Making of Music City.* Chicago: University of Illinois Press, 2007.

"Minnie Pearl Humanitarian Award," *Everything2*, 2001. https://everything2.com/title/Minnie+Pearl+Humanitarian+Award.

Pearl, Minnie. Tape recorded memoir by Sarah Colley Cannon, Nashville, Tennessee. Tape 2, Side B, 1979.

———. *Minnie Pearl Cooks.* Nashville, TN: Aurora Publishing, 1970.

Pearl, Minnie, and Joan Dew. *Minnie Pearl: An Autobiography.* New York: Simon and Schuster, 1980.

Quick, Susan. "Miss Minnie Shares a Piece of Her Mind." *Nashville Scene*, March 14, 1996.

Wills II, Ridley. *Heritage, Highballs, and Hijinks: Colorful Characters I Have Known*. Nashville, TN: Bookland EAN, 2010.

CHAPTER 18

Star-Studded Memories

Looking Back, 1940–1996

Released in 2023, the documentary *Facing the Laughter: Minnie Pearl,* features interviews with a variety of legendary figures. From country and rock musicians to comedians and media personalities, the film showcases the life and enduring influence of Sarah Colley Cannon—better known as Minnie Pearl. Through personal stories and reflections, these stars share their memories of Minnie. The following edited excerpts offer a glimpse into those interviews, courtesy of the film's award-winning director and producer Barbara J. Hall, in collaboration with Nashville PBS.

REBA MCENTIRE

The first time I saw Minnie Pearl, I was around seven years old. We had gone to the Grand Ole Opry—it was one of the few vacations we ever took, besides rodeo trips. I remember being so excited to see Minnie, Roy Acuff, and Rod Brasfield. Rod was actually a distant cousin of my mama. Minnie made such an impression on me. Even then, she was already a legend.

I got to know Minnie better after I moved to Nashville in the late 1980s. . . . Offstage, Minnie was nothing short of regal. . . . We had lunch one day at Green Hills Grille while I was pregnant with my son, Shelby. She'd just finished playing tennis doubles—Minnie was always doing

Cover Art for the documentary film Facing the Laughter: Minnie Pearl produced and directed by Barbara Hall and sponsored by Nashville PBS, 2023. Image courtesy of Nashville PBS.

something active—and we sat down to eat. I was just in awe of her. She was so down-to-earth, funny, and genuinely interested in what you had to say. . . . People still recognized her wherever we went, and she always took the time to greet everyone. That's just who she was. . . . I've never heard anybody say a bad word about Minnie Pearl.

I learned a lot from Minnie about comedic timing. Whether she was on stage with Roy Acuff or Paul Jones, she knew how to play off them perfectly. Minnie knew when to pause, when to deliver the punchline, and how to read the room. Watching her perform was like a masterclass

Minnie Pearl on stage with actor Larry Hagman, 1980. Hagman's most famous role was on the hit television show *Dallas* where he played J. R. Ewing. Image courtesy of The Hope Powell Collection by Singleton/Curb.

in comedy. . . . When she became Minnie Pearl, she transformed into everyone's best friend—someone you could laugh with and feel comfortable around. That was part of her genius.

Whereas Lucille Ball and Carol Burnett were the voices of the city folk, I think Minnie Pearl was the voice for the country folk, the mountain folk, the people on the farm. And it let the world know that people . . . in the country had a great sense of humor and a voice too.

I remember visiting Minnie in the nursing home after her stroke. I tried to make light of things and told her, "This place isn't so bad." She looked me dead in the eye and said, "It's a hellhole. I want to go home." That moment broke my heart. But when she passed, I thought to myself, "Maybe now, Minnie, you finally got to go home.'"

After her death, I was on tour in London. I asked a friend to go to Minnie's estate auction on my behalf—I wanted something to remember her by. They got me a pitcher and a decanter. To this day, I keep them in my China cabinet exactly as I got it—with a newspaper inside the pitcher.

And I tell people I left it there because that was Minnie Pearl's. I have her in my home now.

I think the most impactful part of Minnie Pearl's life was bringing such joy and laughter to the individuals listening to her, whether it was on television or in the audience, wherever they were. She brought a smile. A little hope in your heart. . . . I'm grateful I got to know her, even a little. I miss her with all my heart.

DWIGHT YOAKAM

Minnie Pearl was a therapist. That character was therapy for people. Humor is therapeutic, and the greatest comedians are empaths. She made the audience feel understood—like she was saying, "It's okay, life is bigger than a moment."

She knew the value of making herself the butt of the joke—it was a way to welcome people in, to remove any sense that she looked down on them. By the time she did *Hee Haw,* she was free to push the envelope even further with innuendos and winks . . . that might not have been acceptable on the Opry.

Minnie Pearl's success was on par with the greatest figures in country music—Hank Williams Sr., Bill Monroe, Roy Acuff. I wouldn't say Hank was more famous than Minnie Pearl. She was foundational to the Opry, a bedrock of Nashville's music scene. Roy Acuff knew that and respected her for it. What made Minnie so remarkable was her intuitive sense of people. She could ask a question that cut beyond surface conversations, getting to the heart of things. Her wit and timing were as brilliant as anything from Tennessee Williams or Mark Twain. You can't fake that—it was pure artistic creation.

Ironically, Minnie Pearl was one of the most honest performers in comedy. Her character was pure, and that honesty resonated with people. It's no wonder the greats gravitated toward her—they got it, especially if they ever met her out of character. Her wit wasn't just humor; it was an insight into life. Minnie embodied true inclusiveness. She wasn't part of the sanitized, modern version of inclusion—she lived it in a way that carried humanity with it. Her character made people feel seen and welcomed. That's the magic of Sarah Cannon.

Sarah [literally] stopped me in my tracks at the first CMA Awards I went to . . . in 1986. Before the awards show, I'd been overly candid with the press about my opinions on country music. . . . At the time, I was grappling with the transition from the West Coast scene—Southern California and Bakersfield—into Nashville. I ran into backlash for speaking too freely.

So, I show up at the awards knowing I'd caused some upset with my comments the year before. There were plenty of asides and private remarks from people saying, "You said exactly what I've wanted to say for years," but those comments didn't erase the negativity around me that night. At the end of the show, after I didn't win, we were all leaving, and I felt a hand grab my arm. She spun me around, forcing me to look at her. There she was—Minnie Pearl—but not just Minnie; it was Sarah Cannon, serious and grinning all at once. She looked me dead in the eye and said, "Listen to me. We need you." I was stunned. I had never imagined that anyone in the industry needed me for anything. It was a moment of true humility.

Minnie Pearl had a context and scope that few others had—her career spanned decades, and she saw beyond the moment. She could see through any given situation to the bigger picture. That's the genius of Sarah Cannon. She created a character, a work of art, that resonated deeply with people from vastly different backgrounds. . . . She helped me reset my focus. Her advice wasn't about opinions or winning awards; it was about passion and staying true to the music. She saw the heart of what mattered and knew when to speak with wisdom. I carried that moment with me from then on.

AMY GRANT

When I was in eighth grade, I was thirteen years old in 1974, and our keynote speaker at the closing exercises was Sarah Cannon. I remember being so taken with her talk that day. There were fifty-two of us, and she treated us with such respect—talking about our place in the world. What stayed with me was that she saw us, spoke to us as if we belonged in the same circle.

Sarah was highly involved, well-educated, and invited to speak at many places. She wowed crowds with her mind. It's so important, no matter who you are, what you look like, or what gender you are, to have somebody who's done something amazing. She was a person you could look at and say, "I want to be like that."

As I started singing and doing things publicly, if I was featured in the newspaper, then I'd get a little peach folded notecard: "I saw this, and I

Ball and Carol Burnett. But think about it, I can see a silhouette of Carol Burnett. I can see a silhouette of Lucille Ball. And then I see a silhouette of Minnie. And I bet you ten to one, the most recognizable of those silhouettes simply because of a price tag left on a hat. That would be Miss Minnie.

TEDDY GENTRY [ALABAMA]

She was definitely an entertainer. She didn't have to sing—she entertained without singing. That's the beauty of our industry; it can accept entertainers who don't sing. . . . With comedians, you live and die by that night. If the jokes don't land, there's nothing else to hide behind. I think it's easier being a musician . . . I wouldn't make it as a comic. It's got to be real—people have to feel that it's natural.

With Minnie, it was like a duck in water; she took on that character, and it was perfect. She was brilliant in the realm of what she did—the simplicity of it. You don't normally think of someone really smart and educated creating a character that simple, but that's what made her a genius.

There've been a lot of men who rose to the top in country comedy, but there's never been another female like her who took that chance. . . . It was a pleasure to be in the same business with somebody like her. Being from Lookout Mountain Range and raised on a little cotton farm, getting to sit in the Ryman Auditorium and watch the Grand Ole Opry was a huge inspiration to us. Minnie was part of that inspiration—she made us want to come back and work harder.

RANDY OWEN [ALABAMA]

I remember meeting her early on, and it felt like I was meeting a legend. She had this way of making you feel at home even though she was the biggest star in the room. What made her stand out wasn't just the jokes—it was the kindness behind them. Minnie had a way of making everyone feel important, like they mattered. I think that's what made her comedy timeless.

She taught us something important—if you can make people laugh, they'll listen to you. And if you treat people right, they'll never forget you. Minnie did both. . . . Her character reminded me so much of the people I grew up with—folks who didn't take themselves too seriously, who knew how to laugh at life even when it wasn't easy.

Minnie on the set of a television show taping, c. 1976. From left to right in the foreground: Johnny Cash, Minnie Pearl, Conway Twitty, and Mel Tillis. Image courtesy of The Hope Powell Collection by Singleton/Curb.

She opened doors for all of us. I think every artist who came after her owes her a debt, especially those of us in country music. She showed that being genuine and kind could take you a long way. . . . She was a pioneer in entertainment. Minnie Pearl, to me, was one of the greats—not just for comedy, but for what she represented in our industry. She made people laugh and feel good, and there's nothing more valuable than that.

HENRY CHO

I was born and raised in Knoxville, so the Opry has always been a thing. Even people that didn't know her, anytime someone had anything with a price tag hanging off, you'd make a Minnie Pearl joke. I remember kids in high school with shirts still with price tags, and we'd say, "Hey, you're pulling a Minnie Pearl."

She was a genius for branding, no question. Just iconic. She just invented something that got in the hearts of all of us. How else do you explain it? You got a bunch of teenage boys in Knoxville who didn't care a hoot about anything she ever said on stage. But we knew who she was. Besides, I thought she was hot.

She didn't have the luxury of comedy clubs like we did. In the 1980s, comedy was booming. There were clubs everywhere. But Minnie came from Centerville, Tennessee, and she found her niche at the Grand Ole Opry, where everyone else was singing. That's how brilliant she was—she carved out a space no one else had, and it lasted for decades.

Our whole thing in Southern comedy is not to make fun of people but to make fun with them. Minnie knew that. Nobody ever thought she was making fun of rural folks. She found a way to make herself the butt of the joke, and . . . could push boundaries without being offensive. . . . She paid her dues in ways we can't even imagine today. She toured with musicians in cars, not buses or jets. There were no physical therapists or fancy amenities back then—just a group of people traveling from show to show. . . . It was a different world.

She never stopped being Minnie Pearl. She paved the way for people like Rodney Dangerfield—he had one character, and he stuck to it. That's why she was so successful. She was ahead of her time, in a lot of ways, and paved the way for comedians, especially for women. She held her own in a world dominated by men and created something unique and lasting. Off stage, she treated everyone the same, spoke kindly, and never said a bad word about anybody. That's the kind of hero you want—someone who's kind, considerate, and leaves everyone feeling good.

PAM TILLIS

"Howdy! I'm just so proud to be here!" You know, I've heard that a time or two. But I am proud to be here. I really am. Minnie Pearl meant so much to me, and I'm grateful to be part of something that honors her legacy.

First of all, she was part of my dad's era [singer and songwriting legend Mel Tillis]. They came out of the last vestiges of small-town, rural life. So, she was a link between old hillbilly times and the modern era. From the Opry to The Nashville Network and with Ralph Emery, she spanned both worlds.

The story goes . . . Minnie had a tour going on, and Daddy was a young, skinny kid from Plant City, Florida. He needed a little extra milk money—this was before his career took off. So, she took a couple of guys on the road with her. Daddy played rhythm guitar. A young Roger Miller was also in that band playing fiddle.

Daddy was very bashful about his speech impediment. Minnie noticed he wasn't talking onstage—before or after his songs—and he was letting Roger Miller do all the talking. Miss Minnie pulled Daddy aside one day and asked, "Melvin, what is this all about?" Daddy said, "I can't talk." She told him, "Oh, yes, you can. If you're going to learn to be an entertainer, you better learn to talk to the people. . . . The world loves somebody who knows how to laugh at themselves." That advice really changed him. Daddy even told me once that he learned a lot of his stage timing from Minnie Pearl. . . . She mentored him, and I try to carry that forward a bit myself.

"She never got above her raising," as we say. Even though she lived off Franklin Road in a very nice neighborhood, she carried herself in different circles with ease and always stayed connected to her roots. There are a handful of young artists, like Dwight Yoakam and me, whom Minnie sort of treated like her kids. She thought of me as one of her young'uns.

I met her after my Opry debut at the Ryman . . . when I was eight and sang "Tom Dooley" with my dad. In those days, entertainers didn't have all the production budgets we have now. Their performances were character driven. They had to hook you with their personality, a good story, and a punchline. That's what Minnie did. She held up a mirror to the audience, pointing out things we all struggle with, but in a way that made you laugh. . . . In doing that she was also holding up a mirror to the audience and saying, "I see you." That takes real intelligence.

There weren't many female comedians back then, except for June Carter. But Minnie wanted to blaze the trail for more women. She even told me, "I want you to work on comedy. I want you to follow in my footsteps." My path ended up being more musical, but I do feel like I'm a bit of a bridge between her era and where we are now.

On the Opry stage in the 1980s. Standing behind the microphone from left to right: Porter Wagoner, Minnie Pearl, Dolly Parton, Roy Acuff. Image courtesy of The Hope Powell Collection by Singleton/Curb.

I remember visiting her when she was very frail toward the end of her life, and she looked luminescent, like Katharine Hepburn. She even told me, "When I started out, I wanted to be Katharine Hepburn." Standing there looking at her, I thought, "That's exactly who you remind me of." It was a poetic, precious moment.

I still wear hats a lot, and I usually don't cut the price tag off. Sometimes it sticks out, and people say, "You forgot your tag." And I tell them, "No, no I didn't forget." It's just a little way I keep Minnie with me.

BARBARA MANDRELL

The first time I met her in person, she was wearing this emerald, green sequin dress—very tailored, with a collar and belt at the waist—and matching green satin shoes. She had an evening bag that went perfectly with her outfit, a big emerald ring, and her hair looked wonderful. She just looked dynamite. Minnie loved life, loved people, and she loved entertaining—doing it better than anyone. And yet, she made a living by toning all that down and pretending she couldn't get a guy. She was just so clever.

We had a lot of fun together. Sometimes, we'd sit by the piano, play, and sing old songs—mostly pop songs from World War II, though we did some country, too. She'd start singing, and I'd harmonize. She'd ask, "How do you know the words to these songs?" I'd say, "I love these songs!" We had such fun, swapping stories about things that had happened in the past.

One Easter, when we were on the road together for a show, my daughter, who was about five years old at the time, wanted to color Easter eggs on the bus. I'd bought all the supplies, and Minnie jumped right in to help her. It was such a generous and thoughtful thing to do . . . A year or two later, Minnie did something else for my daughter that I'll never forget. Minnie asked if she could take Jamie on stage with her during a matinee show at the Opry. Minnie even taught her a joke to tell on stage. Minnie didn't have to do that, but that's just who she was. She was always there for you, always thinking of others.

Minnie and Henry were great, too. . . . Henry didn't mean to be, but he was about as funny as she was. He was clever and very witty, and he was also a great businessman. Both Minnie and Henry were so sweet and kind to my husband, Ken. They had a way of making everyone around them feel like family.

After my car accident on September 11, 1984, I was in a dark place. My kids and I had been hit head-on, and I suffered serious injuries, including a head injury. And in my mind, I would say, "I'm never, never going to perform again." I would even speak about Barbara Mandrell in the third person. It was serious.

Minnie came out to my house, even though it was way out of her way. I don't remember much from that time, but I do remember the way she spoke to me—encouraging me, wanting me to come back to work. She cared that much. It wasn't a fun thing for her to do; there I was in a dark bedroom and didn't want any light. I didn't want to see people. But she loved me. She loved me, and I loved her. . . . And I don't know if any woman has ever replaced her or ever could.

RAY STEVENS

I used to live on Curtiswood Lane, where Minnie and Henry lived, right down the street. So, I knew her as a neighbor, as well as from the Grand Ole Opry and other places we'd cross paths. She was always so nice to me and everyone she met—she was a really kind lady. . . . Minnie was respected by everyone, and I never saw her offend anybody. My grandmother was a huge Grand Ole Opry fan, and if you offended her, you were done. But Minnie? Never.

She wasn't known for her singing, but I've never said she couldn't sing. In fact, I made a record called *Southern Hair*, and I got Jerry Clowery and Minnie Pearl to help me on it. And it was a great record that got some airplay. . . . Minnie even sang on a couple of R&B tracks I recorded—just for fun. I still have the masters of those sessions. She did a good job with them, and maybe one day I'll release those songs.

Comedy is comedy, let's face it. And what's funny is funny—whether you're a country music fan or not. Minnie's humor was aimed at rural America at a time when show business didn't think much of that audience. But people out in the country appreciated her—they felt a real kinship with her. I think she knew she was plowing new ground with her act. . . . She created her own niche and filled it to the max.

Minnie's comedic timing was incredible. You can't really learn that—it's something you're born with. Most country singers tell jokes between songs, which sets them apart from pop singers, who usually don't try to make the audience laugh. That kind of humor and music has always been part of country tradition, and Minnie fit right into that.

JEANIE SEELY

I was born the year that Minnie Pearl joined the Grand Ole Opry in 1940. . . . I've often thought about how Minnie influenced me, going back to my childhood. When I speak in the Circle Room at the Opry, I always say that Minnie was one of the reasons I felt that sense of family at the Opry. Before I made it to the Opry, I'd listen to Minnie Pearl, Roy Acuff, Cousin Jody, and Little Jimmy Dickens on the radio. They always sounded like they really liked each other. That connection is what I wanted to find.

When you think about it, Minnie Pearl stepped out into the spotlight during a time when few women did. Kitty Wells was the first female singer to break through, but even then, she had the support of her husband and brother-in-law. Jean Shepard was really the first woman to step out on her own as a solo act, without the backing of a family group. But Minnie did something even more remarkable—she stepped out as a solo female comedian. That's really saying something. As a singer, you at least have a song to fall back on and a band to support you. But Minnie? She was out there all by herself. That takes a lot of guts.

At the Ryman, especially for the women, things were different. . . . There were so few dressing rooms, and the women didn't even have one—we all used the ladies' room. Minnie was right in there with us, joking around. We'd laugh about how all the ruffles on our dresses got in the way. It was like, when one person had their arms up, everyone else had to keep theirs down! But the truth is, even when we could have left, we didn't—because we enjoyed being together. . . . We were all just together, and that made it special.

I mean, we were all out on the road during the week—Minnie was on tour, Bill and Hank Snow were on tour, and we were too. But Saturday night, we'd all come back to the Ryman, and it was like, "Where have you been? Did you get paid? Did you find a good restaurant along the way?" That's what we'd talk about. . . . We'd share stories about where we stopped and stayed. Saturday night was when we caught up before we all went our separate ways again. It was wonderful times. I just hope that some of the younger generation can hold on to that feeling. Maybe sharing these memories will help.

BILL ANDERSON

I remember hearing Minnie long before I ever saw her because I grew up listening to the Opry on the radio. . . . For me, Minnie felt like that wacky aunt or favorite cousin—the kind of person you felt was part of your own family. She had that common touch that connected with people like me—people who didn't live in New York or California, but in what they call "flyover America." And she understood us because she came from that same place. I'll never forget something Minnie once said about her brother: "My brother's not a failure—he just started at the bottom, and he likes it there." That kind of humor resonated with me, and I think it hit home for a lot of people.

I've got a story about Minnie and Henry Cannon that captures their relationship. Someone sent me a picture recently—Minnie had visited their hometown years ago, and they'd taken a photo. In the picture, there's

Minnie as you'd expect, and in the background, there's Henry, standing there holding Minnie's purse. That was Henry in a nutshell. He was the one flying the plane . . . and handling things behind the scenes.

One night in Charlotte, North Carolina, we were standing backstage while Johnny Russell was out on stage, singing his last song. Minnie was next in the lineup, standing there in the wings. As Johnny wrapped up, Minnie turned to me and said, "Bill Anderson"—she always called me by my full name—"do you think we will ever get over being nervous?"

I was stunned and said, "Minnie Pearl, you still get nervous?" And she said, "Well, not nervous like scared, but I still get those little butterflies in the pit of my stomach." We stood there quietly for a moment, and then she said something that has stayed with me ever since. "You know what, though? If we didn't get those little butterflies, it wouldn't mean as much to us." I've shared that story with so many young artists over the years at the Opry . . . They'll say, "I'm in the circle, and I'm so nervous." I always tell them, "If you weren't nervous, it wouldn't mean as much." And that's a lesson I learned from Minnie Pearl.

In 1990, just before her stroke, we had done two shows with the Opry in one night. It was late, and Minnie had only stayed for the first part of the second show. As she was leaving, she was walking down the hall, and I was coming in the door to do my second spot. As we passed each other, I said, "Goodnight, Minnie."

She stopped, reached over and took my arm and said, "Bill Anderson, I love you." I looked at her and said, "Minnie Pearl, I love you, too." That was the last time I saw her. Now, every time I leave the Opry, there's a big picture of Minnie hanging on the wall. And every night, as I walk out, I look at it and say, "Goodnight, Pearl. I love you."

TANYA TUCKER

I met Minnie when I was still a kid just starting out. Right from the start, she made me feel like I belonged. Minnie had this way of being both proper and playful. She could hang out with anyone—from the gutter to the White House. She was the glue that held things together backstage at the Opry. If there was trouble, she'd come in and settle things without a single curse word . . . And I never saw her take a drink either. She was just good, clean fun. And somehow, she managed to be both Minnie Pearl and Sarah Cannon without any conflict. It's not easy to balance two sides

Minnie on stage and the 50th anniversary of the Grand Ole Opry, 1975. Image courtesy of The Hope Powell Collection by Singleton/Curb. From right to left: Charlie Pride, Roy Clark, Dolly Parton, Loretta Lynn, Minnie Pearl, Johnny Cash, Monty Robbins.

like that, but she did it. . . . You never knew where Sarah Cannon ended and Minnie Pearl began, she could be both and still be true to herself.

She also knew how to have fun, and we sure did. One time, I found this tiny kitten in a little town while we were out on the road. I didn't know how I was going to get it home, but Minnie, being Minnie, came up with a plan. She said, "It's fine! We'll sneak it onto the plane." So there we were—Minnie spraying my hair and stuffing the kitten into my purse like it was the most natural thing in the world. Back then, security wasn't what it is now, and somehow, we pulled it off. I remember laughing so hard, thinking, *Only with Minnie Pearl would this happen.*

Minnie always made me feel like her best friend, even though I knew she made everybody feel that way. For my eighteenth birthday, I invited her and Ernest Tubb to my new farm. I couldn't believe Minnie came, and we had the best time—just sitting, talking, and laughing. Most kids my age wouldn't have even known who they were, but I was bowled over.

She gave me all kinds of advice on everything—how to perform, how to carry myself, how to be a lady. She told me things I didn't fully understand back then, but I sure do now. She knew what she was doing. . . . Even today, I find myself thinking about the things she taught me, and I feel lucky to have known her—not just as Minnie Pearl, but as a friend.

BRENDA LEE

Even though I was part of the industry, I was still just a kid and didn't fully understand everyone's role. But when I met Miss Minnie—I was around twelve, and she became like another mother to me. She and my mom both looked out for me while I toured. Her husband, Henry, flew them everywhere, and my husband, Ronnie, got close to him. Henry even asked Ronnie to call him "Uncle Henry," and from then on, that's who he was. Miss Minnie and Henry had a rare relationship built on love and respect. Henry let her shine. They were true partners, and their love for each other was pure magic.

I flew with Miss Minnie, Henry, and their dog on their plane, "The White Poodle," for many shows. They felt like family to me. Miss Minnie was incredibly kind and grounded—one of the most giving people I've ever known. She taught me how to work a stage, show grace, and appreciate people. Even though my mom taught me those things, Minnie extended those lessons on the road. . . . By the 1960s, Minnie was like the "mother hen" of the country music world, the go-to person for advice. Even though she wasn't old enough to be our mother, we always went to her. Sometimes she told us what we didn't want to hear, but she told us anyway.

I always wondered how she created such a brilliant character because she was so refined and well-educated. That persona was entirely hers—no managers or agent, . . . it was all her. People believed in Minnie Pearl so much they thought she was real. No one's ever done anything like it since. . . . I don't think she ever knew her greatness, never cared about her greatness other than she loved to work, and she loved what she did.

After her stroke, I didn't want to see her that way and she didn't want people to see her that way. Towards the end, we talked a lot [by phone], but all of us in the industry knew that time belonged to her and Henry. We gave them space, knowing she was surrounded by love. When she named the cancer center as Sarah Cannon instead of Minnie, it didn't surprise me. She was just as proud of Sarah as she was of Minnie.

Minnie had a deep, quiet faith. She didn't preach, but you could tell she was close to God. I know she was ready when her time came. . . . She was good to go. In my heart, I imagine her still up there, making everyone laugh.

CONCLUSION

The Queen of Country Comedy

A Life Well-Lived, 1912–1996

"Take the backroads, not the highways," Minnie often said. It's a sentiment that captures her life's winding and unexpected journey. Growing up in Centerville, Tennessee, her early years instilled a deep appreciation for small-town community while also inspiring her to dream big. Classically trained as an actress at the Ward-Belmont School, she graduated and joined the Sewell Theater Company, traveling the American South during the Great Depression. By the 1940s, she was performing alongside Grand Ole Opry legends like Pee Wee King, Roy Acuff, and Hank Williams—appearing on the Opry and touring during the week. On the road, she literally and figuratively took the backroads—long before the interstate system existed.

Eventually, her career led to larger stages, including Carnegie Hall and international venues across Europe and Latin America. Along the way, Minnie transitioned from a beloved radio personality to a television star, becoming a household name as a cast member of *Hee Haw*. Even Minnie's off-stage accomplishments reflect an unconventional life of achievement. As a comedian, she earned the rare honor of being inducted into the Country Music Hall of Fame. She not only survived cancer but also founded the Sarah Cannon Research Institute, which remains a global leader in cancer treatment and research. She wasn't just recognized as a

Minnie Pearl, the Queen of Country Comedy, stands on stage at the Grand Ole Opry off of Briley Parkway, 1990. The following year, she suffered a major stroke and was not seen again in public from 1991 until her death in 1996. Image courtesy of the Grand Ole Opry Archives.

humanitarian—she became the namesake of the Minnie Pearl Humanitarian Award.

Whether as Sarah or Minnie, she forged a path entirely her own. Of course, she wasn't perfect, and she lived in an imperfect world. She witnessed physical and substance abuse and navigated a rapidly changing region fraught with race and gender discrimination. With historical hindsight, she made some regrettable choices, but taken as a whole, Sarah/Minnie's life and career were defined by her enduring commitment to use humor to make the world a better place. Her journey stands as a testament to a life well-lived.

Unlike so many performers who fall victim to scandal, addiction, or arrests, Minnie avoided the pitfalls of fame. She could hold her own on the road with a rowdy group of musicians passing around a bottle of whiskey or attend a sophisticated cocktail party at the Belle Meade Country Club. In either case, she ended up at home—safe, sound, and (mostly) sober. In other words, she thrived on human connection and interaction but always kept enough distance to stay grounded. Undoubtedly, her family, faith, and strong personal character played a significant role in shaping her life's trajectory.

The character of Minnie Pearl is both simple and enigmatic. Throughout her career, Cannon skillfully balanced her dual roles as Minnie and Sarah, becoming a bridge between Nashville's country music scene and "high society." In comedy, she was inspirational and influential, admired for her longevity but also her grace in a world where many comedians relied on profanity and insults. There was no "deep, dark, hidden turmoil" in Minnie Pearl's character. Instead, she was a simple girl from a rural world who found joy in laughing at herself—and her audience laughed along with her. Over time, particularly after World War II and her marriage to Henry Cannon, Minnie Pearl evolved into a mentor and matriarch within the world of country comedy. Universally loved and respected, the mere mention of Minnie usually brings a smile.

The evolution and legitimization of country music mirrors the career of Minnie Pearl. For decades, Nashville's upper class dismissed country music as uncultured and unserious. Historian and author Nancy Isenberg described the genre as a symbol of "white trash," but Minnie Pearl disarmed critics by embracing and reinterpreting this stereotype. Her act gave rural America a voice, making those from small towns feel heard

Minnie Pearl at Zibart's Book Store in Nashville, January 1954. Minnie poses with prominent members of Nashville's upper class at a book signing for "Minnie Pearl's Diary." This photo represents the bridge that Sarah/Minnie created between the country music crowd and the more traditional, cultured elite. Image courtesy of the Nashville Public Library Metro Nashville Archives.

and seen. As country music moved from the backwoods to the mainstream in the 1960s, so did Sarah Cannon—a cultured young woman who transformed into the beloved, homespun Minnie Pearl. Together, Sarah and Minnie created a stage on which social elites and "rednecks" could coexist.

In 1970, *Minnie Pearl Cooks* was published. In the preface, Sarah wrote: "Ever since I became two people, Minnie Pearl and Sarah Ophelia Cannon, I've been faced with the problem of when to be Minnie and when to be Sarah Ophelia. In creating this book, I've decided to be both." Historian Kristine McCusker concluded: "And both she was." When her memoir was published a decade later, the front cover featured a colorful, loud and proud Minnie Pearl in full costume. The back cover was black and white, with Sarah dressed in business attire, wearing glasses with her hair in a French twist. A simple caption read: Mrs. Henry Cannon.

This internal conflict demonstrates how Sarah navigated two worlds—one defined by performance and humor, the other by her personal identity as a wife, friend, mentor, aunt, daughter, sister, and community member. The Minnie Pearl persona was carefully crafted to be non-threatening. "She's not pretty. She's not sexy. She's not smart, and people just sort of think they're safe with her," Sarah explained. As McCusker argued, "Minnie walked the fine line between reinforcing and subverting traditional gender norms," creating a character that was "hyperbolically feminine but designed not to challenge the power structures of her time." McCusker also noted the financial implications: "Sarah understood Minnie Pearl as a marketable commodity and wielded that understanding to her advantage."

Sarah/Minnie's duality also reflected her remarkable ability to navigate multiple spaces simultaneously. She was a comedian and a mentor, a small-town girl and a businesswoman, a performer and a philanthropist. As McCusker noted, her success was built on authenticity and adaptability, skillfully balancing tradition with innovation in ways that continue to shape American culture.

Artist and musician, k.d. lang, put it this way: "Minnie Pearl was a visionary. She understood the trajectory of where country music was going and who country music needed to embrace." In other words, though country music originated with Southern Whites, it grew to capture the hearts of people nationwide and worldwide. Minnie Pearl's broad appeal across social, temporal, and geographic divides played a vital role in this growth and diversification.

At the 1977 Country Music Awards, Minnie Pearl and Dolly Parton took the stage to present an award. Minnie, then sixty-five, wore her signature blue-checkered gingham dress, while thirty-one-year-old Dolly stood beside her in a dazzling red, low-cut gown. Minnie seized the moment to showcase her self-deprecating humor. After Dolly delivered her first line, Minnie bantered, "For the benefit of those of you who tuned in late—Minnie Pearl's the one with the hat on!" The audience erupted. This moment was more than just comedic; it was a subtle lesson for Dolly, demonstrating the power of laughing at oneself. Not long after the CMA Awards in 1977, Dolly was asked about her clothes, make-up, and hair

Minnie Pearl with her signature pose, c. 1972. Image courtesy of The Hope Powell Collection by Singleton/Curb.

in an interview. She said, "It costs a lot of money to look this cheap!" Dolly's now-iconic quote perfectly encapsulates her playful approach to her public image—an understanding she gleaned from Minnie.

During the 1980s, Minnie passed the torch to a new generation of performers—artists like Dolly Parton and Reba McEntire—who wove comedy into their country music careers. Country music has since con-

Dolly Parton and Minnie Pearl stand onstage to present an award at the Country Music Awards in 1977. Parton is wearing a sequined red gown with matching flower hair piece while Minnie dons her traditional blue gingham dress and straw hat. Image courtesy of The Hope Powell Collection by Singleton/Curb.

tinued to expand and diversify, evolving far beyond its traditional roots. In 2010, Taylor Swift's album *Fearless* made history by winning both the Grammy Award for Best Country Album and Album of the Year. Then, in 2025, Beyoncé released *Cowboy Carter,* which earned Best Country Album of the Year and Album of the Year at the Grammys, making her the first Black artist to win Best Country Album. But regardless of the artist or genre, anyone who steps onto Ryman Auditorium's hallowed stage first walks by a bronze statue of Minnie Pearl—the "Queen of Country Comedy."

Six months after Sarah Colley Cannon's death a local Nashville network honored her life with a special show. A Tennessee Pearl aired on WDCN, today's PBS Nashville, August 24, 1996. Newspaper clipping, Harpeth Hall Archives.

More than thirty years after Sarah Cannon's death, Minnie Pearl's memory remains a vibrant part of Americana. Her iconic $1.98 price tag is still symbolic of her enduring charm. This biography has captured the many chapters of her life—the person and the persona, the highs and lows, the joy and pain, the people she loved and lost. But whether in a gingham dress or a cashmere sweater, she adhered to one guiding principle as her North Star. For the entirety of her career, she kept this quote framed on her desk: "I expect to pass through this world but once. Any good therefore that I can do or any kindness that I can show . . . let me not defer nor neglect it, for I shall not pass this way again."

With her words as our compass, may we carry forward Sarah's grace and Minnie's heart. In doing so, the circle remains unbroken—linking past to present, and laughter to love..

SOURCES

Isenberg, Nancy. *White Trash: The 400-Year Untold History of Class in America.* New York: Penguin Books, 2016.

McCusker, Kristine M. "Sarah Colley Cannon (Minnie Pearl): Gossiping about Grinder's Switch—The Grand Ole Opry and the Modernization of Tennessee." In *Tennessee Women: Their Lives and Times*, edited by Sarah Wilkerson Freeman and Beverly Bond, 261–80. Athens: University of Georgia Press, 2009.

Pearl, Minnie. *Minnie Pearl Cooks.* Nashville: Aurora Publishing, 1970.

Pearl, Minnie, with Joan Dew. *Minnie Pearl: An Autobiography.* New York: Simon and Schuster, 1980.

INDEX

HOWDY!

Minnie Pearl became my friend in 1964. I was 18, new in town, and Minnie Pearl took me under her wing. She gave me good advice, the how to's, the how not to's, the when to's, and the when not to's. I learned a lot from her as a woman and as a professional entertainer but above all that, as a good, solid human being. Minnie was more than a big laugh. She was a big heart, and I will always love her.

—DOLLY PARTON

HOWDY!

The Minnie Pearl Story

Mary Ellen Pethel and Don Cusic

THE CHARLES K. WOLFE MUSIC SERIES
Ted Olson, *Series Editor*

The University of Tennessee Press
Knoxville

Cloth: 1st printing, 2025; 2nd printing, 2026.

LIBRARY OF CONGRESS CATALOGING-IN-PUBLICATION DATA
Names: Pethel, Mary Ellen author | Cusic, Don author
Title: Howdy! : the Minnie Pearl story / Mary Ellen Pethel and Don Cusic.
Description: Knoxville : The University of Tennessee Press, [2025] |
Series: Charles K. Wolfe music series | Includes bibliographical references. |
Summary: "Sarah Colley Cannon, better known as her stage character, Minnie Pearl, was born in Hickman County, Tennessee, in 1912. After graduating from Ward-Belmont, now Belmont University, she joined a touring theater company and produced and directed plays and musicals throughout the Southeast. In 1940 an executive for WSM radio in Nashville saw her Minni Pearl character and invited her to appear on the Grand Ole Opry. Cannon would play Minnie Pearl on both the Opry stage and the television show Hee Haw for the next fifty years"—Provided by publisher.
Identifiers: LCCN 2025008142 (print) | LCCN 2025008143 (ebook) |
ISBN 9798895270585 hardcover | ISBN 9798895270608 adobe pdf |
ISBN 9798895270592 kindle edition
Subjects: LCSH: Minnie Pearl | Women comedians—United States—Biography |
Women country musicians—United States—Biography | LCGFT: Biographies
Classification: LCC PN2287.C25 P48 2025 (print) | LCC PN2287.C25 (ebook)
LC record available at https://lccn.loc.gov/2025008142
LC ebook record available at https://lccn.loc.gov/2025008143